PENGUIN REFERENCE BOOKS

THE PENGUIN DICTIONARY OF MODERN QUOTATIONS

J. M. Cohen, born in London in 1903, is the author of many Penguin translations, including versions for the Classics of Cervantes, Rabelais and Montaigne. He has also edited the three volumes of *Comic and Curious Verse*, and *Writers in the New Cuba*, and *Latin American Writing Today*. He has written a good deal of criticism, has broadcast on the Third Programme on a variety of subjects, and has read widely in several languages. His particular interests are poetry and the literature of Spanish America, which he has visited several times. He now lives in the country, and, though his vision no longer enables him to read, continues to work and keep up with his favourite subjects.

His third son, M. J. Cohen, is an educational publisher who is married and has three daughters.

This dictionary is intended as a complement to their earlier joint production, *The Penguin Dictionary of Quotations*.

It is a good thing for an uneducated man to read books of quotations.

Winston Churchill, *My Early Life*, Ch. 9

I imagine we're going to find this *full* of quotations!

Ruth Draper, *The Italian Lesson*

I might repeat to myself, slowly and soothingly, a list of quotations beautiful from minds profound; if I can remember any of the damn things.

Dorothy Parker, *The Little Hours*

To say that anything was a quotation was an excellent method, in Eleanor's eyes, for withdrawing it from discussion.

'Saki', *The Jesting of Arlington Stringham*

In the dying world I come from quotation is a national vice. It used to be the classics, now it's lyric verse.

Evelyn Waugh, *The Loved One*

J. M. AND M. J. COHEN

THE PENGUIN
DICTIONARY OF
MODERN
QUOTATIONS

PENGUIN BOOKS

Penguin Books Ltd, Harmondsworth, Middlesex, England
Penguin Books Inc., 7110 Ambassador Road, Baltimore, Maryland 21207, U.S.A.
Penguin Books Australia Ltd, Ringwood, Victoria, Australia

—

First published 1971
Reprinted 1972

—

Copyright © J. M. and M. J. Cohen, 1971

—

Made and printed in Great Britain
by Hazell Watson & Viney Ltd, Aylesbury, Bucks
Set in Monotype Times

FOREWORD

THIS dictionary contains what we hope will be remembered in the year 2000 of the things said and written in the first two thirds of the century. It no doubt contains also a great deal that will have been forgotten by then, and perhaps a good deal that has already been forgotten, but which has amused, impressed or exasperated us at some time in the three years of the sixties in which we have been collecting these four thousand-odd quotations from poets, politicians, novelists, lawyers, comedians and others who somehow get into print or on the air. The bias is predominantly English; translations are given for all sayings in foreign languages. We have set the year 1900 as our starting point, and though we may inadvertently have filched one or two things from the nineties, we have tried to keep strictly to our date.

As we found in compiling the *Penguin Dictionary of Quotations*, it is not always the great who make the best remarks. We are very conscious that some of the finest minds of the century are almost unrepresented. Scientists are seldom brief. Politicians are especially disappointing in their failure to provide the sparks for which we searched the dull embers of their biographies. The great criminal lawyers and judges seldom say anything that seems either impressive or funny out of court. Radio programmes like *Itma* and *The Goon Show*, on the other hand, offer far more

good lines than we can include. Books and the theatre provide the bulk of our offerings; advertisement slogans, music-hall lyrics and remarks on public occasions supply the rest. We have been careful not to include anything that appeared in the *Penguin Dictionary of Quotations* itself. This may inconvenience a reader in search of a line of Shaw or a saying of Churchill's, who has to use two books to find it. But to serve up perhaps a thousand quotations from the first book in the second seemed to us like delivering short weight.

Difficulties in compiling this *Dictionary of Modern Quotations* have been far greater than in making our original dictionary, for which we had every age and many works of reference to draw on. Here we have had to rely on our own judgements and a brief seventy years of history. We have not given dates of birth for our authors (as in so many instances it was not possible to do so), and most of them have fortunately as yet no dates of death. Nor can we be as certain of our accuracy in this book except when using printed sources. Many sayings have had to be marked 'attributed', and many others circulate in more than one form; two newspaper accounts of a speech seldom entirely agree. Many readers will consequently be in the position to correct us in one respect or another. We hope they will do so.

We have had much help in collecting our quotations both from friends and public institutions. It is possible only to name our principal helpers. The B.B.C. allowed us to check our memories of various radio programmes; the *Observer* put its files of *Sayings of the Week* at our disposal, and we have drawn very profitably on them. The *Observer*, the *Sunday Times* and *New Society* published our letters of request for memorable sayings, which produced some interesting suggestions. Among our friends perhaps fifty have contributed a quotation or two or put us on the track of something good. John Gloag, G. M. Lee and Geoffrey Strachan and Peter Ford have been particularly generous in drawing on their reading and memory. We thank everyone who has helped us.

In order to save space, lines of verse are run on and the divisions between lines are indicated by oblique strokes.

We hope that this book will instruct, amuse and entertain, and that the very full index made for us by Anne Robinson will enable readers to find what they want under the key word that they most clearly remember; also that when they look up a familiar word they will find something unknown and impressive that has been said on the subject.

October, 1970

J.M. and M.J.C

PENGUIN DICTIONARY OF
MODERN QUOTATIONS

KING ABDULLA

1 We must not fall into the same errors as the Unbelievers and count up our guns, our bombs, our tanks and our aeroplanes, and pray to them for deliverance. This is a new idolatry, as men once worshipped stones and trees. [Preface to *Memoirs*, quoted in Glubb Pasha, *A Soldier with the Arabs*]

MARK ABRAMS

2 We continue to overlook the fact that work has become a leisure activity. [*Observer*, 'Sayings of the Week', 3 June 1962]

DANNIE ABSE

3 So in the simple blessing of a rainbow, / in the bevilled edge of a sunlit mirror, / I have seen, visible, Death's artifact / like a soldier's ribbon on a tunic tacked. [*The Pathology of Colours*]

GOODMAN ACE

4 Every time a gun goes off in a have-not country another Communist is born. [*Saturday Review*, 12 June 1965]

J. R. ACKERLEY

5 There was so much sculpture that I should certainly have missed the indecencies if Major Pomby had not been considerate enough to mention them. [*Hindoo Holiday*, Pt I, 28 Dec. 1923]

LORD ACTON

6 The atmosphere of accredited mendacity. [*The Study of History*]

ARTHUR ADAMOV

7 The reason why Absurdist plays take place in No Man's Land with only two characters is primarily financial. [Edinburgh International Drama Conference, 13 Sept. 1963]

FRANKLIN P. ADAMS

8 There are seventy stanzas in the Uruguay national anthem, which fact may account for the Uruguay standing army. [Attr.]

HAROLD ADAMSON

9 Comin' in on a Wing and a Prayer. [Title of song]

ALISON ADBURGHAM

10 It was not that she herself [Queen Victoria] was a fashion leader. Probably the most notable garment she ever wore was the nightdress in which she received, that early morning at Kensington Palace, the news of her uncle's death – the nightdress in which she became Queen. [*A Punch History of Manners and Modes*]

11 If you are going to wear a hat at all, be decisive and go the whole hat. In making a courageous choice of millinery, you have nothing to lose but your head. [*The Bedside Guardian 1962*, 'Nothing to Lose but your Head']

SIR FRANK ADCOCK

12 That typically English characteristic for which there is no English name – *esprit de corps*. [Presidential address]

GEORGE ADE

13 Anyone can win, unless there happens to be a second entry. [Quoted in Esar and Bentley, *Treasury of Humorous Quotations*]

14 The house was more covered with mortgages than with paint. [Quoted in *ib.*]

1

15 The music teacher came twice each week to bridge the awful gap between Dorothy and Chopin. [Quoted in *ib.*]

H. AGAR

16 The truth that makes men free is for the most part the truth which men prefer not to hear. [*A Time for Greatness*]

JAMES AGATE

17 Lament we the desperate fix / Of one who sold love *à prix fixe*, / Sole fruit of her womb / Is the worm i' the tomb / And her hope of salvation is nix. [*Ego 1*, 1935]

18 The leader-writer in a great Northern daily said on the morning after King Edward died that if he had not been a king he would have been the best type of sporting publican. [*Ib.*]

19 I like listening to it [Tchaikovsky's 5th] just as I like looking at a fuchsia drenched with rain. [*Ego 8*, 1947]

20 A schoolgirl answered the question 'In what countries are elephants found?' Elephants are very large and intelligent animals, and are seldom lost. [*Ego 9*, quoted in Edward Marsh *Ambrosia and Small Beer*, 'Envoi']

JAMES AGEE

21 If music be the breakfast food of love, kindly do not disturb until lunch time. [On Hollywood musicals, *Age of Film*]

ANNA AKHMATOVA

22 Only the dusty flowers, / the clank of censers, and tracks / leading from somewhere to nowhere. [*Requiem 1935–1940*, v, trans. Richard McKane]

'ALAIN' [pseudonym of Émile Auguste Chartier]

23 What is fictitious in a novel is not so much the story but the method by which thought develops into action, a method which never occurs in daily life. [Quoted in E. M. Forster, *Aspects of the Novel*, III]

EDWARD ALBEE

24 Who's Afraid of Virginia Woolf? [Title of play]

25 Musical beds is the faculty sport around here. [*Who's Afraid of Virginia Woolf?*, I]

26 I know something about history. I know when I'm being threatened. [*Ib.* I]

27 Martha is the only true pagan on the eastern seaboard. [*Ib.*]

28 I have a fine sense of the ridiculous, but no sense of humour. [*Ib.*]

29 Until you start plowing pertinent wives, you really aren't working. The way to a man's heart is through his wife's belly and don't you forget it. [*Ib.* II]

30 You gotta have a swine to show you where the truffles are. [*Ib.*]

31 You just gird your blue-veined loins, girl. [*Ib.* III]

G. S. ALBEE

32 'I don't like to sleep with anybody,' replied Myrthis. 'I wouldn't sleep with my own mother.' [*By the Sea, By the Sea*, Ch. 5]

33 Zee always went naked in the house, except for the brassière she wore when it was her turn to get dinner. Once, cooking French-fried potatoes in a kettle of boiling fat, she had come within an inch of crisping her most striking features. [*Ib.* 6]

RICHARD ALDINGTON

34 Wearily the sentry moves / Muttering the one word: 'Peace'. [*Picket*]

35 Kill winter with your cannon, / Hold back Orion with your bayonets / And crush the spring leaf with your armies. [*In the Trenches*]

TSARINA ALEKSANDRA

36 They accuse Rasputin of kissing women etc. Read the Apostles; they kissed everybody as a form of greeting. [Letter to the Tsar, quoted in Leon Trotsky, *History of the Russian Revolution*, Vol. 1, Ch. 4]

SAMUEL ALEXANDER

37 Evil is not . . . wholly evil; it is misplaced good. [*Space, Time and Deity*]

NELSON ALGREN

38 He [Algren] shunts aside all rules, regulations, and dicta, except for three laws he says a nice old Negro lady once taught him: Never play cards with any man named 'Doc'. Never eat at any place called 'Mom's'. And never, ever, no matter what else you do in your whole life, *never* sleep with anyone whose troubles are worse than your own. [H. E. F. Donohue, *Conversations with Nelson Algren*, Foreword]

HERVEY ALLEN

39 Religions change; beer and wine remain. [*Anthony Adverse*, Pt I, Ch. 3, Sect. xx]

40 Let a man make a remark about the enormous amount of quackery in medicine, for instance, and a woman will immediately wonder how much he owes his physician. [*Ib.* III. 7. l]

ROBERT ALLERTON and TONY PARKER

41 Well, I've known a few parsons and I've known a few whores, and I've always preferred the whores. [*The Courage of his Convictions*, 'Chaplain']

LEO AMERY

42 Speak for Britain. [Said to Arthur Greenwood, spokesman for the Labour Party, in the House of Commons, 2 Sept. 1939, but Harold Nicolson, in his diary, attributes the words to Robert Boothby]

43 You have sat too long here for any good you have been doing. Depart, I say, and let us have done with you. In the name of God, *go*! [Speech, repeating Cromwell's words, addressed to Neville Chamberlain's government, House of Commons, May 1940]

FISHER AMES

44 Monarchy is like a splendid ship, with all sails set; it moves majestically on, then it hits a rock and sinks forever. Democracy is like a raft. It never sinks, but, damn it, your feet are always in the water. [Quoted in D. W. Brogan, *The Free State*]

KINGSLEY AMIS

45 Outside every fat man there was an even fatter man trying to close in. [*One Fat Englishman*, Ch. 3]

46 He was of the faith chiefly in the sense that the church he currently did not attend was Catholic. [*Ib.* 8]

47 A blonde girl wearing a man's shirt but in all other visible respects unmanly to the point of outright effeminacy. [*Ib.*]

48 Never call a Jew a Jew unless you can be sure of making him lose his temper by doing so. [*Ib.*]

49 It was no wonder that people were so horrible when they started life as children. [*Ib.* 14]

50 Work was like cats were supposed to be: if you disliked and feared it and tried to keep out of its way, it knew at once and sought you out and jumped on your lap and climbed all over you to show how much it loved you. Please God, he thought, don't let me die in harness. [*Take A Girl Like You*, Ch. 5]

51 Tapped untalent. [Remark on the *Robbins Report on Higher Education*, which suggested that higher education should cater for 'the untapped talent']

52 The pseudo-light it [Welch's article] threw on non-problems. [*Lucky Jim*, Ch. 1]

53 First making his shot-in-the-back face, Dixon stopped and turned. [*Ib.* 3]

54 I thought of calling her *Amateur Model*. The girl who sat for it's certainly an amateur of a sort, and she acts as a model, at least while she's being painted. [*Ib.* 9]

55 Welch's driving seemed to have improved slightly; at any rate, the only death Dixon felt himself threatened by was death from exposure to boredom. [*Ib.* 18]

56 In the field of evasion-technique, verbal division, and in the physical division of the same field this chap had Welch whacked from the start: self-removal to South America was the traditional climax of an evasive career. [*Ib.* 19]

57 He thought what a pity it was that all his faces were designed to express rage or loathing. Now that something had happened that really deserved a face, he'd none to celebrate it with. As a kind of

token, he made his Sex Life in Ancient Rome face. [*Ib.* 25]

58 Should poets bicycle-pump the heart / Or squash it flat? / Man's love is of man's life a thing apart; / Girls aren't like that. [*Something Nasty in the Bookshop*]

HARRY ANDERSON

59 Beer, beer, glorious beer, / Fill yourself right up to here. [*Beer*]

SHERWOOD ANDERSON

60 The beaten, ignorant, Bible-ridden, white South. [A. M. Schlesinger Jr, *The Politics of Upheaval*, Pt I, Ch. 4, Sect. v]

ANON

61 As Romeo he [Irving] reminds me of a pig who has been taught to play the fiddle. He does it cleverly but he would be better employed in squealing. [Quoted in Ellen Terry, *The Story of My Life*, Ch. 9]

62 All is not queer that titters. [Proverbial in Bayswater, 1964]

63 A bayonet is a weapon with a worker at each end. [British pacifist slogan, 1940]

64 Be a real he-man and wear a Tarzan chest-wig. [Bogus advertisement in *Ballyhoo*, 1930s]

65 Be like Dad, keep Mum. [Ministry of Information slogan, 1941]

66 The best contraceptive is a glass of cold water: not before or after, but instead. [Pakistan delegate at International Planned Parenthood Federation Conference]

67 Body Odour. [Advertising slogan for Lifebuoy soap]

68 Born 1820 – Still Going Strong ['Johnny Walker' advertisement]

69 Clean-limbed American boys are not like any others / Only clean-limbed American boys have mothers. [Said by an anonymous American, quoted in review, *Times Literary Supplement*, 1964]

70 Dancing is a perpendicular expression of a horizontal desire.

71 Delightfully simple. It is refreshing to meet a man who has played the piano for twenty years in a brothel. [On Attlee and the Lynskey Enquiry quoted in O. Brown, *The Extended Tongue*]

72 Down in the jungle / Living in a tent, / Better than a prefab – / No rent! [Quoted in Iona and Peter Opie, *Language and Lore of Schoolchildren*, Ch. 7]

73 Drinka pinta milka day. [Advertising slogan]

74 Even your best friends won't tell you. [American advertisement for Listerine, a deodorant]

75 Every picture tells a story. [Advertisement for Sloan's Backache and Kidney Oils, *c.* 1907]

76 Friday night is Amami Night. [Advertisement for hair-wash, 1920s]

77 The god-men say when die go sky / Through Pearly Gates where river flow, / The god-men say when die we fly / Just like eagle-hawk and crow – / Might be, might-be; but I don't know. [North Australian aborigine version of Christianity]

78 Half of Christendom worships a Jew, and the other half a Jewess. [Quoted in H. L. Mencken, *A New Dictionary of Quotations*]

79 Have you heard? The Prime Minister [Lloyd George] has resigned and Northcliffe has sent for the King. [Popular saying, 1919. Quoted in Hamilton Fyfe, *Northcliffe, an Intimate Biography*, Ch. 16]

80 He is like the woman in an Elinor Glyn novel who describes another by saying 'she is like a figure in an Elinor Glyn novel.' [Quoted in Daniel Boorstin, *The Image*, Ch. 2]

81 Henry's the sort that keeps you guessing as to whether he's going to deliver a sermon or wet the bed. [Said of Henry Wallace by an anonymous American politician. Quoted in A. M. Schlesinger Jr, *The Coming of the New Deal*, Pt I, Ch. 2, sect. v]

82 Here lies the grave of Keelin, / And on it his wife is kneeling; / If he were alive she would be lying, / And he would be kneeling. [Dublin lavatory graffito quoted in Oliver St John Gogarty, *As I was Going Down Sackville Street*, Ch. 4]

83 He's a big shot in steel, but he's a dental cripple all the same. [American insurance advertisement, *c.* 1934]

84 His hands are insured for thousands, but he suffers from athlete's foot. [American insurance advertisement, *c.* 1934]

85 Horsepower was wonderful when only horses had it. [Quoted in *Dramatists' Guild Bulletin*, 1963]

86 How can I know what I think till I see what I say? [Quoted in G. Wallas, *The Art of Thought*]

87 I believe in Stiff Collars on ethical and national grounds. They are a bulwark against lawlessness. [*The Grocer's Handbook*, quoted in M. Bateman, *This England*, selections from the *New Statesman*, Pt I]

88 I don't like the family Stein! / There is Gert, there is Ep, there is Ein. / Gert's writings are punk, / Ep's statues are junk, / Nor can anyone understand Ein. [Quoted in Robert Graves and Alan Hodge, *The Long Weekend*, Ch. 12]

89 If she were cast as Lady Godiva the horse would steal the act. [Of a certain actress]

90 If you're not a rogue you should take a libel action against your face.

1 *Il faut du temps pour être femme.* – It takes time to be a woman.

2 I'll eat when I'm hungry and drink when I'm dry, / If moonshine don't kill me, I'll live till I die. [Song: 'Moonshine'. Quoted in Alan Lomax *Folk Songs of North America* (No. 134)]

3 I'm sixty-one today, / A year beyond the barrier, / And what was once a Magic Flute / Is now a Water Carrier.

4 It isn't the wild ecstatic leap across I deplore. It's the weary trudge home. [On Double Beds versus Single Beds]

5 *Les visages sont si tristes, mais les derrières sont si gais.* – Their faces are so sad, but their bottoms are so gay. [Comment by French diplomat on modern dancing (1918). Quoted in Sir Thomas Beecham, *A Mingled Chime*]

6 Life ain't all you want. It's all you 'ave. So 'ave it!

7 Little nips of whiskey, little drops of gin, / Make a lady wonder where on earth she's bin.

8 Living in the past has one thing in its favour – it's cheaper. [Quoted in *Dramatists' Guild Bulletin*, 1963]

9 Lousy but loyal. [East End slogan at King George V's Jubilee, 1935]

10 Marriage is an attempt to change a night owl into a homing pigeon.

11 Marriage is a very fine institution; no family should be without one.

12 May all the saints be praised! Hell's full at last! [Said by an Irishman when the trapdoor failed to engulf Don Giovanni at a performance of the opera. Story told by Sir Compton Mackenzie]

13 Montezuma's revenge. [Proverbial nickname for digestive complaint suffered by European visitors to Mexico]

14 My brother's a slum missionary / Saving young virgins from sin: / He'll save you a blonde for a shilling – / By God, how the money rolls in. [Song quoted in T. R. Ritchie, *The Singing Street*]

15 ADMIRING FRIEND: 'My, that's a beautiful baby you have there!' MOTHER: 'Oh, that's nothing – you should see his photograph!' [Quoted in Daniel Boorstin, *The Image*, Ch. 1]

16 The Navy's here! [Call on boarding German commerce destroyer *Altmark* carrying British prisoners. Quoted in Winston S. Churchill, *The Gathering Storm*, Ch. 31]

17 Never put a hot baby on a cold slab.

18 A New York actress has just got back to Broadway after a year in Hollywood. She says that she has been so long among the false fronts and papiermâché mansions on the set that nowadays she finds herself sneaking a look at her husband to see if he goes all the way round or is just a profile. [Quoted in P. G. Wodehouse, *Performing Flea*]

19 Now I lay me back to sleep, / The speaker's dull, the subject's deep. / If he should stop before I wake, / Give me a nudge for goodness' sake. [*At a Public Dinner*]

20 Often a bridesmaid, but never a bride. [American advertisement for a deodorant, *c.* 1934]

21 The other one [Pope Pius XII] was nearer to God, but this one [John XXIII] is nearer to us. [Italian]

22 Passion: a glut of feeling sometimes experienced between strangers. [Proverbial definition]

23 A politician is an animal who can sit on a fence and yet keep both ears to the ground. [Quoted in H. L. Mencken, *A New Dictionary of Quotations*]

24 A poor aviator lay dying / At the end of a bright summer's day; / And his comrades were gathered around him / To carry his fragments away. [American airforce song sung in Korea, 1954. Quoted in Alan Lomax, *Folk Songs of North America* (No. 234)]

25 Take the manifolds out of my larynx / And the cylinders out of my brain, / Take the piston rods out of my kidneys, / And assemble the engine again. [*A Poor Aviator*]

26 Pyjamas are safer than nightdresses. [Poster of the Royal Society for the Prevention of Accidents, hanging in waitingroom of Family Planning Association, Streatham, June 1964]

27 Regret cannot come today; have not yet got home yesterday. [Telegram attributed to employee during traffic crisis]

28 Say it with Flowers. [Advertising slogan of American florists, 1920s]

29 Seventeen suburbs in search of a city. [Description of Los Angeles]

30 Take up your cross and relax. [Alleged American slogan of the 1960s. Quoted by Elizabeth Hardwick in radio interview with A. Alvarez, 14 June 1964.]

31 *Teppichfresser!* – Animal that chews the carpet! [Unknown German editor of Adolf Hitler, quoted in W. L. Shirer, *The Rise and Fall of the Third Reich*, Ch. 12]

32 That's Shell, that was. [Advertisement slogan]

33 The Treasury of Human Inheritance, Vol. 1, Pt III (Agioneurotic Oedema, Hermaphroditism, Deaf Mutism, Commercial Ability) 10s. [*Cambridge University Press Catalogue*, 1952, p. 203]

34 'They were married at the church here in the morning,' she said, 'but after that they didn't know how to spend the rest of the day. So they walked into Cambridge to see a man hung. [Old lady quoted in Sybil Marshall, *An Experiment in Education*, Ch. 2]

35 The trains run to time. [Common remark in praise of Italian Fascism]

36 Turn on, tune in, drop out. [Hippie slogan]

37 We aim to please. You aim too, please. [Inscription in gentlemen's lavatory of New York restaurant]

38 We take you in so that the boys will take you out. [Notice in New York corsetière's, 1964]

39 When Lady Jane became a tart, / It almost broke her father's heart. / But blood is blood, and race is race, / And so, to mitigate disgrace, / He bought a most expensive beat / From Asprey's up to Oxford Street. [Quoted in Seymour Hicks, *Vintage Years*]

40 Which Twin has the Toni? [Advertisement slogan]

41 Whiter than white [Detergent advertisement]

42 Your King and Country need you. ['Kitchener' recruiting poster, 1914]

JEAN ANOUILH

43 The object of art is to give life a shape. [*The Rehearsal*, Act I, sc. ii.]

44 What fun it would be to be poor, as long as one was *excessively* poor! Anything in excess is most exhilarating. [*Ring Round the Moon*, Act II]

GUILLAUME APOLLINAIRE

45 *Ah Dieu! que la guerre est jolie / Avec ses chants ses longs loisirs* – Ah God, how pretty war is with its songs, its long rests! [*L'Adieu du Cavalier*]

46 *Voie lactée ô soeur lumineuse / Des blancs ruisseaux de Chanaan / Et des corps blancs des amoureuses / Nageurs morts suivrons-nous d'ahan / Ton cours vers d'autres nébuleuses* – Milky Way, O shining sister of the white streams of Canaan and the white bodies of women in love, shall we follow your track towards other nebulae, panting like dead swimmers? [*La Chanson du mal-aimé*]

47 *Les souvenirs sont cors de chasse / Dont meurt le bruit parmi le vent.* – Memories are hunting-horns, whose noise dies away in the wind. [*Cors de Chasse*]

48 *Bergère ô tour Eiffel le troupeau des ponts bêle ce matin.* – Shepherdess O Eiffel Tower the herd of bridges is bleating this morning. [*Zone*]

SIR EDWARD APPLETON

49 I do not mind what language an opera is sung in so long as it is a language I don't understand. [*Observer*, 'Sayings of the Week', 28 Aug. 1955]

LOUIS ARAGON

50 *O mois des floraisons mois des métamorphoses | Mai qui fut sans nuage et Juin poignardé | Je n'oublierai jamais les lilas ni les roses | Ni ceux que le printemps dans ses plis a gardés.* – O month of flowerings, month of metamorphoses, May without cloud and June that was stabbed, I shall never forget the lilac and the roses, nor those whom the spring has kept in its folds. [*Les lilas et les roses*]

51 *Le démenti des fleurs au vent de la panique | Aux soldats qui passaient sur l'aile de la peur | Aux vélos délirants aux canons ironiques | Au pitoyable accoutrement des faux campeurs.* – The flowers' contradiction of the wind of panic, of the soldiers who passed on the wings of fear, of the delirious bicycles, of the ironic guns, of the pitiable equipment of the bogus campers. [*Ib.*]

52 *Vivre n'est plus qu'un stratagème | Le vent sait mal sécher les pleurs | Il faut haïr tout ce que j'aime | Ce que je n'ai plus donnez-leur | Je reste roi de mes douleurs.* – Living is no more than a trick. The wind is not clever at drying tears. I must hate everything I love. Give them what I no longer possess. I remain king of my griefs. [*Richard II quarante*]

53 *Fuyez les bois et les fontaines | Taisez-vous oiseaux querelleurs | Vos chants sont mis en quarantaine | C'est le règne de l'oiseleur | Je reste roi de mes douleurs.* – Flee the woods and the springs. Be silent, wrangling birds. Your songs are sent to Coventry. It is the reign of the bird-catcher. I remain king of my griefs. [*Ib.*]

54 *Absence abominable absinthe de la guerre | N'en es-tu pas encore amèrement grisée* – Hideous absence, absinthe of war, are you not already horribly in-toxicated with it? [*Les Temps de mots croisés*]

55 *J'ai bu l'été comme un vin doux.* – I drank summer like a sweet wine. [*Zone libre*]

DUKE OF ARGYLL

56 As far as I'm concerned there are only two kinds of people in the world. Those who are nice to their servants and those who aren't. [Attr. by Art Buchwald in *I Chose Caviar*]

MICHAEL ARLEN

57 It is a sorry business to inquire into what men think, when we are every day only too uncomfortably confronted with what they do. [*The Three Cornered Moon*]

58 Nothing is so generally destructive as the spiritual vanity of men who refuse to store up goods in this world. Remember Jesus said he came bringing a sword. But he was so detached from the goods of this world that he left it behind him. [*Man's Mortality*]

59 I have an intellectual leaning towards bloods ... theirs not to reason why, theirs but to do nothing and die. [*Short Stories*, 'Farewell, These Charming People']

60 Well, emotionally she was unimportant, like a play by Mr Noël Coward, but her construction was faultless, like a play by Mr Noël Coward. [*Ib.* 'Portrait of a Lady on Park Avenue']

61 She was of the type early twentieth century, but her gestures and lack of them, were ancient enough, for they were fully expressive of that which really differentiates men from beasts, the social quality of being tired. [*Ib.* 'When the Nightingale Sang in Berkeley Square']

62 My forbears were successful crooks living on the slopes of Mount Ararat. [*Conversation*]

GEORGE ARLISS

63 [After describing himself in a court of law as the greatest living actor, excused his boastfulness with] You see, I am on oath.

PETER ARNO

64 I consider your conduct unethical and lousy. [Caption for cartoon]

65 Wake up, you mut. We're going to be married today. [Caption for cartoon]

66 Have you read any good books lately? [Caption to cartoon of lovers in a clinch]

DAISY ASHFORD

67 Oh Bernard muttered Ethel this is so sudden. No no cried Bernard and taking the bull by both horns he kissed her violently on her dainty face. My bride to be he murmered several times. [*The Young Visiters*, Ch. 9]

ARTHUR ASKEY

68 Hullo playmates! [In wartime broadcasts]

EARL ASQUITH

69 One to mislead the public, another to mislead the Cabinet, and the third to mislead itself. [On the War Office's keeping three sets of figures. Quoted in Alastair Horne, *The Price of Glory*, Ch. 2]

70 Elizabeth told me of an American girl who spoke scoffingly of the Ten Commandments: 'They don't tell you what you ought to do and only put ideas into your head.' [*Letters to a Friend*. Quoted in Samuel, *A Book of Quotations*]

71 Tell him I will give him half-a-crown for the lot. [Message to Lord Beaverbrook when offered the support of his newspapers on certain conditions. Quoted in G. M. Young, *Stanley Baldwin*, Ch. 15]

72 He [Bonar Law] has the mind of a Glasgow Bailie. [Quoted in Robert Blake, *The Unknown Prime Minister*, Pt. V, Ch. 4]

MARGOT ASQUITH

73 He [Lloyd George] could not see a belt without hitting below it. [Quoted in Mark Bonham Carter, Introduction to reprint of her *Autobiography*, 1962]

74 When I told my mother of my engagement, she sank upon a settee, put a handkerchief to her eyes, and said: 'You might as well marry your groom!' [*Autobiography*, Ch. 6]

75 Mary [the Countess of Wemyss] is generally a day behind the fair, and will only hear of my death from the man behind the counter who is struggling to clinch her over a collar for her chow. [Diary note quoted in *ib*. 10]

76 Mr Balfour was difficult to understand . . . because of his formidable detachment. The most that many of us could hope for was that he had a taste in us as one might have in clocks or china. [*Ib*. 11]

77 When my daughter Elizabeth ran into my bedroom at midnight in her nightgown on the 10th November 1918 to tell me that the war was over, I felt as numb as an old piano with broken notes in it. [*Ib*. 21]

JOHN JACOB ASTOR III

78 A man who has a million dollars is as well off as if he were rich. [Attr.]

LADY ASTOR

79 Grass is growing on the Front Bench. [1940. Quoted in *Observer*, 'Sayings of our Times', 31 May 1953]

ALEX ATKINSON and
RONALD SEARLE

80 Although not actually chewing gum, she moved her lower jaw monotonously. The blank stare from her eyes, compounded as it was of accusation, distrust of the elderly, and a kind of meaningless, infantile cunning, was unnerving. She would have been born during the late war. [*The Big City*, 'Night in a London Coffee-House']

81 Even if you're a pro you got to *look* like you're an amacher, otherwise the kids are going to think you're doing something they couldn't do. That way you'd scare them. [*Ib*. 'A Rocking Boy']

W. H. AUDEN

82 To the man-in-the-street, who, I'm sorry to say, / Is a keen observer of life, / The word 'Intellectual' suggests straight away / A man who's untrue to his wife. [*New Year Letter*, Note to line 1277]

83 . . . hinting at the forbidden like a wicked uncle, / Night after night to the farmer's children you beckon. [*The Capital*]

84 Let us honour if we can / The vertical man / Though we value none / But the horizontal one. [*Epigraph*]

85 Within these breakwaters English is spoken; without / Is the immense, improbable atlas. [*Dover*]

86 He knew human folly like the back of his hand, / And was greatly interested in armies and fleets; / When he laughed, respectable senators burst with laughter, / And when he cried the little children died in the streets. [*Epitaph on a Tyrant*]

87 In the nightmare of the dark / All the dogs of Europe bark, / And the living nations wait, / Each sequestered in its hate. [*In Memory of W. B. Yeats*]

88 Intellectual disgrace / Stares from every human face, / And the seas of pity lie / Locked and frozen in each eye. [*Ib.*]

89 And on the issue of their charm depended / A land laid waste, with all its young men slain, / Its women weeping, and its towns in terror. [*In Times of War*]

90 To throw away the key and walk away, / Not abrupt exile, the neighbours asking why / But following a line with left and right, / An altered gradient at another rate. [*The Journey*]

1 About suffering they were never wrong, / The Old Masters. [*Musée des Beaux Arts*]

2 ... even the dreadful martyrdom must run its course / Anyhow in a corner, some untidy spot / Where the dogs go on with their doggy life. [*Ib.*]

3 The glacier knocks in the cupboard, / The desert sighs in the bed, / And the crack in the tea-cup opens / A lane to the land of the dead. [*One Evening*]

4 One tapped my shoulder and asked me 'How did you fall, sir?' / Whereat I awakened. [*1st January 1931*]

5 Attractions for their coming week / Are Masters Wet, Dim, Drip and Bleak. [*The Orators*, Ode, 'Roar Gloucestershire']

6 The Oxford Don: 'I don't feel quite happy about pleasure.' [*Ib.*, 'Journal of an Airman']

7 Three kinds of enemy face – the June bride – the favourite puss – the stone in the rain. [*Ib.*]

8 Only those in the last stage of disease could believe that children are true judges of character. [*Ib.*]

9 But Tennyson, remember, thought trains ran in grooves; / The Queen believed cigars were all one price. [*Ib.*]

10 To ask the hard question is simple. [*The Question*]

11 Verse was a special illness of the ear; / Integrity was not enough. [*Rimbaud*]

12 His truth acceptable to lying men. [*Ib.*]

13 At Dirty Dick's and Sloppy Joe's / We drank our liquor straight, / Some went upstairs with Margery, / And some, alas, with Kate. [*The Sea and the Mirror*, 'Song of the Master and the Boatswain']

14 The nightingales are singing in / The orchards of our mothers, / And hearts that we broke long ago / Have long been breaking others. [*Ib.*]

15 Embrace me, belly, like a bride. [*Ib.*, 'Stephano's Song']

16 O for doors to be open and an invite with gilded edges / To dine with Lord Lobcock and Count Asthma. [*Song*]

17 Noises at dawn will bring / Freedom for some, but not this peace / No bird can contradict. [*Taller Today*]

18 He is not that returning conqueror, / Nor ever the poles' circumnavigator. / But poised between shocking falls on razor-edge / Has taught himself this balancing subterfuge / Of the accosting profile, the erect carriage. [*Watch Any Day*]

19 Be clean, be tidy, oil the lock, / Weed the garden, wind the clock; / Remember the Two. [*The Witnesses*]

20 When I find myself in the company of scientists, I feel like a shabby curate who has strayed by mistake into a drawing-room full of dukes. [*The Dyer's Hand*]

MR JUSTICE AVORY

21 MARSHALL HALL: Are you one of those who believe that no one is mad?
WITNESS: No.
AVORY: I hope you are not one of those, doctor, who believe that everybody is mad. [Quoted in Gordon Lang, *Mr Justice Avory*, Ch. 11]

A. J. AYER

22 No morality can be founded on authority, even if the authority were divine. [*Essay on Humanism*]

B

FRANCIS BACON

1 How can I take an interest in my work when I don't like it? [Quoted by Sir John Rothenstein in his Introduction to *Francis Bacon*]

KENNETH BAINBRIDGE

2 Now we are all sons of bitches. [After first atomic test, of which he was in charge. *The Decision to Drop the Bomb*]

NIGEL BALCHIN

3 Seldom have so many babies been poured out with so little bath water. [Of the philosophy of this age, *Lord, I Was Afraid*]

4 Admirable with tics and hysterical paralysis. Sovereign for claustrophobia and enuresis. Invaluable in depression, anxiety states and all neurotic conditions. But it won't just wash your personal dirty linen. [Of psycho-analysis. *Mine Own Executioner*, Ch. 11]

5 Harrison had been under treatment for nine months, and had just reached the peak of the God Almighty stage. Milne [his analyst] was omniscient, omnipresent, all-powerful. What he said was wisdom and truth. [*Ib.* 13]

JAMES BALDWIN

6 The future is ... black. [*Observer*, 'Sayings of the Week', 25 Aug. 1963]

7 White people in this country will have quite enough to do in learning how to accept and love themselves and each other, and when they have achieved this – which will not be tomorrow and may very well be never – the Negro problem will no longer exist, for it will no longer be needed. [*The Fire Next Time*, 'Down at the Cross']

8 If the concept of God has any validity or use, it can only be to make us larger, freer, and more loving. If God cannot do this, then it is time we got rid of Him. [*Ib.*]

9 Consider the history of labour in a country [U.S.A.] in which, spiritually speaking, there are no workers, only candidates for the hand of the boss's daughter. [*Ib.*]

10 It is a great shock at the age of five or six to find that in a world of Gary Coopers you are the Indian. [Speech at Cambridge Union, 17 Feb. 1965]

STANLEY, EARL BALDWIN

11 One morning they [the millions of un-attached voters] opened their papers and read that Lloyd George had said of Bonar Law that he was 'honest to the verge of simplicity'. And they said, 'By God, that is what we have been looking for.' [Speech at an Oxford dinner, quoted in G. M. Young, *Stanley Baldwin*, Ch. 2]

12 Then comes Winston with his hundred-horse-power mind and what can I do? [*Ib.* 11]

13 Supposing I had gone to the country and said that Germany was rearming and we must rearm.... I cannot think of anything that would have made the loss of the election from my point of view more certain. [Speech, 12 Nov. 1936. *Ib.* 23]

14 The only defence is in offence, which means that you have to kill more women and children more quickly than the enemy if you want to save yourselves. [Speech, Nov. 1932. *Ib.* 17]

15 My lips are not yet unsealed. Were those troubles over I would make a case, and I guarantee that not a man would go into the Lobby against us. [Speech on the Abyssinia crisis, quoted in MacNeil₁ Weir, *The Tragedy of Ramsay Mac-Donald*, Ch. 61]

16 I had noticed once or twice that S.B. did not seem to be attending to me, and presently he passed an open note across the table to Winston, who was sitting beside me. On the note was written / MATCHES / lent at 10.30 A.M. Returned? / [Quoted by Neville Chamberlain in Diary note, 1 Nov. 1925]

17 I would rather be an opportunist and float than go to the bottom with my principles round my neck. [Attr.]

18 The intelligent are to the intelligentsia what a man is to a gent. [Attr.]

ARTHUR, LORD BALFOUR

19 FRIEND: I hear you are going to marry Margot Tennant.
A.J.B.: No, that is not so. I rather think of having a career of my own. [Quoted in Margot Asquith, *Autobiography*, Ch. 9]

20 He has only half learned the art of reading who has not added to it the even more refined accomplishments of skipping and skimming. [Quoted in E. T. Raymond, *Mr Balfour*, Ch. 22]

21 Certitude is the child of Custom, not of Reason. [*Ib.*]

22 Christianity naturally, but why journalism? [Said to a man who claimed that the two greatest curses of civilization were Christianity and journalism. Attr.]

23 Nothing matters very much, and very few things matter at all. [Attr.]

LORD BALFOUR OF BURLEIGH

24 London is a splendid place to live in for those who can get out of it. [*Observer*, 'Sayings of the Week', 1 Oct. 1944]

PIERRE BALMAIN

25 The trick of wearing mink is to look as though you are wearing a cloth coat. The trick of wearing a cloth coat is to look as though you are wearing a mink. [*Observer*, 'Sayings of the Week', 13 Feb. 1955]

DR HASTINGS BANDA

26 I wish I could bring Stonehenge to Nyasaland to show there was a time when Britain had a savage culture. [*Observer*, 'Sayings of the Week', 10 March 1963]

TALLULAH BANKHEAD

27 There is less in this than meets the eye. [Said at the revival of a Maeterlinck play, quoted in Alexander Woollcott, *Shouts and Murmurs*, 'Capsule Criticism']

28 I'm as pure as the driven slush. [*Observer*, 'Sayings of the Week', 24 Feb. 1957]

SIR HENRY CAMPBELL BANNERMAN

29 This is not the end of me. [Dying words quoted in H. H. Asquith, *Memoirs*]

HENRI BARBUSSE

30 I see too deep and too much. [*L'Enfer* (*Hell*), tr. John Rodker]

MAURICE BARING

31 My brain is like a hard boiled egg. [*Verses in a Letter*]

32 We see the contrast between the genius which does what it must and the talent which does what it can. [On Pushkin's *Mozart and Salieri, Russian Literature*]

33 He was forbidden to mention ginger beer or warm affection between a man and woman or the execution of Charles the First. [Describing E. Gosse's dealings with Swinburne's family in letter to E. Marsh, 1917]

WILKIE BARD

34 She cost me seven and sixpence. / I wish I'd bought a dog! [*She Cost Me Seven and Sixpence*]

GEORGE BARKER

35 And as you kissed, clumsy in bathing costumes, / History guffawed in a rosebush. [*To Any Member of My Generation*]

H. GRANVILLE BARKER

36 Do you notice how near the Crystal Palace seems? That means rain. [*The Madras House*, Ch. 1]

37 Some of 'em want to be kissed and some want you to talk politics ... but the principle's the same. [*Ib.* 2]

38 Let us cling to our legends, sir ... they are the spiritual side of facts. [*Ib.* 3]

39 Rightly thought of there is poetry in peaches . . . even when they are canned. [*Ib.*]

40 The ready-made skirt business has appeased your craving, has it, for the eternal feminine? [*Ib.*]

41 The middle-class woman of England, as of America . . . think of her in bulk . . . is potentially the greatest money-spending machine in the world. [*Ib.*]

42 And what we men of business should remember is that art, philosophy and religion can and should, in the widest sense of the term, be made to pay. And it's pay or perish, in this world. [*Ib.*]

43 But oh, the farmyard world of sex! [*Ib.* 4]

44 I think it's a mistake to stand outside a system. There's an inhumanity in that amount of detachment. [*Waste*, Act 1]

45 What is the prose for God? [*Ib.* 2]

46 There's a longer lease for the old gang in letting the youngsters in than in keeping them out, isn't there? [*The Secret Life*, II. i]

47 For you have never found that the whole world's turmoil is but a reflection of the anarchy in your own heart? [*Ib.* II. iii]

48 MOORE: The fame of the actress is transitory.
GRANVILLE BARKER: Not so transitory as the fame of the authors she represents; their works remain to decry them. The actress is more fortunate: she leaves only a name and a legend. [Quoted in George Moore, *Conversations in Ebury Street*, Ch. 18]

DJUNA BARNES

49 When she smiled the smile was only in the mouth, and a little bitter: the face of an incurable yet to be stricken with its malady. [*Nightwood*, Ch. 2.]

50 When she fell in love it was with a perfect fury of accumulated dishonesty; she became instantly a dealer in second-hand and therefore incalculable emotions. [*Ib.* 4]

51 That priceless galaxy of misinformation called the mind, harnessed to that stupendous and threadbare glomerate compulsion called the soul, ambling down the almost obliterated bridle-path of Well and Ill. [*Ib.* 7]

J. M. BARRIE

52 Has it ever struck you that the trouts bite best on the Sabbath? God's critters tempting decent men. [*The Little Minister*, Ch. 8]

53 'It's a kid or a coffin,' he said sharply, knowing that only birth or death brought a doctor here. [*Sentimental Tommy*, Ch. 1]

54 A boy does not put his hand into his pocket until every other means of gaining his end has failed. [*Ib.*]

55 'God's gift!' Tommy shuddered, but he said sourly, 'I wish he would take her back.' [*Ib.* 2]

56 It might be said of these two boys that Shovel knew everything but Tommy knew other things. [*Ib.* 3]

57 'Oh, God, if I was sure I were to die tonight I would repent at once.' It is the commonest prayer in all languages. [*Ib.* 8]

58 Sergeant, I am wishful to scold you, but would you be so obliging as to stand on this paper while I do it? [*Quality Street*, I]

59 Sister, I could bear all the rest; but I have been unladylike. [*Ib.*]

60 Oh, that weary Latin, I wish I had the whipping of the man who invented it. [*Ib.* II]

61 What is algebra exactly; is it those three-cornered things? [*Ib.*]

62 You Scots . . . are such a mixture of the practical and the emotional that you escape out of an Englishman's hand like a trout. [*What Every Woman Knows*, III]

63 He had the most atrocious bow-wow public park manner. [*Ib.*]

64 I have always found that the man whose second thoughts are good is worth watching. [*Ib.*]

65 Every man who is high up likes to feel that he has done it all himself; and the wife smiles, and lets it go at that. It's our only joke. Every woman knows that. [*Ib.* IV]

66 That is ever the way. 'Tis all jealousy to the bride and good wishes to the corpse. [Quoted in Sagittarius and George, *The Perpetual Pessimist*]

67 He was the most brilliant of our company, recently notable in debate at

Oxford, where he was runner-up for the presidency of the Union and only lost it because the other man was less brilliant. [*Dear Brutus*, I (stage direction)]

68 They say that in the wood you get what nearly everybody here is longing for – a second chance. [*Ib.* I]

69 Fame is rot; daughters are the thing. [*Ib.* II]

70 The laugh that children are born with lasts just as long as they have perfect faith. [*Ib.*]

71 There is more in it, you see, than taking the wrong turning; you would always take the wrong turning. [*Ib.* III]

72 The same kind, beaming smile that children could warm their hands at. [*Ib.*]

KARL BARTH

73 Men have never been good, they are not good, they never will be good. [Quoted in *Time*, 12 April 1954]

BERNARD BARUCH

74 The cold war. [Said on 17 April 1947, quoted in *New York Herald Tribune*, 31 Oct. 1949]

75 I will never be an old man. To me, old age is always fifteen years older than I am. [*Observer*, 'Sayings of the Week', 21 Aug. 1955]

JACQUES BARZUN

76 There is no doubt about it, the modern thunderstorm no longer clears the air. [Quoting mythical old lady, *God's Country and Mine*]

ARNOLD BAX

77 One should try everything once, except incest and folk-dancing. [*Farewell to My Youth*]

VICE-ADMIRAL BEATTY

78 There seems to be something wrong with our bloody ships today. [Attr. On sinking of battle-cruisers at Battle of Jutland, 30 May 1916]

GEORGE BEAUCHAMP

79 She was one of the early birds, / And I was one of the worms. [Song: *She was a Sweet Little Dickie Bird*]

SIMONE DE BEAUVOIR

80 *On ne nâit pas femme, on le devient.* – One is not born a woman, one becomes one. [*The Second Sex*, Ch. 2]

LORD BEAVERBROOK

81 He [Lloyd George] did not care in which direction the car was travelling, so long as he remained in the driver's seat. [Quoted in *New Statesman*, 14 June 1963]

82 This is my final word. It is time for me to become an apprentice once more. I have not settled in which direction. But somewhere, sometime, soon. [Speech on 25 May 1964, his last public statement]

SAMUEL BECKETT

83 There is no returning game between a man and his stars. [*Murphy*]

84 Nothing to be done. [*Waiting for Godot*, I]

85 ESTRAGON: ... Let's go.
VLADIMIR: We can't.
ESTRAGON: Why not?
VLADIMIR: We're waiting for Godot. [*Ib.*]

86 We should have thought of it when the world was young, in the nineties. [*Ib.*]

87 It's worse than being at the theatre. [*Ib.*

88 He can't think without his hat. [*Ib.*]

89 Everything oozes. [*Ib.* II]

90 We all are born mad. Some remain so. [*Ib.*]

1 To be buried in lava and not turn a hair, it is then a man shows what stuff he is made of. To know he can do better next time, unrecognizably better, and that there is no next time, and that it is a blessing there is not, there is a thought to be going on with. [*Malone Dies*]

2 They had no conversation properly speaking. They made use of the spoken word in much the same way as the guard of a train makes use of his flags or of his lantern. [*Ib.*]

3 My photograph. It is not a photograph of me, but I am perhaps at hand. It is an ass, taken from in front and close up, at the edge of the ocean, it is not the ocean, but for me it is the ocean. [*Ib.*]

4 For why be discouraged, one of the thieves was saved, that is a generous percentage. [*Ib.*]

5 Death must take me for someone else. [*Ib.*]

6 I have my faults, but changing my tune is not one of them. [*The Unnameable*]

7 If anyone should have a smell, it is I. [*Ib.*]

8 It is suicide to be abroad. But what is it to be at home . . . what is it to be at home? A lingering dissolution. [*All that Fall*]

9 What sky! What light! Ah in spite of all it is a blessed thing to be alive in such weather, and out of hospital. [*Ib.*]

10 This dust will not settle in our time. And when it does some great roaring machine will come and whirl it all skyhigh again. [*Ib.*]

11 We could have saved sixpence. We have saved fivepence. [*Pause*] But at what cost? [*Ib.*]

12 CLOV: Do you believe in the life to come? HAMM: Mine was always that. [*Endgame*]

13 That's what hell must be like, small chat to the babbling of Lethe about the good old days when we wished we were dead. [*Embers*]

14 UPTHEREPUBLIC! [Expressing support for the republican side in the Spanish Civil War. Quoted in Hugh Thomas, *The Spanish Civil War*, Ch. 25]

SIR THOMAS BEECHAM

15 I thought long and earnestly, but never for a moment about music, poetry or pictures. The whole world of beauty and romance was summed up for me in clothes. [*A Mingled Chime*, Ch. 1]

16 Musicians did not like the piece [Strauss's *Elektra*] at all. One eminent British composer on leaving the theatre was asked what he thought of it. 'Words fail me,' he replied, 'and I'm going home at once to play the chord of C major

twenty times over to satisfy myself that it still exists.' [*Ib.* 18]

17 The plain fact is that music *per se* means nothing; it is sheer sound, and the interpreter can do no more with it than his own capacities, mental and spiritual, will allow, and the same applies to the listener. [*Ib.* 33]

18 Concerts in England have no future; I have no future; nobody has any future. [*Observer*, 'Sayings of Our Times', 31 May 1953, quoting from 1926]

MAX BEERBOHM

19 There is disrespect in setting up a dead man's effigy and then not unveiling it. But there would be no disrespect, and there would be no violence, if the bad statues familiar to London were ceremoniously veiled, and their inscribed pedestals left just as they are. [*And Even Now*, 'Mobled King']

20 There is always something rather absurd about the past. [*1880*]

21 To give an accurate and exhaustive account of that period would need a far less brilliant pen than mine. [*Ib.*]

22 The only tribute a French translator can pay Shakespeare is not to translate him — even to please Sarah [Bernhardt]. [*Around Theatres*, 'Hamlet, Prince of Denmark']

23 He [Henry Irving] did not, of course, invent the 'star' system. But he carried it as far as it could be carried. [*Ib.* 'Henry Irving']

24 He cannot see beyond his own nose. Even the fingers he outstretches from it to the world are (as I shall suggest) often invisible to him. [*Ib.* 'A Conspectus of G.B.S.']

25 Humour undiluted is the most depressing of all phenomena. Humour must have its background of seriousness. Without this contrast there comes none of that incongruity which is the mainspring of laughter. [*Ib.*]

26 As a teacher, as a propagandist, Mr Shaw is no good at all, even in his own generation. But as a personality he is immortal. [*Ib.*]

27 The Mote in the Middle Distance by H*nry J*m*s. [Story title in *A Christmas Garland*]

28 Her magnificence was never more obvious than in the pause that elapsed before she all of a sudden remarked, 'They so very indubitably *are*, you know.' [*Ib.*]

29 It is doubtful whether the people of Southern England have even yet realized how much introspection there is going on all the time in the Five Towns. [*Ib.*]

30 The lower one's vitality, the more sensitive one is to great art. [*Seven Men*, 'Enoch Soames']

31 I looked out for what the metropolitan reviewers would have to say. They seemed to fall into two classes: those who had little to say and those who had nothing. [*Ib.*]

32 A hundred eyes were fixed on her, and half as many hearts lost to her. [*Zuleika Dobson*, Ch. 1]

33 She had the air of a born unpacker – swift and firm, yet withal tender. . . . She was one of those born to make chaos cosmic. [*Ib.* 2]

34 On another small table stood Zuleika's library. Both books were in covers of dull gold. On the back of one cover BRADSHAW, in beryls was incrusted; on the back of the other, A.B.C. GUIDE, in amethysts, beryls, chrysoprases and garnets. [*Ib.*]

35 The Duke had an intense horror of unmarried girls. [*Ib.* 3]

36 She was hardly more affable than a cameo. [*Ib.*]

37 It was but a few weeks since he had taken his seat in the Lords; and this afternoon, for want of anything better to do, he strayed in. [*Ib.*]

38 It needs no dictionary of quotations to remind me that the eyes are the windows of the soul. [*Ib.* 4]

39 Women who love the same man have a kind of bitter freemasonry. [*Ib.*]

40 You will find that the woman who is really kind to dogs is always one who has failed to inspire sympathy in men. [*Ib.* 6]

41 Beauty and the lust for learning have yet to be allied. [*Ib.* 7]

42 You will think me lamentably crude: my experience of life has been drawn from life itself. [*Ib.*]

43 He held, too, in his enlightened way, that Americans have a perfect right to exist. But he did often find himself wishing Mr Rhodes had not enabled them to exercise that right in Oxford. [*Ib.* 8]

44 You cannot make a man by standing a sheep on its hind legs. But by standing a flock of sheep in that position you can make a crowd of men. [*Ib.* 9]

45 She had the sensitiveness, though no other quality whatsoever, of the true artist. [*Ib.* 10]

46 Ever since I can remember I have been beset by a recurring doubt as to whether I be or be not quite a gentleman. [*Ib.* 11]

47 Death knocks, as we know, at the door of the cottage and of the castle. He stalks up the front-garden and the steep steps of the semi-detached villa, and plies the ornamental knocker so imperiously that the panels of imitation stained glass quiver in the thin front-door. [*Ib.* 13]

48 There he adjusted his hat with care, and regarded himself very seriously, very sternly, from various angles, like a man invited to paint his own portrait for the Uffizi. [*Ib.* 14]

49 The Socratic manner is not a game at which two can play. Please answer my question to the best of your ability. [*Ib.* 15]

50 And love levels all, doesn't it? Love and the Board school. [*Ib.* 17]

51 Byron! – he would be all forgotten today if he had lived to be a florid old gentleman with iron-grey whiskers, writing very long, very able letters to *The Times* about the Repeal of the Corn Laws. [*Ib.* 18]

52 As for you, little Sir Lily Liver, leaning out there, and, I frankly tell you, looking like nothing so much as a gargoyle hewn by a drunken stonemason for the adornment of a Methodist Chapel in one of the vilest suburbs of Leeds or Wigan. . . . [*Ib.* 22]

53 The skins of some small mammal just not large enough to be used as mats. [Of Pinero's eyebrows. Quoted in Hassall, *Edward Marsh*, Ch. 7]

54 A swear-word in a rustic slum / A simple swear-word is to some, / To Masefield, something more. [Quoted in Graves and Hodge, *The Long Weekend*, Ch. 18]

55 Lytton Strachey ... had, like the rest of us, imperfect sympathies. [*Lytton Strachey*, Rede Lecture, 1943]

56 What were they going to do with the Grail when they found it, Mr Rossetti? [Caption to a cartoon]

BRENDAN BEHAN

57 He was born an Englishman and remained one for years. [*The Hostage*, I]

58 PAT: He was an Anglo-Irishman.
MEG: In the blessed name of God, what's that?
PAT: A Protestant with a horse. [*Ib.*]

59 Call down that brasstitute. [*Ib.*]

60 Meanwhile I'll sing that famous old song, 'The Hound that caught the Pubic Hare'. [*Ib.*]

61 When I came back to Dublin, I was courtmartialled in my absence and sentenced to death in my absence, so I said they could shoot me in my absence. [*Ib.*]

62 I wish I'd been a mixed infant. [*Ib.* II]

63 I met with a Gaelic pawnbroker, / From Killarney's waterfalls, / In sobs he cried, 'I wish I'd died, / The Saxons have stolen my balls.' [*Ib.*]

64 I am a sociable worker. [*Ib.*]

65 I always say that a general and a bit of shooting makes you forget your troubles. [*Ib.* III]

66 Go on, abuse me – your own husband that took you off the streets on a Sunday morning, when there wasn't a pub open in the city. [*Ib.*]

67 How dare you! Men of good taste have complicated me on that carpet. [*Ib.*]

68 We're here because we're queer / Because we're queer because we're here. [*Ib.*]

DOMINIC BEHAN

69 I never heard him say much in favour of the absent living, but, a charitable man, he always spoke well of the dead. [*Teems of Times and Happy Returns*, 'Of Love and Marriage']

70 Then one day they opened a Catholic chapel, which was quickly followed by a pub, a block of shops and eventually a school. The school went up last because there was no profit in it. [*Ib.*, 'The Christian and My Brother']

71 They say the altar wine contains Glauber's salts so as they won't get the taste an' break their pledges. ... [*Ib.* 'Up the Republic']

CLIVE BELL

72 It would follow that 'significant form' was form behind which we catch a sense of ultimate reality. [*Art*, Pt I, Ch. 3]

73 One account ... given me by a good artist, is that what he tries to express in a picture is 'a passionate apprehension of form'. [*Ib.*]

74 Art and Religion are, then, two roads by which men escape from circumstance to ecstasy. [*Ib.* II. 1]

75 I will try to account for the degree of my aesthetic emotion. That, I conceive, is the function of the critic. [*Ib.* II. 3]

76 We are in the age of names and catalogues and genius-worship. Now, genius-worship is the infallible sign of an uncreative age. [*Ib.* III. 2]

77 Let the artist have just enough to eat, and the tools of his trade: ask nothing of him. Materially make the life of the artist sufficiently miserable to be unattractive, and no one will take to art save those in whom the divine daemon is absolute. [*Ib.* V. 1]

78 Culture is far more dangerous than Philistinism, because it is more intelligent and more pliant. It has a specious air of being on the side of the artist. [*Ib.*]

79 Only reason can convince us of those three fundamental truths without a recognition of which there can be no effective liberty: that what we believe is not necessarily true; that what we like is not necessarily good; and that all questions are open. [*Civilization*]

80 Comfort came in with the middle classes. [*Ib.*]

MARTIN BELL

81 Lo! Wild applause proclaims a happy ending. / Vendetta is achieved with

clinking swords. / Sheer from the battlements the Diva is descending, / Rash in black velvet and resplendent chords. [*A Benefit Night at the Opera*]

HILAIRE BELLOC

82 Prince of the Empire, Prince of Timbuctoo, / Prince eight foot round and nearly four foot wide, / Do try to run a little faster, do. / – The ice is breaking up on every side. [*Ballade of Genuine Concern*]

83 Pale Ebenezer thought it wrong to fight, / But Roaring Bill (who killed him) thought it right. [*Epigrams*, 'The Papist']

84 I'm tired of Love: I'm still more tired of Rhyme. / But Money gives me pleasure all the time. [*Epigrams*, 'Fatigue']

85 Compact of ancient tales, and port / And sleep – and learning of a sort. [*Lines to a Don*]

86 You find when you are giving up the ghost, / That those who loved you best despised you most. [Quoted in Sagittarius and George, *The Perpetual Pessimist*]

87 The Servile State [Title of a book]

88 Child! do not throw this book about! / Refrain from the unholy pleasure / Of cutting all the pictures out! [*Dedication on the Gift of a Book to a Child*]

89 Not even this peculiar town / has ever fixed a friendship firmer, / But – one is married, one's gone down, / And one's a Don, and one's in Burmah. [*Dedicatory Ode*]

90 Like many of the Upper Class / He liked the Sound of Broken Glass. [*New Cautionary Tales*, 'About John']

1 He had a lot of stocks and shares / And half a street in Buenos Aires. [*Ib.*]

2 Birds in their little nests agree / With Chinamen, but not with me. [*Ib.* 'On Food']

3 The Moral is (I think, at least) / That Man is an UNGRATEFUL BEAST. [*Ib.* 'A Reproof of Gluttony']

4 We also know the sacred height / Up on Tugela side, / Where those three hundred fought with Beit / And fair young Wernher died. [*Verses to a Lord*]

5 For *deliberate* and *intentional* boring you must have a man of some ability to

practise it well, as you must to practise any art well. [*A Conversation with a Cat*, 'A Guide to Boring']

6 I was and am afraid of any reasonably good woman and of the sea – let alone dentists. [Letter to Mrs Raymond Asquith, 16 March 1925. Quoted in Robert Speaight, *Life of Hilaire Belloc*, Ch. 2]

7 There are few greater temptations on earth than to stay permanently at Oxford in meditation, and to read all the books in the Bodleian. [Interview with Cyril Clemens, *The Mark Twain Journal*, quoted in *Ib.*]

8 Everything in this world has its place and its nature and I hope I shall never see a Duke voting for ending any political abuse whatever. [Speech in House of Commons, 1907, quoted in *Ib.* 11]

9 In further letters to Mrs Asquith he compared faith to 'the knowledge of the real coloured visible world to a man half blind'. [Quoted in *Ib.* 17.]

10 I always like to associate with a lot of priests because it makes me understand anti-clerical things so well. [Letter to E. S. P. Haynes, 9 Nov. 1909, quoted in *Ib.*]

11 Tait and Tout may have been dull dogs, but at least they had their dates right. [Remark quoted in *Ib.* 18]

12 The ideal thing is for the historian to write his history, and then to have a gang of trained slaves who can go through the proofs from various aspects. That is why, take it all in all, gentlemen have made the best historians. [Letter to Arthur Pollen, quoted in *Ib.* 18]

13 The poor darlings [the Jews], I'm awfully fond of them and I'm awfully sorry for them, but it's their own silly fault – they ought to have let God alone. [Letter to R. Speaight, quoted in *Ib.* 19]

14 An edition [of Gray's *Elegy*] with steel engravings of 'Protestant angels brought up on milk pudding'. [Letter to Mrs Wansbrough, 6 Jan. 1926, quoted in *Ib.* 20]

15 All he [Hilaire Belloc] had said to me was that I would most certainly go to hell, and so I had not thought it likely that we should ever make friends. [Maurice Baring, *The Puppet Show of Memory*]

SAUL BELLOW

16 A man may say, 'From now on I'm going to speak the truth.' But the truth hears him and runs away and hides before he's even done speaking. [*Herzog*]

17 I thought myself a bum and had my reasons, the main reason being that I behaved like a bum. [*Henderson the Rain King*, Ch. 1]

18 America is so big, and everyone is working, making, digging, bulldozing, trucking, loading, and so on, and I guess the sufferers suffer at the same rate. [*Ib.* 3]

19 I am true adorer of life, and if I can't reach as high as the face of it, I plant my kiss somewhere lower down. [*Ib.* 12]

20 I think that New York is not the cultural centre of America, but the business and administrative centre of American culture. [Radio interview, *Listener*, 22 May 1969]

L. BEMELMANS

21 An American woman, a tourist, a refugee from a conducted tour of the Châteaux de la Loire. She dismissed the historic safari with the words: 'Nothing but thick walls and running comment.' [*How to Travel Incognito*, Ch. 1]

ROBERT BENCHLEY

22 Even nowadays a man can't step up and kill a woman without feeling just a bit unchivalrous. [*Chips off the Old Benchley*, 'Down in Front']

23 I had just dozed off into a stupor when I heard what I thought was myself talking to myself. I didn't pay much attention to it, as I knew practically everything I would have to say to myself, and wasn't particularly interested. [*Ib.* 'The First Pigeon of Spring']

24 My only solution for the problem of habitual accidents ... is for everybody to stay in bed all day. Even then, there is always the chance that you will fall out. [*Ib.* 'Good Luck']

25 A great many people have come up to me and asked how I manage to get so much work done and still keep looking so dissipated. [*Ib.* 'How to Get Things Done']

26 The biggest obstacle to professional writing today is the necessity for changing a typewriter ribbon. [*Ib.* 'Learn to Write']

27 I have been told by hospital authorities that more copies of my works are left behind by departing patients than those of any other author. [*Ib.* 'Why Does Nobody Collect Me?']

28 I haven't been abroad in so long that I almost speak English without an accent. [*Inside Benchley*, 'The Old Sea Rover Speaks']

29 An Austrian scientist has come out with the announcement that there is no such thing as a hundred per cent male or a hundred per cent female. If this is true, it is really a big step forward. [*Ib.* 'A Talk to Young Men']

30 Often Daddy sat up very late working on a case of Scotch. [*Editha's Christmas Burglar*]

31 The surface of Divorce has not been scratched yet. We are lucky that *everyone* isn't divorced. [*Lucky World*]

32 The wise man thinks once before he speaks twice. [*Maxims from the Chinese*]

33 I think that I am violating no confidence when I say that Nature holds many mysteries which we humans have not fathomed as yet. Some of them may not even be worth fathoming. [*Mysteries from the Sky*]

34 The surest way to make a monkey of a man is to quote him. [*Quick Quotations*]

35 Show me a Sunday paper which has been left in a condition fit only for kite flying, and I will show you an anti-social and dangerous character who has left it that way. [*The Wreck of the Sunday Paper*]

ÉDUARD BENEŠ

36 *Securité collective* – collective security. [Words written on a typed draft put before the League of Nations, 1932. A French delegate is said to have protested, '*Impossible; ce n'est pas français.*' Quoted in G. M. Young, *Stanley Baldwin*, Ch. 17]

37 *Détruisez l'Autriche-Hongrie!* – Destroy Austria-Hungary. [Slogan in First World War]

STEPHEN VINCENT BENET

38 If two New Hampshiremen aren't a match for the devil, we might as well give the country back to the Indians. [*13 O'Clock*, 'The Devil and Daniel Webster']

ALAN BENNETT

39 Life is rather like a tin of sardines – we're all of us looking for the key. [*Beyond the Fringe*]

40 We roll back the lid of the sardine tin of life, we reveal the sardines, the riches of life therein, and we get them out, we enjoy them. But, you know, there's always a little piece in the corner you can't get out. I wonder – I wonder, is there a little piece in the corner of your life? I know there is in mine. [*Ib.*]

ARNOLD BENNETT

41 'What great cause is he identified with?' 'He's identified . . . with the great cause of cheering us all up.' [Last words of *The Card*]

42 The people who live in the past must yield to the people who live in the future. Otherwise the world would begin to turn the other way round. [*Milestones*]

43 A man interested in a strange woman acquires one equine attribute – he can look in two directions at once. [*Riceyman Steps*, Pt 1. Ch. 1]

44 She considered that her sister was in some respects utterly provincial – what they used to call in the Five Towns a 'body'. [*The Old Wives' Tale*, Bk IV, Ch. 2, sect. iii]

45 As with many English novelists, he [Peacock] had not taken the trouble to learn his job. [*Journal*, 4 Jan. 1929]

46 A man accustomed to think in millions – other people's millions. [*Ib.* June 1929]

47 To my mind the most pregnant mystical exhortation ever written is 'Be still and know that I am God.' (Forty-sixth Psalm.) [*Ib.* Dec. 1929]

48 Every Briton is at heart a Tory – especially every British Liberal. [*Ib.* Dec. 1929]

49 Mr Lloyd George . . . spoke for a hundred and seventeen minutes, in which period he was detected only once in the use of an argument. [*Things that have Interested Me*, 'After the March Offensive']

50 She was the sort of girl who while being made love to would calmly reflect that to-morrow was the day for cleaning the parlour. [*Ib.* 'In the Tube']

51 Hang Eddie Marsh! He's a miserable fellow. He enjoys everything. [Quoted in James Agate, *Ego*, Bk I, Ch. 7]

A. C. BENSON

52 I believe in instinct, not in reason. When reason is right, nine times out of ten it is impotent, and when it prevails, nine times out of ten it is wrong! [Letter quoted in C. Hassall, *Edward Marsh*, Ch. 7]

STELLA BENSON

53 Edward had no capacity for being comfortable. He lived in a small room in a cheap hotel in San Francisco, and in that room there was no trace of Edward except Edward himself. [*The Poor Man*, Ch. 2]

54 The fire was so fierce under the frying pan that his characteristically poor contribution was devoured in it like a War-savings stamp in the cost of the Great War. [*Ib.* 3]

55 All the artistic words have changed their meaning in California. *Book* means magazine, *music* means jazz, *act* means behaving, *picture* means a snapshot. They haven't even a place to keep books. [*Ib.* 5]

56 Young brother Cliff was a child of nature, a child, it were, of suburban nature. He had no reticences. [*Ib.*]

NICOLAS BENTLEY

57 He who enjoys a good neighbour, said the Greeks, has a precious possession. Same goes for the neighbour's wife. [Quoted in E. Esar and N. Bentley, *The Treasury of Humorous Quotations*]

58 His was the sort of career that made the Recording Angel think seriously about taking up shorthand. [*Ib.*]

NICHOLAS BERDYAEV

59 The social problem cannot be solved apart from the spiritual problem; unless

there is a Christian renewal of souls, those of the workers above all, the sway of Socialism will become definitely a domination by the bourgeois spirit. [*Christianity and Class War*]

60 Truth nailed upon the cross compels nobody, oppresses no one; it must be accepted and confessed freely; its appeal is addressed to free spirits. . . . Every time in history that man has tried to turn crucified Truth into coercive truth he has betrayed the fundamental principle of Christ. [*Dostoevsky*]

61 In a certain sense, every single human soul has more meaning and value than the whole of history with its empires, its wars and revolutions, its blossoming and fading civilizations. [*The Fate of Man in the Modern World*]

BERNARD BERENSON

62 In figure painting, the type of all painting, I have endeavoured to set forth that the principal if not sole source of life enchantments are Tactile Values, Movement and Space Composition. [*The Decline of Art*]

63 We define genius as the capacity for productive reaction against one's training. [*Ib.*]

64 History is an art which must not neglect the known facts. [Attr.]

IRVING BERLIN

65 My brother down in Texas / Can't even write his name. / He signs his cheques with X's, / But they cash 'em just the same. [*Annie Get Your Gun*, 'Doin' What Comes Naturally']

ISAIAH BERLIN

66 Rousseau was the first militant low-brow. [Quoted in *Observer*, 'Sayings of the Week', 9 Nov. 1952]

J. D. BERNAL

67 The full area of ignorance is not mapped: we are at present only exploring its fringes. [Quoted in Sagittarius and George, *The Perpetual Pessimist*]

JOHN BERRYMAN

68 Blossomed Sarah, and I / blossom. Is that thing alive? I hear a famisht / howl. [*Homage to Mistress Bradstreet*, 21]

69 The moon came up late and the night was cold, / Many men died – although we know the fate / Of none, nor of anyone, and the war / Goes on, and the moon in the breast of man is cold. [*The Moon and the Night and the Men*]

70 I see the dragon of years is almost done, / Its claws loosen, its eyes / Crust now with tears, lust and a scale of lies. [*New Year's Eve*]

71 The statue, tolerant through years of weather, / Spares the untidy Sunday throng its look. [*The Statue*]

72 News of one day, one afternoon, one time. / If it were possible to take these things / Quite seriously, I believe they might / Curry disorders in the strongest brain, / Immobilize the most resilient will, / Stop trains, break up the city's food supply, / And perfectly demoralize the nation. [*World-Telegram*]

JOHN BETJEMAN

73 One bottle more of fizzy lemonade. [*An Archaeological Picnic*]

74 Spirits of well-shot woodcock, partridge, snipe / Flutter and bear him up the Norfolk sky. [*Death of King George V*]

75 As beefy ATS / Without their hats / Come shooting through the bridge, / And 'cheerioh' and 'cheeri-bye' / Across the waste of waters die. [*Henley-on-Thames*]

76 Pam, I adore you, Pam, you great big mountainous sports girl / Whizzing them over the net, full of the strength of five. [*Pot Pourri from a Surrey Garden*]

77 Licensed now for embracement, / Pam and I, as the organ / Thunders over you all. [*Ib.*]

78 The gas was on in the Institute, / The flare was up in the gym. [*A Shropshire Lad*]

79 Miss J. Hunter Dunn, Miss J. Hunter Dunn, / Furnish'd and burnish'd by Aldershot sun. [*A Subaltern's Love-song*]

80 As I struggle with double-end evening

tie, / For we dance at the Golf Club, my victor and I. [*Ib.*]

81 Childhood is measured out by sounds and smells / And sights, before the dark of reason grows. [*Summoned by Bells*, IV]

82 The dread of beatings! Dread of being late! / And, greatest dread of all, the dread of games! [*Ib.* VII]

83 'By the boys, *for* the boys. The boys know best. / Leave it to them to pick the rotters out / With that rough justice decent schoolboys know.' [*Ib.*]

84 Aunt Elsie, aunt of normal Scottish boys, / Adopted aunt of lone abnormal me. [*Ib.* VIII]

85 Spiritually I was at Eton, John. [*Ib.* IX]

86 For, while we ate Virginia hams / Contemporaries passed exams. [*Ib.*]

87 And is it true? And is it true, / This most tremendous tale of all, / Seen in a stained-glass window hue, / A baby in an ox's stall? [*Christmas*]

88 Rumbling under blackened girders, Midland, bound for Cricklewood, / Puffed its sulphur to the sunset where that Land of Laundries stood. [*Parliament Hill Fields*]

89 But I'm dying now and done for? / What on earth was all the fun for? / For I'm old and ill and terrified and tight. [*Sun and Fun*]

90 Broad of Church and broad of mind, / Broad before and broad behind, / A keen ecclesiologist, / A rather dirty Wykehamist. [*The Wykehamist*]

1 Foot and note disease. [Attr.]

2 I can speak only for myself. I would like to be a stationmaster on a small country branch line (single track). [Said when asked to name 'a most suitable second employment' by the *Horizon* questionnaire, 1946]

3 Bournemouth is one of the few English towns that one can safely call 'her'. [*First and Last Loves*]

4 Nothing is more empty than a deserted fairground. [*Ib.*]

5 History must not be written with bias, and both sides must be given, even if there is only one side. [*Ib.*]

ANEURIN BEVAN

6 The language of priorities is the religion of Socialism. [Quoted in Vincent Brome, *Aneurin Bevan*, Ch. 1]

7 He [Churchill] is a man suffering from petrified adolescence. [Quoted in *Ib.* 11]

8 This island is almost made of coal and surrounded by fish. Only an organizing genius could produce a shortage of coal and fish in Great Britain at the same time. [Quoted in *Ib.* 12]

9 Its relationship to democratic institutions is that of the death watch beetle – it [the Communist Party] is not a Party, it is a conspiracy. [Quoted from *Tribune*, in *Ib.* 13]

10 No attempt at ethical or social seduction can eradicate from my heart a deep burning hatred for the Tory Party. . . . So far as I am concerned they are lower than vermin. [Speech at Manchester, 4 July 1949]

11 There is no reason to attack the monkey [Selwyn Lloyd] when the organ-grinder [Harold Macmillan] is present. [Speech in House of Commons. Quoted in L. Harris, *The Fine Art of Political Wit*, Ch. 9]

12 We know what happens to people who stay in the middle of the road. They get run over. [*Observer*, 'Sayings of the Week', 9 Dec. 1953]

13 I read the newspaper avidly. It is my one form of continuous fiction. [*Observer*, 'Sayings of the Week', 3 April 1960]

LORD BEVERIDGE

14 Scratch a pessimist, and you find often a defender of privilege. [*Observer*, 'Sayings of the Week', 17 Dec. 1943]

ERNEST BEVIN

15 We had better do our own washing up. [*Observer*, 'Sayings of the Week', 29 March 1942]

GEORGES BIDAULT

16 The weak have one weapon: the errors of those who think they are strong. [*Observer*, 'Sayings of the Week', 15 July 1962]

AMBROSE BIERCE

17 *Altar*, n. They stood before the altar and supplied / The fire themselves in which their fat was fried. [*The Devil's Dictionary*]

18 When Eve saw her reflection in a pool, she sought Adam and accused him of infidelity. [*Ib.*]

19 Applause is the echo of a platitude. [*Ib.*]

20 *Bore*, n. A person who talks when you wish him to listen. [*Ib.*]

21 *Brain*, n. An apparatus with which we think that we think. [*Ib.*]

22 *Calamity*, n. Calamities are of two kinds: misfortune to ourselves, and good fortune to others. [*Ib.*]

23 *Cannon*, n. An instrument employed in the rectification of national boundaries. [*Ib.*]

24 *Debauchee*, n. One who has so earnestly pursued pleasure that he has had the misfortune to overtake it. [*Ib.*]

25 *Egotist*, n. A person of low taste, more interested in himself than in me. [*Ib.*]

26 *Faith*, n. Belief without evidence in what is told by one who speaks without knowledge, of things without parallel. [*Ib.*]

27 *Future*, n. That period of time in which our affairs prosper, our friends are true and our happiness is assured. [*Ib.*]

28 *Garter*, n. An elastic band intended to keep a woman from coming out of her stockings and desolating the country. [*Ib.*]

29 *Genealogy*, n. An account of one's descent from a man who did not particularly care to trace his own. [*Ib.*]

30 *Hand*, n. A singular instrument worn at the end of a human arm and commonly thrust into somebody's pocket. [*Ib.*]

31 *Marriage*, n. The state or condition of a community consisting of a master, a mistress and two slaves, making in all two. [*Ib.*]

32 *Patience*, n. A minor form of despair, disguised as a virtue. [*Ib.*]

33 *Peace*, n. In international affairs, a period of cheating between two periods of fighting. [*Ib.*]

34 *Philanthropist*, n. A rich (and usually bald) old gentleman who has trained himself to grin while his conscience is picking his pocket. [*Ib.*]

35 *Prejudice*, n. A vagrant opinion without visible means of support. [*Ib.*]

36 *Riot*, n. A popular entertainment given to the military by innocent bystanders. [*Ib.*]

37 Mark how my fame rings out from zone to zone: / A thousand critics shouting, 'He's unknown!' [*Couplet*]

38 All are lunatics, but he who can analyse his delusion is a philosopher. [Quoted in H. L. Mencken, *A New Dictionary of Quotations*]

39 The gambling known as business looks with austere disfavour upon the business known as gambling. [Quoted in *Ib.*]

40 When your friend holds you affectionately by both hands you are safe, for you can watch both his. [Quoted in *Ib.*]

L. BINYON

41 We must be just before we are merciful, and leave it intact. [On Allies' entry into Berlin. Quoted in C. Hassall, *Edward Marsh*, Ch. 15]

F. E. SMITH, EARL OF BIRKENHEAD

42 JUDGE: I have read your case, Mr Smith, and I am no wiser now than I was when I started.
F.E.S.: Possibly not, My Lord, but far better informed. [Quoted in *Life of F. E. Smith* by his son, The Second Earl of Birkenhead, Ch. 9]

43 JUDGE: You are offensive, sir.
F.E.S.: We both are; the difference is that I'm trying to be and you can't help it. [C. E. Bechofen Roberts ('Ephesian'), *Lord Birkenhead*, Ch. 3]

44 He [Churchill] is often right, but when he is wrong – my God! [Dinner-table remark quoted in G. M. Young, *Stanley Baldwin*, Ch. 14]

45 WOODROW WILSON: And what, in your opinion, is the trend of the modern English undergraduate?
F.E.S.: Steadily towards women and drink, Mr President. [Quoted in *ib.* 27]

46 MR JUSTICE DARLING: And who is George Robey?
F.E.S.: Mr George Robey is the Darling of the music-halls, m'lud. [Quoted in A. E. Wilson, *The Prime Minister of Mirth*, Ch. 1]

MORRIS BISHOP

47 'I cannot hear a single word; / Yell if you like,' said Dr Slade. / He patted his Unhearing Aid. [*Free from Speech*]

48 There I stood and humbly scanned / The miracle that sense appals, / And I watched the tourists stand / Spitting in Niagara Falls. [*Public Aid for Niagara Falls*]

49 The lights burn low in the barber-shop / And the shades are drawn with care / To hide the haughty barbers / Cutting each other's hair. [*The Tales the Barbers Tell*]

50 We all know Mumsy was vague and clumsy, / Dithering, drunken and dumb. [*There's Money in Mother and Father*]

JUDGE BLAGDEN

51 A witness cannot give evidence of his age unless he can remember being born. [*Observer*, 'Sayings of the Week', 29 Jan. 1950]

GENERAL TASKER BLISS

52 We ought to get out of Europe, horse, foot and dragoons. [Letter quoted in John dos Passos, *Mr Wilson's War*, Ch. 22]

EDMUND BLUNDEN

53 Old farm-houses with their white faces / Fly, and their ghosts have taken their places; / Even the signposts like grim liars / Point to trapping brakes and briars. [*Evening Mystery*]

54 Can she who shines so calm be fear? / What poison pours she in slumber's ear? [*Ib.*]

55 And nigh this toppling reed, still as the dead / The great pike lies, the murderous patriarch, / Watching the waterpit shelving and dark / Where through the plash his lithe bright vassals tread. [*The Pike*]

56 The field and wood, all bone-fed loam, / Shot up a roaring harvest-home. [*Rural Economy*]

57 A country god to every childish eye. [*The Shepherd*]

58 I saw the sunlit vale, and the pastoral fairy-tale; / The sweet and bitter scent of the may drifted by; / But it looked like a lie, / Like a kindly meant lie. [*The Sunlit Vale*]

WILFRID BLUNT

59 The drawing is on the level of that of an untaught child of seven or eight years old, the sense of colour that of a tea-tray painter, the method that of a schoolboy who wipes his fingers on a slate after spitting on them. [Of the Post-Impressionist Exhibition, Diary: 15 Nov. 1910]

RONALD BLYTHE

60 Constant tact from others had had the effect of making him [the future George VI] far too modest and he had quite lost sight of his own merits, if he ever knew them. He was, in fact, ideally suited for the British Throne. [*The Age of Illusion*, Ch. 11]

61 As for the British churchman, he goes to church as he goes to the bathroom, with the minimum of fuss and no explanation if he can help it. [*Ib.* 12]

ANDREW BONAR LAW

62 If I am a great man, then a good many of the great men of history are frauds. [Said to Sir Max Aitken, afterwards Lord Beaverbrook, during the Ulster crisis.]

63 Do Hon. Members believe that any Prime Minister could give orders to shoot down men whose only crime is that they refuse to be driven out of our community and deprived of the privilege of British citizenship? [Speech in House of Commons on Home Rule Bill, 16 April 1912]

64 We have heard of people being thrown to the wolves, but never before have we heard of a man being thrown to the wolves with a bargain on the part of the wolves that they would not eat him. [Speech in House of Commons on Colonel Seely's proffered resignation as War Minister, March 1914]

65 Look at that man's [Mussolini's] eyes. You will hear more of him later. [Said to a secretary, 1922]

66 I must follow them; I am their leader. [Quoted in E. T. Raymond, *Mr Balfour*, Ch. 15]

67 He [Lord Birkenhead] would sooner keep hot coals in his mouth than a witticism. [Attr.]

EDWARD BOND

68 The English sent all their bores abroad, and acquired the empire as a punishment. [*Narrow Road to the Deep North*, Pt II, sc. 1]

LADY VIOLET BONHAM CARTER

69 Tories are not always wrong, but they are always wrong at the right moment. [*Observer* 'Sayings of the Week', 26 April 1964]

DANIEL BOORSTIN

70 We expect to be inspired by mediocre appeals for 'excellence', to be made literate by illiterate appeals for literacy. [*The Image*, Ch. 1]

71 The celebrity is a person who is known for his well-knownness. [*Ib.* 2]

72 Shakespeare, in the familiar lines, divided great men into three classes: those born great, those who achieve greatness, and those who have greatness thrust upon them. It never occurred to him to mention those who hire public relations experts and press secretaries to make themselves look great. [*Ib.*]

73 In the twentieth century our highest praise is to call the Bible 'the World's Best-Seller'. And it has come to be more and more difficult to say whether we think it is a best-seller because it is great, or vice versa. [*Ib.* 4]

74 A best-seller was a book which somehow sold well simply because it was selling well. [*Ib.*]

JORGE LUIS BORGES

75 I have known uncertainty: a state unknown to the Greeks. [*Ficciones*, 'The Babylonian Lottery']

76 Mir Bahadur Oli is, as we have seen, incapable of evading the most vulgar of art's temptations: that of being a genius. [*Ib.* 'The Approach to Al-Mu'tasim']

77 Unfortunately, Quain had already reached the age of forty; he was totally used to failure and he did not easily resign himself to a change of régime. [*Ib.* 'An Examination of the Work of Herbert Quain']

78 The visible universe was an illusion or, more precisely, a sophism. Mirrors and fatherhood are abominable because they multiply it and extend it. [*Ib.* 'Tlön, Uqbar, Orbis, Tertius']

HORATIO BOTTOMLEY

79 I haven't made a study of the question, but I certainly think it is high time Brighton was relieved. [When questioned on the Jewish National Home, Dec. 1918. Quoted in Julian Symons, *Horatio Bottomley*]

80 VISITOR: Ah, Bottomley, sewing?
BOTTOMLEY: No, reaping. [When discovered sewing mail bags by a prison visitor. Quoted in *ib.*]

81 I HAVE PAID, BUT – [Headline to his story of his life in prison, printed in *Weekly Dispatch* after his release. Quoted in *ib.*]

ELIZABETH BOWEN

82 She had to confess inexperience; her personality was still too much for her, like a punt-pole. [*Friends and Relations*, Pt I, Ch. 1]

83 Today proved to be one of those weekdays, vacant, utterly without character, when some moral fort of a lifetime is abandoned calmly, almost idly, without the slightest assault from circumstance. So religions are changed, celibacy relinquished, marriages broken up, or there occurs a first large breach with personal honour. [*Ib.* II. 3]

84 Proximity was their support; like walls after an earthquake they could fall no further for they had fallen against each other. [*Ib.* II. 7]

85 London was simply a shell to him, stamped with her absence. [*Ib.* III. 4]

86 She was anxious to be someone, and, no one ever having voiced a prejudice in her hearing without impressing her, had come to associate prejudice with identity. You could not be a someone without disliking things. [*The House in Paris*, Pt I, Ch. 1]

87 Meetings that do not come off keep a character of their own. They stay as they were projected. [*Ib*. II. 2]

88 Jealousy is no more than feeling alone among smiling enemies. [*Ib*. II. 8]

89 To talk of books is, for oppressed shut-in lovers, no way out of themselves; what was written is either dull or too near the heart. But to walk into history is to be free at once, to be at large among people. [*Ib*.]

90 They were Amazons in homespuns, Amazons, without a touch of deprivation or pathos; their lives had been one long vigorous walk. Like successful nuns, they both had a slightly married air. [*Look at All Those Roses*, 'The Easter Egg Party']

1 By day she never looked old. She grew up when she was asleep. Then, a map of unwilling adult awareness – lines, tensions and hollows – appeared in her exposed face. [*Ib*. 'A Love Story']

2 Married and so communicative; he dreaded to be involved with her. [*To the North*, Ch. 1]

3 At her confirmation classes they had worked through the Commandments: at the seventh, an evening had been devoted to impure curiosity. [*Ib*. 5]

4 'But all my friends now are so very respectable: they take me to see girls' schools.' 'Dear me,' said her aunt, 'are they widowers?' 'No, they have nieces.' [*Ib*. 11]

5 No never forget! ... Never forget any moment; they are too few. [*Ib*. 28]

SIR MAURICE BOWRA

6 I'm a man / More dined against than dining. [Attr. by J. Betjeman, *Summoned by Bells*, IX]

GEORGE BOYLE

7 The Germans are sending over professors of English to trace out the imaginary itinerary of Joyce's imaginary Mr Bloom through the different pubs he is supposed to have visited. [Oliver St John Gogarty, *As I was Going Down Sackville Street*, Ch. 4]

GENERAL BRABAZON

8 Of the stationmaster at Aldershot he inquired on one occasion in later years: 'Where is the London twain?' 'It has gone, Colonel.' 'Gone! Bwing another!' [Quoted in Churchill, *My Early Life*, Ch. 5]

LORD BRABAZON

9 Space beckons us to the three brass balls of the pawnbroker. [Speech in House of Lords, Nov. 1962]

10 I take the view, and always have done, that if you cannot say what you have to say in twenty minutes, you should go away and write a book about it. [Reported in press, June 1955]

CHARLES BRACKET and BILLY WILDER

11 He was five foot three! I went to a judge. A woman needs a man not a radiator cap. [Film, *Hold Back the Dawn*]

BRENDAN BRACKEN

12 It's a good deed to forget a poor joke. [*Observer*, 'Sayings of the Week', 17 Oct. 1943]

MALCOLM BRADBURY

13 His generation was the one between the wars; the thirties were his stamping ground, and his predominant emotion was a puzzled frustration in the face of the fact that all the passions he had held then almost but not quite fitted the situation of the present time. [*Eating People is Wrong*, Ch. 1]

14 English women do not like me. They despise me because I am circumcised. In my country I have four wives. I do not wish to lie alone. Perhaps there are women in this University of more progressive views. [*Ib*.]

15 'In India,' said the nun ... 'the work of Mr Eliot is very much respected; he is translated; and many people have written his thesis for his doctorate on inclinations of his work.' [*Ib.* 2]

16 Sympathy – for all these people, for being foreigners – lay over the gathering like a woolly blanket; and no one was enjoying it at all. [*Ib.*]

17 With Treece you felt that the world was his fault; by existing himself, he *made* it, and he wanted to apologize for it, as he was sure God would want to if he were here. [*Ib.* 3]

18 'The trouble with me is that I just enjoy more and more things,' said Emma. 'First I just liked milk; then I learned to like tea and coffee; and then cocoa and lemonade; and then port and sherry; and then gin and whisky. Soon I shall like everything.' [*Ib.*]

19 He's sexually unpleasant, Stuart. I call him The Solitary Raper. He's like a walking phallic symbol. [*Ib.* 5]

20 It had always seemed to Louis that a fundamental desire to take postal courses was being sublimated by other people into sexual activity. [*Ib.*]

21 He was one of the Old Boy system who had somehow just not known quite enough Old Boys to get a Cambridge fellowship or into the Diplomatic, and so he had missed the gunboat and was left, continually mystified, among people that no one really mixed with at all. [*Ib.* 6]

22 'It's one of these knee-stroking novels,' said Oliver. 'What are they?' asked Treece. 'Oh you know, all pale young working-class men reading Shelley to one another and saying, "Art thou pale for weariness?" and girls who softly stroke their own knees and say, "You know, you're a very strange person."' [*Ib.* 7]

23 'Are you married, Mr Willoughby?' asked the wife of the Vice-Chancellor. ... 'I don't suppose he believes in it,' said the Vice-Chancellor in disgruntled tones. 'Well, why buy the cow,' asked Willoughby reasonably, 'when you can steal milk through the fence?' [*Ib.* 8]

24 You're what I call flabby genteel. [*Ib.*]

GENERAL OMAR BRADLEY

25 The way to win an atomic war is to make certain it never starts. [*Observer*, 'Sayings of the Week', 20 April 1952]

SIR WILLIAM BRAGG

26 We use the classical theory on Mondays, Wednesdays and Fridays, and the quantum theory on Tuesdays, Thursdays and Saturdays. [Quoted in Whetham, *History of Science*]

CARYL BRAHMS and
S. J. SIMON

27 Art, thought Lord Buttonhooke with a clarity of perception that belongs to the slightly drunk alone, is art. [*Casino for Sale*, Ch. 4]

28 'Pumbleberry,' she directed, 'more *crêpe* on the candelabrum.' [*Don't, Mr Disraeli*, Ch. 1]

29 Together they had read their betrothal gifts (Mr Ruskin in Russian leather – instructive but a little light). [*Ib.*]

30 'And how,' demanded Mr Brandibal, spearing a kidney, 'was the new Ibsen?' 'Bricks without Shaw,' said Mr Gloom, dissecting a kipper. [*Ib.*]

31 The Prince of Esterhazy is entering his coach ... his Hungarian costume so covered with diamonds and jewels that he looks as if he has been caught in a rain of them and come in dripping. [*Ib.*]

32 On his soap box in the Crescent the Crossing Sweeper is eating Gefillte Fish. [*Ib.*]

33 'Do you reverse?' he asks anxiously. Juliet looks at him coldly. 'Only with relations,' she says. [*Ib.*]

34 The rain seeps through the window-sill and stains the carpet that the Turkish Ambassador has been missing for two years. [*Ib.*]

35 Downstairs a billiard saloon, upstairs a brothel – what more can a villain want? [*Ib.*]

36 Uncle Clarence has mistrusted Orientals ever since his ticket failed to win the Calcutta Sweep. [*Ib.*]

37 Down the well-proportioned terraces carved out of Regency butter, black bonneted, black mantled, and black elastic booted, comes an endless procession of governesses. They are on their way to present an Address of Farewell to the First Governess in the Land. [*Ib.*]

38 Dead men tell no solicitors! [*Ib.*]

39 'A shipwreck,' said Shakespeare, tapping the list in front of him. 'An impersonation, three songs for a baritone, a sorting out, and a happy ending. That,' he decided, 'will be forty pounds!' [*No Bed For Bacon*, Ch. 1]

40 For ten pounds Beaumont and Fletcher will give you any one of a dozen plays – each indistinguishable from the other. [*Ib.*]

41 Shakesper / Shakspere / Shekspar / He always practised tracing his signature when he was bored. He was always hoping that one of these days he would come to a firm decision upon which of them he liked best. [*Ib.*]

42 'Ale money,' said Burbage. He laughed bitterly. 'Alms for oblivion.' 'By God!' said Shakespeare. 'That's good. That's genius.' [*Ib.* 8]

43 'I am a little doubtful about this,' admitted Elizabeth. 'Is bright red really suitable, do you think?' For once Lady Meanwell dared to speak the truth. 'Suitable, no Ma'am,' she said. 'But entirely lovable.' [*Ib.* 11]

44 So long as his bears and brothels brought in money, what did he [Burbage] care if he lost some of it on Art. [*Ib.* 13]

45 'I am a business man,' said old man Burbage. 'What I want is results. So you will pardon me if I speak frankly. The trouble with your plays, Master Will, is that you leave far too many characters alive at the end of them.' 'Oh,' said Shakespeare. [*Ib.*]

46 Shakespeare sprang to his feet. 'Master Bacon,' he demanded passionately, 'do I write my plays or do you?' Bacon looked at him. He shrugged. [*Ib.*]

47 The country might hail Marlborough as a military genius, but it ought to know what they thought about him at the War Office. [*No Nightingales*, Ch. 1]

48 'So we've finished the Decline,' said the landlord, well pleased. 'Now for the Fall.' There was a bump outside. Mr Gibbon had not gone to Twickenham. [*Ib.* 8]

49 'Vot,' asked George I courteously, 'is ze difference between a public nuisance and a public Gonvenience?' [*Ib.* 9]

50 'Christ Almighty – another letter from my father!' said the Earl of Chesterfield's son. [*Ib.* 15]

51 You're a pessimist. What are facts? We'd never win a war if we faced facts. [*Ib.* 19]

52 Inside the cab Sarah Siddons tried to find a more comfortable portion of herself to sit upon. [*Ib.* 23]

53 'Tell me,' said Madame la Duchesse in a lecherous whisper, 'where can I get a book by the nottee Miss Austen?' [*Ib.* 28]

54 Have you seen 'Monuments that should be Desecrated' anywhere? [*Ib.* 34]

55 The suffragettes were triumphant. Woman's place was in the gaol. [*Ib.* 37]

56 'He can wait,' said Stroganoff. 'Today I must unpack my soul.' [*Six Curtains for Stroganova*, Ch. 2]

57 'Vladimir,' said Natasha, 'do you love me?' 'Toujours,' said Stroganoff with wariness. An unusual emotion for a honeymooning husband when this particular question crops up. But Stroganoff was lying in the upper berth of a railway compartment and Natasha was in the lower berth so the question could not be an overture to a delightful interlude but merely the prelude to some less delightful demand. [*Ib.* 5]

58 'My dear,' said Kashkavar Jones, 'I am very happy for you.' He wept. [*Ib.* 5]

59 A giant came into the room. He was effulging with astrakhan. [*Ib.* 8]

60 'In Londres,' said Kashkavar Jones, 'there is a bigger circus – the biggest circus in the world where everybody goes. It is called,' he said, 'Pic-a-dolly, I think.' [*Ib.* 12]

61 If there are cat-calls ... you are sure at least that the audience is still there. [*Ib.* 13]

62 Stroganoff gazed at her with the hurt reproach of a hooked mackerel betrayed by its faithful sprat. [*Ib.* 17]

63 He gazed at a drake whose beady eye

reminded him of his bank manager. [*Ib.* 18]

64 'And is this my fault?' he demanded, a truculent camel refusing to break its back with someone else's last straw. [*Ib.*]

ERNEST BRAMAH
[E. B. SMITH]

65 Who has not proved the justice of the saying, 'She who breaks the lid by noon will crack the dish ere nightfall?' [*Kai Lung Unrolls His Mat*, 'The Difficult Progression']

66 It is proverbial that from a hungry tiger and an affectionate woman there is no escape. [*Ib.*]

67 Even if your mind is set on drowning courtesy demands that I who am concerned shall at least provide you with a change of dry apparel in which to do so more agreeably. [*Ib.* 'The Further Continuance']

68 Even a goat and an ox must keep in step if they are to plough together. [*Ib.*]

69 He is capable of any crime, from reviling the Classics to diverting water-courses. [*Ib.* 'The Meeting by the Way with the Warrior of Chi-u']

70 Beware of jealousy. . . . Remember it is written, 'Not everyone who comes down your street enters by your door.' [*Ib.*]

71 It is necessary to have a thin voice now to escape the risk of a thick ear in these questionable times. [*Ib.* 'The Concave-witted Li-loe's Craving']

72 He who can predict winning numbers has no need to let off crackers. [*Ib.* 'How Kai Lung Sought to Discourage']

73 Adequately set forth, the history of the Princess Taik and of the virtuous youth occupies all the energies of an agile story-teller for seven weeks. [*Kai Lung's Golden Hours*, 'The Encountering of Six Within a Wood']

74 Alas, it has been well written: 'He who thinks he is raising a mound may only in reality be digging a pit.' [*Ib.* 'The Inexorable Justice of Shan Tien']

75 It is scarcely to be expected that one who has spent his life beneath an official umbrella should have at his command the finer analogies of light and shade. [*Ib.* 'The Degraded Persistence of the Effete Ming-shu']

76 By, as it were, extending the five-fingered gesture of derision from the organ of contempt, you have invited the retaliatory propulsion of the sandal of authority. [*Ib.*]

77 May bats defile his Ancestral Tablets and goats propagate within his neglected tomb! . . . May the sinews of his hams snap in moments of achievement! [*Ib.* 'The Timely Intervention of the Mandarin Shan Tien's Lucky Day']

78 How is it possible to suspend topaz in one cup of the balance and weigh it against amethyst in the other; or who in a single language can compare the tranquillizing grace of a maiden with the invigorating pleasure of witnessing a well-contested rat-fight? [*Ib.* 'The Incredible Obtuseness of those who had opposed the Virtuous Kai-Lung']

79 Those who walk into an earthquake while imploring heaven for a sign are unworthy of consideration. [*Ib.* 'The Outpassing into a State of Assured Felicity']

80 When struck by a thunderbolt it is unnecessary to consult the Book of Dates as to the precise meaning of the omen. [*The Wallet of Kai Lung*, 'The Transmutation of Ling']

81 I am overwhelmed that I should be the cause of such an engaging display of polished agitation. [*Ib.*]

82 When no-noise had been obtained. [*Ib.*]

83 Wait! all men are but as the black, horn-cased beetles which overrun the inferior cooking-rooms of the city, and even at this moment the heavily-shod and unerring foot of Buddha may be lifted. [*Ib.*]

84 Should a person in returning from the city discover his house to be in flames, let him examine well the change which he has received from the chair-carrier, before it is too late; for evil never travels alone. [*Ib.* 'The Charitable Quen-ki-tong']

85 To what degree do the class and position of her entirely unnecessary parents affect the question? [*Ib.*]

86 To steal insidiously upon a destructively-inclined wild beast and transfix it with one well-directed blow of a spear is

attended by difficulties and emotions which are entirely absent in the case of a wicker-work animal covered with canvas-cloth, no matter how deceptive in appearance the latter may be. [*Ib.* 'The Vision of Yin']

MARLON BRANDO

87 An actor's a guy who, if you ain't talking about him, ain't listening. [*Observer*, 'Sayings of the Year', Jan. 1956]

G. W. BRANDT

88 Surrounded on all sides, I won the war single-handed. [Quoted in *Cassell's Encyclopaedia of Literature*, 'Plot']

BERTOLT BRECHT

89 What they could do with round here is a good war. What else can you expect with peace running wild all over the place? You know what the trouble with peace is? No organization. [*Mother Courage*, I]

90 When he told men to love their neighbour, their bellies were full. Nowadays things are different. [*Ib.* II]

1 In a good country virtues wouldn't be necessary. Everybody could be quite ordinary, middling, and for all I care, cowards. [*Ib.*]

2 I don't trust him. We're friends. [*Ib.* III]

3 Kattrin, beware of thin men! [*Ib.*]

4 When a soldier sees a clean face, there's one more whore in the world. [*Ib.*]

5 THE CHAPLAIN: We're in God's hands now!
MOTHER C.: I hope we're not as desperate as that, but it *is* hard to sleep at night. [*Ib.*]

6 And don't you stand around like Jesus in Gethsemane. [*Ib.*]

7 The finest plans have always been spoiled by the littleness of them that should carry them out. Even emperors can't do it all by themselves. [*Ib.* VI]

8 I say, you can't be sure the war will ever end. Of course it may have to pause occasionally – for breath as it were – it can even meet with an accident – nothing on this earth is perfect – a war of which we could say it left nothing to be desired will probably never exist. [*Ib.*]

9 What happens to the hole when the cheese is gone? [*Ib.*]

10 War is like love, it always finds a way. [*Ib.*]

11 She's not so pretty anyone would want to ruin her. [*Ib.*]

12 Don't tell me peace has broken out. [*Ib.* VIII]

13 THE COOK [*to the Chaplain*]: As a grown man, you should know better than to go round advising people. [*Ib.*]

14 It was never decreed that a god musn't pay hotel bills. [*The Good Woman of Setzuan*, Prologue, trans. Eric Bentley]

15 You can only help one of your luckless brothers / By trampling down a dozen others. [*Ib.* Act IVa]

16 A real superior man is like a bell. If you ring it, it rings, and if you don't, it don't, as the saying is. [*Ib.* VIII]

17 Fearful is the seductive power of goodness. [*The Caucasian Chalk Circle*, Act I, trans. Eric Bentley]

18 A good soldier has his heart and soul in it. When he receives an order, he gets a hard on, and when he drives his lance into the enemy's guts, he comes. [*Ib.* III]

19 Think you can run around with a behind like that and get away with it in court? This is a case of intentional assault with a dangerous weapon! [*Ib.* IV]

20 I love the people with their simple straightforward minds. It's only that their smell brings on my migraine. [*Ib.* V]

21 You want justice, but do you want to pay for it, hm? When you go to a butcher you know you have to pay, but you people go to a judge as if you were off to a funeral supper. [*Ib.*]

22 Take note of what men of old concluded: / That what there is shall go to those who are good for it, / Children to the motherly, that they prosper, / Carts to good drivers, that they be driven well, / the valley to the waterers, that it yield fruit. [*Ib.*]

23 When the shark has had his dinner / There is blood upon his fins. / But Macheath he has his gloves on: / They say nothing of his sins. [*The Threepenny Opera*, Prologue, trans. Desmond I. Vesey and Eric Bentley]

24 A man who sees another man on the street corner with only a stump for an arm will be so shocked the first time he'll give him sixpence. But the second time it'll only be a threepenny bit. And if he sees him a third time, he'll have him cold-bloodedly handed over to the police. [*Ib.* Act I, sc. i]

25 The wickedness of the world is so great you have to run your legs off to avoid having them stolen from under you. [*Ib.* I. iii]

26 What does a man live by? By resolutely / Ill-treating, beating, cheating, eating some other bloke! / A man can only live by absolutely / Forgetting he's a man like other folk. [*Ib.* II. iii]

27 Which Adolf was this? I know two Adolfs. One of them's in a lunatic asylum; the other's Adolf Kokoschka, who collects manure. He's in a concentration camp, because he said you couldn't beat an English thoroughbred for really first-class fertilizer. [*Schweyk in the Second World War*, 1]

JIMMY BRESLIN

28 [President] Nixon is a purposeless man, but I have great faith in his cowardice. [Quoted in *Observer*, 16 Nov. 1969]

ARISTIDE BRIAND

29 People think too historically. They are always living half in a cemetery. [Quoted in H. L. Mencken, *A New Dictionary of Quotations*]

JAMES BRIDIE

30 Macbeth is not sufficient proof that a nervous bloke should not commit a murder. Hamlet, a much more neuropathic gent, should have done it in Act I and lived happy ever after. [Letter of 7 Oct. 1933. Quoted in J. Agate, *Ego*, Bk. 2]

CAPTAIN R. G. BRISCOW, M.P.

31 If only Hitler and Mussolini could have a good game of bowls once a week at Geneva, I feel that Europe would not be as troubled as it is. [Speech reported in *Birmingham Post*, quoted in M. Bateman, *This England*, selections from the *New Statesman* Part I]

COLM BROGAN

32 There is only one word for aid that is genuinely without strings, and that word is blackmail. [Attr.]

D. W. BROGAN

33 The combination of a profound hatred of war and militarism with an innocent delight in playing soldiers is one of these apparent contradictions of American life that one has to accept. [*The American Character*, Pt I. Ch. 5]

J. BRONOWSKI

34 The wish to hurt, the momentary intoxication with pain, is the loophole through which the pervert climbs into the minds of ordinary men. [*The Face of Violence*, Ch. 5]

35 The world is made of people who never quite get into the first team and who just miss the prizes at the flower show. [*Ib.* 6]

VAN WYCK BROOKS

36 His wife not only edited his works but edited him. [*The Ordeal of Mark Twain*, Ch. 5]

'BIG BILL BROONZY'

37 They called everybody's number / But they never did call mine. [Songs 'Black, Brown and White' (Alan Lomax, *Folk Songs of North America*, No. 316)]

HEYWOOD BROUN

38 The best newspaperman who has ever been President of the United States [said of Franklin D. Roosevelt. Quoted in D. Boorstin, *The Image*, Ch. 1]

39 The man who has cured himself of B.O. and halitosis, has learned French to surprise the waiter, and the saxophone to amuse the company, may find that people still avoid him because they do not like him. [Quoted in D. W. Brogan, *The American Character*, Pt I, sect. 6]

OLIVER BROWN

40 A shiver ran through the Scottish M.P.s, frantically looking for a spine to run up. [*The Extended Tongue*]

W. J. BROWN

41 We have not yet lost this war, but we are overdrawn on the Bank of Miracles. [*Observer*, 'Sayings of the Week', 16 Aug. 1942]

W. J. BRYAN

42 Behold a republic gradually but surely becoming the supreme moral factor in disputes. [Quoted in John dos Passos, *Mr Wilson's War*, Pt I, Ch. 1]

FRANCIS BRYCE

43 No one ever goes in a four-wheeler to the theatre. [Said when cross-examined by Sir Edward Carson in the Bryce divorce case]

JOHN BUCHAN, LORD TWEEDSMUIR

44 You have to know a man awfully well in Canada to know his surname. [*Observer*, 'Sayings of the Week', 21 May 1950]

JOHN BUCHAN

45 But for the bold experiment of Fascism the decade has not been fruitful in constructive statesmanship. [*Morning Post*, 31 Dec. 1929]

FRANK BUCHMAN

46 I thank heaven for a man like Adolf Hitler, who built a front line of defence against the anti-Christ of Communism. [Interview quoted in *New York World-Telegram*, 25 Aug. 1936]

ART BUCHWALD

47 The buffalo isn't as dangerous as everyone makes him out to be. Statistics prove that in the United States more Americans are killed in automobile accidents than are killed by buffalo. [*I Chose Caviar*, 'Coward in the Congo']

48 Ascot is so exclusive that it is the only racecourse in the world where the horses own the people. [*Ib*. 'Ordeal at Ascot']

49 I explained to him I had simple tastes and didn't want anything ostentatious, no matter what it cost me. [*Ib*. 'A New Lease on Texas']

J. BURCKHARDT

50 Rationalism for the few and magic for the many. [*19th-century Religion*]

GERALD BULLETT

51 How lovely are the feet of the bottle-laden! [*Mr Godly Beside Himself*]

ALAN BULLOCK

52 The people Hitler never understood, and whose actions continued to exasperate him to the end of his life, were the British. [*Hitler*, Ch. 8, V]

53 Hitler showed surprising loyalty to Mussolini, but it never extended to trusting him. [*Ib*. 11. iii]

IVOR BULMER-THOMAS

54 If ever he [Harold Wilson] went to school without any boots it was because he was too big for them. [Said at annual Conservative Conference, 1949]

BASIL BUNTING

55 Name and date / split in soft slate / a few months obliterate. [*Briggflatts*, 1]

56 It looks well enough on the page, but never / well enough. [*Ib*. 2]

57 It is time to consider how Domenico Scarlatti / condensed so much music into so few bars. [*Ib*. 4]

58 Who / swinging his axe / to fell kings, guesses / where we go? [*Ib*. 'Coda']

LUIS BUÑUEL

59 I am an atheist still, thank God. [Quoted by Ado Kyrou, *Luis Buñuel: an Introduction*]

ANTHONY BURGESS

60 Not a future. At least not in Europe. America's different, of course, but America's really only a kind of Russia. You've no idea how pleasant it is not to have any future. It's like having a totally efficient contraceptive. [*Honey for the Bears*, Pt II, Ch. 6]

61 He said it was artificial respiration, but now I find I am to have his child. [*Inside Mr Enderby*, Pt I, Ch. 4, ii]

62 Five days shalt thou labour, as the Bible says. The seventh day is the Lord thy God's. The sixth day is for football and spreading the word and punishing and suchlike. [*Ib.* I. 5. ii]

63 There's a lot to be said for not being known to the readers of the *Daily Mirror*. [*Ib.* II. 1. iii]

64 Bath twice a day to be really clean, once a day to be passably clean, once a week to avoid being a public menace. [*Ib.* I. 2. i]

65 Laugh and the world laughs with you; snore and you sleep alone. [*Ib.* I. 2. ii]

66 *Pax Romana*. Where they made a desolation they called it a peace. What absolute nonsense! It was a nasty, vulgar sort of civilization, only dignified by being hidden and under a lot of declensions. [*Ib.* I. 2. i]

67 Rome's just a city like anywhere else. A vastly overrated city, I'd say. It trades on belief just as Stratford trades on Shakespeare. [*Ib.* II. 2. i]

68 Would you try it for, say, six months, a poem every week? Preferably set in the form of prose, so as not to offend anyone. [*Ib.* I. 3. ii]

69 Mr Barnaby, like a dog, insisted on shaking hands with everybody at all hours of the day and sometimes, waking everybody gently up for the purpose, in the night. [*Ib.* III. 2. ii]

70 There was also Ballroom Dancing and what was called Homecraft. None of the teachers knew very much about what they taught and it was pathetic, sometimes, the way they tried to make our schooldays happy. [*One Hand Clapping*, Ch. 1]

71 The best thing to do, when you've got a dead body and it's your husband's on the kitchen floor and you don't know what to do about it, is to make yourself a good strong cup of tea. [*Ib.* 26]

FRANCES HODGSON BURNETT

72 Children's as good as 'rithmetic to set you findin' out things. [*The Secret Garden*, Ch. 9]

JOHN BURNS

73 No man is worth more than £500 a year. [Attr. Quoted in MacNeill Weir, *The Tragedy of Ramsay MacDonald*, Ch. 20]

TRISTRAM BUSCH

74 Ever since Sherlock Holmes most Englishmen have been born with a detective novel attached to their umbilical cords. [*Secret Service Unmasked*]

MONTAGU BUTLER

75 Would you, my dear young friends, like to be inside with the five wise virgins, or outside, alone and in the dark with the five foolish ones? [Sermon in Trinity chapel. Quoted in Edward Marsh, *Ambrosia and Small Beer*, Ch. 4]

R. A. BUTLER

76 Land of Hope and Glory, / Country of the Free, / Go on voting Tory / Till eternity. [Parody written at Cambridge, quoted in *Observer*, 31 May 1964]

SAMUEL BUTLER

77 When you have told anyone you have left him a legacy the only decent thing to do is to die at once. [Quoted in Festing Jones, *Samuel Butler: A Memoir*, Vol. 2]

DOUGLAS BYNG

78 I'm Millie, a messy old mermaid. [Song]

79 I'm one of the Queens of England / But I can't remember which. [Song, 'I'm One of the Queens of England']

80 Good Queen Anne looked like a man / And won the Dunmow Flitch. [*Ib.*]

ROBERT BYRON

81 Various incidents enlivened the days. There was the shock of discovering that *chota hasri*, which I had always believed to be a form of suicide, in fact denoted early morning tea. [*First Russia, Then Tibet*, Pt II, Ch. 2]

C

JAMES BRANCH CABELL

1 I shall marry in haste, and repeat at leisure. [*Jurgen*, Ch. 16]

ARTHUR CALDER-MARSHALL

2 'Out of sight, out of mind,' when translated into Russian [by computer] then back again, became 'Invisible maniac'. [*Listener*, 23 April 1964]

NORMAN CAMERON

3 Forgive me, Sire, for cheating your intent, / That I, who should command a regiment, / Do amble amiably here, O God, / One of the neat ones in your awkward squad. [*Forgive me Sire*]

4 You find it no great effort to disclose / Your crimes of murder, bigamy and arson, / But can you tell them that you pick your nose? [*Punishment Enough*]

5 These two hated each other at half sight. [*Rimbaud and Verlaine*]

HERBERT CAMPBELL

6 What I liked about that party was / We was all *so refined.* [Chorus of music hall song, quoted in George Robey, *Looking Back on Life*, Ch. 14]

JOSEPH CAMPBELL

7 As a white candle / In a holy place, / So is the beauty / Of an aged face. [*The Old Woman*]

8 Her brood gone from her / And her thoughts as still / As the water / Under a ruined mill. [*Ib.*]

PATRICK CAMPBELL

9 She preserved her new personality – the Mona Lisa with a tendency towards cocaine. [*Life in Thin Slices*, Ch. 6]

10 The word 'charade' is derived from the Spanish *charrada*, the chatter of clowns. Beyond that, charades have no connection with any kind of entertainment, living or dead. [*A Short Trot with a Cultured Mind*, 'The Chatter of Clowns']

11 Magda was foreign – so foreign, indeed, that it was only possible to place her low down in the Balkans. [*Ib.* 'The Crime in the Cloakroom']

12 It seems to me that you can go sauntering along for a certain period, telling the English some interesting things about themselves, and then all at once it feels as if you had stepped on the prongs of a rake. [*Ib.* 'Let the English Alone']

MRS PATRICK CAMPBELL

13 It doesn't matter what you do in the bedroom as long as you don't do it in the street and frighten the horses. [Quoted in Daphne Fielding, *The Duchess of Jermyn Street*, Ch. 2]

14 Marriage is the result of the longing for the deep, deep peace of the double-bed after the hurly-burly of the chaise-longue. [Attr.]

ROY CAMPBELL

15 Translations (like wives) are seldom faithful if they are in the least attractive. [*Poetry Review*, June/July 1949]

16 I hate 'Humanity' and all such abstracts: but I love *people*. Lovers of 'Humanity' generally hate *people and children*, and keep parrots or puppy dogs. [*Light on a Dark Horse*, Ch. 13]

17 Of all the clever people round me here / I most delight in Me – / Mine is the only voice I care to hear, / And mine the only face I like to see. [*Home Thoughts in Bloomsbury*]

18 The teller, Night, through cloudy bars, / Into his sack with fingers cold / Counted his scanty change of stars. [*In the Town Square*]

19 The bargain is fair and the bard is no robber, / A handful of dirt for a heartful of slobber. [*The Land Grabber* (on a poet who offered his heart for a handful of South African soil)]

20 Who forced the Muse to this alliance? / A Man of more degrees than parts – / The jilted Bachelor of Science / And Widower of Arts. [*On Professor Drenan's Verse*]

21 Far from the vulgar haunts of men / Each sits in her 'successful room', / Housekeeping with her fountain pen / And writing novels with her broom. [*On Some South African Novelists*]

22 And the day burns through their blood / Like a white candle through a shuttered hand. [*The Sisters*]

23 Or like a poet woo the moon, / Riding an arm-chair for my steed, / And with a flashing pen harpoon / Terrific metaphors of speed. [*The Festivals of Flight*]

24 Measuring out my life in flagons / (No coffee-spoon to skim the flood). [*Familiar Daemon*]

25 The English Muse her annual theme rehearses / To tell us birds are singing in the sky ... / Only the poet slams the door and curses, / And all the little sparrows wonder why! [*Georgian Spring*]

26 Now Spring, sweet laxative of Georgian strains, / Quickens the ink in literary veins, / The Stately Homes of England ope their doors / To piping Nancy-boys and Crashing Bores. [*The Georgiad*, I]

27 Attend my fable if your ears be clean, / In fair Banana Land we lay our scene – / South Africa, renowned both far and wide / For politics and little else beside. [*The Wayzgoose*, I]

28 Where, having torn the land with shot and shell, / Our sturdy pioneers as farmers dwell, / And, 'twixt the hours of strenuous sleep, relax / To sheer the fleeces or to fleece the blacks. [*Ib.*]

29 Where pumpkins to professors are promoted / And turnips into Parliament are voted. [*Ib.*]

30 Feed them on Kipling, nourish them on 'Punch' – / And in their works the World will wrap its lunch! [*Ib.*]

31 ... burn, with Athens and with Rome, /

A sacred city of the mind. [*Toledo, July 1936*]

32 Through land and sea supreme / without a rift or schism / Roll on the Wowser's dream – / Fascidemokshvism! [*The Beveridge Plan*]

ALBERT CAMUS

33 I am well aware that an addiction to silk underwear does not necessarily imply that one's feet are dirty. None the less, style, like sheer silk, too often hides eczema. [*The Fall*]

34 A single sentence will suffice for modern man: he fornicated and read the papers. [*Ib.*]

35 How many crimes committed merely because their authors could not endure being wrong! [*Ib.*]

36 You know what charm is: a way of getting the answer yes without having asked any clear question. [*Ib.*]

37 Alas, after a certain age every man is responsible for his face. [*Ib.*]

38 I conceived at least one great love in my life, of which I was always the object. [*Ib.*]

39 It hurts me to confess it, but I'd have given ten conversations with Einstein for a first meeting with a pretty chorus-girl. [*Ib.*]

40 No man is a hypocrite in his pleasures. [*Ib.*]

41 Men are never convinced of your reasons, of your sincerity, of the seriousness of your sufferings, except by your death. [*Ib.*]

42 Bourgeois marriage has put our country into slippers and will soon lead it to the gates of death. [*Ib.*]

43 Don't wait for the Last Judgement. It takes place every day. [*Ib.*]

44 Too many people have decided to do without generosity in order to practise charity. [*Ib.*]

45 A person I knew used to divide human beings into three categories: those who prefer having nothing to hide rather than being obliged to lie, those who prefer lying to having nothing to hide, and finally those who like both lying and the hidden. [*Ib.*]

46 If one denies that there are grounds for suicide one cannot claim them for murder. One cannot be a part-time nihilist. [*The Rebel*, Introduction]

47 What is a rebel? A man who says no. [*Ib*. Ch. 1]

48 The threat of mortality that hangs over us sterilizes everything. Only the cry of anguish can bring us to life; exaltation takes the place of truth. [*Ib*. 2]

49 Every act of rebelling expresses a nostalgia for innocence and an appeal to the essence of being. [*Ib*. 3]

50 From the moment that the free-thinkers began to question the existence of God, the problem of justice became of primary importance. [*Ib*.]

51 In that the supreme value, for the animal, is the preservation of life, consciousness should raise itself above the level of that instinct in order to achieve human value. It should be capable of risking its life. [*Ib*.]

52 Martyrs do not build churches; they are the mortar, or the alibi. They are followed by the priests and bigots. [*Ib*.]

53 All modern revolutions have ended in a reinforcement of the power of the State. [*Ib*.]

54 The first attempt to found a Church on nothingness was paid for by complete annihilation [*Ib*.]

55 What ... is a novel but a universe in which action is endowed with form, where final words are pronounced, where people possess one another completely and where life assumes the aspect of destiny? [*Ib*. 4]

56 In art, rebellion is consummated and perpetuated in the act of real creation, not in criticism or commentary. [*Ib*.]

57 The aim is to live lucidly in a world where dispersion is the rule. [*The Notebooks*]

58 The secret of my universe: just imagine God without man's immortality. [*Ib*.]

59 I am not made for politics because I am incapable of wishing for or accepting the death of my adversary. [*Ib*.]

60 He who despairs over an event is a coward, but he who holds hopes for the human condition is a fool. [*Ib*.]

61 Every fulfilment is slavery. It drives us to a higher fulfilment. [*Ib*.]

ELIAS CANETTI

62 If a mother could be content to be nothing but a mother; but where would you find one who would be satisfied with that part alone? [*Auto da Fé*, Part I, Ch. 1]

63 You have but to know an object by its proper name for it to lose its dangerous magic. [*Ib*. III. 2]

64 To circumvent death, to evade it, is one of the oldest and strongest desires of rulers. [*Crowds and Power*, 'The Crowd in History']

65 A speaker can insult and threaten an assemblage of people in the most terrible way, and they will still love him if, by doing so, he succeeds in forming them into a crowd. [*Ib*. 'The Command']

HUGHIE CANNON

66 Won't you come home Bill Bailey, won't you come home? [Song: *Bill Bailey, won't you please come home?*]

ROBERT CAPA

67 The war correspondent has his stake – his life – in his own hands, and he can put it on this horse or that horse, or he can put it back in his pocket at the very last minute. [Quoted in *Images of War*]

TRUMAN CAPOTE

68 Venice is like eating an entire box of chocolate liqueurs at one go. [*Observer*, 'Sayings of the Week', 26 Nov. 1961]

HOAGY CARMICHAEL

69 Strange as a will-o'-the-wisp, / Crazy as a loon, / Sad as a gipsy / Serenading the moon. [*Skylark*]

JOSEPH COMYNS CARR

70 Bancroft called today and brought me some black grapes – *black*, that's not a very good sign, is it? [Letter written when dying, quoted in Seymour Hicks, *Vintage Years*]

CARSON·CARY

ANTHONY CARSON

71 The civil guard are a secret hard-hatted race like ghosts with rifles who are really longing to be human. [*On to Timbuctoo*, Ch. 2]

72 The girls came over giggling, their bosoms blossoming, their aprons full of insults. [*Ib.*]

73 Pigeons, those dull, unmysterious city unemployables, dressed in their grey, secondhand suits. [*Ib.* 12]

74 He could prune roses, make chicken runs, mend plugs and fuses, and talk fluently about the reasonable things of this world. I envied him. [*A Rose by Any Other Name*, Ch. 3]

75 She was a blonde nearly-young American woman of such dynamism that the tideless waves struggled to get farther up the beach. [*Ib.* 10]

76 Deep down under his eyes there was a great fever of thought, but he blotted it out by constantly reading newspapers. [*Ib.* 13]

77 The gull colony returned from the seaside. They had sad little faces with tiny black spectacles. [*Ib.* 20]

78 He [Inland Revenue official] looked like a cardboard hangman. Poisoned ink, paper clip stilettos and suffocation by forms. [*Ib.* 21]

79 The apples fell and the swallows crossed off the days. [*Ib.*]

80 She was dressed in white, and had black, snapping eyes. When she got up her legs twinkled through the dining-room like swords. She was a challenge. [*Ib.* 28]

81 There is never any doubt, then, that one has arrived in Spain. . . . There is a faint sound of drums, a smell of crude olive-oil, and current of strong, leaking electricity. [*A Train to Tarragona*, Pt I, Ch. 2]

82 Happiness is an extremely simple affair like pulling a plug when the birds are singing. [*Ib.* 4]

83 Facing me sat a stout man with a hard red face like a book of rules. ['The Bonnets of Luxemburg', *New Statesman*, 27 Nov. 1964]

36

SIR EDWARD CARSON

84 [Cross-examining an Irish witness.]
CARSON: Are ye a teetotaller?
WITNESS: No, I'm not.
CARSON: Are ye a modtherate dhrinker?
No answer.
CARSON: Should I be roite if I called ye a heavy dhrinker?
WITNESS: That's my business.
CARSON: Have ye any *other* business?
[H. Montgomery Hyde, *Carson*, Ch. 7, sect. ii]

85 My only great qualification for being put in charge of the Navy is that I am very much at sea. [Said to senior Admiralty staff on formation of Coalition, 1916. Quoted in *Ib.* II. i]

86 [On learning that his daughter had fallen in love with an American] I have written her to be very circumspect as I do not relish foreign relations. [*Ib.* 8. iii]

MARCO CARSON

87 And by my grave you'd pray to have me back, / So I could see how well you looked in black. [*To Any Woman*]

RACHEL CARSON

88 For all at last return to the sea – to Oceanus, the ocean river, like the everflowing stream of time, the beginning and the end. [*The Sea Around Us*, final words]

JOYCE CARY

89 She had a mannish manner of mind and face, able to feel hot and think cold. [*Herself Surprised*, Ch. 7]

90 To abuse a man is a lover-like thing and gives him rights. [*Ib.* 35]

1 The sky was like washed-out Jap silk and there were just a few little clouds coming out of it like down feathers out of an old cushion. [*Ib.* 36]

2 He is an artist, you know, and talks a great deal for his own pleasure. [*Ib.* 83]

3 Sun in a mist. Like an orange in a fried fish shop. [*The Horse's Mouth*, Ch. 1]

4 I never pass an empty telephone box without going in to press button B. Button B has often been kind to me. [*Ib.* 2]

5 Sara could commit adultery at one end and weep for her sins at the other, and enjoy both operations at once. [*Ib.* 8]

6 He has a face like what Cardinal Newman's would have been if he had gone into the army instead of the Church, grown an Old Bill moustache, lost most of his teeth, and only shaved on Saturdays, before preaching. [*Ib.* 11]

7 He hadn't got the right tools. He wasn't using Spinoza then, but some kind of old bible cement mixer. [*Ib.* 14]

8 Remember I'm an artist. And you know what that means in a court of law. Next worst to an actress. [*Ib.*]

9 Old octopus in corner with a green dome and a blue beak, working his arms. Trying to take off his overcoat without losing his chair. [*Ib.* 15]

10 Anarchists who love God always fall for Spinoza because he tells them that God doesn't love them. This is just what they need. A poke in the eye. To a real anarchist a poke in the eye is better than a bunch of flowers. It makes him see stars. [*Ib.* 16]

11 If you want to buy something in a junk shop, ask for something else. As laid down by old Clotheswitz. It causes the enemy to concentrate on the wrong flank and upsets his communications. [*Ib.* 18]

12 Usual modern collection. Wilson Steer, water in water-colour; Matthew Smith, victim of the crime in slaughtercolour; Utrillo, whitewashed wall in mortarcolour; Matisse, odalisque in scortacolour; Picasso, spatchcock horse in tortacolour ... Rouault, perishing Saint in thoughtacolour; Epstein, Leah waiting for Jacob in squawtacolour. [*Ib.* 22]

13 Hell is paved with good intentions, but heaven goes in for something more dependable. Solid gold. [*Ib.*]

14 Rich people are like royalty. They can't afford to be touchy. Richesse oblige. [*Ib.*]

15 The Professor looked like a choir-boy when the paid tenor comes in wrong. Bursting out of his collar with joy. [*Ib.* 27]

16 Men like Wilcher, the real old blackcoat breed, out of Hellfire by *The Times*, get on my nerves. [*Ib.* 28]

17 A little more of the abstract and we'd both have gone potty. What is there to bite on in the abstract? You might as well eat triangles and go to bed with a sewing machine. [*Ib.* 31]

18 The only good government ... is a bad one in the hell of a fright. [*Ib.* 32]

19 It was as dark as the inside of a Cabinet Minister. [*Ib.* 33]

20 You used to be like a boiler, Venus de Silo, but now you've got a front. [*Ib.* 35]

21 Of course, I always liked big women. I suppose I was meant to be a sculptor or architect. [*Ib.* 38]

22 It is very pleasant to be written up, even by a writer. [*Ib.* 41]

23 It was a swing door. You can't bang a pub door. The pubs know a lot, almost as much as the churches. They've got a tradition. [*Ib.* 42]

24 Everybody goes in for pischology these days. It started in Genesis, and it reached the Government about 1930. [*Ib.* 44]

25 It is the misfortune of an old man that though he can put things out of his head he can't put them out of his feelings. [*To be a Pilgrim*, Ch. 8]

26 Julie had the power, belonging to all those who stand outside convention, of making common moral ideas seem ridiculous or artificial. So a wild tree growing through a Roman imperial pavement makes it seem faded and paltry. [*Ib.* 63]

LORD CASEY

27 Relieve us of the humiliations of the weather. [Said at Cloud physics congress. *Observer*, 'Sayings of the Week', 17 Sept. 1961]

SIR HUGH CASSON

28 The British love permanence more than they love beauty. [*Observer*, 'Sayings of the Week', 14 June 1964]

STANLEY CASSON

29 In France there are politicians of merit who began life as professors. But in England politicians seem to have been politicians from birth, with Personal

Advancement as their fairy godmother. [*Progress and Catastrophe*]

CHRISTOPHER CAUDWELL
[pseudonym of **CHRISTOPHER ST JOHN SPRIGG**]

30 With the exhaustion of bourgeois social relations, bourgeois passionate love begins also to wither before the economic blast. [*Studies in a Dying Culture*, 'Love']

31 The mute inglorious Milton is a fallacy. Miltons are made not born. [*Ib.* 'D. H. Lawrence']

CHARLES CAUSLEY

32 You must keep your fingers / To yourself / And your lollipop eye / From another man's shelf. [*Johnny Alleluia*]

33 Ears like bombs and teeth like splinters: / A blitz of a boy is Timothy Winters. [*Timothy Winters*]

34 Don't send me a parcel at Christmas time / Of socks and nutty and wine / And don't depend on a long weekend / By the Great Western railway line. [*Song of the Dying Gunner A.A.1*]

35 You must take off your clothes for the doctor / And stand as straight as a pin, / His hand of stone on your white breastbone / Where the bullets all go in. [*Recruiting Drive*]

LORD DAVID CECIL

36 It does not matter that Dickens' world is not life-like; it is alive. [*Early Victorian Novelists*]

BENNETT CERF

37 The Atomic Age is here to stay – but are we? [*Observer*, 'Sayings of the Week', 12 Feb. 1950]

PAUL CÉZANNE

38 No one shall get his hooks into me. [Quoted in Henri Perruchot, *Cézanne*]

H. CHADWICK

39 One thing about the Arian controversy which is universally agreed is that everyone behaved very badly. [Birkbeck lecture on Athanasius and the Arian controversy]

MARC CHAGALL

40 One cannot be precise and still be pure. [*Observer*, 'Sayings of the Week', 3 May 1964]

NEVILLE CHAMBERLAIN

41 I wonder what you thought of the Honours List. I have never ceased to congratulate myself that I did not figure among that rabble. [Letter, 12 Jan. 1918. Quoted in K. Feiling, *Life of Neville Chamberlain*, 7]

42 What a day! Two salmon this morning, and the offer of the Exchequer this afternoon. [Letter declining office, May 1923. Quoted in *Ib.* 9]

43 Though I never shout at Labour members or insult them, I cannot understand the psychology of some of our men who walked across ... and endeavoured to reason with them. . . . I think this sloppy sentimentality is quite as bad as H.'s rudeness. [Quoted in *Ib.* 9]

44 Stanley [Baldwin] begged me to remember that I was addressing a meeting of gentlemen. I always gave him the impression, he said, when I spoke in the House of Commons, that I looked on the Labour party as dirt. [Diary, 19 June 1927]

45 How horrible, fantastic, incredible it is that we should be digging trenches and trying on gas-masks here because of a quarrel in a far-away country between people of whom we know nothing! [Broadcast of 27 Sept. 1938]

46 One can see already how this war twilight is trying people's nerves. [Letter, 23 Sept. 1939. Quoted in *Ib.* 33]

47 Whatever may be the reason – whether it was that Hitler thought he might get away with what he had got without fighting for it, or whether it was that after all the preparations were not sufficiently complete – however, one thing is certain:

he missed the bus. [Speech to Conservative and Unionist Associations, 4 April 1940]

48 The peace offensive. [Phrase attr. in Winston Churchill, *The Gathering Storm*, Ch. 24]

HARRY CHAMPION

49 I'm Henery the Heighth, I am, I am, / I got married to the widder next door / She's been married seven times before, / Hevery one was a Henery, / She wouldn't have a Willy or a Sam. [Song: *I'm Henery the Heighth*]

50 Ginger, Ye're Barmy [Title of song]

RAYMOND CHANDLER

51 The General spoke again, slowly, using his strength as carefully as an out-of-work showgirl uses her last good pair of stockings. [*The Big Sleep*, Ch. 2]

52 It was a blonde. A blonde to make a bishop kick a hole in a stained-glass window. [*Farewell, My Lovely*, Ch. 13]

53 The house itself was not so much. It was smaller than Buckingham Palace, rather grey for California, and probably had fewer windows than the Chrysler Building. [*Ib.* 18]

54 She gave me a smile I could feel in my hip pocket. [*Ib.*]

55 Why, the thing stands out so far you could break off a yard of it and still have enough left for a baseball bat. [*Ib.* 28]

56 When I split an infinitive, god damn it, I split it so it stays split. [Letter to his English publisher]

CHARLES CHAPLIN

57 I am for people. I can't help it. [*Observer*, 'Sayings of the Week', 28 Sept. 1952]

58 I could support neither my own company nor that of anyone else. And of course, the obvious thing happened: I fell in love. [*My Autobiography*, Ch. 6]

59 All I need to make a comedy is a park, a policeman and a pretty girl. [*Ib.* 10]

60 I remain just one thing, and one thing only – and that is a clown. It places me

on a far higher plane than any politician. [*Observer*, 'Sayings of the Week', 17 June 1960]

M. P. CHARLESWORTH

61 I refuse to consider any theory based on an emendation. [Remark to G. M. Lee]

JOHN CHEEVER

62 He had that spooky bass voice meant to announce that he had entered the kingdom of manhood, but Rosalie knew that he was still outside the gates. [*The Wapshot Chronicle*, Ch. 7]

APSLEY CHERRY-GARRARD

63 Polar exploration is at once the cleanest and most isolated way of having a bad time which has been devised. [*The Worst Journey in the World*, Introduction]

64 Take it all in all, I do not believe anybody on earth has a worse time than an Emperor penguin. [*Ib.*]

G. K. CHESTERTON

65 When all philosophies shall fail, / This word alone shall fit; / That a sage feels too small for life, / And a fool too large for it. [*Ballad of the White Horse*, 8]

66 The wine they drink in Paradise / They make in Haute Lorraine. [*A Cider Song*]

67 The road from heaven to Hereford / Where the apple wood of Hereford / Goes all the way to Wales. [*Ib.*]

68 The men that worked for England / They have their graves at home. [*Elegy in a Country Churchyard*]

69 And they that rule in England, / In stately conclave met, / Alas, alas for England / They have no graves as yet. [*Ib.*]

70 St George he was for England, / And before he killed the dragon / He drank a pint of English ale / Out of an English flagon. [*The Englishman*]

71 Merrily taking twopenny ale and cheese with a pocket-knife; / But these were luxuries not for him who went for the Simple Life. / [*The Good Rich Man*]

72 You will find me drinking gin / In the lowest kind of inn, / Because I am a rigid Vegetarian. [*The Logical Vegetarian*]

73 You have weighed the stars in the balance, and grasped the skies in a span: / Take, if you must have answer, the word of a common man. [*The Pessimist*]

74 'What of vile dust?' the preacher said. / Methought the whole world woke. [*The Praise of Dust*]

75 But who hath seen the Grocer / Treat housemaids to his teas / Or crack a bottle of fish sauce / Or stand a man a cheese? [*The Song against Grocers*]

76 Earth will grow worse till men redeem it, / And wars more evil, ere all wars cease. [*A Song of Defeat*]

77 For the men no lords can buy or sell, / They sit not easy when all goes well. [*Ib.*]

78 The Nothing scrawled on a five-foot page. [*Ib.*]

79 But Higgins is a Heathen, / And to lecture rooms is forced, / Where his aunts, who are not married, / Demand to be divorced. [*The Song of the Strange Ascetic*]

80 I remember my mother, the day that we met, / A thing I shall never entirely forget; / And I toy with the fancy that, young as I am, / I should know her again if we met in a tram. [*Songs of Education*, 3 'For the Crêche']

81 Invoke the philologic pen / To show you that a Citizen / Means Something in the City. [*Ib.* 4, 'Citizenship']

82 And the Cock I used to know, / Where all good fellows were my friends / A little while ago. [*When I came back to Fleet Street*]

83 The villas and the chapels where / I learned with little labour / The way to love my fellow-man / And hate my next-door neighbour. [*The World State*]

84 No psychoanalyst has knocked / The bottom out of Bottom's dream. [*The Apology of Bottom the Weaver*]

85 To be clever enough to get all that money, one must be stupid enough to want it. [*The Innocence of Father Brown*, 'The Paradise of Thieves']

86 Where does a wise man kick a pebble? On the beach. Where does a wise man hide a leaf? In the forest. [*Ib.* 'The Broken Sword']

87 Every work of art has one indispensable mark ... the centre of it is simple, however much the fulfilment may be complicated. [*Ib.* 'The Queer Feet']

88 Journalism largely consists in saying 'Lord Jones Dead' to people who never knew Lord Jones was alive. [*The Wisdom of Father Brown*, 'The Purple Wig']

89 An artist will betray himself by some sort of sincerity. [*The Incredulity of Father Brown*, 'The Dagger with Wings']

90 If you convey to a woman that something ought to be done, there is always a dreadful danger that she will suddenly do it. [*The Secret of Father Brown*, 'The Song of the Flying Fish']

1 When we apply it, you call it anarchy; and when you apply it, I call it exploitation. [*The Scandal of Father Brown*, 'The Crime of the Communist']

2 It isn't that they can't see the solution. It is that they can't see the problem. [*Ib.* 'The Point of a Pin']

3 There is a great man who makes every man feel small. But the real great man is the man who makes every man feel great. [*Charles Dickens*]

4 Circumstances break men's bones; it has never been shown that they break men's optimism. [*Ib.*]

5 America has a new delicacy, a coarse, rank refinement. [*Ib.*]

6 A man looking at a hippopotamus may sometimes be tempted to regard a hippopotamus as an enormous mistake; but he is also bound to confess that a fortunate inferiority prevents him personally from making such mistakes. [*Ib.*]

7 A sober man may become a drunkard through being a coward. A brave man may become a coward through being a drunkard. [*Ib.*]

8 When some English moralists write about the importance of having character, they appear to mean only the importance of having a dull character. [*Ib.*]

9 Either criticism is no good at all (a very defensible position) or else criticism

means saying about an author the very things that would have made him jump out of his boots. [*Ib.*]

10 I am afraid of the Patchwork Peril, which is all colours and none; I am afraid of bits of Bolshevism and bits of insane individualism and bits of independence in the wrong place, floating hither and thither and colliding with they know not what. [*All I Survey*, 'On Dependence and Independence']

11 It is arguable that we ought to put the State in order before there can really be such a thing as a State school. [*Ib.* 'On Education']

12 Unfortunately humanitarianism has been the mark of an inhuman time. [*Ib.* 'On Industrialism']

13 A great deal of contemporary criticism reads to me like a man saying: 'Of course I do not like green cheese: I am very fond of brown sherry.' [*Ib.* 'On Jonathan Swift']

14 The modern world seems to have no notion of preserving different things side by side, of allowing its proper and proportionate place to each, of saving the whole varied heritage of culture. It has no notion except that of simplifying something by destroying nearly everything. [*Ib.* 'On Love']

15 He set out seriously to describe the indescribable. That is the whole business of literature, and it is a hard row to hoe. [*Ib.* 'On Literary Cliques']

16 No animal ever invented anything so bad as drunkenness – or so good as drink. [*All Things Considered*, 'Wine When it is Red']

17 The rich are the scum of the earth in every country. [*The Flying Inn*]

18 Every politician is emphatically a promising politician. [*The Red Moon of Meru*]

19 The word 'orthodoxy' not only no longer means being right; it practically means being wrong. [*Heretics*, Ch. 1]

20 A man's opinion on tramcars matters; his opinion on Botticelli matters; his opinion on all things does not matter. [*Ib.*]

21 As enunciated today, 'progress' is simply a comparative of which we have not settled the superlative. [*Ib.* 2]

22 There is no such thing on earth as an uninteresting subject; the only thing that can exist is an uninterested person. [*Ib.* 3]

23 We ought to see far enough into a hypocrite to see even his sincerity. [*Ib.* 5]

24 Happiness is a mystery like religion, and should never be rationalized. [*Ib.* 7]

25 Every man speaks of public opinion, and means by public opinion, public opinion minus his opinion. [*Ib.* 8]

26 The obvious truth is that the moment any matter has passed through the human mind it is finally and for ever spoilt for all purposes of science. It has become a thing incurably mysterious and infinite; this mortal has put on mortality. [*Ib.* 11]

27 Charity is the power of defending that which we know to be indefensible. Hope is the power of being cheerful in circumstances which we know to be desperate. [*Ib.* 12]

28 Carlyle said that men were mostly fools. Christianity, with a surer and more reverend realism, says that they are all fools. [*Ib.*]

29 Science in the modern world has many uses; its chief use, however, is to provide long words to cover the errors of the rich. The word 'kleptomania' is a vulgar example of what I mean. [*Ib.* 13]

30 Honour is a luxury for aristocrats, but it is a necessity for hall-porters. [*Ib.*]

31 It is quite proper that a British diplomatist should seek the society of Japanese generals if what he wants is Japanese generals. But if what he wants is people different from himself, he had much better stop at home and discuss religion with the housemaid. [*Ib.* 14]

32 To be born into this earth is to be born into uncongenial surroundings, hence to be born into a romance. [*Ib.*]

33 A good novel tells us the truth about its hero; but a bad novel tells us the truth about its author. [*Ib.* 15]

34 The oligarchic character of the modern English commonwealth does not rest, like many oligarchies, on the cruelty of the rich to the poor. It does not even rest on the kindness of the rich to the poor. It rests on the perennial and unfailing kindness of the poor to the rich. [*Ib.*]

35 A third-class carriage is a community, while a first-class carriage is a place of wild hermits. [*Ib.*]

36 The artistic temperament is a disease that afflicts amateurs. [*Ib.* 17]

37 The old are always fond of new things. Young men read chronicles, but old men read newspapers. [*Ib.* 18]

38 When we want any art tolerably brisk and bold we have to go to the doctrinaires. [*Ib.* 20]

39 Bigotry may be roughly defined as the anger of men who have no opinions. [*Ib.*]

40 The modern world is filled with men who hold dogmas so strongly that they do not even know that they are dogmas. [*Ib.*]

41 He was solidly dazed by Westminster Abbey, which is not unnatural since that church became the lumber-room of the larger and less successful statuary of the eighteenth century. [*The Man Who Knew Too Much*, 'The Soul of the Schoolboy']

42 Squire Vane was an elderly schoolboy of English education and Irish extraction. His English education, at one of the great public schools, had preserved his intellect perfectly and permanently at the stage of boyhood. But his Irish extraction subconsciously upset in him the proper solemnity of an old boy, and sometimes gave him back the brighter outlook of a naughty boy. [*Ib.* 'The Trees of Pride']

43 He was himself a robust rationalist, but he went to church to set his tenants an example. Of what, it would have puzzled him to say. [*Ib.*]

44 The human race, to which so many of my readers belong, has been playing at children's games from the beginning, and will probably do it till the end, which is a nuisance for the few people who grow up. [*The Napoleon of Notting Hill*]

45 And Mr Mick not only became a vegetarian, but at length declared vegetarianism doomed ('shedding,' as he called it finely, 'the green blood of the silent animals') and predicted that men in a better age would live on nothing but salt. [*Ib.*]

46 When the chord of monotony is stretched most tight, then it breaks with a sound like a song. [*Ib.*]

47 I never in my life said anything merely because I thought it funny; though, of course, I have an ordinary human vainglory, and may have thought it funny because I had said it. [*Orthodoxy*, Ch. 1]

48 The men who really believe in themselves are all in lunatic asylums. [*Ib.* 2]

49 Poets do not go mad; but chess-players do. [*Ib.*]

50 The madman is not the man who has lost his reason. The madman is the man who has lost everything except his reason. [*Ib.*]

51 The cosmos is about the smallest hole that a man can hide his head in. [*Ib.*]

52 Reason is itself a matter of faith. It is an act of faith to assert that our thoughts have any relation to reality at all. [*Ib.* 3]

53 Thinking means connecting things, and stops if they cannot be connected. [*Ib.*]

54 Mr Shaw is (I suspect) the only man on earth who has never written any poetry. [*Ib.*]

55 Every man who will not have softening of the heart must at last have softening of the brain. [*Ib.*]

56 I came to the conclusion that the optimist thought everything good except the pessimist, and that the pessimist thought everything bad, except himself. [*Ib.* 5]

57 A man's friend likes him but leaves him as he is: his wife loves him and is always trying to turn him into somebody else. [*Ib.*]

58 Courage is almost a contradiction in terms. It means a strong desire to live taking the form of a readiness to die. [*Ib.* 6]

59 All conservatism is based upon the idea that if you leave things alone you leave them as they are. But you do not. If you leave a thing alone you leave it to a torrent of change. [*Ib.* 7]

60 Angels can fly because they take themselves lightly. [*Ib.*]

61 The *rules* of a club are occasionally in favour of the poor member. The drift of a club is always in favour of the rich one. [*Ib.* 9]

62 The primary paradox of Christianity is that the ordinary condition of man is not his sane or sensible condition; that the normal itself is an abnormality. [*Ib.* 11]

63 A debt to Virgil is like a debt to Nature. [*Victorian Literature*]

64 The English statesman is bribed not to be bribed. He is born with a silver spoon in his mouth, so that he may never afterwards be found with the silver spoons in his pocket. [*What's Wrong with the World*]

65 Compromise used to mean that half a loaf was better than no bread. Among modern statesmen it really seems to mean that half a loaf is better than a whole loaf. [*Ib.*]

66 White ermine was meant to express moral purity; white waistcoats were not. [*Ib.*]

67 The meanest man is immortal and the mightiest movement is temporal, not to say temporary. [*Blackfriars*, Jan. 1923]

68 We live in the Tory revival, that is to say, we live in a world in which artists care for nothing but art, and ethicalists for nothing but ethics. [*Daily News*, 1 Aug. 1903]

69 Blasphemy itself could not survive religion; if anyone doubts that, let him try to blaspheme Odin. [*Ib.* 25 June 1904]

70 When you break the big laws, you do not get liberty; you do not even get anarchy. You get the small laws. [*Ib.* 29 July 1905]

71 A dying monarchy is always one that has too much power, not too little; a dying religion always interferes more than it ought, not less. [*Ib.* 11 March 1911]

72 Mankind is not a tribe of animals to which we owe compassion. Mankind is a club to which we owe our subscription. [*Ib.* 10 April 1906]

73 A puritan's a person who pours righteous indignation into the wrong things. [Attr.]

74 New roads: new ruts. [Attr.]

CHIEF CONSTABLE OF GLOUCESTER

75 If you give a woman an inch she'll park a car in it. [Attr.]

CHINESE PROVERB

76 When you have only two pennies left in the world, buy a loaf of bread with one, and a lily with the other. [Current, Shanghai, 1920]

AGATHA CHRISTIE

77 The happy people are failures because they are on such good terms with themselves that they don't give a damn. [*Sparkling Cyanide*]

RANDOLPH CHURCHILL

78 I expect you know my friend Evelyn Waugh, who, like you, your Holiness, is a Roman Catholic. [Said in an audience with the Pope.]

WINSTON S. CHURCHILL

79 The wars of the peoples will be more terrible than those of kings. [Speech in House of Commons on Army Estimates, 1901, quoted in *Maxims and Reflections*, Sect. V]

80 Men will forgive a man anything except bad prose. [Election speech at Manchester, 1906, quoted in R. Speaight, *Hilaire Belloc*, Ch. 10, sect. II]

81 *The Times* is speechless [over Irish Home Rule] and takes three columns to express its speechlessness. [Speech at Dundee, 14 May 1908]

82 He [Lord Charles Beresford] is one of those orators of whom it was well said, 'Before they get up they do not know what they are going to say; when they are speaking, they do not know what they are saying; and when they sit down, they do not know what they have said.' [Speech in House of Commons, 20 Dec. 1912]

83 The grass grows green on the battlefield, but never on the scaffold. [Attr. remark on Irish Rebellion, 1916]

84 Labour is not fit to govern. [Speech at 1920 election]

85 Frightfulness is not a remedy known to the British pharmacopoeia. [Speech in House of Commons, 8 July 1920]

86 They [the British] are the only people who like to be told how bad things are – who like to be told the worst. [Speech in 1921, quoted in *Observer*, 'Churchilliana']

87 You cannot ask us to take sides against arithmetic. You cannot ask us to take sides against the obvious facts of the situation. [Speech in House of Commons, 31 Aug. 1926]

88 A hopeful disposition is not the sole qualification to be a prophet. [Speech in House of Commons, 30 April 1927]

89 I have waited fifty years to see the Boneless Wonder [Ramsay MacDonald] sitting on the Treasury Bench. [*Ib.* 28 Jan. 1931]

90 We know that he [Ramsay MacDonald] has, more than any other man, the gift of compressing the largest amount of words into the smallest amount of thought. [Speech in House of Commons, 23 Mar. 1933]

1 India is a geographical term. It is no more a united nation than the Equator. [Speech in Royal Albert Hall, 18 Mar. 1931]

2 So they [the Government] go on in strange paradox, decided only to be undecided, resolved to be irresolute, adamant for drift, solid for fluidity, all-powerful for impotence. [Speech in Royal Albert Hall, 12 Nov. 1936]

3 We have sustained a defeat without a war. [Describing Munich. Speech in House of Commons, 5 Oct. 1938]

4 I cannot forecast to you the action of Russia. It is a riddle wrapped in a mystery inside an enigma; but perhaps there is a key. That key is Russian national interest. [Speech in London, 1 Oct. 1939]

5 You ask: 'What is our aim?' I can answer in one word: 'Victory!' Victory at all costs, victory in spite of all terror, victory however long and hard the road may be: for without victory there is no survival. [First speech as Prime Minister in House of Commons, 13 May 1940]

6 Learn to get used to it [bombing]. Eels get used to skinning. [Notes for speech, 20 June 1940]

7 You [Hitler] do your worst, and we will do our best. [Speech at Civil Defence Services' Luncheon, 14 July 1941]

8 In my country, as in yours, public men are proud to be servants of the state and would be ashamed to be its masters. [Speech to U.S. Congress, 26 Dec. 1941]

9 I have not become the King's First Minister in order to preside over the liquidation of the British Empire. [Speech at Mansion House, 10 Nov. 1942]

10 The Almighty in His infinite wisdom did not see fit to create Frenchmen in the image of Englishmen. [Speech in House of Commons, 10 Dec. 1942]

11 There is no finer investment for any community than putting milk into babies. [Broadcast, 21 March 1943]

12 A splendid moment in our great history and in our small lives. [On the unconditional surrender of Germany, 1945]

13 There are few virtues which the Poles do not possess and there are few errors they have ever avoided. [Speech in House of Commons after Potsdam Conference, 1945]

14 We must build a kind of United States of Europe. [Speech in Zurich, 19 Sept. 1946]

15 The English never draw a line without blurring it. [Speech in House of Commons, 16 Nov. 1948]

16 The reason for having diplomatic relations is not to confer a compliment, but to secure a convenience. [Speech in House of Commons, 17 Nov. 1949]

17 Perhaps it is better to be irresponsible and right than to be responsible and wrong. [Party Political Broadcast, London, 26 Aug. 1950]

18 Mr Attlee combines a limited outlook with strong qualities of resistance. [Speech in Royal Albert Hall, 27 Apr. 1951]

19 He [Lenin] alone could have led Russia into the enchanted quagmire; he alone could have found the way back to the causeway. He saw; he turned; he perished. . . . The Russian people were left floundering in the bog. Their worst misfortune was his birth, their next worst – his death. [*The World Crisis*, 'Aftermath', Ch. 4]

20 I wrote my name at the top of the page. I wrote down the number of the question '1'. After much reflection, I put a bracket round it thus '(1)'. But thereafter I could not think of anything connected with it that was either relevant or true. . . . It was from these slender indications of scholarship that Mr Weldon drew the conclusion that I was worthy to pass into Harrow. It is very much to his credit. [*My Early Life*, Ch. 2]

21 Thus I got into my bones the essential structure of the ordinary British sentence – which is a noble thing. [*Ib.*]

22 So they told me how Mr Gladstone read Homer for fun, which I thought served him right. [*Ib.*]

23 Headmasters have powers at their disposal with which Prime Ministers have never yet been invested. [*Ib.*]

24 Which brings me to my conclusion upon Free Will and Predestination, namely – let the reader mark it – that they are identical. [*Ib.* 3]

25 Certainly the prolonged education indispensable to the progress of society is not natural to mankind. [*Ib.*]

26 And here I say to parents, especially wealthy parents, 'Don't give your son money. As far as you can afford it, give him horses.' [*Ib.* 4]

27 I had no idea in those days of the enormous and unquestionably helpful part that humbug plays in the social life of great peoples dwelling in a state of democratic freedom. [*Ib.*]

28 I was never tired of listening to his wisdom or imparting my own. [*Ib.* 7]

29 It is a good thing for an uneducated man to read books of quotations. [Of himself. *Ib.* 9]

30 One voyage to India is enough; the others are merely repletion. [*Ib.* 10]

31 Just as the sentence contains one idea in all its fullness, so the paragraph should embrace a distinct episode; and as sentences should follow one another in harmonious sequence, so paragraphs must fit onto one another like the automatic couplings of railway carriages. [*Ib.* 16]

32 Everyone threw the blame on me. I have noticed that they nearly always do. I suppose it is because they think I shall be able to bear it best. [*Ib.* 17]

33 Buller was a characteristic British personality. He looked stolid. He said little, and what he said was obscure. [*Ib.* 18]

34 I have always been against the Pacifists during the quarrel, and against the Jingoes at its close. [*Ib.* 26]

35 Those who can win a war well can rarely make a good peace and those who

could make a good peace would never have won the war. [*Ib.*]

36 In those days we had a real political democracy led by a hierarchy of statesmen and not a fluid mass distracted by newspapers. [*Ib.* 28]

37 This bright, nimble, fierce, and comprehending being – Jack Frost dancing bespangled in the sunshine. [On Bernard Shaw, *Great Contemporaries*]

38 One day President Roosevelt told me that he was asking publicly for suggestions about what the war should be called. I said at once 'the Unnecessary War'. [*The Gathering Storm*, Preface]

39 The redress of the grievances of the vanquished should precede the disarmament of the victors. [*Ib.* Ch. 3]

40 No country is so vulnerable, and no country would better repay pillage than our own.... With our enormous metropolis here, the greatest target in the world, a kind of tremendous, fat, valuable cow tied up to attract the beast of prey, we are in a position in which we have never been before. [Speech in House of Commons, 1934, quoted in *Ib.* 7]

41 Neither of them [Baldwin and Neville Chamberlain] had any wish to work with me except in the last resort. [*Ib.* 12]

42 I have never seen a human being who more perfectly represented the modern conception of a robot. [Comment on Molotov, *Ib.* 20]

43 'Winston is back' [Signal of Board of Admiralty to the Fleet on his return to the Admiralty, 1939. *Ib.* 22]

44 I felt as if I were walking with destiny, and that all my past life had been but a preparation for this hour and this trial. ... My warnings over the last six years had been so numerous, so detailed, and were now so terribly vindicated, that no one could gainsay me.... I was sure I should not fail. Therefore, although impatient for the morning, I slept soundly and had no need for cheering dreams. Facts are better than dreams. [*Ib.* 38, closing words]

45 You must not underrate England. She is a curious country, and few foreigners can understand her mind.... She is very

clever. If you plunge us into another Great War she will bring the whole world against you, like last time. [To Herr von Ribbentrop, 1936]

46 The road across these five years was long, hard and perilous. Those who perished upon it did not give their lives in vain. Those who marched forward to the end will always be proud to have trodden it with honour. [*Their Finest Hour*, Ch. 1]

47 The Mosquito Armada as a whole was unsinkable. In the midst of our defeat glory came to the Island people, united and unconquerable; and the tale of the Dunkirk beaches will shine in whatever records are preserved of our affairs. [*Ib.* 5]

48 We must be very careful not to assign to this deliverance [Dunkirk] the attributes of a victory. Wars are not won by evacuations. [*Ib.*]

49 I longed for more Regular troops with which to rebuild and expand the Army. Wars are not won by heroic militias. [*Ib.* 8]

50 Any chortling by officials who have been slothful in pushing this bomb, over the fact that at present it has not succeeded, will be viewed with great disfavour by me. [Said to General Ismay. *Ib.*]

51 I have often wondered what would have happened if two hundred thousand German storm troops had actually established themselves ashore. The massacre would have been on both sides grim and great. . . . I intended to use the slogan 'You can always take one with you.' [*Ib.* 13]

52 High in the air soared the fighter pilots, or waited serene at a moment's notice around their excellent machines. This was a time when it was equally good to live or die. [*Ib.*]

53 There was some talk in Parliament after the danger had passed away of the 'invasion scare'. Certainly those who knew most were the least scared. [*Ib.* 14]

54 I doubt whether any of the Dictators had as much effective power throughout his whole nation as the British War Cabinet. When we expressed our desires we were sustained by the people's representatives and cheerfully obeyed by all. [*Ib.* 17]

55 When I look back on all these worries I remember the story of the old man who said on his deathbed that he had had a lot of trouble in his life, most of which had never happened. [*Ib.* 23]

56 The Battle of Britain was won. The Battle of the Atlantic had now to be fought. [*Ib.* 31]

57 It is dangerous to meddle with Admirals when they say they can't do things. They have always got the weather or fuel or something to argue about. [*Ib.* 35]

58 In my experience . . . officers with high athletic qualifications are not usually successful in the higher ranks. [*Ib.* Appendix C, 4 Feb. 1941]

59 So far as strategy, policy, foresight, competence are arbiters Stalin and his commissars showed themselves at this moment [Hitler's invasion of Russia] the most completely outwitted bunglers of the Second World War. [*The Grand Alliance*, Ch. 20]

60 I have only one purpose, the destruction of Hitler, and my life is much simplified thereby. If Hitler invaded Hell I would make at least a favourable reference to the Devil in the House of Commons. [*Ib.*]

61 Before Alamein we never had a victory. After Alamein we never had a defeat. [*The Hinge of Fate*, Ch. 33]

62 Tell them from me they are unloading history. [Telegram to the Port Commandant at Tripoli. *Ib.* 40]

63 Well, the principle seems the same. The water still keeps falling over. [When asked whether the Niagara Falls looked the same as when he first saw them. *Closing the Ring*, Ch. 5]

64 I said that the world must be made safe for at least fifty years. If it was only for fifteen to twenty years then we should have betrayed our soldiers. [*Ib.* 20]

65 I then demonstrated with the help of three matches my idea of Poland moving westwards. [*Ib.*]

66 We must have a better word than 'prefabricated'. Why not 'ready-made'? [*Ib.* Appendix C, 2 Apr. 1944]

67 Everybody has a right to pronounce foreign names as he chooses. [*Observer*, 'Sayings of the Week', 5 Aug. 1951]

68 It is always wise to look ahead, but difficult to look farther than you can see. [*Ib.* 27 July 1952]

69 Personally I'm always ready to learn, although I do not always like being taught. [*Ib.* 9 Nov. 1952]

70 Personally I like short words and vulgar fractions. [Speech in Margate, 10 Oct. 1953]

71 'What is your party?' I asked one group. 'We are the Christian Communists,' their chief replied. I could not help saying, 'It must be very inspiring to your party, having the Catacombs so handy.' [*Triumph and Tragedy*, Ch. 7]

72 As I was the host at luncheon I . . . said to the interpreter that if it was the religion of His Majesty [Ibn Saud] to deprive himself of smoking and alcohol I must point out that my rule of life prescribed as an absolutely sacred rite smoking cigars and also the drinking of alcohol before, after, and if need be during all meals and in the intervals between them. [*Ib.* 23]

73 Peace with Germany and Japan on our terms will not bring much rest. . . . As I observed last time, when the war of the giants is over the wars of the pygmies will begin. [*Ib.* 25]

74 In Franklin Roosevelt there died the greatest American friend we have ever known, and the greatest champion of freedom who has ever brought help and comfort from the New World to the Old. [*Ib.* 28]

75 The establishment of the apes on Gibraltar should be twenty-four, and every effort should be made to reach this number as soon as possible and maintain it thereafter. [*Ib.* Appendix C, Minute, 1 Sept. 1944]

76 The difference between him [Mr Asquith] and Arthur [Balfour] is that Arthur is wicked and moral, Asquith is good and immoral. [Quoted in E. T. Raymond, *Mr Balfour*, Ch. 13]

77 In defeat unbeatable; in victory unbearable. [On Viscount Montgomery. Quoted in Edward Marsh, *Ambrosia and Small Beer*, Ch. 5, sect. ii]

78 It is a fine thing to be honest but it is also very important to be right. [Of Mr Baldwin]

79 They consist entirely of clichés – clichés old and new – everything from 'God is Love' to 'Please adjust your dress before leaving'. [Attr., of Anthony Eden's speeches]

80 I am myself an English-speaking union. [Attr.]

81 It was a case of dislike before first sight. [Describing Kitchener's reaction to him]

82 The nation had the lion's heart. I had the luck to give the roar. [Said on his 80th birthday]

JOHN CIARDI

83 One look at the rush-hour jam in the subway and you know why no one rides it any more. ['Manner of Speaking', *Saturday Review*, 8 Aug. 1964]

SIR KENNETH CLARK

84 You have no idea what portrait painters suffer from the vanity of their sitters. [*Observer*, 'Sayings of the Week', 29 March 1959]

GRANT CLARKE and EDGAR LESLIE

85 And then he'd have to get under, / Get out and get under, / And fix up his automobile. [*He'd Have to Get Under*]

PAUL CLAUDEL

86 *Le poème n'est point fait de ces lettres que je plante comme des clous, mais du blanc qui reste sur le papier.* – The poem is not made from these letters that I drive in like nails, but of the white which remains on the paper. [Footnote to *Cinq Grands Odes*, I, '*Les Muses*']

87 *Délivrez-moi de moi-même! délivrez l'être de la condition! / Je suis libre, délivrez-moi de la liberté!* – Deliver me from myself! Deliver my being from its condition! I am free, deliver me from liberty! [*Ib.* II, '*L'Esprit et l'Eau*']

88 *Quelqu'un qui soit en moi, plus moi-même que moi.* – Someone who may be in me, more myself than I. [*Vers d'Exil*]

89 *Nous ne sommes pas seules. Naître, pour tout, c'est connaître. Toute naissance est une connaissance* – We are not alone. To be born for each man is a getting to know. Every birth is a getting to know. [*Traité de la connaissance du monde*]

HARRY CLIFTON

90 Beautiful as a butterfly, and proud as a queen, / Was pretty little Polly Perkins of Paddington Green. [Song: *Polly Perkins*]

1 Paddle Your Own Canoe [Title of music hall song]

J. STORER CLOUSTON

2 'Are you afraid of having your pockets picked?' 'Alas!' replied Mr Beveridge, 'it would take two men to do that.' 'Huh!' snorted the Emperor, 'you are so damned strong are you?' 'I mean,' answered his *vis-à-vis* with his polite smile, 'that it would take one man to put something in and another to take it out.' [*The Lunatic at Large*, Pt I, Ch. 2]

3 'Deformities,' he corrected; 'up to the age of fourteen years I could only walk sideways, and my hair parted in the middle.' [*Ib*. I. 3]

4 'Zey are all noble?' 'In many cases the receipts for their escutcheons are still in their pockets.' [*Ib*. II. 2]

5 'Then it was false?' 'As an address it was perfectly genuine, only it didn't happen to be mine.' [*Ib*. III. 5]

6 'So many virtues in one room reminds me of the virgins of Gomorrah.' 'I beg your pardon? The what?' asked Mr Duggs with a startled stare. Mr Bunker suspected that he had made a slip in his biblical reminiscences. [*Ib*. IV. 2]

HAROLD CLURMAN

7 He [Thornton Wilder] arranges flowers beautifully, but he does not grow them. [*Lies Like Truth*]

IRVIN COBB

8 The mosaic swimming-pool age – just before the era when they had to have a shin-bone of St Sebastian for a clutch-lever. [Quoted in F. Scott Fitzgerald, *Pat Hobby Himself*]

9 I've just learnt about his illness; let's hope it's nothing trivial. [Quoted in Esar and Bentley, *Treasury of Humorous Quotations*]

10 Why should a worm turn? It's probably just the same on the other side. [Quoted in *Ib*.]

CHARLES COBORN

11 ''E's all right when you know 'im, / But you've got to know 'im fust.' ['*E's all right*]

CLAUD COCKBURN

12 He [Maynard Keynes] was the first Englishman since Horace Walpole to tell The Long Run to go jump into a lake. 'In the long run,' said Maynard Keynes, '... we are all dead.' [*Aspects of English History*, 'The Bubble']

13 Lord Rosebery, sometimes called 'Nature's Welfare State'. This is in reference to the fact that by marrying a Rothschild, being Prime Minister and winning the Derby, he demonstrated that it was possible to improve one's financial status and run the Empire without neglecting the study of form. [*Ib*. 'A Good Time Had']

JEAN COCTEAU

14 *Hugo était un fou qui se croyait Hugo.* – Hugo was a madman who believed he was Hugo. [*Opium*]

GEORGE M. COHAN

15 We'll be over, we're coming over, / And we won't come back till it's over, over there. [*Over There*, U.S. song of First World War]

F. MOORE COLBY

16 Self-esteem is the most voluble of the emotions. [Quoted in C. Fadiman, *Reading I Have Liked*]

17 One learns little more about a man from the feats of his literary memory than from the feats of his alimentary canal. [Quoted in *ib*.]

COLETTE

18 I have never had any leanings towards flirtations over a sick-bed – fingers coming into contact over a cup of herbtea, and whisperings behind doors of 'my poor friend'. [*Chance Acquaintances*]

19 Total absence of humour renders life impossible. [*Ib.*]

20 When she raises her eyelids it's as if she were taking off all her clothes. [*Claudine and Annie*]

21 My virtue's still far too small, I don't trot it out and about yet. [*Claudine at School*]

22 Jane is rather like one of those refined persons who go out to sew for the rich because they cannot abide contact with the poor. [*The Other One*]

23 It was towards the end of June that incompatibility became established between them like a new season of the year. [*The Cat*]

24 When Camille was alone, she looked very much like the little girl who did not want to say 'how d'you do?' Her face returned to childhood because it wore that expression of inhuman innocence, of angelic hardness which ennobles children's faces. [*Ib.*]

25 Madame Alvarez had taken the name of a Spanish lover now dead, and accordingly had acquired a creamy complexion, an ample bust, and hair lustrous with brilliantine. [*Gigi*]

26 The three great stumbling-blocks in a girl's education, she says, are *homard à l'Américaine*, a boiled egg, and asparagus. Shoddy table manners, she says, have broken up many a happy home. [*Ib.*]

27 Don't ever wear artistic jewellery; it wrecks a woman's reputation. [*Ib.*]

28 Don't eat too many almonds; they add weight to the breasts. [*Ib.*]

R. G. COLLINGWOOD

29 So, perhaps, I may escape otherwise than by death the last humiliation of an aged scholar, when his juniors conspire to print a volume of essays and offer it to him as a sign that they now consider him senile. [*Autobiography*]

CHAS COLLINS and FRED W. LEIGH

30 My old man said, 'Follow the van, / Don't dilly dally on the way!' / Off went the cart with the home packed in it, / I walked behind with my old cock linnet. / But I dillied and dallied, dallied and dillied, / Lost the van and don't know where to roam. [Song: *The Cock Linnet*]

CHAS COLLINS, E. A. SHEPPARD and FRED TERRY

31 Any Old Iron? [Title of music hall song]

32 You look neat – talk about a treat, / You look dapper from your napper to your feet. [Song: *Any Old Iron?*]

CHAS COLLINS and FRED MURRAY

33 Boiled Beef and Carrots. [Title of music hall song]

CHAS COLLINS and FRED GODFREY

34 Now I Have to Call Him Father. [Title of music hall song]

MICHAEL COLLINS

35 I am signing my death warrant. [On signing the Irish Treaty, 1921. He was assassinated a few months afterwards. Quoted in Longford, *Peace by Ordeal*, Pt 6, Ch. 1]

ALEX COMFORT

36 One is left with a strong impression that Baden-Baden was built on undelivered faeces. [*The Anxiety Makers*, Ch. 4]

IVY COMPTON-BURNETT

37 It would be a good plan to remove all sinks and make all rooms into halls. . . . It would send up the standard of things. [*A Family and a Fortune*, Ch. 1]

38 'Well, of course, people are only human,' said Dudley to his brother, 'but it really does not seem much for them to be.' [*Ib.* 2]

39 I suppose I shall subscribe to hospitals. That's how people seem to give to the poor. I suppose the poor are always sick. They would be, if you think. [*Ib.* 4]

40 People don't resent having nothing nearly as much as too little. I have only just found that out. I am getting the knowledge of the rich as well as their ways. [*Ib.*]

41 It will be a beautiful family talk, mean and worried and full of sorrow and spite and excitement. I cannot be asked to miss it in my weak state. I should only fret. [*Ib.* 10]

42 I cannot help the low quality of people. They seem to be of a different order from myself. [*Mother and Son*, Ch. 1]

43 Many people misjudge the permanent effect of sorrow and their capacity to live in the past. [*Ib.* 2]

44 It was late that feminine helplessness came into fashion. [*Ib.* 9]

45 We must use words as they are used or stand aside from life. [*Ib.*]

46 Myself and I are on the best of terms. [*Ib.*]

47 There is more difference within the sexes than between them [*Ib.* 10]

48 There is probably nothing like living together for blinding people to each other. [*Ib.*]

49 When I die people will say it is the best thing for me. It is because they know it is the worst. They want to avoid the feeling of pity. As though they were the people most concerned. [*The Mighty and Their Fall*, Ch. 4]

50 There are different kinds of wrong. The people sinned against are not always the best. [*Ib.* 7]

51 Of taking pleasure in any human discomfiture, especially in that of the family he served, he was not ashamed, reserving this feeling for such things as threatened his manhood. [*Men and Wives*, Ch. 1]

52 Of course you are not the one man in the world to me. The world is too full of too many men for that, and I am the one woman of too many. The dear old world! [*Ib.* 24]

53 Self-deception? I don't think there is such a thing. When people say they do things unconsciously or subconsciously, I am quite sure they do them consciously. ... I think on the whole people know. [In conversation with Kay Dick. Quoted in 'A Civilized Life', *The Times Saturday Review*, 30 Aug. 1969]

RICHARD CONDON

54 You are you and I am me: and what have we done to each other? [*The Manchurian Candidate*]

MARC CONNELLY

55 GOD: I'll just r'ar back an' pass a miracle. [*The Green Pastures*]

56 Even bein' Gawd ain't a bed of roses. [*Ib.*]

CYRIL CONNOLLY

57 It is closing time in the gardens of the West. [*The Condemned Playground*]

58 When I write after dark the shades of evening scatter their purple through my prose. [*Enemies of Promise*, Ch. 1]

59 A great writer creates a world of his own and his readers are proud to live in it. A lesser writer may entice them in for a moment, but soon he will watch them filing out. [*Ib.*]

60 Contemporary books do not keep. The quality in them which makes for their success is the first to go; they turn overnight. [*Ib.* 2]

61 I shall christen this style the Mandarin, since it is beloved by literary pundits. It is the style of all those writers whose tendency is to make their language convey more than they mean or more than they feel, it is the style of most artists and all humbugs. [*Ib.*]

62 The ape-like virtues without which no one can enjoy a public school. [*Ib.*]

63 An author arrives at a good style when his language performs what is required of it without shyness. [*Ib.* 3]

64 Literature is the art of writing something that will be read twice; journalism what will be grasped at once. [*Ib.*]

65 Peter, calling an art-for-art's sake muezzin to the faithful from the topmost turret of the ivory tower. [*Ib.* 5]

66 Puritanism in other people we admire is austerity in ourselves. [*Ib.* 9]

67 For most good talkers, when they have run down, are miserable; they know that they have betrayed themselves, that they have taken material which should have a life of its own to dispense it in noises upon the air. [*Ib.* 13]

68 Whom the gods wish to destroy they first call promising. [*Ib.*]

69 If, as Dr Johnson said, a man who is not married is only half a man, so a man who is very much married is only half a writer. [*Ib.* 14]

70 There is no more sombre enemy of good art than the pram in the hall. [*Ib.*]

71 I should like to see the custom introduced of readers who are pleased with a book sending the author some small cash token: anything between half-a-crown and a hundred pounds. . . . Not more than a hundred pounds – that would be bad for my character – not less than half-a-crown – that would do no good to yours. [*Ib.*]

72 The best that can happen for a writer is to be taken up very late or very early, when either old enough to take its measure, or so young that when dropped by society he has all life before him. [*Ib.* 15]

73 No one can make us hate ourselves like an admirer. [*Ib.*]

74 Humorists are not happy men. Like Beachcomber or Saki or Thurber they burn while Rome fiddles. [*Ib.* 16]

75 A poet, with the exception of mysterious water-fluent tea-drinking *Auden*, must be a highly-conscious technical expert. [*Ib.*]

76 The health of a writer should not be too good, and perfect only in those periods of convalescence when he is not writing. [*Ib.*]

77 All charming people have something to conceal, usually their total dependence on the appreciation of others. [*Ib.*]

78 I have always disliked myself at any given moment; the total of such moments is my life. [*Ib.* 18]

79 A private school has all the faults of a public school without any of its compensations. [*Ib.* 19]

80 Tall, pale, with his flaccid cheeks, large spatulate fingers and supercilious voice, he was one of those boys who seem born old. [George Orwell at prep school. *Ib.*]

81 The art of getting on at school depends on a mixture of enthusiasm with moral cowardice and social sense. The enthusiasm is for personalities and gossip about them, for a schoolboy is a novelist too busy to write. [*Ib.* 21]

82 Boys do not grow up gradually. They move forward in spurts like the hands of clocks in railway stations. [*Ib.*]

83 In the eighteenth century he would have become Prime Minister before he was thirty; as it was he appeared honourably ineligible for the struggle of life. [On Sir Alec Douglas-Home as a schoolboy. *Ib.* 23]

84 For the first time I was aware of that layer of blubber which encases an English peer, the sediment of permanent adulation. [*Ib.*]

85 Were I to deduce any system from my feelings on leaving Eton, it might be called *The Theory of Permanent Adolescence.* [*Ib.* 24]

86 Even the Jews in England are boyish, like Disraeli, and not the creators of adult philosophies, like Marx or Freud. [*Ib.*]

87 If he is to enjoy leisure and privacy, marry, buy books, travel and entertain his friends, a writer needs upwards of five pounds a day net. If he is prepared to die young of syphilis for the sake of an adjective, he can do on under. [Answer to a *Horizon* questionnaire, quoted in *Ideas and Places*]

88 One of those warm stoves round which expatriates rally. [Of Alma Mahler Werfel]

89 'Pushing up theses', that is the euphemism which men of letters use for being dead; a long littleness of dons lies ahead of us, unless we have been afflicted with the curse of lucidity. [*Previous Convictions*, 'Dylan Thomas']

90 Like many artists he was mildly snobbish and thus fortunately aware of the magical and sombre poetry of the Fall of

the most haunted of all houses of Usher, the aristocratic civilization built up by the English over two hundred years of plenty. [*Ib.* 'Denton Welch']

1 Better to write for yourself and have no public, than write for the public and have no self. [Quoted in *Turnstile One*, ed. V. S. Pritchett]

2 The man who is master of his passions is Reason's slave. [Quoted in *ib.*]

JOSEPH CONRAD

3 A work that aspires, however humbly, to the condition of art should carry its justification in every line. [*The Nigger of the 'Narcissus'*, Preface]

A. J. COOK

4 Not a penny off the pay; not a minute on the day. [Slogan of Coal Strike, 1925]

PETER COOK

5 You know, I go to the theatre to be entertained. . . . I don't want to see plays about rape, sodomy and drug addiction. . . . I can get all that at home. [Caption to cartoon by Roger Law, *Observer*, 8 July 1962]

6 We exchanged many frank words in our respective languages. [*Beyond the Fringe*]

7 I am very interested in the Universe – I am specializing in the universe and all that surrounds it. [*Ib.*]

CALVIN COOLIDGE

8 One with the law is a majority. [Speech of Acceptance, 27 July 1920]

9 The business of America is business. [Speech in Washington, 17 Jan. 1925]

GILES COOPER

10 There was the Reformation and the Civil War and the Repeal of the Corn Laws and the Zeppelin and the Americans, but none of them made much difference, except the Zeppelin, which knocked down an oak tree that the Vikings were supposed to have planted. [*The Forgotten Rotten Borough*, radio drama]

11 Went off to fight the foreigners because they fired off their guns at Lowestoft, where he had a day's holiday on the Saturday after he got married. [*Ib.*]

12 Sudanese, called himself a dervish, swallowed a fish-hook, cut himself open, took it out again. If an uneducated savage can do that, you can cut your own hair. [*Mathry Beacon*, radio drama]

13 EVANS: You'll teach them education and I'll show them how to lay a brick and make a good job of a bit of carpentry.
OLIM: And I'll give them astrology and trumpet playing. [*Ib.*]

14 Plato . . . the only five-lettered philosopher ending in o. [*Ib.*]

15 GEORGE: What are those statues?
AGATHA: My collection.
GEORGE: They're all of him, the General.
AGATHA: What other statues would I collect? [*The Return of General Forefinger*]

16 This one, in Roman style, as you see, was in front of the General Post office at Aden. Most of the mounted ones seem to be from India . . . the prancing one was outside Lucknow gaol. [*Ib.*]

17 Kerry Dick he was called because he nearly went and lived there, but in the end he married a very pale girl from Devonshire, her father drank. [*Ib.*]

18 QUENTIN: Have you got the room with the toadstools on the ceiling?
GEORGE: There is a patch or two of damp.
QUENTIN: They glow in the dark with a dim phosphorescent light, which is just as well, considering there's no bulb upstairs of more than twenty watts. [*Ib.*]

19 You will now say prayers in Kitchener Dorm, turn out all the lights on Cecil Rhodes landing and pull all the plugs in British Honduras. [*Unman, Wittering and Zigo*, radio drama]

20 All schools are hell, nor are we out of them. In a moment you will hear the sound of the second circle: unrestricted boy. [*Ib.*]

21 I'm a connoisseur of failure. I can smell it, roll it round my mouth, tell you the vintage and the side of the hill that grew it. [*Ib.*]

22 He was a delayed failure with quite a strong flavour of success about him. Even I did not recognize it until he had been here a year or two. But then I noticed the way he kept looking at the top of other people's heads to see whether they were getting as bald as he was. [*Ib.*]

23 This place is full of eyes, and they all belong to the Headmaster. [*Ib.*]

WILLIAM COOPER

24 Myrtle might easily have been thinking about El Greco – equally she might have been thinking about the same thing as me. [*Scenes from Provincial Life*, Pt I, Ch. 2]

25 Bolshaw approved of Hitler in so much as he approved the principle of the Führer's function while feeling that he could fulfil it better himself. [*Ib.* I. 3]

26 Unfortunately, thrashing your young woman doesn't make her admire you more as a novelist. [*Ib.* II. 1]

27 If girls aren't ignorant, they're cultured. ... You can't avoid suffering. [*Ib.* III. 2]

28 It takes two to make even a parting. [*Ib.* III. 4]

29 The trouble about finding a husband for one's mistress, is that no other man seems quite good enough. [*Ib.* III. 5]

30 As an absurdity it was so colossal that it took on the air of a great truth. [*Ib.* IV. 4]

31 I think of the string of delights and disasters that have come my way since 1939. And then I think of all the novels I can make out of them – ah, novels, novels, Art, Art, pounds sterling! [*Ib.* IV. 5]

A. E. COPPARD

32 I am able to declare that thus far my autobiography has no more pure fiction in it than my fiction has pure autobiography. [*It's Me, O Lord!*]

GREGORY CORSO

33 The fall of man stands a lie before Beethoven, a truth before Hitler. [*Man*]

BILLY COTTON

34 Wakey-wakey! Rise and shine! [In broadcasts, with his band]

JOHN CORNFORD

35 Only in constant action was his constant certainty found. / He will throw a longer shadow as time recedes. [In *John Cornford, A Memoir*, ed. Pat Sloan, Pt 2, sect. vii: 'Sergei Mironovich Kirov']

R. COULSON

36 Marriage is not all bed and breakfast. [*Reflections*]

NOËL COWARD

37 Though we all disguise our feelings pretty well, / What we mean by 'Very good' is 'Go to hell'. [*Bitter Sweet*, I. ii]

38 Never mind, dear, we're all made the same, though some more than others. [*Collected Sketches and Lyrics*, 'The Café de la Paix']

39 Whatever your Uncle Bob's failings were, he never tucked his serviette into his dickey. [*Ib.*]

40 You always ought to 'ave tom cats arranged, you know – it makes 'em so much more companionable. [*Ib.* 'Cat's Cradle']

41 I've got a cold, wind under the 'eart, I feel sick, and me feet hurt. [*Ib.* 'The English Lido']

42 There's sand in the porridge and sand in the bed, / And if this is pleasure we'd rather be dead. [*Ib.*]

43 When it's raspberry time in Runcorn, / In Runcorn, in Runcorn, / The air is like a draught of wine, / The undertaker cleans his sign, / The Hull express goes off the line, / When it's raspberry time in Runcorn. [*Ib.* 'Fête Galante']

44 I don't know what London's coming to – the higher the buildings the lower the morals. [*Ib.* 'Law and Order']

45 Sunburn is very becoming – but only when it is even – one must be careful not to look like a mixed grill. [*Ib.* 'The Lido Beach']

46 I've over-educated myself in all the things I shouldn't have known at all. [*Ib.* 'Mild Oats']

47 We have no reliable guarantee that the afterlife will be any less exasperating than this one, have we? [*Blithe Spirit*, I]

48 Considering all the time you took forming yourself, Elsie, I'm surprised you're not a nicer little girl than you are. [*Fumed Oak*, II. ii]

49 I belong to a generation of men, most of which aren't here any more, and we all did the same thing for the same reason, no matter what we thought about politics. [*This Happy Breed*, I. iii]

50 Not only people in other countries who want to do us in because they're sick of us ruling the roost – and you can't blame them at that! but people here in England. People who let 'emselves get soft and afraid. People who go on a lot about peace and good will and the ideals they believe in but somehow don't seem to believe in 'em enough to think they're worth fighting for. [*Ib.* III. iii]

51 We know what we belong to, where we come from, and where we're going. We may not know it with our brains, but we know it with our roots. [*Ib.* III. iii]

52 Miss Erikson looked more peculiar than ever this morning. Is her spiritualism getting worse? [*Present Laughter*, I]

53 He drove with an abandon that either betokened nerves of steel or complete lack of imagination. He held strongly developed anti-Semitic views, about which I argued with him whenever we hit a straight piece of road. [*Future Indefinite*, Pt I, 2]

54 Everybody was up to something, especially, of course, those who were up to nothing. [*Ib.* II. 3]

55 There was a saying, much quoted in the war years, that if an Englishman told you he was a secret agent it was a lie, and that if an American told you the same thing it was true. [*Ib.* IV. 2]

56 Mother love, particularly in America, is a highly-respected and much publicized emotion and, when exacerbated by gin and bourbon, it can become extremely formidable. [*Ib.* IV. 3]

57 A gentle austerity was the keynote of breakfast at Government House. There was a copy of the *Malta Times* for everyone present, but Lord Gort, rightly, was the only one who had a sort of lectern on which to prop it. [*Ib.* IV. 15]

58 Divorced couples hob-nobbed with each other, and with each other's co-respondents. [*Present Indicative*]

59 Dear 338171 (May I call you 338?) [Opening of letter to T. E. Lawrence. *Letters to T. E. Lawrence*]

60 Dance, dance, dance little lady, / Leave tomorrow behind. [*This Year of Grace*]

61 The sun never sets on Government House. [*Words and Music*]

62 Mad about the boy. [*Ib.*]

63 Whatever crimes the Proletariat commits / It can't be beastly to the Children of the Ritz. [*Ib.*]

64 Work is much more fun than fun. [*Observer*: 'Sayings of the Week', 21 June, 1963]

SIR EDWARD GORDON CRAIG

65 Farce is the essential theatre. Farce refined becomes high comedy: farce brutalized becomes tragedy. But at the roots of all drama farce is to be found. [*Index to the Story of My Days*]

66 Never take a bit of notice of traffic and it'll never do you any harm. Like wasps. Let them know who's master. [Quoted in M. Swan, *A Small Part of Time*]

67 One day, when I was very small, that man Charles Dodgson came to tea. Tried to divert me with a puzzle about ferrying six cows across a river on a raft. Very tiresome. [Quoted by Kenneth Tynan, *Observer*, 29 July 1956]

HART CRANE

68 Thin squeaks of radio static, / The captured fume of space foams in our ears. [*The Bridge*, 'Cape Hatteras']

69 Stars scribble on our eyes the frosty sagas, / The gleaming cantos of unvanquished space. [*Ib.*]

70 Our Meistersinger, thou set breath in steel; / And it was thou who on the boldest heel / Stood up and flung the

span on even wing / Of that great Bridge, our Myth, whereof I sing. [Ref. to Walt Whitman and Brooklyn Bridge. *Ib.*]

71 You are your father's father, and the stream / A liquid theme that floating niggers swell. [*Ib.* 'The River']

72 The River lifts itself from its long bed, / Poised wholly on its dream. [*Ib.*]

73 And hurry along, Van Winkle – it's getting late. [*Ib.* 'Van Winkle']

74 The phonographs of hades in the brain / Are tunnels that re-wind themselves, and love / A burnt match skating in a urinal. [*Ib.* 'The Tunnel']

75 ... why do I often meet your visage here, / Your eyes like agate lanterns – on and on / Below the toothpaste and the dandruff ads? [Ref. to Walt Whitman. *Ib.*]

76 The bell-rope that gathers God at dawn / Dispatches me as though I dropped down the knell / Of a spent day. [*The Broken Tower*]

77 The Cross alone has flown the wave. / But since the Cross sank, much that's warped and cracked / Has followed in its name, has heaped its grave. [*The Mermen*]

78 And onwards, as bells off San Salvador / Salute the crocus lustres of the stars, / In these poinsettia meadows of her tides. [*Voyages*, II]

BISHOP CREIGHTON

79 The one real object of education is to leave a man in the condition of continually asking questions. [Quoted in C. A. Alington *Things Ancient and Modern*, Ch. 9]

80 Oxford men think they rule the world, and Cambridge men don't care a cent who does. [Attr.]

BENEDETTO CROCE

81 Art is ruled uniquely by the imagination. Images are its only wealth. It does not classify objects, it does not pronounce them real or imaginary, does not qualify them, does not define them; it feels and presents them – nothing more. [*Esthetic*, Ch. 1]

82 Philosophy removes from religion all reason for existing. ... As the science of the spirit, it looks upon religion as a phenomenon, a transitory historical fact, a psychic condition that can be surpassed. [*Ib.* 8]

83 The latter (the most learned of philologists) arrive at the conclusion that they know nothing at all as the result of exhausting toil; while he knew nothing without any effort at all, simply as a generous gift of nature. [A friend's remark, on returning a book, quoted *Ib.*]

BING CROSBY and BOB HOPE

84 Like Webster's Dictionary, we're Morocco bound. [Film: *The Road to Morocco*]

R. H. S. CROSSMAN

85 All the obvious things have been done which were fought for and argued about. And yet, mysteriously enough, ... the ideal, the pattern of values, has not been achieved. We have done them, we have created the means to the good life which they all laid down and said, 'If you do all these things, after that there'll be a classless society.' Well, there isn't. [Fabian lecture, 1950]

E. E. CUMMINGS

86 what i want to know is / how do you like your blueeyed boy / Mister Death. [*Collected Poems* (1938), 31]

87 the flyspecked abdominous female / indubitably tellurian / strolls / emitting minute grins [*Ib.* 68]

88 hurries / elsewhere; to blow / incredible wampum. [*Ib.*]

89 bodies lopped / of every / prettiness, / you hew form truly. [*Ib.* 103]

90 Humanity i love you / because you would rather black the boots of / success than enquire whose soul dangles from his / watch-chain which would be embarrassing for both / parties and because you / unflinchingly applaud all / songs containing the words country home and / mother when sung at the old howard [*Ib.* 107]

1 a pretty girl who naked is / is worth a million statues [*Ib.* 133]

2 in every language even deafanddumb / thy sons acclaim your glorious name by gorry / by jingo by gee by gosh by gum [*Ib.* 147]

3 'then shall the voices of liberty be mute?' / He spoke. And drank rapidly a glass of water [*Ib.*]

4 (dreaming, / et / cetera, of / Your smile / eyes knees and of your Etcetera) [*Ib.* 148]

5 how do you find the sun, ladies? / (graduallyverygradually) 'there is not enough / of it' their, hands / minutely / answered [*Ib.* 158]

6 when i contemplate her uneyes safely ensconced in thick glass / you try if we are a gentleman not to think of (sh) [*Ib.* 201]

7 and the duckbilled platitude lays & lays / and Lays aytash unee [*Ib.* 203]

8 responds, without getting annoyed / 'I will not kiss your f.ing flag.' [*Ib.* 204]

9 Olaf (upon what were once knees) / does almost ceaselessly repeat / 'there is some s. I will not eat' [*Ib.*]

10 unless statistics lie he was / more brave than me: more blond than you. [*Ib.*]

11 lady will you come with me into / the extremely little house of / my mind. [*Ib.* 230]

12 squeeze your nuts and open your face [*Ib.* 246]

13 he sang his didn't he danced his did [*50 Poems*, xxix]

ADMIRAL CUNNINGHAM

14 It takes the Navy three years to build a new ship. It will take three hundred years to build a new tradition. The evacuation [rescue of troops from Crete] will continue. [Quoted in W. S. Churchill, *The Grand Alliance*, Ch. 16]

WILL CUPPY

15 He is known as Alexander the Great because he killed more people of more different kinds than any other man of his time. He did this in order to impress Greek culture upon them. [*The Decline and Fall of Practically Everybody*, II, 'Alexander the Great']

16 Charlemagne's strong point was morals. He was so moral that some people thought he was only fooling. These people came to no good. [*Ib.* III, 'Charlemagne']

17 Philip II of Spain has been called the first modern king because he suffered from arteriosclerosis. [*Ib.* 'Philip the Sap']

18 As Colbert did not believe in supply and demand, he made them illegal and substituted Gimmick's Law, which afterwards led to the Mississippi Bubble. [*Ib.* IV, 'Louis XIV']

19 To give him his due, Louis XIV brought the technique of dressing and undressing in public to a perfection it never reached before or since. [*Ib.*]

20 Unfortunately, this world is full of people who are ready to think the worst when they see a man sneaking out of the wrong bedroom in the middle of the night. [*Ib.* 'Catherine the Great']

21 Henry I ... is on lots of family trees. He was very good at it. He had twenty illegitimate children before he was married, and nobody counted them afterwards. [*Ib.* V, 'William the Conqueror']

22 George I kept his wife in prison because he believed that she was no better than he was. [*Ib.* 'George III']

23 Catherine Parr didn't matter. She never committed even low treason. [*Ib.* 'Henry VIII']

24 The Toltecs invented the Aztec calendar, by means of which everybody lost a great deal of time. There were only five days in each week and twenty days in each month, and you see how that would work out. [*Ib.* VI, 'Montezuma']

25 It's easy to see the faults in people I know; it's hardest to see the good. Especially when the good isn't there. [Attr.]

26 In the mating season Mute Swans entwine their necks and utter low sounds, like everybody else. They mate for life, especially when their wings are clipped so that they cannot fly away. [*How to Attract the Wombat*, 'The Swan']

EARL CURZON OF KEDLESTON

27 I am almost astounded at the coolness, I might even say the effrontery, with which the British government is in the habit of parcelling out the territory of Powers whose independence and integrity it assures them at the same time it has no other intention than to preserve. [Quoted in Ronaldshay, *Life of Lord Curzon*, Vol. III, Ch. 2]

28 I never knew the lower classes had such white skins. [Attr.]

29 Not even a public figure. A man of no experience. And of the utmost in-significance. [Of Stanley Baldwin's appointment as Prime Minister. Quoted in Harold Nicolson, *Curzon: The Last Phase*]

30 In Lord Salisbury's time there stood here [at the Minister's desk in the Foreign Office] an ink-stand of alabaster – what is this contraption of gläss and bräss? [Lewis Broad, *Sir Anthony Eden*, Ch. 22. A different version is given in Ronaldshay, op. cit., III. 12]

31 Better send them a Papal Bull. [Marginal comment on misprint in Foreign Office document: '... even the monks of Mount Athos were violating their cows.' Quoted in *Ib.* III. 15]

D

DAILY MAIL

1 Perhaps the real reason why we have always been able to champion free speech in this country is that we know perfectly well that hardly anybody has got anything to say, and that no one will listen to anyone that has. [Editorial, date unknown]

SIDNEY DARK

2 He [Dean Inge] thought the Kingdom of Heaven was confined to people who had taken a first class degree at Oxford or Cambridge. [Attr. in conversation]

3 Shaw was, of course, the more Christian of the two. [Comparing G. B. Shaw and Dean Inge. Attr. in conversation]

MR JUSTICE DARLING

4 The Law of England is a very strange one; it cannot compel anyone to tell the truth. ... But what the Law can do is to give you seven years for not telling the truth. [Quoted in D. Walker-Smith, *Lord Darling*, Ch. 27]

5 The law-courts of England are open to all men, like the doors of the Ritz Hotel. [Wrongfully (?) attr. See *ib.*]

CLARENCE DARROW

6 When I was a boy I was told that anybody could become President; I'm beginning to believe it. [Quoted in Esar and Bentley, *Treasury of Humorous Quotations*]

CHARLES GALTON DARWIN

7 Water power is the only really big present source of energy that can be counted as income and not capital. [*The Next Million Years*, Ch. 4]

8 At present the most efficient way for a man to survive in Britain is to be almost half-witted, completely irresponsible and spending a lot of time in prison, where his health is far better looked after than outside; on coming out ... he is ready to beget many further children quite promiscuously, and these 'problem children' are then beautifully cared for by various charitable societies and agencies, until ... they have grown old enough to carry on the good work. [*Ib.* 5]

9 Life in the crowded conditions of cities has many unattractive features, but in the long run these may be overcome, not so much by altering them, but simply by changing the human race into liking them. [*Ib.*]

10 The evolution of the human race will not be accomplished in the ten thousand years of tame animals, but in the million years of wild animals, because man is and will always be a wild animal. [*Ib.* 7]

11 It is not simply a change of state that makes for happiness; there must be something unexpected about it. Butler's Erewhonian would very soon have got bored by knowing that he was certain not to be really disappointed. [*Ib.* 9]

WALTER DAVENPORT

12 An editor: a person who knows precisely what he wants – but isn't quite sure. [Quoted by Bennett Cerf in *Saturday Review Reader*, No. 2]

J. T. DAVIES

13 What L.G. doesn't realize is that there is not a man in his [Baldwin's] Cabinet whom he has not insulted at some time or another. [Remark to Countess Lloyd-George, quoted in her introduction to Malcolm Thomson, *David Lloyd-George*]

W. H. DAVIES

14 And hear the pleasant cuckoo, loud and long – / The simple bird that thinks two notes a song. [*April's Charms*]

15 When butterflies will make side-leaps, / As though escaped from Nature's hand / Ere perfect quite. [*Days too Short*]

16 It was the Rainbow gave thee birth, / And left thee all her lovely hues. [*The Kingfisher*]

17 Live with proud Peacocks in green parks. [*Ib.*]

18 A lonely pool, and let a tree / Sigh with her bosom over me. [*Ib.*]

19 I love thee for a heart that's kind – / Not for the knowledge in thy mind. [*Sweet Stay-at-Home*]

CLARENCE DAY

20 'Put your cap on straight,' he added. 'I am trying to bring you up to be a civilized man.' [*Life With Father*, 'A holiday with father']

21 Father nearly burst a blood vessel telling her that he was not anaemic. [*Ib.* 'Father finds guests . . .']

22 I meant to be prompt, but it never occurred to me that I had better try to be early. [*Ib.* 'Father teaches me to be prompt']

23 His instincts were generous. Only it made him cross if he suffered for those generous instincts. [*Ib.* 'Father thumps']

24 Apparently, now that he knew he was in trouble, his thoughts had turned to his God. 'Have mercy!' they heard him shouting indignantly. 'I say have mercy, damn it!' [*Ib.* 'Father is firm . . .']

25 Imagine the Lord talking French! Aside from a few odd words in Hebrew, I took it completely for granted that God had never spoken anything but the most dignified English. [*Ib.* 'Father interferes']

26 Father said he wouldn't mind if people died only once in a while as they used to. [*Ib.* 'Father plans']

27 'If you don't go to other men's funerals,' he told Father stiffly, 'they won't go to yours.' [*Ib.*]

28 Father would get as indignant as though he had been drowning and a life-guard had informed him he would save him tomorrow. [*Ib.*]

29 Father declared he was going to buy a new plot in the cemetery, a plot all for himself. 'And I'll buy one on a corner,' he added triumphantly, 'where I can get out.' Mother looked at him, startled but admiring, and whispered to me, 'I almost believe he could do it.' [*Ib.* final words of book]

C. DAY LEWIS

30 Is it birthday weather for you, dear soul? / Is it fine your way, / With tall moon-daisies alight, and the mole / Busy, and elegant hares at play . . .? [*Birthday Poem for Thomas Hardy*]

31 All is yet same as when I roved the heather / Chained to a demon through the shrinking night. [*Emily Brontë*]

32 It is the logic of our times, / No subject for immortal verse – / That we who lived by honest dreams / Defend the bad against the worse. [*Where are the War Poets?*]

33 Then I'll hit the trail for that promising land; / May catch up with Wystan and Rex my friend, / Go mad in good company, find a good country, / Make a clean sweep or make a clean end. [*The Magnetic Mountain*, 4]

ANTHONY C. DEANE

34 When some visitor commented to a verger on a remarkable reading of a lesson he had heard from Dalton, the verger replied: 'Ah, sir, but you should hear him throw down Jezebel!' [*Time Remembered*]

ARCHBISHOP JOOST DE BLANK

35 Christ in this country [South Africa] would quite likely have been arrested under the Suppression of Communism Act. [*Observer*, 'Sayings of the Week', 27 Oct. 1963]

36 I suffer from an incurable disease – colour blindness. [Attr.]

RÉGIS DEBRAY

37 Revolution in the Revolution? [Book title]

MICHEL DEBRÉ

38 *Europe des patries.* – Europe of the fatherlands. [Speech on taking office as Prime Minister of France, 15 Jan. 1959]

WALTER DE LA MARE

39 Our dreams are tales / Told in dim Eden / By Eve's nightingales. [*All That's Past*]

40 Has anybody seen my Mopser? – / A comely dog is he, / With hair the colour of a Charles the Fifth, / And teeth like ships at sea. [*The Bandog*]

41 In search of a Fairy, / Whose Rozez he knowzez / Were not honeyed for he. [*The Bees' Song*]

42 Only with beauty wake wild memories – / Sorrow for where you are, for where you would be. [*The Cage*]

43 What can a tired heart say, / Which the wise of the world have made dumb? / Save to the lonely dreams of a child, / 'Return again, come!' [*Dreams*]

44 So, when with fickle heart / I joyed in the passing day, / A presence my mood estranged / Went grieved away. [*Estranged*]

45 God in His pity knows / Why, in her bodice stuck, / Reeks a mock rose. [*The Fat Woman*]

46 He is the Ancient Tapster of this Hostel, / To him at length even we all keys must resign. [*Hospital*]

47 I can't abear a Butcher, / I can't abide his meat. [*I Can't Abear*]

48 The world's grimed thumb, / Now hooked securely in his matted hair. [*In the Dock*]

49 And out of her cold cottage never answered Mrs Gill / The Fairy mimbling mambling in the garden. [*The Mocking Fairy*]

50 When music sounds, all that I was I am / Ere to this haunt of brooding dust I came. [*Music*]

51 Ere unto Z / My pen drew nigh; / Leviathan told, / And the honey-fly. [*The Scribe*]

52 Did not those night-hung houses, / Of quiet, starlit stone, / Breathe not a whisper – 'Stay, / Thou unhappy one; / Whither so secret away?' [*The Suicide*]

53 I was that man – in a dream: / And each world's night in vain / I patient wait on sleep to unveil / Those vivid hills again. [*The Three Strangers*]

54 Too tired to yawn, too tired to sleep: / Poor tired Tim! It's sad for him. [*Tired Tim*]

55 Flee into some forgotten night and be / Of all dark long my moon-bright company; / Beyond the rumour even of Paradise come, / There, out of all remembrance, make our home. [*The Tryst*]

56 Somewhere there nothing is; and there lost Man / Shall win what changeless vague of peace he can. [*Ib.*]

SHELAGH DELANEY

57 I'm not frightened of the darkness outside. It's the darkness inside houses I don't like. [*A Taste of Honey* I. i]

58 Women never have young minds. They are born three thousand years old. [*Ib.*]

59 Do you like me more than you don't like me or don't you like me more than you do? [*Ib.* II. ii]

60 The cinema has become more and more like the theatre, it's all mauling and muttering. [*Ib.*]

FREDERICK DELIUS

61 Admirable, but what language was he singing in? [After a recital of his own songs. Quoted in Sir Thomas Beecham, *A Mingled Chime*, Ch. 19]

NIGEL DENNIS

62 Most acts of assent require far more courage than most acts of protest, since courage is clearly a readiness to risk self-humiliation. [*Boys and Girls Come Out to Play*]

LUDWELL DENNY

63 We shall not make Britain's mistake. Too wise to try to govern the world, we shall merely own it. Nothing can stop us. [Written in 1930. *America Conquers Britain*]

DR ALAN DENT

64 JAMES AGATE: Can ghosts be angry? ALAN DENT: What else is there to do in the shades except take umbrage? [Quoted in James Agate, *Ego*, II, 10 March 1934]

PETER DE VRIES

65 Our church is, I believe, the first split-level church in America. It has five rooms and two baths downstairs. . . . There is a small worship area at one end. [*The Mackerel Plaza*, Ch. 1]

66 It is the final proof of God's omnipotence that he need not exist in order to save us. [*Ib.* 2]

67 Let us hope . . . that a kind of Providence will put a speedy end to the acts of God under which we have been labouring. [*Ib.* 3]

68 Mackerel has a long slender face, its rather peevish constituents relieved by red cheeks and blue eyes that have often been termed 'boyish'. Round and yearning, they stand out, among the drawn intellectual's lineaments, like eggs in the wrong nest. [*Ib.* 4]

69 We know the human brain is a device to keep the ears from grating on one another. [*Comfort Me with Apples*, Ch. 1]

70 I think I can say my childhood was as unhappy as the next braggart's. [*Ib.*]

71 They had lived originally in an dinette apartment in town but had begun to drift apart and needed more room. [*Ib.*]

72 He believed that the art of conversation was dead. His own small talk, at any rate, was bigger than most people's large. [*Ib.*]

73 Anglo-Saxon to his fingertips (though of mixed Latin, Celtic and Semitic strains), Nickie liked undercommunicativeness in women, not realizing that Lila had nothing to communicate. [*Ib.* 4]

74 Mrs Thicknesse spoke a patois which on closer hearing turned out to be correct English: 'Had I but been she', she would say, and 'anyone's else' (could that be right?). [*Ib.* 7]

75 'There is no death,' she said. 'No, my dear lady, but there are funerals.' [*Ib.* 8]

76 'If it must be Thomas let it be Mann, and if it must be Wolfe let it be Nero, but let it never be Thomas Wolfe.' This of course my friend appreciated as a paraphrase of the old Viennese coffee-shop *mot*, 'If it must be Richard let it be Wagner and if it must be Strauss let it be Johann, but let it never be Richard Strauss.' [*Ib.*]

77 Mrs Thicknesse and I agreed that a business of his own was probably the only solution for him because he was obviously unemployable. [*Ib.*]

78 Once you're marked as a moral leopard – [*Ib.*]

79 . . . The inscription *Gott Mit Uns*. I must ceaselessly resolve this legend as a declaration that one had gloves. [*Ib.* 15]

80 Gluttony is an emotional escape, a sign something is eating us. [*Ib.*]

81 Probably a fear we have of facing up to the real issues. Could you say we were guilty of Noel Cowardice? [*Ib.*]

82 This person was a deluge of words and a drizzle of thought. [*Ib.* 17]

83 I wanted to be bored to death, as good a way to go as any. [*Ib.*]

84 I wished now that I had gone to the restaurant across the street where the food had at least the merit of being taste-less. [*Ib.* 18]

85 I smiled with Christianity out of one side of my face while with the other I expressed outrage. [*Ib.* 19]

86 There are times when parenthood seems nothing but feeding the mouth that bites you. [*Tunnel of Love*, Ch. 5]

87 And when I can no longer bear to think of the victims of broken homes, I begin to think of the victims of intact ones. [*Ib.* 8]

88 The value of marriage is not that adults produce children but that children produce adults. [*Ib.* 8]

89 I was thinking that we all learn by experience, but some of us have to go to summer school. [*Ib.* 14]

LORD DEWAR

90 There are two classes of pedestrians in these days of reckless motor traffic: the quick and the dead. [Quoted in George Robey, *Looking Back on Life*, Ch. 28]

SERGEI DIAGHILEV

1 Exactly what I wanted. [After the stormy reception of Stravinsky's *Sacre du Printemps*. Quoted in Igor Stravinsky and Robert Craft, *Conversations*]

WILHELM DIBELIUS

2 England is the single country in the world that, in looking after its own interest with meticulous care, has at the same time something to give to others; the single country where patriotism does not represent a threat or challenge to the rest of the world. [*England*, Bk. I, Ch. 4, Sect. iv]

WALT DISNEY

3 Whistle While You Work. [Song title in *Snow White and the Seven Dwarfs*; words by Larry Morey]

BONAMY DOBRÉE

4 It is difficult to be humble. Even if you aim at humility, there is no guarantee that when you have attained the state you will not be proud of the feat. [*John Wesley*, opening sentences, Ch. 1]

KEN DODD

5 The trouble with Freud is that he never played the Glasgow Empire Saturday night. [Interview in A.T.V. Programme, 'The Laughter Makers', quoted in *The Times*, 7 Aug. 1965]

SIR GERALD DODSON
(Recorder of London)

6 Sometimes people commit bigamy to please the landlady. [*Observer*, 'Sayings of the Week', 18 Oct. 1942]

J. P. DONLEAVY

7 I got disappointed in human nature as well and gave it up because I found it too much like my own. [*Fairy Tales of New York*, 2]

8 Well, ghosts won't bother me on a full stomach and certainly never if I had a full sex life. [*The Ginger Man*, Ch. 2]

9 To marry the Irish is to look for poverty. [*Ib.*]

10 I'm all for Christianity but insolence must be put down. [*Ib.* 4]

11 But Jesus, when you don't have any money, the problem is food. When you have money, it's sex. When you have both it's health, you worry about getting ruptured or something. If everything is simply jake then you're frightened of death. [*Ib.* 5]

12 When I die I want to decompose in a barrel of porter and have it served in all the pubs in Dublin. I wonder would they know it was me? [*Ib.* 31]

JOHN DOS PASSOS

13 Rumours of peace talks worried him [Pershing]. Peace would ruin his plans for an American army. [*Mr Wilson's War*, Ch. 21]

JAMES DOUGLAS

14 I would rather put a phial of prussic acid in the hands of a healthy boy or girl than the book in question. [Reviewing Radclyffe Hall's *The Well of Loneliness* in the *Sunday Express*]

15 If only men could love each other like dogs, the world would be a paradise. [From *Sunday Express*, quoted in M. Bateman, *This England*, selections from the *New Statesman*, Pt I]

NORMAN DOUGLAS

16 It is the drawback of all sea-side places that half the landscape is unavailable for purposes of human locomotion, being covered by useless water. [*Alone*, 'Mentone']

17 Education is a state-controlled manufactory of echoes. [*How about Europe?*]

18 Roman Catholics have shaken off the nightmare of monotheism. Their Trinity is broken up, the Holy Ghost having evaporated in the course of years, as spirits often do. [*Ib.*]

19 There is a beauty in fitness which no art can enhance. [*Siren Land*, 'The Cove of Crapolla']

20 Bouillabaisse is only good because cooked by the French, who, if they cared to try, could produce an excellent and nutritious substitute out of cigar stumps and empty matchboxes. [*Ib.* 'Rain on the Hills']

21 The bishop was feeling rather sea-sick. Confoundedly sea-sick, in fact. [*South Wind*, Ch. 1]

22 I am what we call a 'Returned Empty'. It is a phrase we apply in England to Colonial bishops who come back from their dioceses. [*Ib.*]

23 Don Francesco was a fisher of men, and of women. He fished *ad maiorem Dei gloriam*, and for the fun of the thing. It was his way of taking exercise. [*Ib.* 2]

24 ... Impoverished them to such an extent that for three consecutive months they could barely afford the most unnecessary luxuries of life. [*Ib.* 20]

SIR ALEC DOUGLAS-HOME

25 There are two problems in my life. The political ones are insoluble and the economic ones are incomprehensible. [Speech, Jan. 1964]

LADY CAROLINE DOUGLAS-HOME

26 He is used to dealing with estate workers. I cannot see how anyone can say he is out of touch. [On her father's becoming Prime Minister. Reported by Jon Akass, *Daily Herald*, 21 Oct. 1963]

SIR ARTHUR CONAN DOYLE

27 It is an old maxim of mine that when you have excluded the impossible, whatever remains, however improbable, must be the truth. [*The Beryl Coronet*]

28 You know my method. It is founded upon the observance of trifles. [*The Boscombe Valley Mystery*]

29 Depend upon it, there is nothing so unnatural as the commonplace. [*A Case of Identity*]

30 I can never bring you to realize the importance of sleeves, the suggestiveness of thumb-nails, or the great issues that may hang from a bootlace. [*Ib.*]

31 Crime is common. Logic is rare. Therefore it is upon the logic rather than upon the crime that you should dwell. [*The Copper Beeches*]

32 A man should keep his little brain attic stocked with all the furniture that he is likely to use, and the rest he can put away in the lumber-room of his library, where he can get it if he wants it. [*Five Orange Pips*]

33 I shall be my own police. When I have spun the web they may take the flies, but not before. [*Ib.*]

34 A study of family portraits is enough to convert a man to the doctrine of reincarnation. [*The Hound of the Baskervilles*]

35 A cast of your skull, sir, until the original is available, would be an ornament to any anthropological museum. [*Ib.*]

36 When I find a man who keeps his cigars in the coal-scuttle, his tobacco in the toe-end of a Persian slipper, and his unanswered correspondence transfixed by a jack-knife into the very centre of his wooden mantelpiece, then I begin to give myself virtuous airs. [*The Musgrave Ritual*]

37 I read nothing except the criminal news and the agony column. The latter is always instructive. [*The Noble Bachelor*]

38 A bicycle certainly, but not *the* bicycle. I am familiar with forty-two impressions left by tyres. [*The Priory School*]

39 My life is spent in one long effort to escape from the commonplaces of existence. [*The Red-Headed League*]

40 Now, Watson, the fair sex is your department. [*The Second Stain*]

41 In an experience of women that extends over many nations and three separate continents, I have never looked upon a face which gave a clearer promise of a refined and sensitive nature. [Dr Watson in *The Sign of Four*]

42 The most winning woman I ever knew was hanged for poisoning three little children for their insurance money. [*Ib.*]

43 I never make exceptions. An exception disproves the rule. [*Ib.*]

44 The unofficial force – the Baker Street irregulars. [*Ib.*]

45 Rather an irregular proceeding.... However the whole thing is irregular, and I suppose we must wink at it. [*Ib.*]

46 When a doctor does go wrong he is the first of criminals. He has nerve and he has knowledge. [*The Speckled Band*]

47 Where there is no imagination there is no horror. [*A Study in Scarlet*]

48 The giant rat of Sumatra, a story for which the world is not yet prepared. [*The Sussex Vampire*]

49 'I am inclined to think –' said I. 'I should do so,' Sherlock Holmes remarked impatiently. [*The Valley of Fear*]

RUTH DRAPER

50 Number seven.... What's it meant to be, dear? ... A 'Study'? ... It doesn't say what of? ... Well, that's an easy way out for an artist. [*At an Art Exhibition in Boston*]

51 Aren't the artists brave to go out and paint a sea as rough as that? ... I don't see how he kept his canvas dry. [*Ib.*]

52 Well, perhaps nobody wanted to come – perhaps they'd *all* like to go – but they're *not* going. ... Because they're going to behave – and that's what we *all* have to learn in life – we *have* to learn to behave! [*The Children's Party*]

53 Now listen, Christopher, you must not cry, darling – just because a lady kicks you. ... You *mustn't* cry. ... Because in one way or another everybody gets kicked. ... Certainly – we *all* get kicked. Daddy gets kicked and *he* doesn't cry.... No – I don't kick him. ... But somebody else may. [*Ib.*]

54 Sometimes I think I'll not send him to school – but just let his individuality develop. [*Ib.*]

55 Green bloomers? – Oh, no – green is a lovely shade. Any shade that is near to nature is dear to me. [*A Class in Greek Poise*]

56 And when you lie down, your bodies will take beautiful, sinuous curves, relaxed as if on clouds – like the famous Fates on the Parthenon frieze. [*Ib.*]

57 What is one of the lowest forms of life? ... The earth-worm – exactly! And what does he teach us? ... *To stretch – precisely!* ... He's probably the greatest stretcher in the world! [*Ib.*]

58 Do I believe in Platonic friendship? I certainly *do*. I think it's the most *wonderful* relation between a man and a girl.... I mean, to begin with ... I mean, you know where *you* are – and I like knowing where *I* am. [*A Débutante at a Dance*]

59 He said I was the most sensitive person he had ever seen – that I belonged to the hyper-hyper type and we *rarely* survive! Of course, I was examined, and so was the éclair, and they found that the éclair contains *every*thing my system lacks. So I take three a day and I feel like a new woman. [*Doctors and Diets*]

60 And so she went to this doctor – it seems he examines you in regard to the way you react to colour – he is what they call a Colour Analyst. [*Ib.*]

61 You see – he's got a perfectly new idea. He never sees his patients. He's not interested in individuals, he prefers to treat a crowd. And he's organized these mass cures. ... And he cures thirty thousand people every Thursday. [*Ib.*]

62 'To the left is the monument of General[1] Carlo Trembolo who fell in the battle of Scaputra in 1427.' Bessie, you're the girl for battles, do you know that one? ... Never mind, I'll look it up in my battle-book.... I have one at home. [*In a Church in Italy*]

63 I wish I knew more saints. ... I hardly know a saint. ... Oh, there's St Lawrence with his grill. ... Well, he was broiled as a martyr, dear, and in the pictures he always carries a grill. ... I want to get a postcard of him. [*Ib.*]

64 'In the middle of the road.' That's not very poetical. In English I don't think one *could* begin a poem with 'in the middle of the road'. [*The Italian Lesson*]

65 Of course he was a genius, wasn't he – like Shakespeare? ... He and Dante seem to have known *everything* ... known what would always be true. ... I imagine we're going to find this *full* of quotations! [*Ib.*]

66 You know, Billy is a very sensitive child. ... He's a *peculiarly* sensitive child – I'm afraid he's not quite like other children, and he simply *hates* Mathematics. [*Ib.*]

67 As a matter of fact, you know I am rather sorry you should see the garden now, because, alas! it is not looking at its best. Oh, it doesn't *compare* to what it was last year. [*Showing the Garden*]

68 And as for my poor *Glubjullas*, they never came up at all! ... I can't think why, because I generally have great luck with my *Glubjullas*. [*Ib.*]

69 It's going to give me a little *vista*, which will be rather exciting, I think! I shall see more sky – which is always desirable. I hope I shall see the horizon – which would be *very* jolly! ... Then, I shall have a sense of space – of distance. ... A little glimpse into the beyond, as it were. [*Ib.*]

HUGH DRUMMOND

70 Ladies and Gentlemen I give you a toast. It is 'Absinthe makes the tart grow fonder.' [Quoted in Seymour Hicks, *Vintage Years*]

GEORGES DUHAMEL

71 Courtesy is not dead – it has merely taken refuge in Great Britain. [*Observer*, 'Sayings of Our Times', 31 May 1953]

J. FOSTER DULLES

72 If E.D.C. [European Defence Community] should fail, the United States might be compelled to make an 'agonizing reappraisal' of its basic policy. [Speech at North Atlantic Council in Paris, 14 Dec. 1953]

73 If you are scared to go to the brink, you are lost. [Quoted in *Life* Magazine, 16 Jan. 1956]

74 An obsolete conception, and except under very exceptional circumstances it is an immoral and short-sighted conception. [On neutralism, speech at Iowa State College, 9 June 1956]

AMERIGO DUMINI

75 My name is Dumini, twelve assassinations. [Quoted in George Seldes, *Sawdust Caesar*]

ELAINE DUNDY

76 When I felt the horns of my dilemma actually toss me into the air, I lit out of the hotel and landed in the street. [*The Dud Avocado*, Ch. I]

77 I was merely a disinterested spectator at the Banquet of Life. [*Ib.*]

78 I hate champagne more than anything in the world next to Seven-up. [*Ib.*]

79 I find I always have to write SOMETHING on a steamed mirror. [*Ib.*]

80 It was one of those nights when the air is blood temperature and it's impossible to tell where you leave off and it begins. [*Ib.* 9]

81 I mean, the question actors most often get asked is how they can bear saying the same things over and over again night after night, but God knows the answer to *that* is, don't we all *anyway*; might as well get paid for it. [*Ib.*]

FINLEY PETER DUNNE

82 I don't know what a chamber of commerce is unless 'tis a place where business men go to sleep. [*Mr Dooley on the Amateur Ambassadors*]

83 Vice ... is a creature of such heejus mien ... that the more ye see it th' better ye like it. [*The Crusade Against Vice*]

JAMES DUNNE

84 The English and the Irish are very much alike, except that the Irish are more so. [In conversation, during the Irish Troubles]

85 The quiet Irishman is about as harmless as a powder magazine built over a match factory. [*Ib.*]

WILL DURANT

86 The finger that turns the dial rules the air. [*What is Civilization?*]

LEO DUROCHER

87 Nice guys finish last. [Attr. by Denis Brogan, *Observer*, 16 May 1965]

LAURENCE DURRELL

88 Hollis who had wives killed under him like horses / And that man of destiny / Ramon de something who gave lectures / From an elephant. [*Mythology*]

89 He gave asylum to aged chairs in his home, / Lampposts and crockery, everything that / Seemed to him suffering he took in / Without mockery. [*Ib.*]

90 O men of the Marmion class, sons of the free. [*Ib.*]

1 The city, half-imagined (yet wholly real), begins and ends in us, lodged in our memory. [*Balthazar*, Pt I]

2 BRITAIN TO BUY SERBIAN TIT-PROPS [*Esprit de Corps*, 'Flying the Flag']

3 A poem is what happens when an anxiety meets a technique. [Reported remark]

4 Poggio's, where people go to watch each other watch each other. [*Tunc*, Ch. 1]

5 No more about sex, it's too boring. Everyone's got one. Nastiness is a real stimulant though – but poor honest sex, like dying, should be a private matter. [*Ib.*]

ELENORA DUSE

6 To save the Theatre, the Theatre must be destroyed, the actors and actresses all die of the Plague ... they make art impossible. [Quoted in A. Symons, *Studies in Seven Arts*]

E

MAX EASTMAN

1 I don't know why it is that we are in such a hurry to get up when we fall down. You might think we would lie there and rest awhile. [*The Enjoyment of Laughter*]

LORD ECCLES

2 A small acquaintance with history shows that all Governments are selfish and the French Governments more selfish than most. [*Observer*, 'Sayings of the Year', 29 Dec. 1962]

SIR A. EDDINGTON

3 Electrical force is defined as something which causes motion of electrical charge; an electrical charge is something which exerts electric force. [*The Nature of the Physical World*]

4 Matter is what Mr X knows. [*Science and the Unseen World*]

5 When Dr Watson watches rats in mazes, what he knows, apart from difficult inferences, are certain events in himself. [*Ib.*]

SIR ANTHONY EDEN

6 I am wondering whether there is anything more I could have done to prevent this. [After Chamberlain's broadcast in Sept. 1939 announcing that war had been declared. Quoted in Lewis Broad, *Sir Anthony Eden*, Ch. 13]

7 REPORTER: If Mr Stalin dies, what will be the effect on international affairs?
A.E.: That is a good question for you to ask, not a wise question for me to answer. [*Ib.* Conversation on board *Queen Elizabeth*, 4 March 1953]

8 We are living in slightly exceptional times. [1944. *Observer*, 'Sayings of Our Times', 31 May 1953]

9 Everybody is always in favour of general economy and particular expenditure. [*Observer*, 'Sayings of the Week', 17 June 1956]

10 We are not at war with Egypt. We are in an armed conflict. [Speech in House of Commons, 4 Nov. 1956]

LADY CLARISSA EDEN

11 During the last few weeks I have felt that the Suez Canal was flowing through my drawing room. [At time of Suez crisis, 1956]

DUKE OF EDINBURGH

12 I include 'pidgin-English' ... even though I am referred to in that splendid language as 'Fella belong Mrs Queen'. [Speech to English-Speaking Union Conference at Ottawa, 29 Oct. 1958]

13 There are many things which we do which don't seem to have any particular point or tangible result. Take today; a lot of time and energy has been spent on arranging for you to listen to me take a long time to declare open a building which everybody knows is open already. [Speech at Opening of Chesterfield College of Technology, 21 Nov. 1958]

14 Just at this moment we are suffering a national defeat comparable to any lost military campaign, and what is more it is self-inflicted. .... I think it is about time we pulled our finger out. [Speech to businessmen, 17 Oct. 1961]

15 The rest of the world most certainly does not owe us a living. [*Ib.*]

16 All money nowadays seems to be produced with a natural homing instinct for the Treasury. [*Observer*, 'Sayings of the Week', 26 May 1963]

17 I never see any home cooking. All I get is fancy stuff. [*Observer*, 'Sayings of the Week', Dec. 1962]

18 The biggest waste of water in the country by far. You spend half a pint and flush two gallons. [Attr. in Speech, 1965]

THOMAS EDISON

19 They say Wilson has blundered. Perhaps he has but I notice he usually blunders forward. [Quoted in John dos Passos, *Mr Wilson's War*, Ch. 2, Sect. x]

KING EDWARD VII

20 You can tell when you have crossed the frontier into Germany because of the badness of the coffee. [Quoted in Lord Haldane, *Autobiography*]

21 Let me introduce you to the last king of England. [To Lord Haldane on introducing him to the Prince of Wales – afterwards George V. Quoted in Dudley Sommer, *Haldane of Cloan*, Ch. 15]

EDWARD VIII

22 There is no central machinery to provide a substitute for the good neighbour. [1932. *Observer*, 'Sayings of Our Times', 31 May 1953]

23 Something must be done. [Said during tour of unemployment areas in South Wales]

24 But you must believe me when I tell you that I have found it impossible to carry the heavy burden of responsibility and to discharge my duties as King as I would wish to do, without the help and support of the woman I love. [Abdication speech, 11 Dec. 1936]

ILYA EHRENBURG

25 What he [Churchill] was congratulating me on I did not know, but I smiled back and congratulated him, on what I did not know either. [*The War: 1941–5*]

ALBERT EINSTEIN

26 I know why there are so many people who love chopping wood. In this activity one immediately sees the results. [Quoted in Carl Seelig, *Albert Einstein*, Ch. 4]

27 *Car moi, je ne crois pas à la mathématique.* – I don't believe in mathematics. [Said to Gustave Ferrière. Quoted in *ib.* 5]

28 *Gott ist raffiniert, aber boshaft ist er nicht.* – God is subtle but he is not malicious. [Quip carved above the fireplace of Fine Hall, the Mathematical Institute of Princeton University. *Ib.* 8]

29 I can, if the worst comes to the worst, still realize that the Good Lord may have created a world in which there are no natural laws. In short, a chaos. But that there should be statistical laws with definite solutions, i.e. laws that compel the good Lord to throw the dice in each individual case, I find highly disagreeable. [To James Franck, quoted in *ib.*]

30 The release of atom power has changed everything except our way of thinking, and thus we are being driven unarmed towards a catastrophe. ... The solution of this problem lies in the heart of humankind. [Speech to National Commission of Nuclear Scientists, May 1946. Quoted in *ib.*]

31 If only I had known, I should have become a watchmaker. [Of his making the atom bomb possible. Quoted in *New Statesman*, 16 April 1965]

32 I cannot believe that God plays dice with the cosmos. [*Observer*, 'Sayings of the Week', 5 April 1954]

33 You have got the impression that contemporary physics is based on concepts somewhat analogous to the smile of the absent cat. [Comment on Viscount Samuel, *Essay in Physics*. Quoted in John Bowle, *Viscount Samuel*, Ch. 19]

PRESIDENT EISENHOWER

34 There is one thing about being President – nobody can tell you when to sit down. [*Observer*, 'Sayings of the Week', 9 Aug. 1953]

35 Whatever America hopes to bring to pass in this world must first come to pass in the heart of America. [Inaugural Address, 1953]

SIR EDWARD ELGAR

36 Music is in the air – you simply take as much of it as you want. [Attr.]

T. S. ELIOT

37 The red-eyed scavengers are creeping / From Kentish Town and Golder's Green. [*A Cooking Egg*]

38 Over buttered scones and crumpets / Weeping, weeping multitudes / Droop in a hundred A.B.C.'s. [*Ib.*]

39 Here I am, an old man in a dry month, / Being read to by a boy. [*Gerontion*]

40 In the juvescence of the year / Came Christ the tiger. [*Ib.*]

41 An old man in a draughty house / Under a windy knob. [*Ib.*]

42 After such knowledge, what forgiveness? Think now / History has many cunning passages, contrived corridors / And issues. [*Ib.*]

43 Unnatural vices / are fathered by our heroism. [*Ib.*]

44 Tenants of the house, / Thoughts of a dry brain in a dry season. [*Ib.*]

45 The hippopotamus's day / Is passed in sleep; at night he hunts; / God works in a mysterious way – / The Church can feed and sleep at once. [*The Hippopotamus*]

46 To hear the latest Pole / transmit the Preludes, through his hair and fingertips. [*Portrait of a Lady*]

47 Discuss the late events, / Correct our watches by the public clocks. / Then sit for half an hour and drink our bocks. [*Ib.*]

48 You will see me any morning in the park / Reading the comics and the sporting page. / Particularly I remark / An English countess goes upon the stage. [*Ib.*]

49 The worlds revolve like ancient women / Gathering fuel in vacant lots. [*Preludes*]

50 Midnight shakes the memory / As a madman shakes a dead geranium. [*Rhapsody on a Windy Night*]

51 'Put your shoes at the door, sleep, prepare for life.' / The last twist of the knife. [*Ib.*]

52 The host with someone indistinct / Converses at the door apart, / The nightingales are singing near / The Convent of the Sacred Heart. [*Sweeney among the Nightingales*]

53 Yet we have gone on living, / Living and partly living. [*Murder in the Cathedral*, Pt I]

54 Only / the fool, fixed in his folly, may think / He can turn the wheel on which he turns. [*Ib.*]

55 Human kind cannot bear very much reality. [*Ib.* II]

56 Clear the air! clean the sky! wash the wind! take stone from stone and wash them. [*Ib.*]

57 We like to appear in the newspapers, / So long as we are in the right column. [*The Family Reunion*, I]

58 We can say of Shakespeare, that never has a man turned so little knowledge to such great account. [*The Classics and the Man of Letters*, lecture]

59 I do not wish to be accused of inventing a new heresy to the effect that salvation depends on getting a first in classics. [*Ib.*]

60 A good deal of confusion could be avoided, if we refrained from setting before the group, what can be the aim only of the individual; and before society as a whole, what can be the aim only of a group. [*Mass Civilization and Minority Culture*]

61 [Wit] involves, probably, a recognition, implicit in the expression of every experience, of other kinds of experience that are possible. [*Selected Essays*, 'Andrew Marvell']

62 It is our business, as readers of literature, to know what we like. It is our business as Christians, as *well* as readers of literature, to know what we ought to like. It is our business as honest men not to assume that what we like is what we ought to like. [*Ib.* 'Charles Whibley']

63 The majority of poems one outgrows and outlives, as one outgrows and outlives the majority of human passions. Dante's is one of those that one can only just hope to grow up to at the end of life. [*Ib.* 'Dante']

64 Dryden is distinguished, principally, by his *poetic* ability. [*Ib.* 'John Dryden']

65 No poet, no artist of any sort, has his complete meaning alone. His significance, his appreciation is the appreciation of his relation to the dead poets and artists. [*Ib.* 'Tradition and the Individual Talent']

66 We can only say that it appears likely that poets in our civilization, as it exists at present, must be *difficult*. [*Ib.* 'The Metaphysical Poets']

67 The majority of people live below the level of belief or doubt. It takes application and a kind of genius to believe anything, and to believe anything ... will probably become more and more difficult as time goes on. [*The Enemy*, Jan. 1927]

68 I confess that I am seldom interested in what he [Ezra Pound] is saying, but only in the way he says it. ['Isolated Superiority', article in *The Dial*, Jan. 1928]

69 The more perfect the artist, the more completely separate in him will be the man who suffers and the mind which creates. [Quoted in 'Palinurus' (Cyril Connolly), *The Unquiet Grave*]

ELIZABETH, THE QUEEN MOTHER

70 My favourite programme is 'Mrs Dale's Diary'. I try never to miss it because it is the only way of knowing what goes on in a middle-class family. [From the *Evening News*, quoted in M. Bateman, *This England*, selections from the *New Statesman*, Pt IV]

DUKE ELLINGTON

71 Saddest tale told on land or sea / Is the tale they told / When they told the truth on me. [*Saddest Tale*]

MAXINE ELLIOTT

72 I would not marry God. [Cable when her engagement was rumoured. Quoted in D. Forbes Robertson, *Maxine*]

HENRY HAVELOCK ELLIS

73 What we call progress is the exchange of one nuisance for another nuisance. [Quoted in Sagittarius and George, *The Perpetual Pessimist*]

EDWARD ELLSWORTH

74 Force one day was served to him. / Since then they've called him Sunny Jim. [Advertisement for Force, early 20th-century breakfast cereal]

PAUL ELUARD

75 *Adieu tristesse | Bonjour tristesse | Tu es inscrite dans les lignes du plafond.* – Farewell sadness, / good day sadness. / You are written in the lines on the ceiling. [*La Vie immédiate*]

76 *Qui n'a pas vu les ruines du ghetto | Ne connaît pas le destin de son corps.* – Anyone who has not seen the ruins of the ghetto does not know the destiny of his body. [*Varsovie la ville fantastique*]

WILLIAM EMPSON

77 Johnson could see no bicycle would go; / 'You bear yourself and the machine as well.' [*Invitation to June*]

78 Slowly the poison the whole blood stream fills. / The waste remains, the waste remains and kills. [*Missing Dates*]

79 But Alice showed her pup Ulysses' bough / Well from behind a thistle, wise with dread. [*The Scales*]

80 There was a period of the cult of Pure Sound when infants were read passages from Homer, and then questioned as to their impressions, not unlike Darwin playing the trombone to his French beans. [*Seven Types of Ambiguity*, Ch. 1]

D. J. ENRIGHT

81 What odds / Whether the couples walk on the campus and look at / The moon or walk on the moon and look at the earth? / Just so long as there's somewhere left to walk, to sit, to cycle, / And something left to look at. [*Addictions*]

SIR ARTHUR EVANS

82 I come back every fifty years. [On revisiting the prison of Ragusa in old age. Quoted in Joan Evans, *Time and Chance*, Ch. 20]

BERGAN EVANS

83 The wisdom of silent men is beyond proof, though proverbial in every language. What basis it has seems to consist in our assumption that anyone who has not spoken to the contrary must agree with

us and is, therefore, a fellow of infinite wisdom. [*The Natural History of Nonsense*, Ch. 13]

84 While the car may limit the size of the family, it is certainly instrumental in getting one started. There is no more irresistible mating call than the imperious horn at the kerb. [*The Spoor of Spooks*, Ch. 13]

DAME EDITH EVANS

85 When a woman behaves like a man, why doesn't she behave like a nice man?

[*Observer*, 'Sayings of the Week', 30 Sept. 1956]

EVENING STANDARD

86 My own personal reaction is that most ballets would be quite delightful if it were not for the dancing. [Quoted in M. Bateman, *This England*, selections from the *New Statesman*, Pt I]

KURT EWALD

87 Our family is not yet so good as to be degenerating. [*My Little Boy*]

F

HERBERT FARJEON

1 I've danced with a man, who's danced with a girl, who's danced with the Prince of Wales. [*Picnic*]

KING FAROUK

2 There will soon be only five kings left – the Kings of England, Diamonds, Hearts, Spades and Clubs. [Said to Lord Boyd-Orr, 1951]

ROBERT FARQUHARSON

3 Look at her! A moth entirely surrounded by candles. [Of B.B.C. actress amidst admiring males.]

WILLIAM FAULKNER

4 The Swiss . . . are not a people so much as a neat clean solvent business. [*Intruder in the Dust*]

5 Between grief and nothing I will take grief. [*The Wild Palms*]

6 No man can cause more grief than that one clinging blindly to the vices of his ancestors. [*Intruder in the Dust*, Ch. 3]

7 Maybe the only thing worse than having to give gratitude constantly all the time, is having to accept it. [*Requiem For a Nun*, Act II, sc. i]

JULES FEIFFER

8 Artists can colour the sky red because they *know* it's blue. Those of us who aren't artists must colour things the way they really are or people might think we're stupid. [*Crawling Arnold*]

9 Her male friendships had been restricted to several Y.M.C.A. secretaries with whom she read poetry. For years she had not stared at a man below the first button on his suit. [*Harry, the Rat with Women*, I]

10 I know she's alive. I saw her lip curl. [*Sick, Sick, Sick*]

11 There *are* no more policemen. Only police dogs. We've eliminated the middle man. [*Observer*, 7 July 1963]

MARTY FELDMAN

12 Comedy, like sodomy, is an unnatural act. [Quoted in *The Times*, 9 June 1969]

RACHEL FERGUSON

13 The kind of actress Agate would call husky and orchidaceous. [*A Child in the Theatre*. Quoted in James Agate, *Ego 1*, 2, 1933]

LAWRENCE FERLINGHETTI

14 And he is the mad eye of the fourth person singular / of which no body speaks. [*He*]

EUGENE FIELD

15 Mr Clarke played the King all evening as though under constant fear that someone else was about to play the Ace. [On a production of *King Lear*. Quoted in Alexander Woollcott, *Shouts and Murmurs*, 'Capsule Criticism']

'MICHAEL FIELD' [Katherine Bradley and Edith Cooper]

16 His [George Moore's] smile is like sunshine on putty. [*Journals*]

GABRIEL FIELDING

17 It's not what men fight for. They fight in the last resort to impress their mothers. [*The Birthday King*, Ch. 3]

GRACIE FIELDS

18 Wish Me Luck as You Wave Me Good-bye. [Title of song; words by Phil Park]

19 What Can You Give a Nudist On His Birthday? [Title of song]

20 We're going to string old Hitler / From the very highest bough / Of the biggest aspidistra in the world. [Song: *The Biggest Aspidistra*]

W. C. FIELDS

21 Anybody who hates children and dogs can't be all bad. [Quoted in *Radio Times*, 12 Aug. 1965]

EDWARD A. FILENE

22 Why shouldn't the American people take half my money from me? I took all of it from them. [Quoted in A. M. Schlesinger Jr, *The Coming of the New Deal*, Pt 7, Ch. 2, Sect. iv]

RONALD FIRBANK

23 For I yearn for those kisses you gave me once / On the steps by Bakerloo. [*Caprice*, I]

24 'O God, help me, Dear,' she prayed, 'this little once, O Lord. For Thou knowest my rights.' [*Ib*. III]

25 'I hear it's the Hebrew in Heaven, sir – Spanish is seldom spoken,' he exclaimed seraphically. [*The Eccentricities of Cardinal Pirelli*, Ch. 8]

26 She made a ravishing corpse. [*Ib.*]

27 'I've never travelled,' Dona Consolation blandly confessed, 'but I dare say, dear, you can't judge Egypt by *Aïda.*' [*Ib*. 9]

28 'She reads at such a pace,' she complained, 'and when I asked her where she had learnt to read so quickly she replied "On the screens at cinemas."' [*The Flower Beneath the Foot*, Ch. 1]

29 His Weariness the Prince entered the room in all his tinted Orders. [*Ib.*]

30 Ah! How clever Shakespeare. . . . I once knew a speech from 'Julia Sees Her!' . . . perhaps his greatest oeuvre of all. [*Ib*. 2]

31 She's shy – of the Violet persuasion, but that's not a bad thing in a young girl. [*Ib*. 2]

32 Beneath the strain of expectation even the little iced sugar cakes upon the tea-table looked green with worry. [*Ib*. 3]

33 Mrs Barleymoon's position, as a captain's widow with means, unquestionably came before Mrs Montgomery's, who drew a salary and hadn't often an h. [*Ib*. 4]

34 I feel his books are all written in hotels with the bed unmade at the back of the chair. [*Ib*. 4]

35 I remember the average curate at home was something between a eunuch and a snigger. [*Ib*. 4]

36 'Basta!' his master replied with all the brilliant glibness of the Berlitz-school. [*Ib*. 5]

37 But I'm so sensitive . . . I seem to *know* when I talk to a man the colour of his braces . . . ! I say to myself: 'Yours are violet . . .'. [*Ib*. 5]

38 She looks at other women as though she would inhale them. [*Ib*. 5]

39 Her dreaminess was making ready a few private telegrams, breaking without undue harshness the melancholy news, 'Poor Lizzie has ceased articulating.' [*Ib*. 6]

40 There's few can mix as I can, yet I don't never get no rise!' the shy youth exclaimed, producing a card that was engraved: *Harry Cummings, Salad-Dresser to the King.* [*Ib*. 13]

41 It is said, I believe, that to behold the Englishman at his *best* one should watch him play tip-and-run. [*Ib*. 14]

42 I always like to be on the right side of my profile! [*Prancing Nigger*, Ch. 10]

43 Fo' a villa so grand, dair must be mo' dan one privy? [*Ib.*]

44 A quietly silly woman, Madam Ruiz was often obliged to lament the absence of intellect at her door: accounting for it as the consequence of a weakness for negroes, combined with a hopeless passion for the Regius Professor of Greek at Oxford. [*Ib*. 12]

45 To be sympathetic without discrimination is so very debilitating. [*Vainglory*, Ch. 7]

46 All millionaires love a baked apple. [*Ib.* 13]

47 Valmouth, with its ancient bridge and great stone church, that from the country had the scheming look of an ex-cathedral. [*Valmouth*, Ch. I]

48 She stands, I fear, poor thing, now, for something younger than she looks. [*Ib.*]

49 Love in the East Mrs Yaj, I presume, is *only* feasible indoors? [*Ib.* 3]

50 'I know of no joy,' she airily began, 'greater than a cool white dress after the sweetness of confession.' [*Ib.* 4]

51 And *so* poorly and *so* run down. She says her blood is nothing but rose-water. [*Ib.*]

52 Some ninety hours afterwards the said young novice brought into the world the Blessed St Elizabeth Bathilde, who, by dint of skipping, changed her sex at the age of forty and became a man. [*Ib.* 6]

53 There was really no joy in pouring out one's sins while he sat assiduously picking his nose. [*Ib.*]

LOUIS FISCHER

54 But you can burn your fingers on your own chestnuts. [Comment on Stalin's 'burning chestnuts' speech, *The Nation*, 6 Jan. 1940]

H. A. L. FISHER

55 Men wiser and more learned than I have discerned in history a plot, a rhythm, a predetermined pattern. These harmonies are concealed from me. I can see only one emergency following on another. [*A History of Europe*, Preface]

56 W.C. [Winston Churchill] is a bigger danger than the Germans by a long way in what is just now imminent in the Dardanelles. [Letter to Bonar Law, May 1915, quoted in Robert Blake, *The Unknown Prime Minister*]

CLYDE FITCH

57 The Woman in the Case [Title of play]

F. SCOTT FITZGERALD

58 She had once been a Catholic, but discovering that priests were infinitely more attentive when she was in process of losing or regaining faith in Mother Church, she maintained an enchantingly wavering attitude. [*This Side of Paradise*, Bk I, Ch. 1]

59 Monsignor was forty-four then, and bustling – a trifle too stout for symmetry, with hair the colour of spun gold, and a brilliant, enveloping personality. When he came into a room clad in his full purple regalia from thatch to toe, he resembled a Turner sunset. [*Ib.*]

60 Mother always feels the girl is safe if she's with me. . . . If I start to hold somebody's hand they laugh at me, and *let* me, just as if it wasn't part of them. As soon as I get hold of a hand they sort of disconnect it from the rest of them. [*Ib.*]

61 He differed from the healthy type that was essentially middle-class – he never seemed to perspire. [*Ib.* I. 2]

62 Life was a damned muddle . . . a football game with everyone off-side and the referee gotten rid of – everyone claiming the referee would have been on his side. [*Ib.* II. 5]

63 Beware of the artist who's an intellectual also. The artist who doesn't fit. [*Ib.*]

64 The idea that to make a man work you've got to hold gold in front of his eyes is a growth, not an axiom. We've done that for so long that we've forgotten there's any other way. [*Ib.*]

65 One thing I know. If living isn't a seeking for the grail it may be a damned amusing game. [*Ib.*]

66 'I know myself,' he cried, 'but that is all.' [*Ib.*]

67 A big man has no time really to do anything but just sit and be big. [*Ib.* III. 2]

68 One of those men who reach such an acute limited excellence at twenty-one that everything afterward savours of anti-climax. [*The Great Gatsby*, Ch. 1]

69 She told me with pride that her husband had photographed her a hundred and twenty-seven times since they had been married. [*Ib.* 2]

70 Mrs Eberhardt. She goes around looking at people's feet in their own homes. [*Ib.*]

71 I was so excited that when I got into a taxi with him I didn't hardly know I wasn't getting into a subway train. [*Ib.*]

72 I was one of the few guests who had actually been invited. People were not invited – they went there. [*Ib.* 3]

73 I've been drunk for about a week now, and I thought it might sober me up to sit in a library. [*Ib.*]

74 Everyone suspects himself of at least one of the cardinal virtues, and this is mine: I am one of the few honest people that I have ever known. [*Ib.*]

75 I understand you're looking for a business gonnegtion. [*Ib.* 4]

76 He went to Oggsford College in England. [*Ib.*]

77 There are only the pursued, the pursuing, the busy, and the tired. [*Ib.*]

78 If you want to kiss me any time during the evening, Nick, just let me know and I'll be glad to arrange it for you. Just mention my name. [*Ib.* 6]

79 'What'll we do with ourselves this afternoon?' cried Daisy, 'and the day after that, and the next thirty years?' [*Ib.* 7]

80 Her voice is full of money. [*Ib.*]

81 When I was a young man it was different – if a friend of mine died, no matter how, I stuck with them to the end. [*Ib.* 9]

82 Gatsby believed in the green light, the orgastic future that year by year recedes before us. It eluded us then, but that's no matter – tomorrow we will run faster, stretch out our arms further.... And one fine morning – So we beat on, boats against the current, borne back ceaselessly into the past. [*Ib.*]

83 Three British nannies sat knitting the slow pattern of Victorian England, the pattern of the forties, the sixties, and the eighties, into sweaters and socks, to the tune of gossip as formalized as incantation. [*Tender is the Night*, Bk. I, Ch. 1]

84 Though the Jazz Age continued, it became less and less an affair of youth. The sequel was like a children's party taken over by the elders. [*The Crack Up*, 'Echoes of the Jazz Age']

85 The less sought-after girls who had become resigned to sublimating a probable celibacy came across Freud and Jung in seeking their intellectual recompense and came tearing back into the fray. [*Ib.*]

86 His life was a sort of dream, as are most lives with the mainspring left out. [*Notebooks*, C]

87 A man says to another man: 'I'd certainly like to steal your girl.' Second man: 'I'd give her to you, but she's part of a set.' [*Ib.* E]

88 Show me a hero and I will write you a tragedy. [*Ib.*]

89 Switzerland is a country where very few things begin, but many things end. [*Ib.*]

90 Hospitality is a wonderful thing. If people really want you, they'll have you even if the cook has just died in the house of small-pox. [*Ib.*]

1 She was one of those people who would just as soon starve in a garret with a man – if she didn't have to. [*Ib.*]

2 She's got to be a loyal, frank person if she's got to bitch everyone in the world to do it. [*Ib.*]

3 'What kind of man was he?' 'Well, he was one of those men who come in a door and make any woman with them look guilty.' [*Ib.*]

4 When he buys his ties he has to ask if gin will make them run. [*Ib.*]

5 S.F.: The rich are different from us.
ERNEST HEMINGWAY: Yes, they have more money. [Conversation, reported in *ib.*]

6 He was not the frock-coated and impressive type of millionaire which has become so frequent since the war. He was rather the 1910 model – a sort of cross between Henry VIII and 'our Mr Jones will be in Minneapolis on Friday'. [*Ib.* H]

7 I entertained on a cruising trip that was so much fun that I had to sink my yacht to make my guests go home. [*Ib.* K]

8 Once tried to get up a ship's party on a ferry boat. [*Ib.*]

9 When he urinated, it sounded like night prayer. [*Ib.* M]

10 Listen, little Elia, draw your chair up close to the edge of the precipice and I'll tell you a story. [*Ib.* N]

11 A great social success is a pretty girl who plays her cards as carefully as if she were plain. [From an undated letter to Frances Scott Fitzgerald]

12 All good writing is *swimming under water* and holding your breath. [*Ib.*]

13 An author ought to write for the youth of his own generation, the critics of the next, and the schoolmasters of ever afterwards. [Quoted in the *Guardian*, 13 Nov. 1964]

BOB FITZSIMMONS

14 The bigger they come the harder they fall· [Pugilist's boast]

BUD FLANAGAN

15 Underneath the arches / We dream our dreams away. [Song: *Underneath the Arches*]

16 Run, Rabbit [Title of song; words by Noel Gay]

MICHAEL FLANDERS

17 Eating People is Wrong [Title of song]

18 Have Some Madeira, M'Dear. [Title of song]

JAMES ELROY FLECKER

19 Plunge not the finger of enquiry into the pie of impertinence, O my uncle. [*Hassan*, I. ii]

20 Since when did a door of good reputation open on to this street, my masters? [*Ib.*]

21 Shall I then drop the needle of insinuation and pick up the club of statement? [*Ib.* II. i]

22 I shall study the reasons of the excessive ugliness of the pattern of this carpet. [*Ib.*]

23 We have walked with the Friend of Friends in the Garden of the Stars, and He is pitiable to poor lovers who are pierced by the arrows of this ghostly world. [*Ib.* III. iii]

24 You have left the Garden of Art for the Palace of Action. [*Ib.* V. i]

25 Why should the dead be wiser than the living? The dead know only this – that it was better to be alive. [*Ib.*]

26 And such sweet jams meticulously jarred / As God's Own Prophet eats in Paradise. [*Ib.* V. ii]

27 We are the Pilgrims, master; we shall go / Always a little further; it may be / Beyond that last blue mountain barred with snow / Across that angry or that glimmering sea. [*Ib.*]

28 What would ye, ladies? It was ever thus. / Men are unwise and curiously planned. [*Ib.*]

IAN FLEMING

29 Dangerous at both ends and uncomfortable in the middle. [Attr. description of the horse. Quoted in *Sunday Times*, 9 Oct. 1966]

A. G. N. FLEW

30 Hope is free! [In private letter]

MARSHAL FOCH

31 *Victoire, c'est la Volonté!* – The will to conquer is the first condition of victory. [Quoted in Tuchman, *The Guns of August*]

HENRY FORD

32 Exercise is bunk. If you are healthy, you don't need it: if you are sick, you shouldn't take it. [Attr.]

33 I did not say it [history] *was* bunk. It was bunk to *me*. ... I did not need it very bad. [Quoted in Allan Nevins, *Ford: Expansion and Challenge*]

FORD MADOX FORD

34 You cannot be absolutely dumb when you live with a person unless you are an inhabitant of the North of England or the State of Maine. [*The Good Soldier*, Pt III, Ch. 4]

35 We [Americans] haven't got peerages and social climbing to occupy us much, and decent people do not take interest in politics or elderly people in sport. [*Ib.* IV. 2]

E. M. FORSTER

36 What the world most needs today are negative virtues – not minding people, not being huffy, touchy, irritable or revengeful. Positive ideals are becoming a curse, for they can seldom be achieved without someone being killed, or maimed or interned. [*Picture Post*, 'Tolerance', July 1939]

37 American women shoot the hippotamus with eyebrows made of platinum. [Quoted in James Thurber, *Alarms and Diversions*]

38 Only connect! [*Howards End*, Epigraph]

39 They [railway termini] are our gates to the glorious and the unknown. Through them we pass out into adventure and sunshine, and to them, alas! we return. [*Ib.* Ch. 2]

40 Brahms, for all his grumbling and grizzling, had never guessed what it felt like to be suspected of stealing an umbrella. [*Ib.* 5]

41 We are not concerned with the very poor. They are unthinkable, and only to be approached by the statistician or the poet. [*Ib.* 6]

42 He believed in sudden conversion, a belief which may be right, but which is peculiarly attractive to the half-baked mind. [*Ib.*]

43 To speak against London is no longer fashionable. The Earth as an artistic cult has had its day. [*Ib.* 13]

44 Give Mr Bast money and don't worry about his ideals. He'll pick up those for himself. [*Ib.* 15]

45 Ronny approved of religion as long as it endorsed the National Anthem, but he objected when it attempted to influence his life. [*A Passage to India*, Ch. 5]

46 She felt increasingly ... that, though people are important, the relations between them are not. [*Ib.* 13]

47 'Can you always tell whether a stranger is your friend?' 'Yes.' 'Then you are an Oriental.' [*Ib.* 36]

48 The historian must have ... some conception of how men who are not historians behave. Otherwise he will move in a world of the dead. [*Abinger Harvest*, 'Captain Edward Gibbon']

49 It is pleasant to be transferred from an office where one is afraid of a sergeant-major into an office where one can intimidate generals, and perhaps this is why History is so attractive to the more timid among us. We can recover self-confidence by snubbing the dead. [*Ib.* 'The Consolations of History']

50 It is not that the Englishman can't feel – it is that he is afraid to feel. He has been taught at his public school that feeling is bad form. He must not express great joy or sorrow, or even open his mouth too wide when he talks – his pipe might fall out if he did. [*Ib.* 'Notes on the English Character']

51 How rare, how precious is frivolity! How few writers can prostitute all their powers! They are always implying 'I am capable of higher things.' [*Ib.* 'Ronald Firbank']

52 Yes – oh dear, yes – the novel tells a story. [*Aspects of the Novel*, Ch. 2]

53 Look at them [the Jews] in the railway carriage now. Their faces are anxious and eloquent of past rebuffs. But they are travelling First. [*Pharos and Pharillon*, 'Philo's Little Trip']

54 If I had to choose between betraying my *country* and betraying my *friend*, I hope I should have the guts to *betray* my country. [*What I Believe*]

55 Spoon feeding in the long run teaches us nothing but the shape of the spoon. [*Observer*, 'Sayings of the Week', 6 Oct. 1951]

56 One has two duties – to be worried and not to be worried. [*Observer*, 'Sayings of the Week', 4 Jan. 1959]

H. E. FOSDICK

57 An atheist is a man who has no invisible means of support. [Attr.]

S. C. FOSTER

58 The sun shines bright in the old Kentucky home. [*My Old Kentucky Home*]

M. FOUREST

59 It is sad that so many people appear to be interested in God because no one is interested in them. [Attr.]

FRAGA IRIBARNE

60 A free economy presupposes a free social order. [Said during visit to England. *Observer*, 'Sayings of the Year', 1963]

ANATOLE FRANCE

61 *Dans tout état policé, la richesse est chose sacrée; dans les démocraties elle est la seule chose sacrée.* – In every well-governed state wealth is a sacred thing; in democracies it is the only sacred thing. [*L'Île des Pingouins*]

GENERAL FRANCO

62 The destiny of history has united you with myself and the Duce in an indissoluble way. [Letter to Adolf Hitler]

HANS FRANK

63 Our Constitution is the will of the Fuehrer. [Quoted in A. Bullock, *Hitler*, Ch. 7, Sect. vi]

SIR OLIVER FRANK

64 The Pentagon, that immense monument to modern man's subservience to the desk. [*Observer*, 'Sayings of the Week', 30 Nov. 1952]

MICHAEL FRAYN

65 There is something about a blurb-writer paying his respects to a funny book which puts one in mind of a short-sighted lord mayor raising his hat to a hippopotamus. [Introduction to *The Best of Beachcomber*]

66 The Euroglise will be staffed by a carefully chosen team of Divine Relations Officers, and the services will be conducted in Basic Eurish. [*Shouts and Murmurs*, 'Us Poor Blighters in Public Relations']

67 The Government has made small slips before, of course. It has made minor errors of economic policy. It has occasionally deported the wrong people. It has gambled on the wrong defence system. It invaded the wrong country. All these peccadilloes could be forgiven. ... But now a member of the Government has *slept with the wrong woman*, and as a consequence severely strained this country's newsprint resources. [Comment on Profumo case in *Observer*, 1963]

68 To be absolutely honest, what I feel really bad about is that I don't feel worse. There's the ineffectual liberal's problem in a nutshell. [*Observer*, 8 Aug. 1965]

R. M. FREEMAN

69 Let us have the numbers [of casualties] made instantly public; however large they be they shall never approach the figures arrived at by the reckless arithmetic of rumour. [*Pepys and Wife Go to It*]

WILLIAM PERCIVAL FRENCH

70 Where the mountains of Mourne sweep down to the sea. [Song: The Mountains of Mourne]

CLEMENT FREUD

71 If you resolve to give up smoking, drinking and loving, you don't actually live longer; it just seems longer. [Attr. to 'a third-rate comedian in Sloane Square'. *Observer*, 27 Dec. 1964]

SIGMUND FREUD

72 The myth of King Oedipus, who killed his father and took his mother to wife, reveals, with little modification, the infantile wish, which is later opposed and repudiated by the *barrier against incest*. Shakespeare's *Hamlet* is equally rooted in the soil of the incest-complex, but under a better disguise. [*Five Lectures on Psycho-Analysis*, IV]

73 A culture which leaves unsatisfied and drives to rebelliousness so large a number of its members neither has a prospect of continued existence nor deserves it. [*The Future of an Illusion*]

74 We believe that civilization has been built up, *under the pressure of the struggle for existence*, by sacrifices in gratification of the primitive impulses. [*Introductory Lectures*]

75 I do not think our successes can compete with those of Lourdes. There are so many more people who believe in the miracles of the Blessed Virgin than in the existence

of the unconscious. [*New Introductory Lectures*, Lecture XXXIV]

76 I repeatedly addressed my patient as Mrs Smith ... when her real name is Mrs James. My attention having been called to it, I soon discovered that I had another patient called Mrs James, who refused to pay for her treatment. Mrs Smith was also my patient and paid her bills promptly. [*Psychopathology of Everyday Life*, 5]

77 Two women stopped in front of a drugstore, and one said to her companion, 'If you will wait a few moments I'll soon be back,' but she said *movements* instead. She was on her way to buy some castoroil for her child. [*Ib.*]

78 A woman who is very anxious to get children always reads *storks* instead of *stocks*. [*Ib.* 6]

79 I wished to make merry with an intimate friend over a statement made by my wife only a few hours earlier, but I found myself hindered by the noteworthy fact that I had entirely forgotten the statement. I had first to beg my wife to recall it to me. [*Ib.* 7]

80 Occasionally I have had to admit to myself that the annoying, awkward stepping aside on the street, whereby for some seconds one steps here and there, yet always in the same direction as the other person, until finally both stop facing each other ... conceals erotic purposes under the mask of awkwardness. [*Ib.* 8]

81 When a member of my family complains that he or she has bitten his tongue, bruised her finger, and so on, instead of the expected sympathy I put the question, 'Why did you do that?' [*Ib.*]

82 Due to unknown motives, Jones left a letter for several days on his desk, forgetting each time to post it. He ultimately posted it, but it was returned to him from the Dead-letter Office because he forgot to address it. After addressing it and posting it a second time, it was again returned to him, this time without a stamp. He was then forced to recognize the unconscious opposition to the sending of the letter. [*Ib.* 11]

83 Psycho-analysis has revealed to us that the totem-animal is really a substitute for the father, and this really explains to us

the contradiction that it is usually forbidden to kill the totem animal, that the killing of it results in a holiday, and that the animal is killed and yet mourned. [*Totem and Taboou*, Ch. IV, Sect. v.]

MAX FRISCH

84 Technology ... the knack of so arranging the world that we don't have to experience it. [Quoted in D. J. Boorstin, *The Image*, title page epigraph]

85 Travel is atavistic, the day will come when there will be no more traffic at all and only newlyweds will travel. [Quoted in *Ib.* Ch. 3]

ROBERT FROST

86 I never dared be radical when young / For fear it would make me conservative when old. [*Precaution*]

87 Lord forgive all the little tricks I play on you, and I'll forgive the great big one you played on me. [Attr.]

88 Earth's the right place for love: / I don't know where it's likely to go better. [*Birches*]

89 One could do worse than be a swinger of birches. [*Ib.*]

90 Part of the moon was falling down the west / Dragging the whole sky with it to the hills. [*The Death of the Hired Man*]

1 'Home is the place where, when you have to go there, / They have to take you in.' / 'I should have called it / Something you somehow haven't to deserve.' [*Ib.*]

2 Why make so much of fragmentary blue / In here and there a bird, or butterfly, / Or flower, or wearing-stone, or open eye, / When heaven presents in sheets the solid hue? [*Fragmentary Blue*]

3 The land was ours before we were the land's. / She was our land more than a hundred years / Before we were her people. [*The Gift Outright*]

4 Keep cold, young orchard. Goodbye and keep cold. / Dread fifty above more than fifty below. [*Goodbye and Keep Cold*]

5 Friends make pretence of following to the grave, / But before one is in it, their minds are turned / And making the best of their way back to life / And living people, and things they understand. [*Home Burial*]

6 This as it will be seen is other far / Than with brooks taken otherwhere in song. / We love the things we love for what they are. [*Hyla Brook*]

7 For them there was really nothing sad. / But though they rejoiced in the nest they kept. / One had to be versed in country things / Not to believe the phoebes wept. [*The Need of Being Versed in Country Things*]

8 I met a Californian who would / Talk California – a state so blessed, / He said, in climate, none had ever died there / A natural death. [*New Hampshire*]

9 No wonder poets sometimes have to *seem* / So much more business-like than business men. / Their wares are so much harder to get rid of. [*Ib.*]

10 I knew a man who failing as a farmer / Burned down his farmhouse for the fire insurance, / And spent the proceeds on a telescope / To satisfy a life-long curiosity / About our place among the infinities. / And how was that for other-worldliness? [*Ib.*]

11 The bird would cease and be as other birds / But that he knows in singing not to sing. / The question that he frames in all but words / Is what to make of a diminished thing. [*The Oven Bird*]

12 Pressed into service means pressed out of shape. [*The Self-Seeker*]

13 The best way out is always through. [*A Servant to Servants*]

14 Never tell me that not one star of all / That slip from heaven at night and softly fall / Has been picked up with stones to build a wall. [*A Star in a Stone-Boat*]

15 So near to paradise all pairing ends: / Here loveless birds now flock as winter friends, / Content with bud-inspecting. [*A Winter Eden*]

16 People are inexterminable – like flies and bed-bugs. There will always be some that survive in cracks and crevices – that's us. [*Observer*, 'Sayings of the Week', 29 March 1959]

CHRISTOPHER FRY

17 If every man gave up women in God's name, / Where in God's name would be the men / To give up women in a generation's time? [*Curtmantle*, I]

18 Time walks by your side, ma'am, unwilling to pass. [*Ib.* II]

19 What a man knows he has by experience, / But what a man is precedes experience. [*Ib.*]

20 I apologize / For boasting, but once you know my qualities / I can drop back into a quite brilliant / Humility. [*The Lady's Not for Burning*, I]

21 Or Alexander, wearing / His imperial cobwebs and breastplate of shining worms / Wakens and looks for his glasses, to find the empire / Which he knows he put beside his bed. [*Ib.*]

22 Your innocence is on at such a rakish angle / It gives you quite an air of iniquity. [*Ib.*]

23 What after all / Is a halo? It's only one more thing to keep clean. [*Ib.*]

24 THOMAS: I have come to be hanged, do you hear.
TYSON: Have you filled in the necessary forms? [*Ib.*]

25 When it [the Day of Judgement] comes it will come in the autumn. / Heaven, I am quite sure, wouldn't disappoint / The bulbs. [*Ib.*]

26 Too unusual / Not to be corrupt. [*Ib.* II]

27 We don't want to put ourselves wrong / With anything as positive as evil. [*Ib.*]

28 Where did I put my better half ? I laid it / Aside. [*Ib.*]

29 Always fornicate / Between clean sheets and spit on a well-scrubbed floor. [*Ib.*]

30 And I'll live too, if it kills me. [*Ib.*]

31 The moon is nothing / But a circum-ambulating aphrodisiac / Divinely sub-sidized to provoke the world / Into a rising birth-rate. [*Ib.* III]

32 I know tears when I see them, / My wife has them. [*Ib.*]

33 I wish to be alone with my own convictions. [*Ib.*]

34 Peace on earth and good tall women. [*Ib.*]

35 But life and death / Is cat and dog in this double-bed of a world. [*A Phoenix Too Frequent*]

36 He was so punctual, you could regulate / The sun by him. [*Ib.*]

37 Death's a new interest in life. [*Ib.*]

38 Despair / Abroad can always nurse pleasant thoughts of home. [*Ib.*]

39 How easy to swear if you're properly educated. [*Ib.*]

40 When you belong / To an upper class, the nether world might come strange. / Now I was born nether, madam, though not / As nether as some. [*Ib.*]

41 He was caught / Red-handed with the silver, and his Grace / Being short of staff at the time, asked him to stay / And clean it. [*Venus Observed*, I]

42 But how I longed / As a boy for the groves and grooves of Academe. [*Ib.*]

43 You mustn't / Drift into Gothic, when your physique is so / Stubbornly Norman. [*Ib.*]

44 A spade is never so merely a spade as the word / Spade would imply. [*Ib.* II]

45 I know an undesirable character / When I see one; I've been one myself for years. [*Ib.*]

46 The patter of tiny criticism. [Attr.]

ROGER FRY

47 Manet and the Post-Impressionists. [Name of exhibition 'struck out in talk with a journalist'. Virginia Woolf, *Roger Fry*, Ch. 7]

48 There has been nothing like this outbreak of militant Philistinism since Whistler's day. [Letter to his mother, on Post-Impressionist exhibition. Quoted in *Ib.*]

49 We make buildings for our need, and then, sacrificing our pockets to art, cover them with a mass of purely nonsensical forms which we hope may turn them into fine architecture. [Letter to *The Times*, 1912. Quoted in *Ib.* 8]

50 Art is significant deformity. [Quoted in *Ib.*]

51 No bombardment [of Rheims Cathedral] can do anything like the damage that the last restoration did. [Quoted in *Ib.* 9]

52 I've found a perfect description of mysticism – it's the attempt to get rid of mystery. [Quoted in *Ib.* 11]

53 Bach almost persuades me to be a Christian. [Quoted in *Ib.*]

ROGER FULFORD

54 As with most Regency houses, the bedrooms were sacrificed to the living rooms. [On Brighton Pavilion, *The Prince Consort*]

ROY FULLER

55 As horrible thoughts, / Loud fluttering aircraft slope above his head / At dusk. The ridiculous empires break like biscuits. [*The Middle of a War*]

56 Tonight I'd like to bring / The poets from their safe and paper beds, / Show them my comrades and the silver pall / Over the airfield, ask them what they'd sing. [*A Wry Smile*]

57 The poets get a quizzical ahem. / They reflect time, I am the very ticking. [*Ib.*]

58 It [the news] half convinces me that some great faculty, / Like hands, has been eternally lost and all / Our virtues now are the high and horrible / Ones of a streaming wound which heals in evil. [*October 1942*]

DOUGLAS FURBER

59 Any time you're Lambeth way, / Any evening, any day, / You'll find us all doin' the Lambeth walk. [Song: *Doin' the Lambeth Walk*]

G

ZSA ZSA GABOR

1 I never hated a man enough to give him diamonds back. [*Observer*, 'Sayings of the Week', 28 Aug. 1957]

HUGH GAITSKELL

2 Surely the right course is to test the Russians, not the bombs. [*Observer*, 'Sayings of the Week', 23 June 1957]

J. K. GALBRAITH

3 Wealth is not without its advantages, and the case to the contrary, although it has often been made, has never proved widely persuasive. [*The Affluent Society*, Ch. 1, sect. 1]

4 One of the best ways of avoiding necessary and even urgent tasks is to seem to be busily employed on things that are already done. [*Ib.* ii]

5 No society seems ever to have succumbed to boredom. Man has developed an obvious capacity for surviving the pompous reiteration of the commonplace. [*Ib.* 2. vi]

6 Wealth has never been a sufficient source of honour in itself. It must be advertised, and the normal medium is obtrusively expensive goods. [*Ib.* 7. v]

7 With increasing well-being all people become aware, sooner or later, that they have something to protect. [*Ib.* 8. iii]

8 It is easy to overlook the absence of appreciable advance in an industry. Inventions that are not made, like babies that are not born, are rarely missed. [*Ib.* 9. iii]

9 Consumer wants can have bizarre, frivolous, or even immoral origins, and an admirable case can still be made for a society that seeks to satisfy them. But the case cannot stand if it is the process of satisfying wants that creates the wants. [*Ib.* 11. ii]

10 It is a far, far better thing to have a firm anchor in nonsense than to put out on the troubled seas of thought. [*Ib.* IV]

11 One of the tolerable features of old-fashioned wars was that the military planner could proceed with his task in the reasonably secure knowledge that in the event of hostilities someone else would be killed. [*Ib.* 12. vi]

12 Few things are as immutable as the addiction of political groups to the ideas by which they have once won office. [*Ib.* 13. iv]

13 The greater the wealth the thicker will be the dirt. This indubitably describes a tendency of our time. [*Ib.* 18. iii]

14 In the world of minor lunacy the behaviour of both the utterly rational and the totally insane seems equally odd. [*Ib.* 20. ii]

15 The modern liberal rallies to protect the poor from the taxes which in the next generation, as the result of a higher investment for their children, would eliminate poverty. [*Ib.* 22. iv]

16 We have barely noticed that the leisured class has been replaced by another and much larger class to which work has none of the older connotation of pain, fatigue, or other mental or physical discomfort. We have failed to observe the emergence of this New Class, as it may be simply called. [*Ib.* 24. iv]

17 The test will be less the effectiveness of our material investment than the effectiveness of our investment in men. [*Ib.* 25. iv]

JOHN GALSWORTHY

18 When a Forsyte died – but no Forsyte had as yet died; death being contrary to their principles, they took precautions against it. [*The Forsyte Saga: The Man of Property*, Pt I, Ch. 1]

19 'Very haughty!' he said, 'the wild Buccaneer.' [*Ib.*]

20 He would be setting up as a man of property next, with a place in the country. [*Ib.*]

21 Keep faith! We've all done that. It's not enough. [*Loyalties*, III]

22 What is it that gets loose when you begin to fight, and makes you what you think you're not? ... Begin as you may, it ends in this – skin game. [*The Skin Game*, III]

23 When we began this fight, we had clean hands – are they clean now? What's gentility worth if it can't stand fire? [*Ib.*]

ARCHBISHOP C. GARBETT

24 Any fool can criticize, and many of them do. [Attr.]

GRETA GARBO

25 I want to be alone. [Attr.]

JOSÉ GARCÍA OLIVER

[Anarchist Minister of Justice during the Civil War]

26 Justice, I firmly believe, is so subtle a thing that to interpret it one has only need of a heart. [Quoted in Hugh Thomas, *The Spanish Civil War*, Ch. 43]

LEON GARFIELD

27 Nature herself had created them to be storesmen. They had the very air of having been not so much born as indented for. [*The Drummer Boy*, Ch. 6]

J. L. GARVIN

28 Dear Mr Lansbury stands for our happy exposure to perfect annihilation. With broad amiability he is ready any day for the Gadarene gallop on the back of his own whole hog. [*Observer*, 1937]

GENERAL DE GAULLE

29 France has lost the battle but she has not lost the war. [In 1940]

30 I myself have become a Gaullist only little by little. [*Observer*, 'Sayings of the Year', 29 Dec. 1963]

31 I have come to the conclusion that politics are too serious a matter to be left to the politicians. [Attr.]

32 Events have made me the guide of the nation. [Attr.]

KING GEORGE V

33 I can't understand it. I'm really quite an ordinary sort of chap. [Attr. remark at his Jubilee in 1935]

34 Is it possible that my people live in such awful conditions? ... I tell you, Mr Wheatley, that if I had to live in conditions like that I would be a revolutionary myself. [On hearing Mr Wheatley's life story. Quoted in L. MacNeill Weir, *The Tragedy of Ramsay MacDonald*, Ch. 16]

DANIEL GEORGE

35 O Freedom, what liberties are taken in thy name! [*The Perpetual Pessimist*]

WILLIAM GERHARDI

36 None of them [the Russians on the train] could understand the Admiral's interpretation of No. They had all grown up with the idea that No meant Yes after an adequate amount of pressure and insistence. [*Futility*, Pt III, Ch. 4]

37 She even sighed offensively ... as if she meant to charge me with the necessity of doing so. [*Ib.* 5]

38 There are as many fools at a university as elsewhere. ... But their folly, I admit, has a certain stamp – the stamp of university training, if you like. It is trained folly. [*The Polyglots*, Ch. 7]

39 Instead of shaving in the clean manly way as he should, he used a fiendish contrivance ... for burning off his facial growth, making an unholy stink in the doing – regularly on the fourth day. ... The voyage across the Pacific ... took us fourteen days, during which time Major Beastly made a stink in our cabin three times. [*Ib.*]

40 We are like icebergs in the ocean: one-eighth part consciousness and the rest submerged beneath the surface of articulate apprehension. [*Ib.* 14]

41 What attracted me was that she did not even pretend to think that her un-intellectuality could be anything but interesting to me, an intellectual. [*Ib.* 20]

42 All day long she sang a sad, sad song of a strong Slavonic flavour that, however, seemed an improvisation, for it had no recognizable melody, though lots and lots of feeling. [*Ib.* 28]

43 He had a passion for life, which to him was identified with the intimate charm of the feminine form in its greatest variety; and so he spent his days in quest of the red light. [*Ib.* 32]

WILLA GIBBS

44 The three kinds of services you generally find in the Episcopal churches. I call them either low-and-lazy, broad-and-hazy, or high-and-crazy. [*The Dean*]

KAHLIL GIBRAN

45 Forget not that modesty is for a shield against the eye of the unclean. And when the unclean shall be no more, what were modesty but a fetter and a fouling of the mind? [*The Prophet*]

W. W. GIBSON

46 But we, how shall we turn to little things / And listen to the birds and winds and streams / Made holy by their dreams, / Nor feel the heart-break in the heart of things? [*A Lament*]

L. WOLFE GILBERT

47 *Waitin' for the* Robert E Lee. [Title of song]

W. S. GILBERT

48 Sir, I view the proposal to hold an international exhibition at San Francisco with an equanimity bordering on in-difference. [Quoted in Hesketh Pearson, *Gilbert, His Life and Strife*, Ch. 19]

49 Funny without being vulgar. [Attr. remark on Irving's *Hamlet*]

GILES

50 Fred's just heard the first cuckoo – and GOT it. [Caption of cartoon quoted in Colin MacInnes, *England, Half English*, 'The Express Families']

HERMIONE GINGOLD

51 What we at home call draught, Americans refer to as cross-ventilation. [*Observer*, 'Sayings of the Week', 8 Nov. 1953]

52 There are too many men in politics and not enough elsewhere. [*Observer*, 'Say-ings of the Week', 2 Oct. 1958]

ALLEN GINSBERG

53 America I'm putting my queer shoulder to the wheel. [*America*]

NORMAN GINSBURY

54 You must be prepared to sacrifice the Divine Passion to your Divine Right. That is the noble tragedy of Royalty. [*The Last Gentleman*, I. ii]

55 If it weren't for his good manners, Leopold could easily pass for an English-man. [*The First Gentleman*, II. i]

56 I never snub anybody accidentally. [*Viceroy Sarah*, I. ii]

57 To me, one political party is very much like another, especially in office. [*Ib.* III. i]

JEAN GIRAUDOUX

58 Beauty is always the first to hear about the sins of the world. [*Duel of Angels*, I]

59 Limousin, the country which has bred more popes and fewer lovers than any other in the world. [*Ib.*]

60 I said that virtue was the weakness of strong generals, and the strength of weak magistrates. [*Ib.*]

61 You spit with great charm, like a shocked schoolgirl [*Ib.*]

62 Heroes are men who glorify a life which they can't bear any longer. [*Ib.* III]

63 You know women as well as I do. They are only willing when you compel them, but after that they're as enthusiastic as you are. [*Tiger at the Gates*, I]

64 On horseback, in the usual style of seducers, leaving a heap of horse manure under the windows. [*Ib.*]

65 Blonde beauty doesn't usually last for ever. [*Ib.*]

66 Ask any soldier. To kill a man is to merit a woman. [*Ib.*]

67 A man has only one way of being immortal on this earth: he has to forget he is mortal. [*Ib.*]

68 It's odd how people waiting for you stand out far less clearly than people you are waiting for. [*Ib.*]

69 Often I don't recognize faces, but I always recognize the jewellery. [*Ib.*]

70 As soon as war is declared it will be impossible to hold the poets back. Rhyme is still the most effective drum. [*Ib.*]

71 But the annihilation of a people doesn't alter in the least their superior moral position. [*Ib.*]

72 There's no better way of exercising the imagination than the study of law. No poet ever interpreted nature as freely as a lawyer interprets truth. [*Ib.*]

73 The life of a wife and husband who love each other is never at rest. Whether the marriage is true or false, the marriage portion is the same: elemental discord. [*Ib.* II]

74 I can tell the sex of a seagull thirty yards off. [*Ib.*]

75 I forgot they were talking about me. They sound so wonderfully convincing. [*Ib.*]

76 One of the privileges of the great is to witness catastrophes from a terrace. [*Ib.*]

77 Nations, like men, die by imperceptible disorders. We recognize a doomed people by the way they sneeze or pare their nails. [*Ib.*]

78 One way to recognize error is the fact that it's universal. [*Ib.*]

JOHN GLOAG

79 Our Georgian forerunners had faculties that we have lost ... they ignored the natural smells of sweat and dung and dirt, as we ignore the artificial smells of petrol fumes and industrial effluents, but they rejoiced in an unimpaired sense of sight. [*Georgian Grace*, Ch. 1]

80 England is a living guide-book to over two thousand years of civilization. [*2,000 Years of England*, Ch. 1]

81 When we have outgrown the current nostalgia for the Victorian Age, we may come to regard it as a period of vigorous decadence. [*Victorian Taste*, 'The Character']

82 Architecture cannot lie, and buildings, although inanimate, are to that extent morally superior to men. [*The Significance of Historical Research in Architectural and Industrial Design*, a paper read to the Royal Society of Arts, 20 March 1963]

83 Since the early nineteenth century we have depended almost exclusively on what used to be called book learning, so much so that we have become visually illiterate. [*Ib.*]

CHARLES GODFREY

84 When we go to meet the foe, / It's the English speaking race against the world. [Song: *We're Brothers of the Selfsame Race*]

FRED GODFREY and MARK SHERIDAN

85 Who were you with last night? / Out in the pale moonlight. [Song: *Who Were You with Last Night?*]

JOSEF GOEBBELS

86 You can tell those tales to the marines, you honest old British Jack Tar. [In letter to Commander King-Hall, 1939]

87 The Iron Curtain. [*Das Reich*]

88 This was the Angel of History! We felt its wings flutter through the room. Was that not the fortune we awaited so anxiously? [On hearing of Roosevelt's death. *Diary*]

HERMANN GOERING

89 They [the British] entered the war to prevent us from going into the East, not to have the East come to the Atlantic. [On the possibilities of splitting the Grand Alliance. Quoted in G. M. Gilbert, *Nuremburg Diary*]

90 I herewith commission you to carry out all preparations with regard to . . . a *total solution* of the Jewish question in those territories of Europe which are under German influence. [Instructions to Heydrich, 31 July 1941. Quoted in W. L. Shirer, *The Rise and Fall of the Third Reich*, Bk V, Ch. 27]

OLIVER ST JOHN GOGARTY

1 In spite of his faith in one medicine for many unseen and unknown diseases, he [the Englishman] cannot accept miracles; he burks at the infallibility of the Pope, but unquestioningly accepts the infallibility of the pill. 'Just as much as will fit on a threepenny-piece' instead of as many angels as will stand on the point of a needle. [*As I was Going Down Sackville Street*, Ch. 3]

2 O Boys, the times I've seen! / The things I've done and known! / If you knew where I have been / Or half the joys I've had, / You never would leave me alone. [*O Boys! O Boys!*]

WILLIAM GOLDING

3 Philip is a living example of natural selection. He was as fitted to survive in this modern world as a tapeworm in an intestine. [*Free Fall*, Ch. 2]

4 I kept my drinking from Beatrice because she thought of pubs as only one degree less damned than the Church of England. [*Ib.* 4]

5 Sleep is when all the unsorted stuff comes flying out as from a dustbin upset in a high wind. [*Pincher Martin*, Ch. 6]

SAMUEL GOLDWYN

6 Anybody who goes to see a psychiatrist ought to have his head examined. [Attr.]

7 Every director bites the hand that lays the golden egg. [Attr.]

8 If Roosevelt were alive he'd turn in his grave. [Attr.]

9 I'll give you a definite maybe. [Attr.]

10 It's more than magnificent – it's mediocre. [Attr.]

11 A verbal contract isn't worth the paper it's written on. [Attr.]

12 'Why only twelve?' 'That's the original number.' 'Well, go out and get thousands.' [During the filming of *The Last Supper*. Attr.]

13 [To a man who said, 'What beautiful hands your wife has':] Yes, I'm going to have a bust made of them. [Attr.]

14 You ought to take the bull between the teeth. [Attr.]

15 Chaplin is no business man – all he knows is that he can't take anything less. [Quoted in Charles Chaplin, *My Autobiography*, Ch. 19]

16 My *Toujours* Lautrec! [Quoted in Lillian Ross, *Picture*, 'Throw the Little Old Lady Down the Stairs']

17 Let's have some new clichés. [*Observer*, 'Sayings of the Week', 24 Oct. 1948]

18 Why should people go out and pay money to see bad films when they can stay at home and see bad television for nothing? [*Observer*, 'Sayings of the Week', 9 Sept. 1956]

19 I read part of the book right the way through. [Attr. Quoted in Philip French, *The Movie Moguls*]

DR I. J. GOOD

20 When I hear the word 'gun' I reach for my culture. [*The Scientist Speculates*]

21 I have had so many deadlines to keep, it is a wonder I am still alive. [In conversation]

RICHARD GORDON

22 The birds on the Liver building, that are unfairly supposed by Liverpool seafarers to flap their wings when passed by a woman of untarnished virtue, wept ceaselessly on to the bleak pierhead. [*Doctor at Sea*, Ch. 1]

23 She was a girl called Wendy, a blonde, but of the arid sort, like the stubble in a wheatfield after a hot harvest. [*Ib.* 2]

24 I began to suffer an attack of *terror celebans*, or bachelor's panic. [*Ib.*]

25 She clapped me to her bosom like a belladonna plaster and pushed me on the dance floor. . . . It was like being lashed to an upholstered pneumatic drill. [*Ib.* 10]

26 The staff at St Swithin's had come to out-number the patients by four to one and now seemed to be expanding naturally, like a water-lily covering a small pond. [*Doctor in the House*, Ch. 1]

27 To my mind the most important function of the St Swithin's nursing school is that it provides competent wives to help in general practice anywhere in the world. [*Ib.* 2]

28 The established English custom of drop-ping the national mantle of self-conscious-ness at Christmastime and revealing the horrible likeness of the charade under-neath. [*Ib.* 10]

BISHOP GORE

29 Can you lend me a Bible? I remembered my pipe but have forgotten my Bible. [To an ultra-pious vicar and curate before preaching in their church. G. L. Prestige, *Life of Bishop Gore*, Ch. 16, sect. ii]

30 An octave is something idolatrous and wicked and smells of incense and witch-craft. [To a lady puzzled on a point of ritual. Quoted in John Gore, *Charles Gore*, Ch. 5]

31 If there *is* to be a resurrection, we must hold on to our toasting forks. [In delirium. Quoted in C. A. Alington, *Things Ancient and Modern*, Ch. 5]

32 I am increasingly convinced that the *Church Times* is now edited by the Devil in person. [Quoted in *ib.*]

33 But for the miracles, I should consider Nero the ideal man. [Attr.]

MAXIM GORKY

34 Everyone knows that it is much harder to turn word into deed than deed into word. ['On Plays', quoted in *U.S.S.R. in Construction*, Apr. 1937]

EDMUND GOSSE

35 We were as nearly bored as enthusiasm would permit. [On a Swinburne play. Quoted in Christopher Hassall, *Edward Marsh*, Ch. 6]

36 Gosse amused him one day by pointing to an advertisement in a newspaper: Messrs Gunter send their celebrated Invalid Turtle to all parts of the King-dom, remarked, 'I conceive of it travelling with a lacklustre eye'. [Quoted in *ib.*]

37 There always seemed to me a worm slumbering at the root of his talent. [On Flecker's death. Letter to Edward Marsh, Jan. 1915]

GERALD GOULD

38 The telephone directory is, because of its rigorous selection and repression, a work of art compared to the wastepaper basket. And [James Joyce's] *Ulysses* is a waste-paper basket. [*The English Novel*]

RUPERT T. GOULD

39 A member of that unfortunate fraternity to whom the world has never listened, because they have not prophesied accep-table things. [*Oddities*, 'The Wizard of Mauritius']

SIR ERNEST GOWERS

40 Our use of gentleman, like that of esquire, is being affected by our progress towards a classless society, but in the opposite way: we are all esquires now, and we are none of us gentlemen any more. [*Fowler's Dictionary of Modern English Usage*, 2nd edition]

VIRGINIA GRAHAM

41 Lully my darling, till atom bombs fall, / When up will go baby and mummy and all. [*A Lullaby in Poor Taste*]

W. S. GRAHAM

42 So here we are, you and I, / Thought up out of silence for an instant here / Under the ancient hardware of the sky. [*In Memoriam: Burns Singer*]

ROBERT GRAVES

43 We spurred our parents to the kiss, / Though doubtfully they shrank from this. [*Children of Darkness*]

44 Children are dumb to say how hot the day is, / How hot the scent is of the summer rose. [*The Cool Web*]

45 A gaping silken dragon, / Puffed by the wind, suffices us for God. [*The Cuirassiers of the Frontier*]

46 Yet love survives, the word carved on the sill / Under antique dread of the headsman's axe. [*End of Play*]

47 How not terrible / When the event outran the alarm / And suddenly we were free. [*The Fallen Tower of Siloam*]

48 I dung on my grandfather's doorstep, / Which is a reasonable and loving due / To hold no taint of spite or vassalage / And understood only by him and me. [*Front Door Soliloquy*]

49 This house is jealous of its nastiness. [*Ib.*]

50 To be mad is not easy, / Will earn him no money, / But a niche in the news. [*The Halls of Bedlam*]

51 These dusty-featured Lollocks / Have their nativity in all disordered / Backs of cupboard drawers. [*Lollocks*]

52 Is it not the height of silent humour / To cause an unknown change in the earth's climate? [*The Meeting*]

53 Stirring suddenly from long hibernation, / I knew myself once more a poet / Guarded by timeless principalities / Against the worm of death. [*Mid-Winter Waking*]

54 Any honest housewife would sort them out, / Having a nose for fish, an eye for apples. [*The Poets*]

55 What, then, was war? No mere discord of flags / But an infection of the common sky / That sagged ominously upon the earth / Even when the season was the airiest May? [*Recalling War*]

56 Fortune enrolled me among the second-fated / Who have read their own obituaries in *The Times*. [*The Second-Fated*]

57 Take your delight in momentariness, / Walk between dark and dark – a shining space / With the grave's narrowness, though not its peace. [*Sick Love*]

58 Love is a universal migraine / A bright stain on the vision / Blotting out reason. [*Symptoms of Love*]

59 They carry / Time looped so river-wise about their house / There's no way in by history's road / To name or number them. [*Through Nightmare*]

60 To bring the dead to life / Is no great magic. / Few are wholly dead: / Blow on a dead man's embers / And a live flame will start. [*To Bring the Dead to Life*]

61 Subdue your pen to his handwriting / Until it prove as natural / To sign his name as yours. [*Ib.*]

62 To evoke posterity / Is to weep on your own grave, / Ventriloquizing for the unborn. [*To Evoke Posterity*]

63 It's an old story – f's for s's – / But good enough for them, the suckers. [*Wm. Brazier*]

64 Nowadays, to curse effectively one cannot rely merely on breaches of religious or semi-religious taboos; a reality or at least a plausibility must be invoked. [*Occupation: Writer*, 'Lars Porsena']

65 Among the working classes one of the unforgivable words of abuse is 'bastard' – because they take bastardy seriously. [*Ib.*]

66 For a woman to have a *liaison* is almost always pardonable, and occasionally, when the lover chosen is sufficiently distinguished, even admirable; but in love as in sport, the amateur status must be strictly maintained. [*Ib.*]

67 As for the Freudian, it is a very low, Central European sort of humour. [*Ib.* 'Mrs Fisher']

68 The poet is the unsatisfied child who dares to ask the difficult question which arises from the schoolmaster's answer to his simple question, and then the still more difficult question which arises from that. [*The White Goddess*, Ch. 6]

69 Nine-tenths of English poetic literature is the result either of vulgar careerism, or of a poet trying to keep his hand in. Most poets are dead by their late twenties. [Quoted in *Observer*, 11 Nov. 1962]

70 To be a poet is a condition rather than a profession. [In *Horizon* questionnaire, 1946]

71 The remarkable thing about Shakespeare is that he is really very good – in spite of all the people who say he is very good. [*Observer*, 'Sayings of the Week', 6 Dec. 1964]

72 The thundering text, the snivelling commentary. [*Ogres and Pygmies*]

73 I should define a good poem as one that makes complete sense; and says all it has to say memorably and economically, and has been written for no other than poetic reasons. [*Steps*, 'Talk on the Legitimate Criticism of Poetry']

ROBERT GRAVES and ALAN HODGE

74 He [Tarzan] was unaware that he was the lost child of a distinguished explorer and his wife; and when he fell in love with a girl whom he saved from the gangs of savage beasts, a delicate scruple prevented him from marrying her. She could not fathom the reason. Then it came out: 'My mother was an ape,' he said simply! [*The Long Week End*, Ch. 4]

75 When greeted by his Bishop on Easter morning with the ancient salutation 'Christ is Risen' he had boorishly withheld the expected response, 'He is Risen indeed,' and said instead: 'Yes, Sir!' [*Ib.* 7]

76 At the superior nudist camps, a nice class distinction was made: the butlers and maids who brought along the refreshments were forced to admit their lower social standing by wearing loincloths and aprons respectively. [*Ib.* 16]

GRAHAM GREENE

77 At one with the One, it didn't mean a thing beside a glass of Guinness on a sunny day. [*Brighton Rock*, Pt I, Ch. 1]

78 'Of course there's Hell. Flames and damnation,' he said ... 'torments.' [*Ib.* II. 1]

79 He trailed the clouds of his own glory after him; hell lay about him in his infancy. He was ready for more deaths. [*Ib.* 2]

80 Ida Arnold was on the right side. She was cheery, she was healthy, she could get a bit lit with the best of them. She liked a good time. [*Ib.* III. 1]

81 Those who marry God ... can become domesticated too – it's just as hum-drum a marriage as all the others. [*A Burnt-Out Case*, Ch. 1]

82 To me comfort is like the wrong memory at the wrong place or time: if one is lonely one prefers discomfort. [*The End of the Affair*, Pt I, Ch. 1]

83 'I see you were at the old place.... Those were the days, eh? ... I don't suppose you'd remember old Tester (six months for indecent assault). I try to keep up with them. Whose house were you?' [*England Made Me*, Pt II]

84 He spoke with the faintest foreign accent and it was difficult to determine whether he was Jewish or of an ancient English family. He gave the impression that very many cities had rubbed him smooth. [*A Gun for Sale*, Ch. 4, iii]

85 Hail Mary, quite contrary! [*Our Man in Havana*]

86 Fame is a powerful aphrodisiac. [Quoted in *Radio Times*, 10 Sept. 1964]

JULIAN GRENFELL

87 And he is dead who will not fight; / And who dies fighting has increase. [*Into Battle*]

W. GRENFELL

88 When one comes to think of it, it's odd that there should be so much admiration for prowess in drinking, which after all is merely a domestic virtue. [Quoted in Christopher Hassall, *Edward Marsh*, Ch. 8]

SIR EDWARD GREY

89 The United States is like a gigantic boiler. Once the fire is lighted under it there is no limit to the power it can generate. [Quoted in Winston S. Churchill, *Their Finest Hour*, Ch. 32]

JOHN GRIGG [formerly LORD ALTRINCHAM]

90 Lloyd George would have a better rating in British mythology if he had shared the fate of Abraham Lincoln. [*Observer*, 'Sayings of the Week', 7 Apr. 1963]

GEORG GRODDECK

1 Whatever you blame, that you have done yourself. [Quoted in 'Palinurus' (Cyril Connolly), *The Unquiet Grave*, Pt III]

GEORGE GROSSMITH
(The Younger)

2 Yip-i-addy-i-ay, i-ay, yip-i-addy-i-ay! [Song]

THE GUARDIAN [See also *Manchester Guardian*]

3 As for our Lord Himself, of course there are those who think of our Lord's sex life in the terms of Robert Graves, but here again there is more evidence on the other side. [Letter, Nov. 1962]

GIOVANNI GUARESCHI

4 I had to do everything to stay alive and succeeded almost completely by dedicating myself to a precise programme which is summarized in my slogan 'I will not die even if they kill me.' [*The Little World of Don Camillo*, 'How I Got Like This']

PHILIP GUEDALLA

5 Biography, like big-game hunting, is one of the recognized forms of sport, and it is as unfair as only sport can be. [*Supers and Supermen*]

6 No picture of life in Calais was too ludicrous to be believed in Dover; that is one of the advantages of being an Island Race. [*Ib.*]

7 An Englishman is a man who lives on an island in the North Sea governed by Scotsmen. [*Ib.*]

8 One would think that poetry was a form of deep breathing. Even Mr Chesterton seems to be suffering from a hearty degeneration of the fat. [Quoted in Stephen Potter, *Sense of Humour*, I]

9 The twentieth century is only the nineteenth speaking with a slight American accent. [Attr.]

TEXAS GUINAN

10 Hello, sucker! [Said to night-club customers]

ARTHUR GUITERMAN

11 Then came the prophet Sam-u-el / Upon the only Cam-u-el – [*The Legend of the First Cam-u-el*]

12 Don't tell your friends about your indigestion: / 'How are you!' is a greeting, not a question. [*A Poet's Proverbs*, 'Of Tact']

SACHA GUITRY

13 If a playwright is funny, the English look for the serious message, and if he is serious they look for the joke. [*Observer*, 'Sayings of the Week', 19 Apr. 1957]

THOM GUNN

14 The group's name on the left, The Knights, / And on the right the slogan Born to Lose. [*Black Jackets*]

15 I saw that lack of love contaminates. / You know I know you know I know you know. [*Carnal Knowledge*]

16 We stand on a white terrace and confer; / This is the last camp of experience. [*From the Highest Camp*]

17 One is always nearer by not keeping still. [*On the Move*]

18 Ours is the only country deliberately founded on a good idea. [*Inside U.S.A.*]

GEORGE GURDJIEFF

19 [Man] is a machine, everything with him *happens.* . . . He lives in a subjective world. . . . He does not see the real world. The real world is hidden from him by the wall of imagination. *He lives in sleep.* [Quoted in P. D. Ouspensky, *In Search of the Miraculous*]

20 There is a war going on at the present moment. What does it signify? It signifies that several millions of sleeping people are trying to destroy several millions of other sleeping people. They would not do this, of course, if they were to wake up. [Quoted in *ib.*]

H

EARL HAIG

1 *Foch: Est-ce-que les hommes sont en bon état?* – Are the men in good heart?
Haig: They never were in better heart, and are longing for a fight. [*Diaries*, 12 Sept. 1915]

EMPEROR HAILE SELASSIE OF ABYSSINIA

2 We have finished the job, what shall we do with the tools? [Telegram in 1941 to Winston Churchill. Quoted in Edward Marsh, *Ambrosia and Small Beer*, Ch. 4]

J. B. S. HALDANE

3 Einstein – the greatest Jew since Jesus. I have no doubt that Einstein's name will still be remembered and revered when Lloyd George, Foch and William Hohenzollern share with Charlie Chaplin that ineluctable oblivion which awaits the uncreative mind. [*Daedalus or Science and the Future*]

4 Shelley and Keats were the last English poets who were at all up to date in their chemical knowledge. [*Ib.*]

5 The conservative has but little to fear from the man whose reason is the servant of his passions, but let him beware of him in whom reason has become the greatest and most terrible of passions. [*Ib.*]

6 If human beings could be propagated by cutting, like apple trees, aristocracy would be biologically sound. [*The Inequality of Man*, title essay]

7 Christian Science is so often therapeutically successful because it lays stress on the patient's believing in his or her own health rather than in Noah's Ark or the Ascension. [*Possible Worlds*, 'The Duty of Doubt']

8 An angel whose muscles developed no more power weight for weight than those of an eagle or a pigeon would require a breast projecting for about four feet to house the muscles engaged in working its wings, while to economize in weight, its legs would have to be reduced to mere stilts. [*Ib.* 'On Being the Right Size']

9 The conclusion forced upon me in the course of a life devoted to natural science is that the universe as it is assumed to be in physical science is a spiritual universe in which spiritual values count for everything. [*The Sciences and Philosophy*]

VISCOUNT HALDANE

10 I was a little exhausted when I arrived [at the War Office] . . . and asked the tall ex-Guards soldier in attendance for a glass of water. 'Certainly, sir: Irish or Scotch?' [Letter quoted in Dudley Sommer, *Haldane of Cloan*, Ch. 8]

11 Yes, I consider Lötze's classroom was my spiritual home. [Remark at Mrs Humphry Ward's, later distorted by Professor Oncken, so that it referred to Germany. *Ib.* 22]

12 The trouble with Lloyd George is that he thinks in images, not in concepts. [Said during the Victory election, 1919. *Ib.* 26]

GENERAL FRANZ HALDER

13 It is hardly too much to say that the campaign against Russia has been won in fourteen days. [Diary note, 3 July 1941, quoted in W. L. Shirer, *The Rise and Fall of the Third Reich*, Ch. 23]

ÉLIE HALÉVY

14 The Socialists believe in two things which are absolutely different and perhaps even contradictory: freedom and organization. [Quoted in W. R. Inge *The End of an Age*]

GLANVIL HALL

15 The British habit of drinking whilst standing up is barbaric. [*Observer*, 'Sayings of the Week', 19 Feb. 1961]

PROFESSOR HALLSTEIN

16 *Wer in europaischen Angelegenheiten nicht an Wunder glaubt ist kein Realist.* – Anyone who does not believe in miracles in European affairs is no realist. [*On the Common Market*]

MARK HAMBOURG

17 The finest Elijah in the world, dear boy. But what a pity he plays Bridge like Elijah! [Of well-known singer. Quoted in James Agate, *Ego 1*, Pt II, 1933]

GENERAL, SIR IAN HAMILTON

18 Dig, dig, dig! [*Instructions at Gallipoli*]

PATRICK HAMILTON

19 Sleep is gross, a form of abandonment, and it is impossible for anyone to awake and observe its sordid consequences save with a faint sense of recent dissipation, of minute personal disquiet and remorse. [*Slaves of Solitude*]

DAG HAMMARSKJOLD

20 Pray that your loneliness may spur you into finding something to live for, great enough to die for. [*Diaries*, 1951]

21 In our era the road to holiness necessarily passes through the world of action. [*Ib.* 1955]

22 In the last analysis, it is our conception of death which decides our answers to all the questions that life puts to us. [*Ib.* 1958]

IRENE HANDL

23 They are silly. They asked me if I'd mind having a slight moustache in this film – and I've got one anyhow. [Quoted in Edward Marsh, *Ambrosia and Small Beer*, Ch. 3]

JAMES HANLEY

24 That is the art of living that your price shall suit everybody. [*Drift*, Ch. 2]

25 You talk about walking in the wilderness, but what else *is* the world but that, and besides, aren't we all walking in one kind of wilderness or another, since only we can make them. [*A Walk in the Wilderness*, title story]

MAJOR-GENERAL HARBORD

26 I met the great little man [Colonel House], the man who can be silent in several languages. [John dos Passos, *Mr Wilson's War*, Ch. 3, Sect. XV]

GILBERT HARDING

27 I would like to quote what a judge said not long ago – that all his experience both as Counsel and Judge had been spent in sorting out the difficulties of people who, upon the recommendation of people they did not know, signed documents which they did not read, to buy goods they did not need, with money thay had not got. [Television answer to question on subject of hire purchase. Quoted in *Gilbert Harding and His Friends*]

28 I've never consciously striven for worldly success. But once I was aware I had it I must say that I'm terrified of losing it. [*Ib.*]

29 WYNFORD VAUGHAN THOMAS: Try and seem full of the milk of human kindness. G.H.: I am full of the stuff, damn it. My trouble is that it gets clotted so easily. [*Ib.*]

30 [To Mae West's manager, who had asked, 'Can't you sound a bit more sexy when you interview her'] If, sir, I possessed the power of conveying unlimited sexual attraction through the potency of my voice, I would not be reduced to accepting a miserable pittance from the BBC for interviewing a faded female in a damp basement. [*Ib.*]

31 I've often thought I'd like to join a monastery. But then I'd have to behave myself much more than I'm able to do. [*Ib.*]

THOMAS HARDY

32 Where once we danced, where once we sang, Gentlemen, / The floors are shrunken, cobwebs hang. [*An Ancient to Ancients*]

33 Yet hear – no doubt to your surprise – / I am grieving, for his sake, / That I have escaped the sacrifice / I was distressed to make! [*Cross-currents*]

34 Smile out; but still suffer: / The paths of love are rougher / Than thoroughfares of stones. [*The End of the Episode*]

35 She chose her bearers before she died / From her fancy-men. [*Julie-Jane*]

36 Here's not a modest maiden elf / But dreads the final Trumpet, / Lest half of her should rise herself, / And half some sturdy strumpet! [*The Levelled Churchyard*]

37 'Well, though it seems / Beyond our dreams,' / Said Liddell to Scott, / 'We've really got / To the very end.' [*Liddell and Scott*]

38 Queer are the ways of a man I know. [*The Phantom Horsewoman*]

39 The Roman Road runs straight and bare / As the pale parting-line in hair. [*The Roman Road*]

40 There was Life – pale and hoar; / And slow it said to me, / 'Twice-over cannot be!' [*A Second Attempt*]

41 You were the sort that men forget; / Though I – not yet! – / Perhaps not ever. [*You Were the Sort That Men Forget*]

42 Oh, but I admire the *Iliad* greatly. Why, it's in the *Marmion* class! [Said to T. E. Lawrence, quoted in Robert Graves, *Good-bye to All That*]

EARL OF HAREWOOD

43 Benjamin Britten is a metropolitan composer with a longing for a micropolitan existence. [Quoted in Murray Schafer, *British Composers in Interview*, Ch. 10, 'Benjamin Britten']

WILLIAM HARGREAVES

44 P.C.49 [Title of music hall song]

J. P. HARRINGTON

45 Everything in the Garden's Lovely! [Title of music hall song, sung by Marie Lloyd]

46 Now your country calls you far across the sea, / To do a soldier's duty / For England, home and beauty. [Song: *The Girls You Leave Behind You*]

FRANK HARRIS

47 I remember once an article appearing in a London paper, putting me among the first writers of the time, and declaring that I was a better talker than Oscar Wilde. [*My Life and Adventures*, Ch. 31]

LORENZ HART

48 Bewitched, Bothered and Bewildered. [Title of song in *Babes in Arms*]

49 That's Why the Lady Is a Tramp. [Title of song in *ib.*]

CHRISTOPHER HASSALL

50 She's genuinely bogus. [Attr. remark on Dame Edith Sitwell]

LEWIS HASTINGS

51 By the way, why is it that of all people on earth the only one who is dignified by the name of 'producer' is a fat guy with a large cigar who fusses about in the early stages of a theatrical show or movie? [*Dragons are Extra*, Ch. 7]

52 The fact is that the possession of a highly sensitive social conscience about large-scale issues is no guarantee whatever of reasonable conduct in private relations. [*Ib.* 8]

53 It's an awful thing, this cult of trousers in native Africa. . . . It began about sixty years ago, when a storm battalion of the London Missionary Society, waving their braces like a banner, swept into the astonished kraals . . . and crammed the unwilling black limbs into these twin tubes. There ought to be another Freedom added to the Famous Four, so far as Africa is concerned – Freedom from Clothes. [*Ib.*]

IAN HAY

54 There is nothing so thoroughly enthuses the feminine mind as an imaginary injustice perpetrated upon someone unknown to her and under circumstances of which she knows nothing. [*The Knight on Wheels*]

JOHN HAYWARD

55 ... A French master at Eton who, after teaching there for 30 years, brought out a little book of instructional dialogues, the first of which began: 'One of the boys in our house has three balls.' 'Has he? Hurrah!' The book had to be recalled, and another first page substituted. [Quoted in Edward Marsh, *Ambrosia and Small Beer*, Ch. 5, Sect. ii]

TIM HEALY, K.C.

56 Gentlemen, we have witnessed today the greatest miracle since Moses struck the rock: tears from my learned friend [When Mr Campbell, later Lord Glenavy, wept at the close of a divorce action in which he represented the plaintiff. Quoted in St John Gogarty, *As I was Going Down Sackville Street*, Ch. 7]

W. R. HEARST

57 Stop running those dogs on your page. I wouldn't have them peeing on my cheapest rug. [Comment to editor who was publishing Thurber's drawings. Quoted in James Thurber, *The Years with Ross*]

FRED HEATHERTON

58 I've got a loverly bunch of cocoanuts, / There they are a-standing in a row, / Big ones, small ones, some as big as your head. [Song, *I've Got a Lovely Bunch of Cocoanuts*]

59 Singing roll or bowl a ball, a penny a pitch. [*Ib.*]

MARTIN HEIDEGGER

60 We are too late for the gods, too early for Being. [Quoted in review, *Times Literary Supplement*, 1 July 1965]

JOSEPH HELLER

61 He was working hard at increasing his life span. He did it by cultivating boredom. Dunbar was working so hard at increasing his life span that Yossarian thought he was dead. [*Catch-22*, Ch. 1]

62 It was truly a splendid structure, and Yossarian throbbed with a mighty sense of accomplishment each time he gazed at it and reflected that none of the work that had gone into it was his. [*Ib.* 2]

63 'You're crazy,' Clevinger shouted vehemently, his eyes filling with tears. 'You've got a Jehovah complex.' [*Ib.*]

64 He was a self-made man who owed his lack of success to nobody. [*Ib.* 3]

65 He had decided to live for ever or die in the attempt. [*Ib.*]

66 He had opposed his daughter's marriage to Colonel Moodus because he disliked attending weddings. [*Ib.* 4]

67 He disapproved of Adolf Hitler, who had done such a great job of combating un-American activities in Germany. [*Ib.*]

68 Even when he cheated he couldn't win, because the people he cheated against were always better at cheating too. [*Ib.*]

69 I've got these rubber models in my office with all the reproductive organs of both sexes, that I keep locked up in separate cabinets to avoid a scandal. [*Ib.* 5]

70 He could barely read or write and had been assigned to Captain Black as assistant intelligence officer. [*Ib.*]

71 There was only one catch and that was Catch-22, which specified that a concern for one's own safety in the face of dangers that were real and immediate was the process of a rational mind. [*Ib.*]

72 So convincing were these dreams of lying awake that he awoke from them each morning in complete exhaustion and fell right back to sleep. [*Ib.* 6]

73 He knew everything about literature except how to enjoy it. [*Ib.* 8]

74 There was little she hadn't tried and less she wouldn't. [*Ib.*]

75 She was a crazy mathematics major from the Wharton School of Business who could not count to twenty-eight each month without getting into trouble. [*Ib.*]

76 Some men are born mediocre, some men achieve mediocrity, and some men have mediocrity thrust upon them. With Major Major it had been all three. [*Ib.* 9]

77 Hungry Joe collected lists of fatal diseases and arranged them in alphabetical order so that he could put his finger without delay on any one he wanted to worry about. [*Ib.* 17]

78 Good God, how much reverence can you have for a Supreme Being who finds it necessary to include such phenomena as phlegm and tooth-decay in His divine system of Creation? [*Ib.* 18]

79 Frankly, I'd like to see the government get out of war altogether and leave the whole field to private industry. [*Ib.* 24]

80 I want those letters to be sincere letters. I want them filled up with lots of personal details so there'll be no doubt I mean every word you say. [*Ib.* 25]

81 General Peckem liked listening to himself talk, liked most of all listening to himself talk about himself. [*Ib.* 29]

82 Prostitution gives her an opportunity to meet people. It provides fresh air and wholesome exercise, and it keeps her out of trouble. [*Ib.* 33]

ROBERT HELPMAN

83 I'm going to introduce sex into *Romeo and Juliet*. [*Observer*, 'Sayings of the Year', Jan. 1957]

ERNEST HEMINGWAY

84 A serious writer is not to be confounded with a solemn writer. A serious writer may be a hawk or a buzzard or even a popinjay, but a solemn writer is always a bloody owl. [Quoted in Cyril Connolly, *Enemies of Promise*, Ch. 8]

85 I started out very quiet and I beat Mr Turgenev. Then I trained hard and I beat Mr de Maupassant. I've fought two draws with Mr Stendhal, and I think I had an edge in the last one. But nobody's going to get me in any ring with Mr Tolstoy unless I'm crazy or I keep getting better. [Quoted in Lillian Ross, *Portrait of Hemingway*]

86 An analyst once wrote me, What did I learn from psychoanalysts. I answered,

Very little but hope they had learned as much as they were able from my published works. [*Ib.*]

LEON HENDERSON

87 I got my job by hollering, and no day passes but what I holler about something. [Arthur Schlesinger Jr, *The Coming of the New Deal*, Pt II, Ch. 10, Sect. iv]

SIR NEVILLE HENDERSON

88 He [Göring] may be a blackguard, but not a dirty blackguard. [Speech at Sleaford, reported in *News Chronicle*. Quoted in M. Bateman *This England*, selections from the *New Statesman*, Pt II]

O. HENRY [W. S. PORTER]

89 I guess I must have had New England ancestors away back and inherited some of their staunch and rugged fear of the police. [*Conscience in Art*]

90 Esau, that swapped his copyright for a partridge. [*Cupid à la Carte*]

1 There was always something in her voice that made you think of lorgnettes, of accounts at Tiffany's, of sledges smoothly gliding on the trail from Dawson to Forty Mile, of the tinkling of pendant prisms on your grandmother's chandeliers, of snow lying on a convent roof; of a police sergeant refusing bail. [*The Defeat of the City*]

2 The road lay curling around wood and dale like a ribbon lost from the robe of a careless summer. [*Ib.*]

3 Busy as a one-armed man with the nettle-rash pasting on wall-paper. [*The Ethics of Pig*]

4 The true adventurer goes forth aimless and uncalculating to meet and greet unknown fate. A fine example was the Prodigal Son – when he started back home. [*The Green Door*]

5 About the only job left that a woman can beat a man in is female impersonator in vaudeville. [*The Hand that Rules the World*]

6 Men to whom life had appeared as a reversible coat – seamy on both sides. [*The Hiding of Black Bill*]

7 We made the acquaintance of drinks invented by the Creoles during the period of Louey Cans, in which they are still served at the side doors. [*Hostages to Momus*]

8 Of course there was nothing the matter with me, but I was very ill. I couldn't work, sleep, eat or bowl. The only way I could get any sympathy was to go without shaving for four days. [*Let Me Feel Your Pulse*]

9 The bride sat in the rocker with her feet resting upon the world. She was wrapt in rosy dreams and a kimono of the same hue. [*Little Speck in Garnered Fruit*]

10 Bagdad-on-the-Subway. [Said of New York in *A Madison Square Arabian Night*, also in other stories]

11 A burglar who respects his art always takes his time before taking anything else. [*Makes the Whole World Kin*]

12 He had the artistic metempsychosis which is half drunk when sober and looks down on airships when stimulated. [*A Midsummer Masquerade*]

13 Satan ... is a hard boss to work for. ... When other people are having their vacation is when he keeps you the busiest. As old Dr Watts or St Paul or some other diagnostician says: 'He always finds somebody for idle hands to do.' [*Ib.*]

14 A kind of mixture of fools and angels – they rush in and fear to tread at the same time. [*The Moment of Victory*]

15 He was brought up with the idea that to be beautiful was to make good. [*Next to Reading Matter*]

16 She would have made a splendid wife, for crying only made her eyes more bright. [*No Story*]

17 Whenever he saw a dollar in another man's hands he took it as a personal grudge, if he couldn't take it any other way. [*The Octopus Marooned*]

18 There are two times when you never can tell what is going to happen. One is when a man takes his first drink; and the other is when a woman takes her latest. [*Ib.*]

19 He was outwardly decent and managed to preserve his aquarium, but inside he was impromptu and full of unexpectedness. [*Ib.*]

20 The room was about full of curly-headed Cubans and South-American brunettes of different shades and the atmosphere was international with cigarette smoke, lit up by diamond rings, and edged off with a whisper of garlic. [*On Behalf of the Management*]

21 And I thinks to myself some about this marrying business, and how it seems to be the same kind of game as that Mrs Delilah played. She give her old man a hair cut, and everybody knows what a man's head looks like after a woman cuts his hair. And then when the Pharisees came around to guy him he was so 'shamed he went to work and kicked the whole house down on top of the whole outfit. [*Ib.*]

22 Ready to melt in the crucible of her ire a little more gold plating from the wrought steel chains of matrimony. [*The Pendulum*]

23 He wrote love stories, a thing I have always kept free from, holding the belief that the well-known and popular sentiment is not properly a matter for publication, but something to be privately handled by the alienists and the florists. [*The Plutonian Fire*]

24 There is always hope for a man who, when sober, will not concede or acknowledge that he was ever drunk. [*The Rubaiyat of a Scotch Highball*]

25 A straw vote only shows which way the hot air blows. [*A Ruler of Men*]

26 Raw and astringent as a schoolgirl – of the old order – young May breathed austerely among the budding trees. [*The Shocks of Doom*]

27 The best grafts in the world are built up on copybook maxims and psalms and proverbs and Esau's fables. They seem to kind of hit off human nature. [*A Tempered Wind*]

28 There was too much scenery and fresh air. What I need is a steam-heated flat with no ventilation or exercise. [Letter, 15 April 1910]

A. P. HERBERT

29 Bring porridge, bring sausage, bring fish for a start, / Bring kidneys and mushrooms and partridges' legs, / But let the foundation be bacon and eggs. [*A Book of Ballads*, 'Bacon and Eggs']

30 Don't let's go to the dogs tonight, / For mother will be there. [*Ib.* 'Don't let's go']

31 Nor should we be plied with unsuitable liquors, / For two of our number are married to vicars. [*Ib.* 'Don't Look at Us!']

32 For Kings and governments may err / But never Mr Baedeker. [*Ib.* 'Mr Baedeker, or Britons Abroad']

33 Other people's babies – / That's my life! / Mother to dozens, / And nobody's wife. [*Ib.* 'Other People's Babies']

34 For I don't have no adventures in the street, / Men don't register emotion when we meet: / Jack don't register Love's Sweet Bliss, / Jack just registers an ordinary kiss. [*Ib.* 'It May Be Life']

35 Come to the pictures and have a good cry. / For it's jolly old Saturday, / Mad-as-a-Hatter-day, / Nothing-much-matter-day-night. [*Ib.* 'Saturday Night']

36 And when the film was finished quite / It made my bosom swell / To find that by electric light / I loved her just as well. [*Ib.* ''Twas at the Pictures, Child, We Met']

37 Nature, I'm perfectly sure, sir, / Did not intend me to be poor. / I've the kind of a character which / Is only of use to the rich. [*Come to the Ball*, an adaptation of *Die Fledermaus*]

38 For I should be a perfect dear / On fifty thousand pounds a year. [*Ib.*]

39 These early 'smellies' made a great sensation, particularly *Fish*, a strong story written 'around the life of a San Francisco fishwife of homicidal tendencies'. [*Look Back and Laugh*, 'The Smellies']

40 The critical period in matrimony is breakfast time. [Attr.]

41 The Treasury are never happy; even in Paradise they will be worried about excessive imports. [*Observer*, 'Sayings of the Week', 19 Apr. 1964]

ÉDOUARD HERRIOT

42 When it's a question of peace one must talk to the Devil himself. [*Observer*, 'Sayings of the Week', 21 Sept. 1953]

LORD HEWART

43 A long line of cases shows that it is not merely of some importance, but it is of fundamental importance, that justice should not only be done, but should manifestly and undoubtedly be seen to be done. [R. Jackson, *The Chief*]

SEYMOUR HICKS

44 You will recognize, my boy, the first sign of age: it is when you go out into the streets of London and realize for the first time how young the policemen look. [Quoted in Pulling, *They Were Singing*, Ch. 7]

GEOFFREY HILL

45 He considers the lilies, the rewards. / There is no substitute for a rich man. [*To the (Supposed) Patron*]

JOE HILL

46 You'll get pie in the sky when you die. [Quoted in Alan Lomax, *Folk Songs of North America*, No. 222]

SIR EDMUND HILLARY

47 Because it was there. [When asked why he had climbed Mt Everest. Attr.]

48 There is precious little in civilization to appeal to a Yeti. [*Observer*, 'Sayings of the Week', 3 June 1960]

HEINRICH HIMMLER

49 We shall never be rough and heartless when it is not necessary, that is clear. We Germans, who are the only people in the world who have a decent attitude towards animals, will also assume a decent attitude towards these human animals. [Speech, 4 Oct. 1943]

PAUL HINDEMITH

50 Today unexplored regions of the stringed instruments' fingerboard are non-existent; even the arctic zones of the eternal rosin (near the bridge) have become a habitable abode for fearless climbers. [*A Composer's World*, Ch. 7, Sect. ii]

51 How, then, would the perfect musician exercise his art? 'He would take his horse [answered a Chinese musician] and ride to a mountain far away from houses and men. There he would play his instrument and sing for his own enlightenment.' [*Ib*. Ch. 7, Sect. v]

52 The worst blow the admirers of the hammer-keyboard ever received was the discovery of physicists that in the sound-tracks of an oscillator no difference can be seen between tones produced by the adept touch of a great artist's hand and those stemming from manipulation with an umbrella. Piano antagonists liked to gloat over this humiliating experiment. [*Ib*. Ch. 8, Sect. vii]

ALFRED HITCHCOCK

53 I never think you should judge a country by its politics. After all, we English are quite honest by nature, aren't we? [Lines spoken by 'Miss Froy' in film, *The Lady Vanishes*]

ADOLF HITLER

54 With a suitcase full of clothes and underwear in my hand and an indomitable will in my heart, I set out for Vienna. . . . I too hoped to become 'something'. [*Mein Kampf*, Vol. I, Ch. 1]

55 All those who are not racially pure are mere chaff. [*Ib*. 2]

56 The broad masses of the people can be moved only by the power of speech. All great movements are popular movements, volcanic eruptions of human passions and emotional sentiments, stirred either by the cruel Goddess of Distress or by the firebrand of the word hurled among the masses. [*Ib*. 3]

57 The art of leadership . . . consists in consolidating the attention of the people against a single adversary and taking care that nothing will split up that attention. [*Ib*.]

58 Only constant repetition will finally succeed in imprinting an idea on the memory of the crowd. [*Ib*. 6]

59 I have never delivered a firebrand speech. [In 1933. *Observer*, 'Sayings of Our Times', 31 May 1953]

60 The victor will not be asked afterwards whether he told the truth or not. In starting and waging a war it is not right that matters, but victory. [Quoted in W. L. Shirer, *The Rise and Fall of the Third Reich*, Ch. 16]

61 I can see no reason why this war must go on. [Speech after the fall of France, quoted in *Ib*. 21]

62 When Barbarossa [the invasion of Russia] commences, the world will hold its breath and make no comment. [To Gen. Franz Halder, quoted in *Ib*. 23]

63 The essential thing is the formation of the political will of the nation: that is the starting point for political action. [Speech at Düsseldorf, 27 Jan. 1932. Quoted in Alan Bullock, *Hitler*, Pt I, Ch. 4]

64 According to the English there are two countries in the world today which are led by adventurers: Germany and Italy. But England, too, was led by adventurers when she built her Empire. Today she is ruled merely by incompetents. [Remarks to Ciano, Quoted in *Ib*. VI. 6]

65 I go the way that Providence dictates with the assurance of a sleepwalker. [Quoted in *Ib*. VII. 1]

66 It almost causes me pain to think that I should have been selected by Fate to deal the final blow to the structure which these men [the British government] have already set tottering. . . . Mr Churchill ought, perhaps, for once to believe me when I prophesy that a great Empire will be destroyed which it was never my intention to destroy or even to harm. [Speech to the Reichstag, 19 July 1940. Quoted in *Ib*. X. 3]

67 I can only be grateful to Providence that it entrusted me with the leadership in this historic struggle, which, for the next five hundred or a thousand years, will be described as decisive, not only for the history of Germany but for the whole of Europe and indeed the whole world. A historical revision on a unique scale has been imposed on us by the Creator. [Speech on declaring war on the U.S.A. Quoted in *Ib*. XII. 2]

68 The little affair of operational command is something that anybody can do. [To General Halder. Quoted in *Ib*.]

69 We have mastered a destiny which broke another man [Napoleon] a hundred and thirty years ago. [Speech to the Reichstag, 26 Apr. 1942. Quoted in *Ib*. XII. 3]

70 The man should have shot himself. . . . What hurts me most, personally, is that I promoted him to Field-Marshal. . . . That's the last Field-Marshal I shall appoint in this war. [On von Paulus's surrender at Stalingrad. Quoted in *Ib*. XII. 4]

71 On land I am a hero, but on water I am a coward. [Words to von Runstedt quoted in Shulman, *Defeat in the West*]

72 I don't see much future for the Americans. . . . Everything about the behaviour of American society reveals that it's half judaized, and the other half negrified. How can one expect a state like that to hold together? [*Hitler's Secret Conversations*]

73 We cannot tolerate any more the tutelage of governesses. [Ref. to Great Britain after Munich. Quoted in Winston S. Churchill, *The Gathering Storm*, Ch. 18]

74 Rather than go through it [his meeting with Franco] again, . . . I would prefer to have three or four of my teeth out. [To Mussolini. Quoted from Ciano's *Diplomatic Papers* in Winston S. Churchill, *Their Finest Hour*, Ch. 26]

75 I am not annoyed with Hungary, but she has missed the bus. [Conversation with Darányi, quoted in A. J. P. Taylor, *The Origins of the Second World War*, Ch. 9]

76 GOERING: It is time to stop this *va banque*.
HITLER: It is the only call I ever make. [Conversation of 29 Aug. 1939, quoted from Weizsäcker in *Ib*. 11]

77 Who says I am not under the special protection of God? [Attr. After attempt on his life, 20 July 1944]

78 Well, he [Chamberlain] seemed such a nice old gentleman, I thought I would give him my autograph as a souvenir. [After Munich. Attr.]

HAROLD HOBSON

79 The United States, I believe, are under the impression that they are twenty years in advance of this country; whilst, as a matter of actual verifiable fact, of course, they are just about six hours behind it. [*The Devil in Woodford Wells*, Ch. 8]

ROLF HOCHHUTH

80 Cursed are the peacemakers. [*The Representative*, Act I, scene i]

81 The Holy See / must remain a sanctuary of *neutrality*. [*Ib*. IV.]

M. J. C. HODGART

82 A critic is a haunter of unquiet graves. He tries to evoke the presence of a living art, but usually succeeds only in disturbing the peace of the dead. [*The Ballads*, Ch. 1]

RUDOLF HOESS [*Commandant of Auschwitz*]

83 Another improvement that we made . . . was that we built our gas-chambers to accommodate two thousand people at one time. [Affidavit, quoted in Alan Bullock, *Hitler*, Ch. 12]

SAMUEL HOFFENSTEIN

84 The stars, like measles, fade at last. [*The Mimic Muse*, V]

85 Though women tempt you more than plenty, / Your rate is half a girl in twenty. / In short, from grace you never fell yet − / And what do you get? On all sides hell yet! [*Poems in Praise of Practically Nothing*, First Series]

86 You buy some flowers for your table; / You tend them tenderly as you're able; / You fetch them water from hither and thither − / What thanks do you get for it all? They wither. [*Ib*. Second Series]

87 I think of all the corpses / Worm-eaten in the shade; / I cannot chew my peanuts / Or drink my lemonade: / Good God, I am afraid! [*The Shropshire Lad's Cousin*]

88 Babies haven't any hair; / Old men's heads are just as bare; − / Between the cradle and the grave / Lies a haircut and a shave. [*Songs of Faith in the Year after Next*, VIII]

COLONEL MAX HOFFMAN

89 LUDENDORFF: The English soldiers fight like lions.
HOFFMAN: True. But don't we know that they are lions led by donkeys. [Of 1915 battles, quoted in A. Clark, *The Donkeys*]

LANCELOT HOGBEN

90 This is not the age of pamphleteers. It is the age of engineers. The spark-gap is mightier than the pen. Democracy will not be salvaged by men who talk fluently, debate forcefully and quote aptly. [*Science for the Citizen*]

QUINTIN HOGG, M.P.

1 The Conservatives do not believe it necessary, and, even if it were, we should oppose it. [Reported in the *Oxford Mail*, quoted in M. Bateman, *This England*, selections from the *New Statesman*, Pt III]

SIR WILLIAM HOLFORD

2 Large buildings in London and elsewhere today are too often designed in the lift going down to lunch. [*Observer*, 'Sayings of the Week', 5 June 1960]

JOHN H. HOLMES

3 The universe is not hostile, nor yet is it friendly. It is simply indifferent. [*Sensible Man's View of Religion*]

MIROSLAV HOLUB

4 But above all / we have / the ability / to sort peas, / to cup water in our hands, / to seek / the right screw / under the sofa / for hours. / This / gives us / wings. [*Wings*, trans. Ian Milner and George Theiner]

GERARD HOPKINS

5 Why do people lament their follies for which their friends adore them. [Quoted in V. S. Pritchett, *Great Turnstile*, under initials G. H.]

ALISTAIR HORNE

6 To sum up on Joffre, it might be said that the war was very nearly lost with him, but that it would almost certainly have been lost without him. [*The Price of Glory*, Ch. 2]

KENNETH HORNE and RICHARD MURDOCH

7 Oh, jolly D.! [Dudley Davenport in *Much Binding in the Marsh* radio series, *passim*]

8 Good morning sir – was there something? [Sam Costa in *ib.*]

DONALD HORNIG

9 Aside from being tremendous it was one of the most aesthetically beautiful things I have ever seen. [On first atomic test. *The Decision to Drop the Bomb*]

COLONEL EDWARD HOUSE

10 My ambition has been so great it has never seemed to me worth while to try to satisfy it. [John dos Passos, *Mr Wilson's War*, Ch. 1, Sect. ii]

11 Saturday was a remarkable day. . . . We actually got down to work at half past ten and finished remaking the map of the world as we would have it, at half past twelve o'clock. [Diary note, quoted in *ib.* 4. xvi]

A. E. HOUSMAN

12 About the woodlands I will go / To see the cherry hung with snow. [*A Shropshire Lad*, II]

13 Lie down, lie down, young yeoman; / The sun moves always west; / The road one treads to labour / Will lead one home to rest, / And that will be the best. [*Ib.* VII]

14 White in the moon the long road lies. [*Ib.* XXXVI]

15 Into my heart an air that kills / From yon far country blows: / What are those blue remembered hills, / 'What spires, what farms are those? [*Ib.* XL]

16 The Queen of air and darkness / Begins to shrill and cry, / 'O young man, O my

slayer, / To-morrow you shall die.' [*Last Poems*, III]

17 May will be fine next year as like as not: / Oh ay, but then we shall be twenty-four. [*Ib.* IX]

18 For so the game is ended / That should not have begun. / My father and my mother / They had a likely son, / And I have none. [*Ib.* XIV]

19 Until from grass and clover / The upshot beam would fade, / And England over / Advanced the lofty shade. [*Ib.* XLI]

20 If you want to get poetry out of me you must be either a relative or a duchess, and you are neither. [When asked to contribute to *Georgian Poetry*. Quoted in Christopher Hassall *Edward Marsh*, Ch. 9]

21 This University, which once saw Wordsworth drunk and Porson sober, will now see a better scholar than Wordsworth and a better poet than Porson betwixt and between. [Inaugural lecture in the Chair of Latin at Cambridge]

22 I just stand up and spout. [When asked what he did in his lectures. Attr.]

23 I find Cambridge an asylum, in every sense of the word. [On coming from Oxford. Attr.]

24 I'll tell that story on the golden floor. [On being told a joke when he was dying. Attr. by the late Rev. J. Plowden-Woodlaw, Vicar of St Clement's, Cambridge]

REV. P. F. HOW

25 Yes, that's the worst of living, you get older every day. [Sermon at Runnell Hospital, 1946]

ELBERT HUBBARD

26 One machine can do the work of fifty ordinary men. No machine can do the work of one extraordinary man. [*Roycroft Dictionary and Book of Epigrams*]

27 Little minds are interested in the extraordinary; great minds in the commonplace. [*Ib.*]

BARON VON HUGET

28 I myself have been on excellent terms with matter as long as I can remember and I am quite contented. [Quoted by E. H. W. Meyerstein in a letter, 12 June 1911]

TED HUGHES

29 The world rolls under the long thrust of his heel. / Over the cage floor the horizons come. [*The Jaguar*]

30 It took the whole of Creation / To produce my foot, my each feather: / Now I hold creation in my foot. [*Hawk Roosting*]

JOHN HUSTON

31 A left-handed form of human endeavour. [Definition of crime in film *The Asphalt Jungle*. Quoted in Lillian Ross, *Picture*]

ALDOUS HUXLEY

32 He was immensely proud of his Anglo-Saxon descent and the derivation of his name from Old English *lycam*, a corpse. [*Limbo*, 'Cynthia']

33 The loss of the work of any ancient writer gave him the keenest sorrow. I rather think he had written a version of the unrecovered books of Petronius. [*Ib.*]

34 It is very difficult to flagelate yourself with a cane in a room so small that any violent gesture imperils the bric-à-brac. [*Ib.* 'Farcical History of Richard Greenow']

35 The process of balancing the horoscopes of two elevens one against the other was a very delicate and difficult one. A match between the Spurs and the Villa entailed a conflict in the heavens so vast and so complicated that it was not to be wondered at if she sometimes made a mistake about the outcome. [*Crome Yellow*, Ch. 2]

36 'Which of the contemporary poets do you like best?' 'Blight, Mildew, and Smut,' he replied, with the laconism of one who is absolutely certain of his own mind. [*Ib.* 10]

37 *Certaine Priuy Counsels* by *One of Her Maiestie's Most Honourable Priuy Counsel, F. L. Knight*, in which the whole matter is treated with great learning and elegance. [*Ib.* 11]

38 Seven volumes of the *Tales of Knockes-potch*. [*Ib.* 14]

39 Carminative: for me the word was as rich in content as some tremendous, elaborate work of art; it was a complete landscape with figures. [*Ib.* 20]

40 'A mental carminative,' said Mr Scogan reflectively. 'That's what you need.' [*Ib.*]

41 He liked to think of himself as a merciless vivisector probing into the palpitating entrails of his own soul; he was Brown Dog to himself. [*Ib.* 24]

42 'But I should like to come,' Miss Spence protested, throwing a rapid Gioconda at him. [*Mortal Coils*, 'The Gioconda Smile', i]

43 She was a machine-gun riddling her hostess with sympathy. [*Ib.* ii]

44 It's a pity they should have chosen the day of the Eton and Harrow match for the funeral. [*Ib.* iii]

45 Most of one's life . . . is one prolonged effort to prevent oneself thinking. [*Ib.* 'Green Tunnels']

46 Miss Penny laughed, and rattled the miniature gallows of her ears. [*Ib.* 'Nuns at Luncheon']

47 She was one of those indispensables of whom one makes the discovery, when they are gone, that one can get on quite as well without them. [*Ib.*]

48 I'll get you a hedgehog at once. . . . They're sure to have some at Whiteley's. [*Ib.* 'The Tillotson Banquet', iii]

49 Ah, you've noticed my Order. . . . It was given me by the Grande Porte, you know, for services rendered in the Russo–Turkish War. It's the Order of Chastity, the second class. [*Ib.*]

50 What I glory in is the civilized, middle way between stink and asepsis. [*Antic Hay*, Ch. 4]

51 Christlike in my behaviour, / Like every good believer, / I imitate the Saviour, / And cultivate a beaver. [*Ib.*]

52 He was only the Mild and Melancholy one foolishly disguised as a Complete Man. [*Ib.* 9]

53 There are few who would not rather be taken in adultery than in provincialism. [*Ib.* 10]

54 On the other side of the party-wall . . . a teeming family of Jews led their dark, compact, Jewish lives with a prodigious intensity. At this moment they were all passionately quarrelling. [*Ib.* 11]

55 Sweet, sweet and piercing, the saxophone pierced into the very bowels of compassion and tenderness, pierced like a revelation from heaven, pierced like the angel's treacly dart into the holy Teresa's quivering and ecstasiated flesh. [*Ib.* 15]

56 What's he to Hecuba? / Nothing at all. / That's why there'll be no wedding on Wednesday week, / Way down in old Bengal. [*Ib.*]

57 Mr Mercaptan went on to preach a brilliant sermon on that melancholy sexual perversion known as continence. [*Ib.* 18]

58 Lady Capricorn, he understood, was still keeping open bed. [*Ib.* 21]

59 I don't know which direction civilization marches – whether north towards Kilburn and Golder's Green, or over the river to the Elephant and Clapham and Sydenham and all those other mysterious places. [*Ib.*]

60 There are no more genuine mermaids in the Edgware Road. [*Ib.*]

61 The picture-papers are more than half-filled with photographs of bathing nymphs – photographs that make one understand the ease with which St Anthony rebuffed his temptations. [*On the Margin*, 'Beauty in 1920']

62 She pictured to herself a Calamy who was one of Nature's Guardsmen, touched, as Guardsmen sometimes are, with that awed and simple reverence for the mysteries of art. [*Those Barren Leaves*, Pt I, Ch. 1]

63 I'm afraid of losing my obscurity. Genuineness only thrives in the dark. Like celery. [*Ib.*]

64 At thirty-three . . . Lilian Aldwinkle appealed to all the instinctive bigamist in one. She was eighteen in the attics and widow Dido on the floors below. [*Ib.* I. 2]

65 Mrs Aldwinkle didn't want her guests to lead independent existences out of her sight. [*Ib.*]

66 Mrs Aldwinkle had even bought the stars. [*Ib.* I. 4]

67 We are native where we walk / Through the dim streets of Camden Town. / But hopeful still through twice-breathed air / The Holy Ghost comes shining down. [*Ib.* II. 1]

68 'The Rabbit Fanciers' Gazette' with which, as every schoolboy knows, is incorporated 'The Mouse Breeders' Record'. [*Ib.* II. 2]

69 My father ... considered a walk among the mountains as the equivalent of church-going. [*Ib.* II. 4]

70 'But the only surroundings that really inspire me,' said Chelifer, 'are the lower middle class quarters of London, north of the Harrow Road, for example.' [*Ib.* III. 1]

71 I always notice that the most grave and awful denunciations of obscenity in literature are to be found precisely in those periodicals whose directors are most notoriously alcoholic. [*Ib.* III. 2]

72 'I sometimes doubt,' she said, 'whether he takes any interest in women at all. Fundamentally, unconsciously, I believe he's a homosexualist.' 'Perhaps,' said Irene gravely. She knew her Havelock Ellis. [*Ib.* III. 11]

73 'An admirable place for playing halma,' said Chelifer, as they entered the Teatro Metastasio. [*Ib.* IV. 2]

74 'Charming language,' he said, 'charming! Ever since I learned that the Etruscans used to call the god of wine Fufluns, I've taken the keenest interest in their language.' [*Ib.* IV. 5]

75 It's the great dead language of the future. If Etruscan didn't exist, it would be necessary to invent it. [*Ib.*]

76 If we wrote it ourselves, we might find Etruscan literature interesting. Etruscan literature composed by Etruscans would be as boring as any other ancient literature. [*Ib.*]

77 'It's like the question of the authorship of the *Iliad*,' said Mr Cardan. 'The author of that poem is either Homer or, if not Homer, somebody else of the same name.' [*Ib.* V. 4]

78 Compare the music of *The Beggar's Opera* with the music of a contemporary revue. They differ as life in the garden of Eden differed from life in the artistic quarter of Gomorrah. [*Along the Road,* 'Popular Music']

79 Since Mozart's day composers have learned the art of making music throatily and palpitatingly sexual. [*Ib.*]

80 In the spiritual home of the Peddleys there was only a bed-room and a lecture-room – no sentimental boudoir for confidences, no quiet study pleasantly violated from time to time by feminine intrusion. [*Two or Three Graces*, title story]

81 Gazing at the pianist as St Theresa might have gazed at the uplifted Host. [*Ib.*]

82 In the eighteenth century, when logic and science were the fashion, women tried to talk like the men. The twentieth century has reversed the process. [*Ib.*]

83 Kingham made a habit of telling all his acquaintances, sooner or later, what he thought of them – which was invariably disagreeable. He called this process a 'clearing of the atmosphere'. [*Ib.*]

84 ... Forgetting that several excuses are always less convincing than one. [*Point Counter Point*, Ch. 1]

85 Is it illusion or the revelation of profoundest truth? Who knows? Pongileoni blew, the fiddlers drew their resined horsehair across the stretched intestines of lambs; through the long Sarabande the poet slowly meditated his lovely and consoling certitude. [*Ib.* 2]

86 What was one day a sheep's hind leg and leaves of spinach was the next part of the hand that wrote, the brain that conceived the slow movement of the Jupiter Symphony. [*Ib.* 3]

87 He had cured her, he remembered, of a passion for Burne-Jones, but never, alas, of her prejudice in favour of virtue. [*Ib.* 4]

88 A correspondence course of passion was, for her, the perfect and ideal relationship with a man. [*Ib.* 5]

89 My stepfather's a perfect specimen of Intelligence, Military. [*Ib.* 7]

90 A good housewife, she knew how to hash up the conversational remains of last night's dinner to furnish out this morning's lunch. [*Ib.*]

1 The clock ticked. The moving instant which, according to Sir Isaac Newton, separates the infinite past from the infinite future advanced inexorably through the dimension of time. [*Ib.* 11]

2 Putting the bottom in again is one of the traditional occupations of the aged. [*Ib.*]

3 It takes two to make a murder. There are born victims, born to have their throats cut, as the cut-throats are born to be hanged. You can see it in their faces. [*Ib.* 12]

4 He had such a pure, childlike and platonic way of going to bed with women, that neither they nor he ever considered that the process really counted as going to bed. [*Ib.* 13]

5 Work gives them the comfortable illusion of existing, even of being important. If they stopped working, they'd realize they simply weren't there at all, most of them. Just holes in the air, that's all. [*Ib.* 17]

6 Brought up in an epoch when ladies apparently rolled along on wheels, Mr Quarles was peculiarly susceptible to calves. [*Ib.* 20]

7 The instinct of acquisitiveness has more perverts, I believe, than the instinct of sex. At any rate, people seem to me odder about money than about even their amours. [*Ib.* 22]

8 Happiness is like coke – something you get as a by-product in the process of making something else. [*Ib.* 30]

9 The umbrellas were like black mushrooms that had suddenly sprouted from the mud. [*Ib.*]

10 If Don Juans and Don Juanesses only obeyed their desires, they'd have very few affairs. They have to tickle themselves up imaginatively before they can start being casually promiscuous. [*Ib.* 34]

11 Judd remained for him the Oldest Friend whom one definitely dislikes. [*Brief Candles*, 'After the Fireworks']

12 ... Lives in Rome ... because he likes to get his popery straight from the horse's mouth. [*Ib.*]

13 I've lived most of my life posthumously ...; in reflections and conversations after the fact. [*Ib.* 'Chawdron']

14 He was fifty. It's the age when clergymen first begin to be preoccupied with the underclothing of little schoolgirls in trains, the age when eminent archaeologists start taking a really passionate interest in the Scout movement. [*Ib.*]

15 What's the highest ethical ideal in Christianity? It's expressed in À Kempis's formula – 'The Imitation of Christ.' So that the organized Churches turn out to be nothing but vast and elaborate Academies of Dramatic Art. [*Ib.*]

16 She authenticated the not-facts by simply repeating that they had happened. [*Ib.*]

17 Even if she hadn't loved him she would have married him on principle, just because his father *was* a draper and because all this class business was an irrelevant nonsense. [*Ib.* 'The Claxtons']

18 Recognizableness is an artistic quality which most people find profoundly thrilling. [*Music at Night*, 'Art and the Obvious']

19 The God of Industry supplies his worshippers with objects and can only exist on condition that his gifts are gratefully accepted. In the eyes of an Industrialist the first duty of man is to collect as many objects as he can. [*Ib.* 'History and the Past']

20 You never see animals going through the absurd and often horrible fooleries of magic and religion. ... Only man behaves with such gratuitous folly. It is the price he has to pay for being intelligent but not, as yet, quite intelligent enough. [*Texts and Pretexts*, 'Amor Fati']

21 The male soul, in immaturity, is *naturaliter ferrovialis*. [*Eyeless in Gaza*, Ch. 9]

22 The fact that the Matthew Passion, for example, the Hammerklavier Sonata, had had human authors was a source of hope. It was just conceivable that humanity might some day and somehow be made a little more John-Sebastian-like. [*Ib.* 22]

23 People will insist ... on treating the *mons Veneris* as though it were Mount Everest. [*Ib.* 30]

24 Death. ... It's the only thing we haven't succeeded in completely vulgarizing. [*Ib.* 31]

25 How can you expect to think in anything but a negative way, when you've got chronic intestinal poisoning? [*Ib.* 49]

26 There seems no obvious connection between the Webbs and the Soviets on the one hand and Modern Catholicism on the other. But what profound subterranean resemblances! ... For English Catholics, sacraments are the psychological equivalents of tractors in Russia. [*Ib.* 50]

27 For Lawrence, existence was one continuous convalescence; it was as though he were newly reborn from a mortal illness every day of his life. What these convalescent eyes saw, his most casual speech would reveal. [*The Olive Tree*, 'D. H. Lawrence']

28 Good is that which makes for unity; Evil is that which makes for separateness. [*Ends and Means*]

29 The sort of pose that a new arrival in the seraglio would be taught by the eunuchs to assume at her first interview with the sultan. [*After Many a Summer*, Pt I, Ch. 4]

30 Why should human females become sterile in the forties, while female crocodiles continued to lay eggs into their third century? [*Ib.* 5]

31 Past time is only evil at a distance. [*Ib.* 8]

32 If we were consistently human the percentage of mental cases would rise from twenty to a hundred. But fortunately most of us are incapable of consistency – the animal always resuming its rights. [*Ib.* 9]

33 He had managed, in the nick of time, to get himself converted to Catholicism. ... Thenceforward, he had been able to pack up the moral responsibility for his share in the general iniquity, take it to Farm Street and leave it there in camphor, so to speak, with the Jesuit Fathers. [*Ib.* II. 1]

34 With a course of thiamin chloride and some testosterone I could have made him as happy as a sandboy. Has it ever struck you ... what a lot of the finest romantic literature is the result of bad doctoring? [*Ib.* 6]

35 Talk of unction! It couldn't have been oilier in an English cathedral. Like vaseline with a flavour of port wine. [*Ib.* III. 1]

36 Christianity accepted as given a metaphysical system derived from several already existing and mutually incompatible systems. [*Grey Eminence*, Ch. 3]

37 If hell is paved with good intentions, it is, among other reasons, because of the impossibility of calculating consequences. [*Ib.* 10]

38 The political activity that seems to be least compatible with theocentric religion is that which aims at increasing a certain special type of social efficiency – the efficiency required for waging or threatening large-scale war. [*Ib.*]

39 The quality of moral behaviour varies in inverse ratio to the number of human beings involved. [*Ib.*]

40 A Don Juan without the courage of his conversation. [*Time Must Have a Stop*, Ch. 2]

41 Think of the inexpugnable retreats for microbes prepared by Michelangelo in the curls of Moses' beard! [*Ib.* 3]

42 All that good money going on a mere picture, when it might have been spent on something really useful, like a drinking fountain or a public lavatory. [*Ib.* 4]

43 ... In spite of that tiresome religiosity of his. Nothing but the Gaseous Vertebrate! [*Ib.*]

44 The nipple [his cigar] was coffee-coloured and six inches long. [*Ib.* 5]

45 How appallingly thorough these Germans always managed to be, how emphatic! In sex no less than in war – in scholarship, in science. Diving deeper than anyone else and coming up muddier. [*Ib.* 6]

46 There's only one corner of the universe you can be certain of improving, and that's your own self. [*Ib.* 7]

47 It [champagne] had the taste, he thought, of an apple peeled with a steel knife. [*Ib.* 12]

48 Give me Catholicism every time. Father Cheeryble with his thurible; Father Chatterjee with his liturgy. What fun they have with all their charades and conundrums. If it weren't for the Christianity they insist on mixing with it, I'd be converted tomorrow. [*Ib.*]

49 Only one more indispensable massacre of Capitalists or Communists or Fascists or

Christians or Heretics, and there we are – there we are in the Golden Future. [*Ib.*]

50 Talking of shamelessness ... I knew a girl once who lost her virginity on the night of Good Friday, at Jerusalem – just above the Church of the Holy Sepulchre. [*Ib.* 14]

51 And each new problem would require a new crusade, and each new crusade would leave fresh problems for yet further crusades to solve and multiply in the good old way. [*Ib.* 20]

52 Girls who had seen a spiral nebula got a big bottle of scent the next day, with a playful invitation, embossed with a coronet and signed, 'Yours very affectionately, W.,' to come again another time and really explore the Moon. [*Ib.* 22]

53 You mean what everybody means nowadays. ... Ignore death up to the last moment; then, when it can't be ignored any longer, have yourself squirted full of morphia and shuffle off in a coma. [*Ib.* 26]

54 Knowledge is proportionate to being. ... You know in virtue of what you are. [*Ib.*]

55 In a place where even the king goes on foot – *enfin*, the toilet cabinet. [*Ib.* 27]

56 There isn't any formula or method. You learn to love by loving – by paying attention and doing what one thereby discovers has to be done. [*Ib.* 30]

57 Beauty is intrinsically edifying; gossip, daydreaming and mere self-expression, intrinsically unedifying. [*Ib.*]

58 One can either go on listening to the news – and of course the news is always bad, even when it sounds good. Or alternatively one can make up one's mind to listen to something else. [*Ib.*]

59 There is one anthology, potentially the most interesting of them all, which, to the best of my knowledge, has never yet been compiled; I mean, the Anthology of Later Works. [*Themes and Variations*, 'Variations on Goya']

60 A seventeenth century palace was totally without privacy. Architects had not yet invented the corridor. To get from one part of the building to another, one simply walked through a succession of other people's rooms, in which literally anything might be going on. [*The Devils of Loudun*, Ch. 1]

61 In the intervals of love the young Bishop occupied himself chiefly with war. [*Ib.* 2]

62 In medieval and early modern Christendom the situation of sorcerers and their clients was almost precisely analogous to that of Jews under Hitler, capitalists under Stalin, Communists and fellow travellers in the United States. [*Ib.* 5]

63 Few people now believe in the devil; but very many enjoy behaving as their ancestors behaved when the Fiend was a reality as unquestionable as his Opposite Number. [*Ib.*]

64 Henry IV's feet and armpits enjoyed an international reputation. [*Ib.* 10]

65 We participate in a tragedy; at a comedy we only look. [*Ib.* 11]

66 I was seeing what Adam had seen on the morning of his creation – the miracle, moment by moment, of naked existence. [*The Doors of Perception*]

67 'Bed,' as the Italian proverb succinctly puts it, 'is the poor man's opera.' [*Heaven and Hell*]

68 Your maiden modesty would float face down, / And men would weep upon your hinder parts. [*Leda*, 'Second Philosopher's Song']

69 Consistency is contrary to nature, contrary to life. The only completely consistent people are the dead. [*Do What you Will*, 'Wordsworth in the Tropics']

70 The physicists and psychologists have revealed the universe as a place, in spite of everything, so fantastically queer, that to hand it over to be enjoyed by footmen would be a piece of gratuitous humanitarianism. Servants must not be spoiled. [*Vulgarity in Literature*, Ch. 2, 1]

71 The aristocratic pleasure of displeasing is not the only delight that bad taste can yield. One can love a certain kind of vulgarity for its own sake. [*Ib.* Ch. 4]

72 He [T. S. Eliot] likes to look on the bile when it's black. [Quoted in Edward Marsh, *Ambrosia and Small Beer*, Ch. 5, Sect. i]

73 Armaments, universal debt and planned obsolescence – those are the three pillars of Western prosperity. [*Island*, Ch. 9]

JULIAN HUXLEY

74 Spiritual progress is our one ultimate aim; it may be towards the dateless and irrevoluble; but it is inevitably dependent upon progress intellectual, moral and physical – progress in this changing, revolving world of dated events. [*Essays of a Biologist*, I]

75 We all know how the size of sums of money appears to vary in a remarkable way according as they are being paid in or paid out. [*Ib*. V]

76 The change in our conception of God necessitates the stressing of religious experience as such, as against belief in particular dogma, or in the efficacy of special ritual. [*Ib*. VI]

77 Sooner or later, false thinking brings wrong conduct. [*Ib*. VII]

78 Operationally, God is beginning to resemble not a ruler but the last fading smile of a cosmic Cheshire cat. [*Religion without Revelation*]

EDWARD HYAMS

79 The consequences of acquiring knowledge are always incalculable and seldom beneficial. [*William Medium*]

80 Assassination ... should be used as the vote should ideally be used, that is, bearing in mind only the public good and regardless of personal interest. [*Killing No Murder*, Ch. 10]

I

DOLORES IBARRURI ('LA PASIONARIA')

1 It is better to die on your feet than to live on your knees! [Republican slogan broadcast in the Spanish Civil War, but first coined by Emiliano Zapata in Mexico in 1910. Quoted in Hugh Thomas, *The Spanish Civil War*, Ch. 16]

HAROLD L. ICKES

2 I have heard of various kinds of government, such as oligarchies, monarchies and democracies, but this is the first time that I have ever heard of a farmocracy. [Speech against the U.S. Department of Agriculture, 1935]

3 I am against government by crony. [On resigning as Secretary of the Interior, Feb. 1946]

4 The trouble with Senator Long is that he is suffering from halitosis of the intellect. That's presuming Emperor Long has an intellect. [Quoted in A. M. Schlesinger Jr, *The Politics of Upheaval*, Pt II, Ch. 14, sect. v]

W. R. INGE, DEAN OF ST PAUL'S

5 What we know of the past is mostly not worth knowing. What is worth knowing is mostly uncertain. Events in the past may roughly be divided into those which probably never happened and those which do not matter. [*Assessments and Anticipations*, 'Prognostications']

6 To predict the future . . . is not only the most important part of the work of an historian; it is the most scientific and least imaginative part of his duties. Our chief interest in the past is as a guide to the future. [*Ib.*]

7 When our first parents were driven out of Paradise, Adam is believed to have remarked to Eve: 'My dear, we live in an age of transition.' [*Ib.* 'Work']

8 I called democracy a superstition and a fetish: and I repeat that it is plainly both. [*The Church and the Age*, Preface]

9 I confess that any hopefulness for the future of civilization is based on the reasonable expectation that humanity is still only beginning its course. [*Ib.*]

10 I have found myself dubbed 'the gloomy dean', in contrast with certain more popular ecclesiastics who, because they can always conscientiously shout with the largest crowd, are naturally cheerful deans. [*Ib.* Ch. 2]

11 The aim of education is the knowledge not of fact but of values. [*The Church in the World*, Oct. 1932]

12 The proper time to influence the *character* of a *child* is about a *hundred* years before he is born. [*Observer*, 21 June 1929]

13 A nation is a society united by a delusion about its ancestry and by a common hatred of its neighbours. [Quoted in Sagittarius and George, *The Perpetual Pessimist*]

14 Universal suffrage almost inevitably leads to government by mass bribery, an auction of the worldly goods of the unrepresented minority. [*The End of an Age*, Ch. 1]

15 The Lutheran separation of public and private morals is utterly false and pernicious. [*Ib.* 2]

16 The operation of flogging a dead horse is always popular and is very congenial to rhetoricians. Dickens was careful to castigate abuses which were being reformed. [*Ib.*]

17 Man is an amphibious animal. He lives partly in a world of concrete facts, and partly in a world of timeless values, which are not all connected with religion, for mathematics ignores time. [*Ib.*]

18 Hatred and the feeling of solidarity pay a high psychological dividend. The statistics of suicide show that, for non-combatants at least, life is more interesting in war than in peace. [*Ib.* 3]

19 The enemies of Freedom do not argue; they shout and they shoot. [*Ib.* 4]

20 There are many crowd movements which we are unable to explain, since possession by good or evil spirits is now considered unscientific. [*Ib.* 5]

21 Most of us, though we are bidden to look forward to an eternity of calm fruition, cannot spend an evening without trying to escape from a gentleman whom we know slightly and find, it seems, an intolerable bore – ourselves. [*Ib.* 6]

22 The effect of boredom on a large scale in history is underestimated. It is a main cause of revolutions, and would soon bring to an end all the static Utopias and the farmyard civilization of the Fabians. [*Ib.*]

23 Revivals are shallow things, since they aim at reproducing what never existed or what has perished with the age that gave it birth. [*Ib.*]

24 The distinction between literature and journalism is becoming blurred; but journalism gains as much as literature loses. [*England*]

25 The command 'Be fruitful and multiply' [was] promulgated according to our authorities, when the population of the world consisted of two persons. [*More Lay Thoughts of a Dean*, Pt I, Ch. 6]

26 The vulgar mind always mistakes the exceptional for the important. [*Ib.* Pt III, Ch. I, 'Private Notebooks']

27 Many people believe that they are attracted by God, or by Nature, when they are only repelled by man. [*Ib.*]

28 If George III had had the political sagacity of Queen Victoria, should we have lost America? And, if not, would the political connection between the two countries have been terminated in the twentieth century by a glorious war of independence waged by Great Britain? [*Ib.* III. 3]

29 If ... an outbreak of cholera might be caused either by an infected water supply or by the blasphemies of an infidel mayor, medical research would be in confusion. [*Outspoken Essays*, Second Series, I, i, 'Confessio Fidei']

30 To become a popular religion, it is only necessary for a superstition to enslave a philosophy. [*Ib.* II. iii, 'The Idea of Progress']

31 It is ... an unproved assumption that the domination of the planet by our own species is a desirable thing, which must give satisfaction to its creator. [*Ib.*]

32 Christianity promises to make men free; it never promises to make them independent. [*The Philosophy of Plotinus*]

33 Religion is a way of walking, not a way of talking. [Attr.]

34 We tolerate shapes in human beings that would horrify us if we saw them in a horse. [Attr.]

35 I prudently brought in a book, but the boredom of the six hours in the Abbey was extreme. [On the coronation of George V. Diary entry]

36 Our day of political pride is over. A great race we are and shall remain; a great power we have been and are no longer. [*Ib.* Sept. 1914]

37 The world is a much worse place than I ever thought it. [*Ib.* 7 July 1917]

38 Christ says, 'Judge not,' *but we must judge.* [Attr.]

39 When Arthur Balfour launched his scheme for peopling Palestine with Jewish immigrants, I am credibly informed that he did not know there were Arabs in the country. [From *Evening Standard*, quoted in M. Bateman, *This England*, selections from the *New Statesman*, Pt I]

SIR THOMAS INSKIP

40 The years that the locust hath eaten. [Applying Joel 2:25 to wasted years, 1931–5. Said 1939, quoted in W. S. Churchill, *The Gathering Storm*, Ch. 5]

EUGÈNE IONESCO

41 AMÉDÉE: He's got geometrical progression.
MADELEINE: Geometrical progression?
AMÉDÉE: Yes ... the incurable disease of the dead. [*Amédée*, I]

42 Yoghurt is very good for the stomach, the lumbar regions, appendicitis and apotheosis. [*The Bald Prima Donna*]

43 He never prescribes anything he hasn't first tried out on himself. Before he made Parker go through that operation last year he had himself operated on, for liver, you know, although there was nothing wrong with him at the time. [*Ib.*]

44 He made the best-looking corpse in Great Britain! And he never looked his age. Poor old Bobby! He'd been dead for four years and he was still warm. A living corpse if ever there was one. [*Ib.*]

45 As they had the same name, when you saw them together, you could never tell one from the other. [*Ib.*]

46 Then, Madam, we must live in the same room and sleep in the same bed, dear Madam. Perhaps that is where we have met before. [*Ib.*]

47 It's a useless but absolutely vital precaution. [*Ib.*]

48 Describe a circle, stroke its back and it turns vicious. [*Ib.*]

49 The Pope's eloped! The Pope's no soap. [*Ib.*]

50 We haven't the time to take our time. [*Exit the King*]

51 Many people have delusions of grandeur but you're deluded by triviality. [*Ib.*]

52 There's an idiotic cloud that can't restrain itself. Like an old man, weak in the bladder. [*Ib.*]

53 Everything that has been will be, everything that will be is, everything that will be has been. [*Ib.*]

54 Heart attacks are reserved for businessmen. [*Ib.*]

55 What if I decided to stop wanting things, to just stop wanting, and decided not to decide! [*Ib.*]

56 Characters in a play don't always have to be bigger fools than in everyday life. [*Foursome*]

57 Just because she's our only daughter it doesn't mean she's sterile. [*The Future is in Eggs*]

58 Once, in a large country town, in the middle of the street, during the summer, I saw a young shepherd, about three o'clock in the afternoon, who was embracing a chameleon. . . . It was such a touching scene I decided to turn it into a tragic farce. [*Improvisation*]

59 As you're not a scholar, you've no right to have ideas. [*Ib.*]

60 Autocriticism does honour to the writer, dishonour to the critic. [*Ib.*]

61 IONESCO: A vicious circle can have its virtues too!
BARTOLOMEO I: So long as you get out of it in time. [*Ib.*]

62 It's not his fault if he doesn't understand. He's an intellectual. A man of the theatre ought to be stupid! [*Ib.*]

63 Only the ephemeral is of lasting value. [*Ib.*]

64 You've always made the mistake of being yourself. [*Ib.*]

65 The critic should describe, and not prescribe. [*Ib.*]

66 Look at yourself with one eye, listen to yourself with the other! [*Ib.*]

67 I'm going into the next room to pack my bags and you'll never see me again, except at mealtimes and at odd moments during the day and night for a cup of tea and a bun. [*Jacques or Obedience*]

68 When I was born I was nearly fourteen. That's why I found it easier than most people to realize what life was all about. [*Ib.*]

69 A civil servant doesn't make jokes. [*The Killer*, I]

70 Yes, the rich are probably as poor as us, if there's any left these days. [*Ib.* II]

71 Crime doesn't pay. So stop being a criminal and we'll pay you. [*Ib.* III]

72 GIRL ADMIRER: But ... but ... the leader hasn't got a head!
ANNOUNCER: What's he need a head for when he's got genius? [*The Leader*]

73 How, for example, would you say, in English, the roses of my grandmother are as yellow as my grandfather who was born in Asia? [*The Lesson*]

74 You'll probably say that progress can be good or bad, like Jews or Germans or films! ... [*Maid to Marry*]

75 [The Lady's daughter comes in. She is a man, about thirty years old, robust and virile, with a bushy black moustache, wearing a grey suit.] [*Ib.* Stage direction]

76 A nose that can see is worth two that sniff. [*The Motor Show*]

77 Life is an abnormal business. [*Rhinoceros*, I]

78 There are more dead people than living. And their numbers are increasing. The living are getting rarer. [*Ib.* II]

79 But you'll never become a rhinoceros, really you won't . . . you haven't got the vocation! [*Ib.* III]

80 You can only predict things after they've happened. [*Ib.*]

81 The government's urging all the citizens of the big towns to cultivate detachment. [*Victims of Duty*]

82 You're often going to the cinema; you must be very fond of the theatre. [*Ib.*]

VALENTIN IREMONGER

83 Where, then, is Wilbur [contemporary American poet]? Practising, in a lonely room, in front of a full length gilded mirror and talking, I am afraid, to the wall. [Review in *Guardian*, 7 Dec. 1962]

CHRISTOPHER ISHERWOOD

84 I am a camera with its shutter open, quite passive, recording, not thinking. [*A Berlin Diary*. First four words are title of a drama based on Isherwood's Berlin stories by John van Druten.]

85 The other day I made an epigram. I said, Anni's beauty is only *sin*-deep. [*Mr Norris Changes Trains*]

W. W. JACOBS

1 'Dealing with a man,' said the night-watchman thoughtfully, 'is as easy as a teetotaller walking along a nice wide pavement; dealing with a woman is like the same teetotaller, arter four or five whiskies, trying to get up a step that ain't there.' [*Deep Water*, 'Husbandry']

2 A man I knew once – he's dead now, poor chap, and left three widders mourning their unrepairable loss – said that with all 'is experience, wimmin was as much a riddle to 'im as when he fust married. [*Light Freights*, 'A Question of Habit']

3 A nice, quiet gal she was, and there wasn't much went on that she didn't hear. I've known 'er to cry for hours with the ear-ache, pore gal. [*Odd Craft*, 'Dixon's Return']

4 He was an orderly man, and had hung them [his trousers] every night for over twenty years on the brass nob on his side of the bed . . . and now they had absconded with a pair of red braces just entering their teens. [*Ship's Company*, 'Fine Feathers']

5 Mr Joseph Gibbs finished his half-pint . . . with the slowness of a man unable to see where the next was coming from. [*Ib.* 'Friends in Need']

6 When I told my missis once I should never dream of being jealous of *her*, instead of up and thanking me for it, she spoilt the best frying-pan we ever had. [*Ib.* 'Good Intentions']

7 The landlady always kept cotton-wool in 'er ears, not 'aving been brought up to the public line. [*Ib.* 'Skilled Assistance']

HENRY JAMES

8 'You mean the youngsters are – unfortunate?' 'No, they're only, like all the modern young, I think, mysteries, terrible little baffling mysteries.' [*The Awkward Age*, Bk I, Ch. 1]

9 London doesn't love the latent or the lurking, has neither time, nor taste, nor sense for anything less discernible than the red flag in front of the steam-roller. It wants cash over the counter and letters ten feet high. [*Ib.* 2]

10 Little Aggie presented, up and down, an arrangement of dress exactly in the key of her age, her complexion, her emphasized virginity. [*Ib.* II. 8]

11 Experience was to be taken as showing that one might get a five-pound note as one got a light for a cigarette; but one had to check the friendly impulse to ask for it in the same way. [*Ib.* IV. 13]

12 He had not supposed at the moment – in the fifties and the sixties – that he passed for old-fashioned, but life couldn't have left him so far in the rear had the start between them originally been fair. [*Ib.* V. 17]

13 Little Aggie differed from any young person he had ever met in that she had been deliberately prepared for consumption and in that furthermore the gentleness of her spirit had immensely helped the preparation. [*Ib.* 18]

14 The men, the young and the clever ones, find it a house . . . with intellectual elbow-room, with freedom of talk. Most English talk is a quadrille in a sentry-box. [*Ib.* 19]

15 People talk about the conscience, but it seems to me one must just bring it up to a certain point and leave it there. You can let your conscience alone if you're nice to the second housemaid. [*Ib.* VI. 23]

16 He was so particularly the English gentleman and the fortunate settled normal person. Seen at a foreign table-d'hôte, he suggested but one thing: 'In what perfection England produces them!' He had kind safe eyes and a voice which, for all its clean fullness, told the quiet tale

of its having never had once to raise itself. [*The Wings of the Dove*, Bk I, Ch. 1]

17 He was young for the House of Commons, he was loose for the Army. He was refined, as might have been said, for the City and, quite apart from the cut of his cloth, sceptical, it might have been felt, for the Church. [*Ib.* II. 1]

18 It was an oddity of Mrs Lowder's that her face in speech was like a lighted window at night, but that silence immediately drew the curtain. [*Ib.* 2]

19 She was all for scenery – yes; but she wanted it human and personal, and all she could say was that there would be in London – wouldn't there? – more of that kind than anywhere else. [*Ib.* III. 2]

20 He was for ever carrying one well-kept Italian hand to his heart and plunging the other straight into her pocket, which, as she had instantly observed him to recognize, fitted it like a glove. [*Ib.* VII. 3]

21 For a man in whom the vision of her money should be intense, in whom it should be most of the ground for 'making up' to her, any prospective failure on her part to be long for this world might easily count as a positive attraction. [*Ib.* 4]

22 Strether had at this very moment to recognize the truth that wherever one paused in Paris the imagination reacted before one could stop it. [*The Ambassadors*, Bk II, Ch. 2]

23 'Decent men don't go to Cannes with the – well with the kind of ladies you mean.' 'Don't they?' Strether asked with an interest in decent men that amused her. 'No; elsewhere, but not to Cannes. Cannes is different.' [*Ib.* III. 2]

24 She seemed, with little cries and protests and quick recognitions, movements like the darts of some fine high-feathered free-pecking bird, to stand before life as before some full shop window. You could fairly hear, as she selected and pointed, the tap of her tortoise-shell against the glass. [*Ib.* V. 1]

25 One of those types who don't keep you explaining – minds with doors as numerous as the many-tongued cluster of confessionals at St Peter's. You might confess to her with confidence in Roumelian, and even Roumelian sins. [*Ib.* 3]

26 She made him, as under the breath of some vague western whiff, homesick and freshly restless; he could really for the time have imagined himself stranded with her on a far shore, during an ominous calm, in a quaint community of ship-wreck. Their little interview was like a picnic on a coral strand; they passed each other with melancholy smiles and looks sufficiently allusive, such cupfuls of water as they had saved. [*Ib.* IX. 3]

27 The Prince's notion of a recompense to women – similar in this to his notion of an appeal – was more or less to make love to them. [*The Golden Bowl*, Bk I, Pt i, Ch. 1]

28 She would have liked for instance ... to marry ; and nothing in general is more ridiculous, even when it has been pathetic, than a woman who has tried and has not been able. [*Ib.* ii. 10]

29 His lordship had been a person ... in connexion with whom there was almost nothing but the pure monotony of his success to mention. [*The Abasement of the Northmores*]

30 Sitting down by a receptacle daily emptied for the benefit of the dustman, she destroyed, one by one, the gems of the collection in which each piece had been a gem. [*Ib.*]

31 What could the thing that was to happen to him be, after all, but just this thing that had begun to happen? Her dying, her death, his consequent solitude – *that* was what he had figured as the beast in the jungle. [*The Beast in the Jungle*]

32 She had indeed no sense of humour and, with her pretty way of holding her head on one side, was one of those persons whom you want, as the phrase is, to shake, but who have learnt Hungarian by themselves. [*The Figure in the Carpet*]

33 He lacked ... the light hand with which Corvick had gilded the gingerbread – he laid on the tinsel in splotches. [*Ib.*]

34 In her position – that of a young person spending, in framed and wired confinement, the life of a guinea-pig or a magpie. [*In the Cage*, Ch. 1]

35 During the three months ... after her consent, she had often asked herself what it was that marriage would be able to add to a familiarity so final. [*Ib.*]

36 Nothing could equal the frequency and variety of his communications to her ladyship but their extraordinary, their abysmal propriety. [*Ib.* 4]

37 She managed just the accent they had at Paddington when they stared like dead fish. [*Ib.* 23]

38 The flowers at Waterbath would probably go wrong in colour and the nightingales sing out of tune; but she remembered to have heard the place described as possessing those advantages that are usually spoken of as natural. [*The Spoils of Poynton*, Ch. 1]

39 He might have been a fine young man with a bad toothache, with the first even of his life. What ailed him, above all, she felt, was that trouble was new to him. [*Ib.* 8]

40 The point at which the soft declivity of Hampstead had at that time to confess in broken accents to St John's Wood. [*The Tree of Knowledge*]

41 Splendid Rupert [Brooke] to be the soldier that could beget them on the Muse! and lucky Muse, not less, which could have an affair with a soldier and yet feel herself not guilty of the least deviation. [Letter about *Soldier Sonnets*, 28 Mar. 1915]

42 But then I'm a battered old novelist and it's my business to comprehend. [Letter to Edward Marsh, 1915]

43 It was like morning prayers in a workhouse. [On a would-be Elizabethan production of *Hamlet*. Attr.]

44 Summer afternoon – summer afternoon; to me those have always been the two most beautiful words in the English language. [Quoted in Edith Wharton, *A Backward Glance*, Ch. 10]

45 So here it is at last, the distinguished thing! [Said by a 'voice' heard as he suffered his first stroke, often wrongly described as his last words. Quoted in *ib.*]

46 Dearest Alice, I could come back to America (could be carried back on a stretcher) to die – but never, never to live. [Letter to his sister-in-Law, Alice James. *The Letters of Henry James*, sel. and ed. by Percy Lubbock, Vol. 2]

47 Are you acquainted with the terrible, the devastating words, if I may call them so,

the fiat of Doom: 'I don't know if you know, sir'? As when the housemaid comes into your bedroom in the morning and says, 'I don't know if you know, sir, that the bath has fallen through the kitchen ceiling!' [Quoted in Ford Madox Ford, *Return to Yesterday*]

48 Kidd, turn off the light to spare my blushes. [Said to the maid after Edmund Gosse had told him he had been awarded the O.M. Quoted in James S. Bain, *A Bookseller Looks Back*]

49 It is art that *makes* life, makes interest, makes importance, for our consideration and application of these things, and I know of no substitute whatever for the force and beauty of its process. [Letter to H. G. Wells. Quoted in H. Montgomery Hyde, *Henry James at Home*, Ch. 7, sect. iii]

50 This place in which I find myself is the strangest mixture of Edinburgh and Dublin and New York and some other place I don't know. [Said during his last illness. Quoted in *ib*. 7. iv]

51 Tell the boys to follow, to be faithful, to take me seriously. [Last recorded words, said to Alice James. Quoted in *ib.*]

52 However British you may be, I am more British still. [Said to two English friends in 1914. Quoted in *ib*. 7. v]

WILLIAM JAMES

53 The human as distinct from the German mind. [Attr.]

54 The perfection of rottenness. [Comment on a book by Santayana. Attr.]

SIR JAMES JEANS

55 Life exists in the universe only because the carbon atom possesses certain exceptional properties. [*The Mysterious Universe*, Ch. 1]

56 One tiny corner at least, and possibly several tiny corners, of this universe of atoms had chanced to become conscious for a time, but was designed in the end, still under the action of blind mechanical forces, to be frozen out and again leave a lifeless world. [*Ib.* 5]

57 The universe shows evidence of a designing or controlling power that has ... the tendency to think in the way which, for want of a better word, we describe as mathematical. [*Ib.*]

58 Science should leave off making pronouncements; the river of knowledge has too often turned back on itself. [*Ib.*]

REV. EDWARD JEFFREY

59 People expect the clergy to have the grace of a swan, the friendliness of a sparrow, the strength of an eagle and the night hours of an owl – and some people expect such a bird to live on the food of a canary. [*Observer*, 'Sayings of the Week', 14 June 1964]

LENA JEGER

60 It is a sad woman who buys her own perfume. [*Observer*, 'Sayings of the Week', 20 Nov. 1955]

VISCOUNT JELLICOE

61 I had always to remember that I could have lost the war in an afternoon. [On battle of Jutland]

ELIZABETH JENNINGS

62 Now deep in my bed / I turn and the world turns on the other side. [*In the Night*]

PAUL JENNINGS

63 So, cousins all, / A fortnight hence we bid you all to Wales / To tell sad tories of the death of things. ['History of Harold and the Common Market', reprinted in *Shouts and Murmurs* from the *Observer*]

64 In this concept of Activated Sludge two perfectly opposite forces are held in perfect equilibrium, like all those electrons, mesons, neutrons, protons and morons in the atom. [*The Jenguin Pennings*, 'Activated Sludge']

65 Spring-cleaning is a basic human experience. Faced in the right way, it sets the seal on married love. [*Ib.* 'Advice to Husbands']

66 *Fernsprechbeamtin* has already provoked a vision of a placid, fair-haired, semi-mythical Teutonic figure, a kind of Telephone Queen, deep in some German forest – the Far-Speaking Beaming One. [*Ib.* 'Far Speaking']

67 Ventre offers us a grand vision of the Universe as One Thing – the Ultimate Thing (Dernière Chose). And it is against us. [*Ib.* 'Report on Resistentialism']

68 Of all musicians, flautists are most obviously the ones who know something we don't know. [*Ib.* 'Flautists Flaunt Afflatus']

69 They have collective farms, why not the collective unconscious? [*Ib.* 'Intourist on Capital']

70 Wembley, adj. Suffering from a vague *malaise*. 'I feel a bit w. this morning.' [*Ib.* 'Ware, Wye, Watford']

71 It is difficult to decide whether translators are heroes or fools. They must surely know that the Afrikaans for 'Hamlet, I am my father's ghost' sounds something like 'Omlet, ek is de papa spook.' [*Observer*, 'On Beatrix Potter Translated', quoted in Stephen Potter, *Sense of Humour*, Ch. 3]

JEROME K. JEROME

72 I want a house that has got over all its troubles; I don't want to spend the rest of my life bringing up a young and inexperienced house. [*They and I*]

73 I never read a patent medicine advertisement without being impelled to the conclusion that I am suffering from the particular disease therein dealt with in its most virulent form. [*Three Men in a Boat*, Ch. 1]

74 It is a curious fact, but nobody ever is sea-sick – on land. [*Ib.*]

75 You never saw such a commotion, up and down a house, in all your life, as when my Uncle Podger undertook to do a job. [*Ib.* 3]

76 Nothing satisfies us on Christmas Eve but to hear each other tell authentic anecdotes about spectres. It is a genial, festive season, and we love to muse upon graves, and dead bodies, and murder, and blood. [*Told after Supper*]

C. E. M. JOAD

77 It all depends what you mean by . . . [In *The Brains Trust* radio series, *passim*]

78 The nineteenth century regarded European civilization as mature and late, the final expression of the human spirit; we are only now beginning to realize that it is young and childish. [*Guide to Modern Thought*, Ch. 1]

79 Conscience was the barmaid of the Victorian soul. Recognizing that human beings were fallible and that their failings, though regrettable, must be humoured, conscience would permit, rather ungraciously perhaps, the indulgence of a number of carefully selected desires. Once the appointed limit was reached, conscience would rap on the bar of the soul. 'Time's up, gentlemen,' she would say, 'we close at ten-thirty.' [*Under the Fifth Rib*, Ch. 9]

80 I have come to the conclusion that the degree of my difference from most people exceeds the average of most people's difference from one another; or, to put it more briefly, that my reactions to many things don't conform to popular patterns. [*A Year More or Less*, 3 May 1947]

81 Whenever I look inside myself I am afraid. [*Observer*, 'Sayings of the Week', 8 Nov. 1942]

82 I've not had a new idea for the last twenty years. [*Ib.* 31 Oct. 1943]

83 My life is spent in a perpetual alternation between two rhythms, the rhythm of attracting people for fear I may be lonely and the rhythm of trying to get rid of them because I know that I am bored. [*Ib.* 12 Dec. 1948]

84 There was never an age in which useless knowledge was more important than in our own. [*Ib.* 30 Sept. 1951]

85 It will be said of this generation that it found England a land of beauty and left it a land of beauty spots. [*Observer*, 'Sayings of our Times', 31 May 1953]

POPE JOHN XXIII

86 I offer my life as a sacrifice for the successful outcome of the Ecumenical Council and for peace among men. [Words to his confessor, reported in *Guardian*, 31 May 1963]

87 I am able to follow my own death step by step. Now I move softly towards the end. [Said two days before his death. Reported in *Guardian*, 3 June 1963]

AUGUSTUS JOHN

88 W. R. RODGERS: What do you think of life?
A.J.: There's nothing more terrifying. [*Sunday Times*, 1 Dec. 1963]

GLYNIS JOHNS

89 I think the Swiss have sublimated their sense of time into clock-making. [Attr.]

ALVA JOHNSON

90 Anyone who extends to him [Mayor La Guardia] the right hand of fellowship is in danger of losing a couple of fingers. [Arthur Schlesinger Jr, The *Politics of Upheaval*, Pt I, Ch. 8, Sect. iii]

HIRAM JOHNSON

1 The first casualty when war comes is truth. [Quoted in Johnson, *Common English Quotations*]

LYNDON B. JOHNSON

2 Every man has a right to a Saturday night bath. [*Observer*, 'Sayings of the Week', 13 March 1960]

3 For the first time in our history it is possible to conquer poverty. [*Ib.* 22 Mar. 1964]

4 I am going to build the kind of nation that President Roosevelt hoped for, President Truman worked for and President Kennedy died for. [Quoted in *Sunday Times*, 27 Dec. 1964]

HANNS JOHST

5 When I hear anyone talk of culture I reach for my revolver. [*Schlageter*, 1932. Usually attr. H. Goering]

HENRY ARTHUR JONES and HENRY HERMAN

6 I backed the right horse, and then the wrong horse went and won. [*The Silver King*, 1]

L. E. JONES

7 The sheer babyhood of the human race against the background of incalculable time makes anything but a questing agnosticism absurdly presumptuous. [*I Forgot to Tell You*]

RICHARD JONES

8 The sun's gonna shine in my back do' some day. ['Troubled in Mind'. Alan Lomax, *Folk Songs of North America*, No. 313]

MICHAEL JOSEPH

9 Authors are easy enough to get on with – if you are fond of children. [*Observer*, 'Sayings of the Week', 29 May 1949]

BENJAMIN JOWETT

10 MARGOT ASQUITH: What was your lady-love like, dear Master?
B.J.: Violent ... very violent. [*Margot Asquith, Autobiography*, Ch. 7]

JAMES JOYCE

11 Ireland is the old sow that eats her farrow. [*Portrait of the Artist as a Young Man*]

12 The snotgreen sea. The scrotumtightening sea. [*Ulysses* (Bodley Head, 1937), p. 3]

13 When I makes tea I makes tea, as old mother Grogan said. And when I makes water I makes water. [*Ib.* p. 10]

14 The Roman, like the Englishman who follows in his footsteps, brought to every new shore on which he set his foot (on our shore he never set it) only his cloacal obsession. He gazed about him in his toga and he said: It is meet to be here. Let us construct a water-closet. [*Ib.* p. 122]

15 As we read in the first chapter of Guinness'es. [*Ib.* p. 122]

16 I caught a cold in the park. The gate was open. [*Ib.* p. 126]

17 We call it D.B.C. because they have damn bad cakes. [*Ib.* p. 235]

18 Saint Thomas – writing of incest from a standpoint different from that of the new Viennese school. [*Ib.* p. 309]

19 A face on him as long as a late breakfast. [*Ib.* p. 309]

20 They believe in rod, the scourger almighty, creator of hell upon earth and in Jacky Tar, the son of a gun, who was conceived of unholy boast, born of the fighting navy, suffered under rump and dozen, was sacrificed flayed and curried, yelled like bloody hell, the third day he arose again from the bed, steered into haven, sitteth on his beamend till further orders whence he shall come to drudge for a living and be paid. [*Ib.* p. 313]

21 There's a bloody sight more pox than pax about that boyo. [Of Edward VII. *Ib.* p. 315]

22 I dream of wellfilled hose. [*Ib.* p. 351]

23 There have been cases of shipwreck and somnambulism in my client's family. [*Ib.* p. 442]

24 I belong to the *faubourg Saint-Patrice* called Ireland for short [*Ib.* p. 606]

25 riverrun, past Eve and Adam's, from swerve of shore to bend of bay, brings us by a commodius vicus of recirculation back to Howth Castle and Environs. [*Finnegans Wake* (1939) Pt I, p. 1]

26 the redaction known as the Sayings Attributive to H. C. Earwicker, prize on schillings, postlots free. [*Ib.* p. 36]

27 Have you heard of one Humpty Dumpty / How he fell with a roll and a rumble / And curled up like Lord Olofa Crumble / By the butt of the Magazine Wall, / (Chorus) Of the Magazine Wall, / Hump helmet and all? [*Ib.* 'The Ballad of Persse O'Reilly', p. 45]

28 He was fafafather of all schemes to bother us / Slow coaches and immaculate contraceptives for the populace. [*Ib.*]

29 Like the bumping bull of the Cassidys / All your butter is in your horns. [*Ib.*]

30 Mind my duvetyne dress above all! It's golded silvy, the newest sextones with princess effect. For Rutland blue's got out of passion. [*Ib.* p. 148]

31 The Mookse and the Gripes. Gentes and laitymen, fullstoppers and semicolonials, hybreds and lubberds! Eins within a space and a wearywide space it wast ere wohned a Mookse. [*Ib.* p. 152]

32 Nuvoletta in her lightdress, spunn of sisteen shimmers, was looking down on them, leaning over the bannistars and listening all she childishly could. [*Ib.* p. 157]

33 Shem is as short for Shemus as Jem is joky for Jacob. [*Ib.* p. 169]

34 Shem was a sham and a low sham and his lowness creeped out first via food-stuffs. [*Ib.* p. 170]

35 O / tell me all about / Anna Livia! I want to hear all / about Anna Livia. Well, you know Anna Livia? Yes, of course, we all know Anna Livia. Tell me all. Tell me now. [*Ib.* p. 196]

36 Can't hear with the waters of. The chittering waters of. Flittering bats, fieldmice bawk talk. Ho! Are you not gone ahome? [*Ib.* p. 215]

37 Dark hawks near us. Night! Night! My ho head halls. I feel as heavy as yonder stone. [*Ib.*]

38 Beside the rivering waters of, hitherand-thithering waters of. Night! [*Ib.* p. 216]

39 Voyaging after maidens, belly jonah hunting the polly joans. [*Ib.* II, p. 323]

40 Reefer was a wenchman. One can smell off his westments how he is coming from a beach of promisck. [*Ib.*]

41 The Gracehoper was always jigging a jog, hoppy on akkant of his joyicity. [*Ib.* III. p. 414]

42 *The thing pleased him andt, and andt, / He larved ond he larved on he merd such a nauses / The Gracehoper feared he would mixplace his fauces.* [*Ib.* p. 418]

43 Write it, damn you, write it! What else are you good for? [*Giacomo Joyce*]

44 Envoy: Love me, love my umbrella. [*Ib.*]

45 The devil mostly speaks a language called Bellsybabble which he makes up himself as he goes along but when he is very angry he can speak quite bad French very well though some who have heard him say that he has a strong Dublin accent. [*The Cat and the Devil*]

C. G. JUNG

46 Among all my patients in the second half of life – that is to say over thirty-five – there has not been one whose problem in the last resort was not that of finding a religious outlook on life. [*Modern Man in Search of His Soul*]

47 Nowadays we can see as never before that the peril which threatens all of us comes not from nature, but from man, from the psyches of the individual and the mass. . . . If certain persons lose their heads nowadays, a hydrogen bomb will go off. [*Memories, Dreams, Reflections,* Ch. 4]

48 Encounters with people of so many different kinds and on so many different psychological levels have been for me incomparably more important than fragmentary conversations with celebrities. The finest and most significant conversations of my life were anonymous. [*Ib.* 4]

49 The pendulum of the mind oscillates between sense and nonsense, not between right and wrong. [*Ib.* 5]

50 I was never able to agree with Freud that the dream is a 'façade' behind which its meaning lies hidden – a meaning already known but maliciously, so to speak, withheld from consciousness. To me dreams are a part of nature, which harbours no intention to deceive but expresses something as best it can, just as a plant grows or an animal seeks its food as best it can. [*Ib.*]

51 All the eagles and other predatory creatures that adorn our coats of arms seem to me to be apt psychological representations of our true nature. [*Ib.* 9. ii]

52 A man who has not passed through the inferno of his passions has never overcome them. [*Ib.* 9. iv]

53 As far as we can discern, the sole purpose of human existence is to kindle a light in the darkness of mere being. [*Ib.* 11]

54 Every form of addiction is bad, no matter whether the narcotic be alcohol or morphine or idealism. [*Ib.* 12]

55 We need more understanding of human nature, because the only real danger that exists is man himself. . . . We know nothing of man, far too little. His psyche should be studied because we are the origin of all coming evil. [In BBC television 'Face to Face' interview with John Freeman]

ERNST JÜNGER

56 Evolution is far more important than living. [Quoted in Albert Camus, *The Rebel,* Ch. 3]

K

KANEKO MITSUHARU

1 This I believe: to oppose / Is the only
fine thing in life. / To oppose is to live. /
To oppose is to get a grip on the very
self. [Opposition, trans. Geoffrey Bownas
and Anthony Thwaite in *Penguin Book of
Japanese Verse*]

FRANZ KAFKA

2 You've been taken on as Land Surveyor,
as you say, but, unfortunately, we have
no need of a Land Surveyor. There
wouldn't be the least use for one here.
The frontiers of our little state are
marked out and all officially recorded.
[*The Castle*, Ch. 5]

3 It's a working principle of the Head
Bureau that the very possibility of error
must be ruled out of account. The ground
principle is justified by the consummate
organization of the whole authority. [*Ib.*]

4 There's no fixed connection with the
Castle, no central exchange which trans-
mits our calls further. When anybody
calls up the Castle from here the instruments in all the subordinate departments
ring, or rather they would ring if practically all the departments ... didn't leave
their receivers off. [*Ib.*]

5 Officials are highly educated, but one-
sided; in his own department an official
can grasp whole trains of thought from a
single word, but let him have something
from another department explained to
him by the hour, he may nod politely, but
he won't understand a word of it. [*Ib.*
15. 'Petitions']

6 If you have the right eye for these things,
you can see that accused men are often
attractive. It's a remarkable phenomenon,
almost a natural law. [*The Trial*, Ch. 8]

7 It's often safer to be in chains than to be
free. [*Ib.*]

8 Let me remind you of the old maxim:
people under suspicion are better moving
than at rest, since at rest they may be
sitting in the balance without knowing it,
being weighed together with their sins.
[*Ib.*]

9 If the French were German in their
essence, then how the Germans would
admire them! [*The Diaries of Franz
Kafka*, 17 Dec. 1910]

10 Don't despair, not even over the fact that
you don't despair. [*Ib.* 21 Jul. 1913]

11 If there is a transmigration of souls, then
I am not yet on the bottom rung. My life
is a hesitation before birth. [*Ib.* 24 Jan.
1922]

ERICH KÄSTNER

12 *Kennst Du das Land, wo die Kanonen
blühn? Du kennst es nicht? Du wirst es
kennenlernen.* – Do you know the land
where the cannon flower grew? You
don't? But you will. [*Bei Durchsicht
meiner Bücher, 'Kennst Du das Land, wo
die Kanonen blühn?'*]

13 *Da hat mir kürzlich und mitten im Bett
eine Studentin der Jurisprudenz erklärt:
Jungfernschaft sei, möglicherweise, ganz
nett, besäsz aber kaum noch Sammlerwert.*
– Recently and in the middle of bed, a
girl student of law informed me that
virginity might possibly be quite nice, but
had now hardly any collector's value. [*Ib.*
'Moralishe Anatomie'].

14 *Wo sonst die Linie 56 hält | war eine
Art von Urwald aufgestellt. | Und Orang
Utans hingen in den Zweigen.* – Where
once the number 2 bus used to stop /
They'd set a kind of pristine jungle up /
And apes – orang-outangs – hung on the
trees. [*Doktor Erich Kästners Lyrische
Hausapotheke, Gefährliches Lokal'.* Tr.
by Michael Hamburger]

15 *Weil man mich dann zum Telephone rief /
(ein Kunde wollte mich geschäftlich
sprechen), war ich genötigt, plötzlich
aufzubrechen. / Als ich zurückkam, sah
ich, dasz ich schlief ...* – Because they
called me to the phone (old Deeping, /
My senior clerk, to tell me he was sick) /
I was obliged to make my exit quick. /
When I came back I saw that I was sleeping. [*Ib.*]

16 *Wenn Frauen Fehler machen wollen, /
dann soll man ihnen nicht in Wege stehen.* –
When women want to make mistakes,
one should not prevent them. [*Ib.
'Hotelsolo für eine Mannerstimme'*]

17 *Nun bin ich beinah 40 Jahre / und habe
eine kleine Versfabrik.* – Now I am almost
40 and have a little verse-factory. [*Ib.
'Kurzgefaszter Lebenslauf'*]

18 Password *Emil.* [*Emil and the Detectives*,
Ch. 9]

PRESIDENT KAUNDA OF ZAMBIA

19 Inability of those in power to still the
voices of their own consciences is the
great force leading to desired changes.
[*Observer*, 'Sayings of the Week', 27
July 1965]

TED KAVANAGH

20 'After you, Claude.' / 'No, after you,
Cecil.' [*Itma*, BBC radio comedy series]

21 Boss, boss! Something terrible's happened. [*Ib.*]

22 Dan! Dan! You dilatory old man. [And
variations. *Ib.*]

23 Down, Upsey! [*Ib.*]

24 Excuse please, mister. You buy saucy
savings stamps – very grimy – oh blimey!
[And variations. *Ib.*]

25 I go – I come back. [*Ib.*]

26 It's being so cheerful as keeps me going.
[Mona Lott. *Ib.*]

27 'The Mater would be most distressed' [or
variations]. 'What – Crafty Clara ... ?'
[*Ib.*]

28 My pappa [Chief Bigga Banga], he say ...
[*Ib.*]

29 Now, now – come-come – that'll do –
don't dilly-dally! [*Ib.*]

30 Poppy Poopah's outside. [And variations. *Ib.*]

31 Sir Short Supply of the Ministry of
Food. [*Ib.*]

32 T.T.F.N. [Ta-ta for now. *Ib.*]

NIKOS KAZANTZAKIS

33 The doors of heaven and hell are adjacent
and identical: both green, both beautiful.
[*The Last Temptation*, Ch. 18]

JOHN KETAS

34 The automobile changed our dress,
manners, social customs, vacation habits,
the shape of our cities, consumer purchasing patterns, common tastes and
positions in intercourse. [*The Insolent
Chariots*, Ch. 1]

35 If Detroit is right ... there is little wrong
with the American car that is not wrong
with the American public. [*Ib.*]

36 In the beginning ... a car was a status-symbol, like a boar's tusk in a Papuan's
nose. [*Ib.* 3]

37 The automobile did not put the adventure
of travel within reach of the common
man. Instead, *it first gave him the opportunity to make himself more and more
common.* [*Ib.* 7]

HENRY KEMBLE

38 Young man, in the course of a long life I
have never heard anyone utter such
foolish things as you have tried to pass off
for wit tonight. ... I am sorry I made a
hasty remark to you ... I was wrong. I
once did. It was nineteen years ago in a
public house in Oldham. Good night, sir.
The next time we meet I shall not be
there. [Quoted in Hesketh Pearson,
Beerbohm Tree, Ch. 5]

PRESIDENT JOHN F. KENNEDY

39 We stand today on the edge of a new
frontier. [Speech on his adoption as
Democratic presidential candidate, 15
July 1960]

40 Ask not what your country can do for you; ask what you can do for your country. [Inaugural address as President, 20 Jan. 1961]

41 Let the word go forth from this time and place, to friend and foe alike, that the torch has been passed to a new generation of Americans – born in this century, tempered by war, disciplined by a hard and bitter peace. [*Ib.*]

42 Those who foolishly sought power by riding on the back of the tiger ended up inside. [*Ib.*]

43 We must use time as a tool not as a couch. [*Observer*, 'Sayings of the Week', 10 Dec. 1961]

44 The war against hunger is truly mankind's war of liberation. [Speech at opening of World Food Congress, 4 June 1963]

45 The United States has to move very fast to even stand still. [*Observer*, 'Sayings of the Week', 21 July 1963]

46 When power narrows the areas of man's concern, poetry reminds him of the richness and diversity of his existence. When power corrupts, poetry cleanses. [Address at Dedication of the Robert Frost Library, Nov. 1963]

47 In free society art is not a weapon. . . . Artists are not engineers of the soul. [*Ib.*]

48 If we cannot now end our differences, at least we can help make the world safe for diversity. [*Observer*, 'Sayings of the Year', 1963]

49 I believe in an America that is on the march. ['Ideas, Attitudes, Purposes from His Speeches and Writings', *Saturday Review*, 7 Dec. 1963]

50 The people of the world respect a nation that can see beyond its own image. [*Ib.*]

51 Mr Krushchev made one point which I wish to pass on. . . . It is easy to dismiss as Communist-inspired every anti-government or anti-American riot, every overthrow of a corrupt régime or every mass protest against misery and despair. [*Ib.*]

52 Let us begin anew – remembering on both sides that civility is not a sign of weakness, and sincerity is always subject to proof. Let us never negotiate out of fear. But let us never fear to negotiate. [*Ib.*]

53 The basic problems facing the world today are not susceptible to a military solution. [*Ib.*]

54 Our purpose is not to buy friends or hire allies. Our purpose is to defeat poverty. . . . Our goal is to again influence history instead of merely observing it. [*Ib.*]

ROBERT KENNEDY

55 One fifth of the people are against everything all the time. [*Observer*, 'Sayings of the Week', 10 May 1964]

HUGH E. KEOUGH

56 The race is not always to the swift, but that is where to look. [Quoted by F. P. Adams in *Atlantic Monthly*, Aug. 1942]

JEROME KERN

57 Ol' Man River / He jus' keeps rollin' along. [Song: *Ol' Man River*; words by Oscar Hammerstein II]

58 Tired o' living, / And scared of dying. [*Ib.*]

JACK KEROUAC

59 We tiptoed around each other like heart-breaking new friends. [*On the Road*, Pt I, Ch. 1]

60 You can't teach the old maestro a new tune. [*Ib.*]

61 We're really all of us bottomly broke. I haven't had time to work in weeks. [*Ib.* I. 7]

62 Do you know you can go to jail for putting the American flag upside down on a government pole? [*Ib.* I. 11]

63 I had nothing to offer anybody except my own confusion. [*Ib.* II. 3]

GERALD KERSH

64 Prem . . . remembered the woman as a superb brunette, with a contralto voice like hot, damp fur. [*An Ape, a Dog and a Serpent*]

65 Only great poets can talk of love without making bores or fools of themselves. None but the exceedingly great can talk of love from the molehill of personal experience without betraying kinship with

121

the spaniel or the goat. [*Clean, Bright and Slightly Oiled*, 'Love, Capital and Labour']

66 His pale and insipid soul was dotted with silly little prejudices and principles as feeble as the vestigial seeds of a banana. [*Neither Man nor Dog*, 'The Conqueror Worm']

67 When Irish eyes are smiling, watch your step; and when you hear the lilt of Irish laughter, take care to arm yourself either with a quart bottle or a fire-extinguisher. [*Ib.* 'Macagony's Fist']

68 The habitual liar always imagines that his lie rings true. No miracle of belief can equal his childlike faith in the credulity of the people who listen to him; and so it comes to pass that he fools nobody as completely as he fools himself. [*Night and the City*]

69 Her lips moved, and her eyes became blank; flat and empty, like holes punched in a magazine-cover, with specks of sky visible through them. [*Ib.*]

70 The dark, flat houses cling under the railway bridges like ticks on the belly of a rhinoceros. [*The Nine Lives of Bill Nelson*]

71 Those bright brown eyes ... may now be likened to a couple of cockroaches desperately swimming in two saucers of boiled rhubarb. [*Prelude to a Certain Midnight*]

72 Mrs Kipling ... had, in her day, danced suggestive dances and sung lewd songs in East End music halls, but ... now (as visitors said) was like something out of the Book of Revelation. [*Ib.*]

J. MAYNARD KEYNES

73 He [Clemenceau] had only one illusion – France; and only one disillusion – mankind. [Quoted in Robert L. Heilbroner, *The Worldly Philosophers*, Ch. 9]

74 Like Odysseus, he [Woodrow Wilson] looked wiser when seated. [Quoted in *ib.*]

75 Whenever you save 5s. you put a man out of work for a day. [In 1931. *Observer*, 'Sayings of Our Times', 31 May 1953]

76 'Sound' finance may be right psychologically; but economically it is a depressing influence. [1932, *Ib.*]

77 The recent gyrations of the dollars have looked to me more like a gold standard on the booze than the ideal managed currency which I hope for. [1933, *Ib.*]

78 Does that mean that because Americans won't listen to sense, you intend to talk nonsense to them? [Remark to Treasury official on the way to international money conference, 1944 or '45]

79 It is Enterprise which builds and improves the world's possessions. ... If Enterprise is afoot, wealth accumulates whatever may be happening to Thrift; and if Enterprise is asleep, Wealth decays, whatever Thrift may be doing. [*Treatise on Money*]

80 If the Treasury were to fill old bottles with banknotes, bury them at suitable depths in disused coalmines which are then filled up to the surface with town rubbish, and leave it to private enterprise on well-tried principles of *laissez-faire* to dig the notes up again ... there need be no more unemployment and, with the help of the repercussions, the real income of the community ... would probably become a good deal larger than it actually is. [*General Theory of Employment*, Bk III, Ch. 10]

81 It is better that a man should tyrannize over his bank balance than over his fellow citizens. [*Ib.* Bk VI, Ch. 24]

82 The Economic Problem, as one may call it for short, the problem of want and poverty and the economic struggle between classes and nations, is nothing but a frightful muddle, a transitory and *unnecessary* muddle. [*Essays in Persuasion*, Preface]

83 It's a good thing to make mistakes so long as you're found out quickly. [Attr.]

84 No, I don't know his telephone number. But it was up in the high numbers. [Attr.]

HUGH KINGSMILL

85 What still alive at twenty-two, / A clean, upstanding chap like you! / Sure, if your throat is hard to slit, / Slit your girl's and swing for it. [Parody on Housman. Quoted in H. Pearson and M. Muggeridge, *About Kingsmill*]

86 But bacon's not the only thing / That's cured by hanging from a string. [Parody on Housman quoted in *ib.*]

87 A gentleman has all the qualities of a saint except saintliness. [Quoted in Michael Holroyd, *Hugh Kingsmill*]

88 Society is based on the assumption that everyone is alike and no one is alive. [*Ib.*]

RUDYARD KIPLING

89 Seven men from all the world back to town again, / *Rollin' down the Ratcliffe Road drunk and raising Cain.* [*The Ballad of the 'Bolivar'*]

90 It was not preached to the crowd, / It was not taught by the State. / No man spoke it aloud, / When the English began to hate. [*The Beginnings*]

1 There's a little red-faced man, / Which is Bobs, / Rides the tallest 'orse 'e can – / *Our Bobs.* [*Bobs* – Lord Roberts]

2 We have fed our sea for a thousand years / And she calls us, still unfed, / Though there's never a wave of all her waves / But marks our English dead. [*The Coastwise Lights*]

3 Until thy feet have trod the Road / Advise not wayside folk. [*The Comforters*]

4 O they're hangin' Danny Deever in the mornin'! [*Danny Deever*]

5 The 'eathen in 'is blindness must end where 'e began, / But the backbone of the Army is the Non-commissioned Man! [*The 'Eathen*]

6 Who are neither children nor Gods, but men in a world of men! [*England's Answer*]

7 They are lifting their heads in the stillness to yelp at the English Flag! [*The English Flag*]

8 Because to force my ramparts your nutshell navies came. [*Ib.*]

9 Cock the gun that is not loaded, cook the frozen dynamite – / But oh, beware my Country, when my Country grows polite! [*Et Dona Ferentes*]

10 Buy my English posies! / Kent and Surrey may – / Violets of the Undercliff / Wet with Channel spray. [*The Flowers*]

11 God help us, for we knew the worst too young! [*Gentlemen-Rankers*]

12 But when it comes to slaughter / You will do your work on water, / An' you'll lick the bloomin' boots of 'im that's got it. [*Gunga Din*]

13 So I'll meet 'im later on / At the place where 'e is gone – / Where it's always double drill and no canteen. / 'E'll be squattin' on the coals / Givin' drink to poor damned souls, / An' I'll get a swig in hell from Gunga Din! [*Ib.*]

14 Ere yet we loose the legions – / Ere yet we draw the blade, / Jehovah of the Thunders, / Lord God of Battles aid! [*Hymn before Action*]

15 No doubt but ye are the People – your throne is above the King's. / *Whoso speaks in your presence must say acceptable things.* [*The Islanders*]

16 There's times when you'll think that you mightn't, / There's times when you know that you might; / *But the things you will learn from the Yellow and Brown, / They'll 'elp you a lot with the White!* [*The Ladies*]

17 I've taken my fun where I've found it / An' now I must pay for my fun. [*Ib.*]

18 Have it *jest* as you've a mind to, but I've proved it time on time, / If you want to change her nature you have *got* to give her lime. [*The Land*]

19 'Hev it *jest* as you've a mind to, *but*' – and so he takes command. / For whoever pays the taxes old Mus' Hobden owns the land. [*Ib.*]

20 Thus said the Lord in the Vault above the Cherubim, / Calling to the Angels and the Souls in their degree. [*The Last Chantey*]

21 Then said the Soul of the Angel of the Off-shore Wind: / (He that bits the thunder when the bull-mouthed breakers flee). [*Ib.*]

22 And Ye take mine honour from me if Ye take away the sea! [*Ib.*]

23 Then cried the soul of the stout Apostle Paul to God. [*Ib.*]

24 Loud sang the souls of the jolly, jolly mariners, / Plucking at their harps, and they plucked unhandily. [*Ib.*]

25 Then stooped the Lord, and he called the good sea up to Him, / And 'stablishèd its borders unto all eternity. [*Ib.*]

26 *And the ships shall go abroad | To the Glory of the Lord | Who heard the silly sailor-folk and gave them back their sea!* [*Ib.*]

27 There be triple ways to take, of the eagle or the snake, / Or the way of a man with a maid. [*The Long Trail*]

28 Though Thy Power brings / All skill to naught, Ye'll understand a man must think o' things. [*McAndrew's Hymn*]

29 Lord, send a man like Robbie Burns to sing the Song o' Steam! [*Ib.*]

30 And I'm learnin' 'ere in London what the ten-year soldier tells: / 'If you've 'eard the East a-callin', you won't never 'eed naught else.' [*Mandalay*]

31 Ten thousand men on the pay-roll, and forty freighters at sea! [*The 'Mary Gloster'*]

32 'Not least of our merchant princes'. Dickie, that's me, your dad! [*Ib.*]

33 Weak, a liar, and idle, and mean as a collier's whelp / Nosing for scraps in the galley. [*Ib.*]

34 King Solomon drew merchantmen, / Because of his desire / For peacocks, apes and ivory, / From Tarshish unto Tyre. [*The Merchantmen*]

35 Here, when they heard the horse-bells ring, / The ancient Britons dressed and rode / To watch the dark Phoenicians bring / Their goods along the Western Road. [*Just So Stories*, 'Merrow Down']

36 I will out and batter the family priest, / Because my Gods have afflicted me! [*Natural Theology*]

37 To my own Gods I go. / It may be they shall give me greater ease / Than your cold Christ and tangled Trinities. [*Plain Tales from the Hills*, 'Lisbeth', chapter heading]

38 ... King over all the children of pride / Is the Press – the Press – the Press! [*The Press*]

39 Gawd, 'oo knows all I cannot say, / Look after me in Thamesfontein [London]. [*The Return*]

40 There's never a law of God or man runs north of Fifty-three. [*The Rhyme of the Three Sealers*]

41 *Brother, thy tail hangs down behind!* [*Road-Song of the 'Bandar-Log'*]

42 Grey gun-'orses in the lando, / An' a rogue is married to a whore. [*The Sergeant's Weddin'*]

43 Shillin' a day, / Bloomin' good pay – / Lucky to touch it, a shillin' a day. [*Shillin' a Day*]

44 The God of Fair Beginnings / Hath prospered here my hand – [*The Song of Diego Valdez*]

45 Hold ye the Faith – the Faith our Fathers sealèd us; / Whoring not with visions – overwise and overstale. [*A Song of the English*]

46 Keep ye the Law – be swift in all obedience – / Clear the land of evil, drive the road and bridge the ford. [*Ib.*]

47 Through the Jungle very softly flits a shadow and a sigh – / He is Fear, O Little Hunter, he is Fear! [*The Song of the Little Hunter*]

48 To these from birth is Belief forbidden; from these till death is Relief afar. / They are concerned with matters hidden – under the earth-line their altars are. [*The Sons of Martha*]

49 Our blunt, bow-headed, whale-backed Downs. [*Sussex*]

50 The sheep-bells and the ship-bells ring / Along the hidden beach. [*Ib.*]

51 Here through the strong and shadeless days / The tinkling silence thrills; / Or little, lost, Down churches praise / The Lord who made the hills. [*Ib.*]

52 And the Long Man of Wilmington / Looks naked towards the shires. [*Ib.*]

53 And ... the faith that ye share with Berkeley Square uphold you, Tomlinson! [*Tomlinson*]

54 Once I ha' laughed at the power of Love and twice at the grip of the Grave, / And thrice I ha' patted my God on the head that men might call me brave. [*Ib.*]

55 The Devil he blew upon his nails, and the little devils ran, / And he said: 'Go husk this whimpering thief that comes in the guise of a man.' [*Ib.*]

56 Ye have scarce the soul of a louse,' he said, / 'But the roots of sin are there.' [*Ib.*]

57 For it's Tommy this, an' Tommy that, an' 'Chuck him out, the brute!' / But it's 'Saviour of 'is country' when the guns begin to shoot. [*Tommy*]

58 There are whose study is of smells, / And to attentive schools rehearse / How something mixed with something else / Makes something worse. [*A Translation, Horace,* Bk V, Ode 3]

59 England shall bide till Judgment Tide / By Oak, and Ash, and Thorn! [*A Tree Song*]

60 Each in his place, by right, not grace, / Shall rule his heritage – / The men who simply do the work / For which they draw the wage. [*The Wage-Slaves*]

61 And no one shall work for money, and no one shall work for fame, / But each for the joy of working. [*When Earth's Last Picture is Painted*]

62 When 'Omer smote 'is bloomin' lyre, / He'd 'eard men sing by land an' sea; / An' what he thought 'e might require, / 'E went an' took – the same as me! [*When 'Omer Smote*]

63 By all ye cry or whisper, / By all ye leave or do, / The silent, sullen peoples / Shall weigh your Gods and you. [*The White Man's Burden*]

64 Hands off o' the sons o' the Widow, / Hands off o' the goods in 'er shop. [*The Widow at Windsor*]

65 And you can't refuse when you get the card, / And the Widow gives the party. [*The Widow's Party*]

66 They rest awhile in Zion, / Sit down and smile in Zion; / Ay, even jest in Zion; / In Zion, at their ease. [*Zion*, 1914–18]

67 The Waddy is an infectious disease. [*Wee Willie Winkie*, 'A Second-Rate Woman']

68 A man-cub is a man-cub, and he must learn *all* the Law of the Jungle. [*The Jungle Book* 'Kaa's Hunting']

69 What the *Bandar-log* think now the jungle will think later. [*Ib.*]

70 Nothing but foolish words, and little picking thievish hands. [*Ib.*]

71 'We be of one blood, thou and I,' Mowgli answered, '. . . my kill shall be thy kill if ever thou art hungry.' [*Ib.*]

72 The Russian is a delightful person till he tucks in his shirt. As an Oriental he is charming. It is only when he insists on being treated as the most easterly of western peoples instead of the most westerly of easterns that he becomes a racial anomaly extremely difficult to handle. [*Life's Handicap*, 'The Man Who Was']

73 Under the rules of the R-royal Humane Society, ye must give me hot whisky and water. [*Many Inventions*, 'Brugglesmith']

74 The two men seemed to agree about everything, but when grown-ups agree they interrupt each other almost as much as if they were quarrelling. [*Rewards and Fairies*, 'The Wrong Thing']

75 'How are you, sir?' 'Loungin' round and sufferin', my son.' [*Debits and Credits*, 'The United Idolaters']

76 He was confined to heavings and shruggin's and copious *Mong Jews*! The French are very badly fitted with relief-valves. [*A Diversity of Creatures*, 'The Horse Marines']

77 He was in a highly malleable condition and full o' *juice de spree*. [*Ib.*]

78 When our combination has finished with Sir Thomas Ingell, Bart, M.P. . . . . Sodom and Gomorrah will be a winsome bit of Merrie England beside 'em. [*Ib.* 'The Village that Voted the Earth was Flat']

79 Then he left, in a good deal of astrachan collar and nickel-plated limousine, and the place felt less crowded. [*Ib.*]

80 He spoke and wrote trade-English – a toothsome amalgam of Americanisms and epigrams. [*Ib.*]

81 Politics are not my concern. . . . They impressed me as a dog's life without a dog's decencies. [*Ib.*]

82 The Law of the Jungle – which is by far the oldest law in the world. [*The Second Jungle Book*, 'How Fear Came to the Jungle']

83 What matter? I have killed Fear. [*Ib.*]

84 He was without form and void, so far as I remember, but desperately earnest. [*Stalky and Co.*, 'The Flag of Their Country']

85 We've got him – got him on the Caudine Toasting-fork! [*Ib.* 'In Ambush']

86 We ain't goin' to have any beastly Erickin'. [*Ib.* 'The Moral Reformers']

87 'Twiggez-vous?' 'Nous twiggons.' [*Ib.* 'Slaves of the Lamp']

88 The God who Looks after Small Things had caused the visitor that day to receive two weeks' delayed mails in one. [*Traffics and Discoveries*, 'The Captive']

89 I despise exaggeration – 'tain't American or scientific. [*Ib.*]

90 He laughed one of those thick, big-ended British laughs that don't lead anywhere. [*Ib.*]

LORD KITCHENER

1 I don't mind your being killed, but I object to your being taken prisoner. [To the Prince of Wales, on his asking to go to the Front. Quoted in Viscount Esher, *Journal*, 18 Dec. 1914]

PAUL KLEE

2 An *active* line on a walk, moving freely, without goal. A walk for a walk's sake. [*Pedagogical Sketchbook*, I. 1]

3 The purest mobile form, the cosmic one, ... is only created through the liquidation of gravity (through elimination of material ties). [*Ib.* IV. 35]

4 The father of the arrow is the thought: how do I expand my reach? [*Ib.* IV. 37]

5 I cannot be grasped in this world, for I am as much at home with the dead as with the yet unborn – a little closer to the heart of creation than is usual, if still not close enough. [Extract from *Diary*, inscribed on his grave as an epitaph]

JOHN KNAPPSWOOD

6 Commit no thesis. [Inscription for a poet's tomb]

E. V. KNOX

7 I never knew what Life nor Art meant, / I wrote 'Reserved' on my compartment, / And once (I was a guilty man) / I swapped the labels in guard's van. [*The Everlasting Percy*]

GENERAL KNOX

8 What is wanted is the Cossacks. This people needs the whip! A dictatorship – that is just what it needs. [Quoted in Leon Trotsky, *History of the Russian Revolution*, Pt II, Ch. 9]

RONALD KNOX

9 A rescue-the-poor young man, / A waiter-look-sharp young man, / A ride-in-a-motory / Keep-to-your-coterie / Friend-of-the-world young man. [Parody in *Isis*. Quoted in Evelyn Waugh, *Ronald Knox*, Pt I, Ch. 4]

10 The baby doesn't understand English and the Devil knows Latin. [When asked to perform a baptism in English. Quoted in *ib.* I. 5]

11 We love the windows bright / With red and yellow paints / Presenting to our sight / The better class of Saints. [Hymn parody. Quoted in *ib.*]

12 It is so stupid of modern civilization to have given up believing in the devil when he is the only explanation of it. [*Let Dons Delight*]

13 Are creature comforts more demoralizing when consciously enjoyed or when taken for granted? [*Pensée*]

14 Greet him like Etonians without a single word, / Absolutely silent and indefinitely bored. [*On the Right Method of Greeting a New Headmaster*]

BERNARD KOPS

15 We must set the example but that doesn't mean we must follow it. [*Enter Solly Gold*, Sc. iii]

NIKITA S. KRUSHCHEV

16 We will bury you. [Quoted in *New York Herald Tribune*, 17 Sept. 1959]

17 They talk about who won and who lost. Human reason won. Mankind won. [On the Cuban crisis. Quoted in *Observer*, 11 Nov. 1962]

18 When you are skinning your customers, you should leave some skin on to grow so that you can skin them again. [Addressing British businessmen. Quoted in *Observer*, 'Sayings of the Week', 28 May 1961]

19 If you start throwing hedgehogs under me, I shall throw two porcupines under you. [Quoted in *Observer*, 'Sayings of the Week', 10 Nov. 1963]

STANLEY KUBRICK

20 The great nations have always acted like gangsters, and the small nations like prostitutes. [Quoted in *Guardian*, 5 June 1963]

L

R. D. LAING

1 The statesmen of the world who boast and threaten that they have Doomsday weapons are far more dangerous, and far more estranged from 'reality', than many of the people on whom the label 'psychotic' is affixed. [*The Divided Self*, Preface to the Pelican edition]

2 Freud was a hero. He descended to the 'Underworld' and met there stark terrors. He carried with him his theory as a Medusa's head which turned these terrors to stone. [*Ib.* Ch. 1]

3 Schizophrenia cannot be understood without understanding despair. [*Ib.* 2]

4 Few books today are forgivable. [*The Politics of Experience*, Introduction]

5 We are born into a world where alienation awaits us. [*Ib.*]

6 Before we can ask such an optimistic question as 'What is a personal relationship?', we have to ask if a personal relationship is possible, or, *are persons possible* in our present situation? [*Ib.* Ch. 1]

7 We are effectively destroying ourselves by violence masquerading as love. [*Ib.* 13]

8 Madness need not be all breakdown. It may also be break-through. It is potential liberation and renewal as well as enslavement and existential death. [*Ib.* 6]

OSBERT LANCASTER

9 Oh hark to the groans of the wounded and dying, / Of the mother who casts a last lingering look / At her infant aloft, understandably crying, / Impaled on the spear of a Bashi Bazook. [*Drayneflete Revisited*]

10 The resulting style, known as Bankers Georgian, always preserves something of the air of a Metro-Goldwyn-Mayer production of *The School for Scandal*. [*Pillar to Post*, 'Bankers Georgian']

11 Architectural Association (or Beggar's Opera) Georgian ... may be distinguished by its invincible refinement. [*Ib.*]

12 'Fan vaulting' ... an architectural device which arouses enormous enthusiasm on account of the difficulties it has all too obviously involved but which from an aesthetic standpoint frequently belongs to the 'Last-Supper-carved-on-a-peach-stone' class of masterpiece. [*Ib.* 'Perpendicular']

13 In attitudes of acute discomfort nymphs and tribal deities of excessive female physique and alarming size balanced precariously on broken pediments, threatening the passer-by with a shower of stone fruit from the cavernous interiors of their inevitable cornucopia. [*Ib.* 'Edwardian Baroque']

14 A hundred and fifty accurate reproductions of Anne Hathaway's cottage, each complete with central heating and garage. [*Ib.* 'Stockbrokers Tudor']

ANDREW LANG

15 Miracles do not happen? It's a miracle if they don't. [Quoted by Basil Willey in paper on *Robert Elsmere*, read before the English Association]

HALVARD LANGE

16 We do not regard Englishmen as foreigners. We look on them only as rather mad Norwegians. [*Observer*, 'Sayings of the Week', 9 Mar. 1957]

DAVID LARDNER

17 The plot was designed in a light vein that somehow became varicose. [Quoted in Bennett Cerf, *Try and Stop Me*]

PHILIP LARKIN

18 Hatless, I take off / My cycle-clips in awkward reverence. [*Church-going*]

19 A serious house on serious earth it is. [*Ib.*]

20 Marrying left your maiden name disused. [*Maiden Name*]

21 Why should I let the toad *work* / Squat on my life? [*Toads*]

22 To prove / Our almost-instinct almost true: / What will survive of us is love. [*An Arundel Tomb*]

23 Get stewed: / Books are a load of crap. [*A Study of Reading Habits*]

24 I thought of London spread out in the sun, / Its postal districts packed like squares of wheat. [*The Whitsun Weddings*]

HAROLD LASKI

25 The meek do not inherit the earth unless they are prepared to fight for their meekness. [Attr.]

26 De mortuis nil nisi bunkum. [Attr.]

CHARLES LAUGHTON

27 I had to throw too many of his kind out of our hotel when I was sixteen. [On refusing to play Falstaff. Quoted in James Agate, *Ego 1*, 1933]

PIERRE LAVAL

28 If peace is a chimaera, I am happy to have caressed her. [1935. *Observer*, 'Sayings of Our Times', 31 May 1953]

D. H. LAWRENCE

29 Creatures that hang themselves up like an old rag, t o sleep; / And disgustingly upside down. / Hanging upside down like rows of disgusting old rags / And grinning in their sleep. / Bats! [*Bats*]

30 And so, I missed my chance with one of the lords / Of life. / And I have something to expiate; / A pettiness. [*Ib.*]

31 Me or the Mexican who comes to chop wood / All the same, / All humanity is jam to you. [*Bibbles*]

32 You must always be a-waggle with LOVE. [*Ib.*]

33 Is it the secret of the long-nosed Etruscans? / The long-nosed, sensitive footed, subtly-smiling Etruscans, / Who made so little noise outside the cypress groves? [*Cypresses*]

34 Evil, what is evil? / There is only one evil, to deny life / As Rome denied Etruria / And mechanical America Montezuma still. [*Ib.*]

35 Don't be sucked in by the su-superior, / don't swallow the culture-bait. [*Don'ts*]

36 O pity the dead that are dead, but cannot make / the journey, still they moan and beat / against the silvery adamant walls of life's exclusive city. [*The Houseless Dead*]

37 Thought is not a trick, or an exercise, or a set of dodges. / Thought is a man in his wholeness wholly attending. [*Thought*]

38 Cuckoos, like noise falling in drops off the leaves. [*Fantasia of the Unconscious*, Ch. 4]

39 The Romans and Greeks found everything human. Everything had a face, and a human voice. Men spoke, and their fountains piped an answer. [*Ib.*]

40 The refined punishments of the spiritual mode are usually much more indecent and dangerous than a good smack. [*Ib.*]

41 Morality which is based on i deas, or on an ideal, is an unmitigated evil. [*Ib.* 7]

42 We think that love and benevolence will cure anything. Whereas love and benevolence are our poison, poison to the giver, and still more poison to the receiver. [*Ib.*]

43 When Eve ate this particular apple, she became aware of her own womanhood, mentally. And mentally she began to experiment with it. She has been experimenting ever since. So has man. To the rage and horror of both of them. [*Ib.*]

44 Every race which has become self-conscious and idea-bound in the past has perished. [*Ib.*]

45 To make the mind an absolute ruler is as good as making a Cook's tourist-interpreter a king and a god, because he can speak several languages and make an Arab understand that an Englishman wants fish for supper. [*Ib.* 11]

46 Death is the only pure, beautiful conclusion of a great passion. [*Ib.* 15]

47 Better passion and death than any more of these 'isms'. No more of the old purpose done up in aspic. Better passion and death. [*Ib.*]

48 We have all lost the war. All Europe. [*The Ladybird*, title story]

49 And all lying mysteriously within the Australian underdark, that peculiar, lost weary aloofness of Australia. There was the vast town of Sydney. And it didn't seem to be real, it seemed to be sprinkled on the surface of a darkness into which it never penetrated. [*Kangaroo*, Ch. 1]

50 You may be the most liberal Liberal Englishman, and yet you cannot fail to see the categorical difference between the responsible and the irresponsible classes. [*Ib.*]

51 But Somers was of the people himself, and he had that alert *instinct* of the common people, the instinctive knowledge of what his neighbour was wanting and thinking, and the instinctive necessity to answer. [*Ib.* 2]

52 'We don't like to have anybody overhead here,' said Kangaroo. 'We don't even care to go upstairs, because then we're one storey higher than our true, ground-floor selves.' [*Ib.* 6]

53 The very best that is in the Jewish blood: a faculty for pure disinterestedness, and warm, physically warm love, that seems to make the corpuscles of the blood glow. [*Ib.*]

54 What do the facts we know *about* a man amount to? Only two things we can know of him, and this by pure soul-intuition: we can know if he is true to the flame of life and love which is inside his heart, or if he is false to it. [*Ib.* 7]

55 They were over-ripe; they had been in the sun of prosperity too long, and all their tissues were soft and sweetish. How could they react with any sharpness to any appeal on earth? [*Ib.* 8]

56 The indifference – the fern-dark indifference of this remote golden Australia. Not to care – from the bottom of one's soul, not to care. [*Ib.* 10]

57 Man lives according to his own idea of himself. When circumstances begin really to run counter to his idea of himself, he damns circumstances. When the running-counter persists, he damns the nature of things. And when it *still* persists, he becomes a fatalist. A fatalist or an opportunist – anything of that sort. [*Ib.* 13]

58 The spontaneous soul must extricate itself from the *almost* automatic white octopus of the human ideal, the octopus of humanity. [*Ib.*]

59 Life makes no absolute statement. It is all Call and Answer. [*Ib.*]

60 The highest function of *mind* is its function of messenger. [*Ib.* 16]

61 Man's ultimate love for man? Yes, yes, but only i n the separate darkness of man's love for the present, unknowable God. [*Ib.* 17]

62 He daren't quite bite. Not that he was really afraid of the others. He was afraid of himself, once he let himself go. [*St Mawr*]

63 It always seemed to me that men wore their beards, like they wear their neckties, for show. I shall always remember Lewis for saying his beard was part of him. [*Ib.*]

64 Clever men are mostly such unpleasant *animals*. [*Ib.*]

65 The modern pantheist not only sees the god in everything, he takes photographs of it. [*Ib.*]

66 It was one of those places where the spirit of aboriginal England still lingers, the old savage England, whose last blood flows still in a few Englishmen, Welshmen, Cornishmen. [*Ib.*]

67 Ideal mankind would abolish death, multiply itself million upon million, rear up city upon city, save every parasite alive, until the accumulation of mere existence is swollen to a horror. [*Ib.*]

68 Judas is the last god, and, by heaven, the most potent. [*Ib.*]

69 And suddenly she craved again for the more absolute silence of America. English stillness was so soft, like an inaudible murmur of voices, of presences. [*Ib.*]

70 You may have my husband, but not my horse. My husband won't need emasculating, and my horse I won't have you meddle with. I'll preserve one last male thing in the museum of this world, if I can. [*Ib.*]

71 Her own peculiar dynamic force was stronger than the force of Mind. She could make Mind kiss her hand. [*Ib.*]

72 There's nothing so artificial as sinning nowadays. I suppose it once was real. [*Ib.*]

73 'It [Mexico] is a country where men despise sex, and live for it,' said Ramón. 'Which is suicide.' [*The Plumed Serpent*, Ch. 25]

74 The young Cambridge group, the group that stood for 'freedom' and flannel trousers and flannel shirts open at the neck, and a well-bred sort of emotional anarchy, and a whispering, murmuring sort of voice, and an ultra-sensitive sort of manner. [*Lady Chatterley's Lover*, Ch. 1]

75 It's all this cold-hearted fucking that is death and idiocy. [*Ib.* 14]

76 This is John Thomas marryin' Lady Jane. [*Ib.* 15]

77 A man's most dangerous moment ... is when he's getting into his shirt. Then he puts his head in a bag. [*Ib.*]

78 But tha mun dress thysen, an' go back to thy stately homes of England, how beautiful they stand. Time's up! Time's up for Sir John, an' for little Lady Jane! Put thy shimmy on, Lady Chatterley! [*Ib.*]

79 The identifying ourselves with the visual image of ourselves has become an instinct; the habit is already old. The picture of me, the me that is *seen*, is me. [*Phoenix*, 'Art and Morality']

80 You can't *invent* a design. You recognize it, in the fourth dimension. That is, with your blood and your bones, as well as with your eyes. [*Ib.*]

81 This is the agony of our human existence, that we can only feel things in conventional feeling-patterns. [*Ib.* 'The Good Man']

82 Neither can you expect a revolution, because there is no new baby in the womb of our society. Russia is a collapse, not a revolution. [*Ib.*]

83 Sentimentalism is the working off on yourself of feelings you haven't really got. [*Ib.* 'John Galsworthy']

84 Pornography is the attempt to insult sex, to do dirt on it. [*Ib.* 'Pornography and Obscenity']

85 Russia will certainly inherit the future. What we already call the greatness of Russia is only her pre-natal struggling. [*Ib.* Preface to Leo Shestov, *All Things are Possible*]

86 Away with all ideals. Let each individual act spontaneously from the for ever incalculable prompting of the creative well-head within him. There is no universal law. [*Ib.*]

87 No matter how much of a shabby animal you may be, you can learn from Dostoyevsky and Chekhov, etc., how to have the most tender, unique, coruscating soul on earth. [*Ib.* 'Preface to Mastro-don Gesualdo']

88 It is no good casting out devils. They belong to us, we must accept them and be at peace with them. [*Ib.* 'The Reality of Peace']

89 We know these new English Catholics. They are the last words in Protest. They are Protestants protesting against Protestantism. [*Ib.* Review of Eric Gill, *Art Nonsense*]

90 I am a man, and alive.... For this reason I am a novelist. And being a novelist, I consider myself superior to the saint, the scientist, the philosopher, and the poet, who are all great masters of different bits of man alive, but never get the whole hog. [*Ib.* 'Why the Novel Matters']

1 Only in the novel are *all* things given full play. [*Ib.*]

2 My destiny has been cast among cocksure women. Perhaps when man begins to doubt himself, woman, who should be nice and peacefully hen-sure, becomes instead insistently cocksure. She develops convictions, or she catches them. And then woe betide everybody. [*Ib.* 'Women are so Cocksure']

3 To every man who struggles with his own soul in mystery, a book that is a book flowers once, and seeds, and is gone. [*Ib.* A Bibliography of D.H.L.]

4 One realizes with horror, that the race of men is almost extinct in Europe. Only Christ-like heroes and woman-worshipping Don Juans, and rabid equality-mongrels. [*Sea and Sardinia*, Ch. 3]

5 To the Puritan all things are impure. [*Etruscan Places*]

6 Whatever the sun may be, it is certainly not a ball of flaming gas. [Quoted in Ogden and Richards, *Meaning of Meaning*]

7 I think more of a bird with broad wings flying and lapsing through the air, than anything, when I think of metre. [Letter to Edward Marsh, Nov. 1913]

8 I like to write when I feel spiteful; it's like having a good sneeze. [Letter to Lady Cynthia Asquith, Nov. 1913]

9 The ordinary novel would trace the history of the diamond – but I say, 'Diamond, what! This is carbon.' And my diamond may be coal or soot and my theme is carbon. [Letter to Edward Garnett, 5 June 1914]

10 I cannot get any sense of an enemy – only of a disaster. [Letter to Edward Marsh, Autumn 1914]

11 I am tired of being told there is no such animal by animals who are merely different. [Letter to J. Middleton Murry, 20 May 1929]

12 Individuals do not *vitally* concern me any more. Only a *purpose* vitally concerns me. [Letter to Lady Ottoline Morrell, 29 July 1915]

13 Nothing is more painful than to be plunged back into the world of the past, when that past is irrevocably gone by, and a new thing far away is struggling to come to life in one. [Letter to Lady Cynthia Asquith, 24 Dec. 1915]

14 They are great parables, the novels [Dostoyevsky's], but false art. They are only parables. All the people are *fallen angels* – even the dirtiest scrubs. This I cannot stomach. People are not fallen angels, they are merely people. [Letter to J. Middleton Murry and Katherine Mansfield, 17 Feb. 1916]

15 Now it is time for us to leave our Christian-democratic epoch, as it was time for Europe in Michael Angelo's day to leave the Christian-aristocratic epoch. But we cannot leap away, we slip back. [Letter to Lady Ottoline Morrell, 7 April 1916]

16 I am only half there when I am ill, and so there is only half a man to suffer. To suffer in one's whole self is so great a violation, that it is not to be endured.

[Letter to Catherine Carswell, 16 April 1916]

17 One has a certain order inviolable in one's soul. There one sits, as in a crow's nest, out of it all. . . . Life mustn't be taken seriously any more, at least the outer, social life. The social being I am has become a spectator at a knockabout dangerous farce. [Letter to Lady Cynthia Asquith, 26 April 1916]

18 I think people ought to fulfil sacredly their desires. And this means fulfilling the deepest desire, which is a desire to live unhampered by things that are extraneous, a desire for pure relationships and living truth. [Letter to Catherine Carswell, 16 July 1916]

19 I'm not sure if a mental relation with a woman doesn't make it impossible to love her. To know the *mind* of a woman is to end in hating her. Love means the pre-cognitive flow . . . it is the honest state before the apple. [Letter to Dr Trigant Burrow, 3 Aug. 1927]

T. E. LAWRENCE

20 All men dream: but not equally. Those who dream by night in the dusty recesses of their minds wake in the day to find that it was vanity: but the dreamers of the day are dangerous men, for they may act their dream with open eyes, to make it possible. [*Seven Pillars of Wisdom*, Ch. 1]

21 We were a self-centred army without parade or gesture, devoted to freedom, the second of man's creeds, a purpose so ravenous that it devoured all our strength, a hope so transcendent that our earlier ambitions faded in its glare. [*Ib.*]

22 Before me lay a vista of responsibility and command, which disgusted my thought-riddled nature. I felt mean to fill the place of a man of action; for my standards of value were a wilful reaction against theirs, and I despised their happiness. [*Ib.* XLVIII]

23 Many men would take the death-sentence without a whimper to escape the life-sentence which fate carries in her other hand. [*The Mint*, Pt I, Ch. 4]

24 The trumpets came out brazenly with the last post. . . . Our eyes smarted against our wills. A man hates to be moved to folly by a noise. [*Ib.* Pt III, Ch. 9]

25 I meant once to write a book on the background of Christ ... Galilee and Syria, social, intellectual and artistic of 40 B.C. It would make an interesting book. As good as Renan's *Life of Jesus* should have been, if only he had had the wit to leave out the central figure. [Letter to Sir Herbert Baker, 20 Jan. 1928]

26 I fancy, for myself, that they are rather out of touch with reality; by reality I mean shops like Selfridges, and motor buses, and the *Daily Express* [Of James Joyce and fellow expatriate authors in Paris. Letter to W. Hurley, 1 Apr. 1929]

27 I'm re-reading it [*Lady Chatterley's Lover*] with a slow deliberate carelessness. [Letter to Edward Marsh, 18 Apr. 1929]

28 In some ways it's a horrible little book. Like over-brewed tea. [*Ib*. Of *The Mint*]

STEPHEN LEACOCK

29 The classics are only primitive literature. They belong in the same class as primitive machinery and primitive music and primitive medicine. [*Homer and Humbug*]

30 A single room is that which has no parts and no magnitude. [*Literary Lapses*, 'Boarding-House Geometry']

31 Any two meals at a boarding-house are together less than two square meals. [*Ib*.]

32 The pleasure of getting out of a cold bed and creeping into a hot bath beats a cold plunge to death. [*Ib*. 'How to Live to be 200']

33 Get your room full of good air, then shut up the windows and keep it. It will keep for years. Anyway, don't keep using your lungs all the time. Let them rest. [*Ib*.]

34 The more we mix together the better I like the things we mix. [*Ib*. 'How to Make a Million Dollars']

35 I detest life-insurance agents; they always argue that I shall some day die, which is not so. [*Ib*. 'Insurance Up to Date']

36 The great man ... walks across his century and leaves the marks of his feet all over it, ripping out the dates on his goloshes as he passes. [*Ib*. 'The Life of John Smith']

37 Astronomy teaches the correct use of the sun and the planets. [*Ib*. 'A Manual of Education']

38 There are no handles to a horse, but the 1910 model has a string to each side of its face for turning its head when there is anything you want it to see. [*Ib*. 'Reflections on Riding']

39 It takes a good deal of physical courage to ride a horse. This, however, I have. I get it at about forty cents a flask, and take it as required. [*Ib*.]

40 Broad, comfortable waistcoats, a yard and a half round the equator. [*Ib*. 'Self-Made Men']

F. R. LEAVIS

41 The only way to escape misrepresentation is never to commit oneself to any critical judgement that makes an impact – that is, never *say* anything. [*The Great Tradition*, Ch. 1]

42 Poetry can communicate the actual quality of experience with a subtlety and precision unapproachable by any other means. But if the poetry and the intelligence of the age lose touch with each other, poetry will cease to matter much and the age will be lacking in finer awareness. [*New Bearings in English Poetry*, Ch. 1]

43 He [Rupert Brooke] energized the Garden-Suburb ethos with a certain original talent and the vigour of a prolonged adolescence. [*Ib*.]

44 The question 'This is so, isn't it?' expecting the answer 'Yes, but –' [Lectures, *passim*]

45 The accepted valuations are a sort of paper currency based upon a very small proportion of gold. To the state of such a currency the possibilities of fine living at any time bear a close relation. [*Mass Civilization and Minority Culture*]

FRED W. LEIGH

46 Tiddley-om-Pom! [Title of music hall song]

HARPER LEE

47 Being Southerners, it was a source of shame to some members of the family that we had no recorded ancestors on either side of the Battle of Hastings. [*To Kill a Mockingbird*, Pt I, Ch. 1]

48 Shoot all the bluejays you want, if you can hit 'em, but remember it's a sin to kill a mockingbird. [*Ib.* II. 10]

49 Everybody in Maycomb, it seemed, had a streak: a Drinking Streak, a Gambling Streak, a Mean Streak, a Funny Streak. [*Ib.* II. 12]

LAURIE LEE

50 Effie M. was a monster. Six foot high and as strong as a farm horse. No sooner had she decided that she wanted Uncle Tom than she knocked him off his bicycle and told him. [*Cider with Rosie*, 'The Uncles']

THÉO LEFÈVRE [Belgium Prime Minister]

51 In Western Europe there are now only small countries – those that know it and those that don't know it yet. [*Observer*, 'Sayings of the Year', 1963]

SIR FREDERICK LEITH-ROSS

52 Inflation is like sin; every government denounces it and every government practises it. [*Observer*, 'Sayings of the Week', 30 June 1957]

C. A. LEJEUNE

53 A real regular English home it is, just like yours or mine, or Mr Anthony Eden's, with a Great Dane on the hearthrug, yards of mullion round the windows, and Miss Marlene Dietrich sleeping in the best bedroom. [*Observer* 'Dietrich as an Angel', quoted in Stephen Potter, *Sense of Humour*, Ch. 3]

VLADIMIR I. LENIN

54 If it were necessary to give the briefest possible definition of imperialism we should have to say that imperialism is the monopoly stage of capitalism. [*Imperialism, the Highest Stage of Capitalism*, Ch. 7]

55 We can (and must) begin to build up Socialism, not with the fantastic human material especially created by our imagination, but with the material bequeathed us by Capitalism. ['*Left-Wing*' *Communism*, Ch. 6]

56 History generally, and the history of revolutions in particular, is always richer in content, more varied, more many-sided, more lively and more 'subtle' than even the best parties and the most class-conscious vanguards of the most advanced classes imagine. [*Ib.* 10]

57 One step forward, two steps back. . . . It happens in the lives of individuals, and it happens in the history of nations and in the development of parties. [*One Step Forward, Two Steps Back*]

58 In its struggle for power the proletariat has no other weapon but organization. [*Ib.*]

59 Under capitalism we have a state in the proper sense of the word, that is, a special machine for the suppression of one class by another. [*The State and Revolution*, Ch. V, sect. ii]

60 A bourgeois revolution is *absolutely* necessary in the interests of the proletariat. The more complete, determined and consistent the bourgeois revolution, the more assured will be the proletarian struggle against the bourgeoisie for Socialism. [*Two Tactics of Social-Democracy*, Ch. 6]

61 'A decisive victory of the revolution over tsarism' is the *revolutionary-democratic dictatorship of the proletariat and the peasantry.* [*Ib.*]

62 A Social-Democrat must never forget that the proletariat will inevitably have to wage a class struggle for Socialism even against the most democratic and republican bourgeoisie and petty bourgeoisie. [*Ib.* 10]

63 Revolutionary Social-Democracy always included, and now includes, the fight for reforms in its activities. But it utilizes 'economic' agitation for the purpose of presenting to the government, not only demands for all sorts of measures, but also (and primarily) the demand that it cease to be an autocratic government. [*What is to be Done?*, Ch. 3, sect. A]

64 We must have a committee of professional *revolutionaries*. [*Ib.* 4. C]

65 We are passing from the sphere of history to the sphere of the present and partly to the sphere of the future. [*Ib.* 'Conclusions']

66 To proclaim in advance the dying away of the state will be a violation of historical perspective. [Said at 7th Party Congress, March 1918]

67 A good man fallen among Fabians. [Attr. remark about Bernard Shaw]

JOHN LENNON

68 It was strange for a man whom have everything and a wife to boot. [*In His Own Write*, 'A Sad Michael']

69 A typical quimmty old hag who spread these vile ruperts was Mrs Weatherby – a widow by her first husbands. [*Ib.* 'Victor Triumphs']

70 Yea, though I wart through the valet of thy shadowy hut I will feed no norman. [*Ib.* 'No Flies on Frank']

71 His wife, a former beauty queer, regarded him with a strange but burly look. [*Ib.*]

72 Hanyway he carried on putting ub the desicrations and muzzletoe. [*Ib.* 'Randolf's Party']

73 For the past 17 years the fabled fibe had been forming into adventures on varicose islands and secrete vallets with their famous ill bred dog. [*Ib.* 'The Famous Five']

74 'Belay there me 'earty scabs,' says Large John Saliver entering. [*Ib.* 'Treasure Ivan']

75 That seems to be the crutch of the matter. [*Ib.* 'The Fingeltoad Resort']

76 It was something special, a day amongst days ... a red lettuce day. [*Ib.* 'Nicely Nicely Clive']

77 Jumble Jim, whom shall remain nameless, was slowly but slowly asking his way through the underpants. [*Ib.* 'On Safairy']

DAN LENO

78 I see the world as a football, kicked about by the higher powers, with me clinging on by my teeth and toenails to the laces. [Quoted in Desmond MacCarthy, *Theatre*]

79 For five and twenty years I've had my eye on Jim, / And if he won't marry me, I'll marry him. [Song: *I'll Marry Him*]

ALAN JAY LERNER

80 An Englishman's way of speaking absolutely classifies him / The moment he talks he makes some other Englishman despise him. [*My Fair Lady*, I, i]

81 All I want is a room somewhere, / Far away from the cold night air; / With one enormous chair ... / Oh, wouldn't it be loverly? [*Ib.*]

82 They're always throwin' goodness at you / But with a little bit of luck / A man can duck! [*Ib.* I. ii]

83 I'd be equally as willing / For a dentist to be drilling / Than to ever let a woman in my life. [*Ib.*]

84 Just you wait, 'enry 'iggins, just you wait! / You'll be sorry but your tears will be too late! [*Ib.*]

85 There he was, that hairy hounde / From Budapest. / Never leaving us alone, / Never have I ever known / A ruder pest. [*Ib.* II. i]

86 Oozing charm from every pore, / He oiled his way around the floor. [*Ib.*]

87 Don't talk of June! / Don't talk of fall! / Don't talk at all! / Show me! [*Ib.* II. ii]

88 I'm getting married in the morning! / Ding dong! the bells are gonna chime. / Pull out the stopper! / Let's have a whopper! / But get me to the church on time! [*Ib.* II. iii]

89 Why can't a woman be more like a man? / Men are so honest, so thoroughly square; / Eternally noble, historically fair. [*Ib.* II. iv]

90 I've grown accustomed to the trace / Of something in the air, / Accustomed to her face. [*Ib.* II. vi]

DORIS LESSING

1 When old settlers say 'One has to understand the country,' what they mean is, 'You have to get used to our ideas about the native.' They are saying, in effect, 'Learn our ideas, or otherwise get out; we don't want you.' [*The Grass is Singing*, Ch. 1]

2 When a white man in Africa by accident looks into the eyes of a native and sees the human being (which it is his chief preoccupation to avoid), his sense of guilt, which he denies, fumes up in resentment and he brings down the whip. [*Ib.* 8]

ALFRED LESTER

3 Call out the Boys of the Old Brigade, / Who made Old England free – / Call out my Mother, my Sister and my Brother, / But for God's sake don't send me! [*Conscientious Objector's Lament*]

W. R. LETHABY

4 Art is not a special sauce applied to ordinary cooking; it is the cooking itself if it is good. [*Form in Civilization*, 'Art and Workmanship']

5 Art is thoughtful workmanship. [*Ib.*]

ADA LEVERSON

6 It is an infallible sign of the second-rate in nature and intellect to make use of everything and everyone. [*The Limit*]

7 But she could carry off anything; and some people said that she did. [*The Little Otleys*]

8 People were not charmed with Eglantine because she herself was charming, but because she was charmed. [*Love at Second Sight*]

9 You don't know a woman until you have had a letter from her. [*Tenterhooks*]

10 'No hurry, no hurry,' said Sir James, with that air of self-denial that conveys the urgent necessity of intense speed. [*The Twelfth Hour*, Ch. 2]

11 He pondered a few moments about nothing whatever. [*Ib.*]

12 Before he left, Aunt William pressed a sovereign into his hand, as if it were conscience money. He, on his side, took it as though it were a doctor's fee, and both ignored the transaction. [*Ib.* 4]

13 He had a triangular face, the details of which were vague though the outline was clear, like a negative that had been left too long in the sun. [*Ib.* 5]

14 Ridokanaki looked at the clock. It immediately struck ten, tactfully, in a clear subdued tone. [*Ib.* 9]

15 One really rare possession she certainly had – a husband who, notwithstanding that he felt a mild dislike for her merely, bullied her and interfered with her quite as much as if he were wildly in love. [*Ib.* 13]

16 [When told by Wilde that a devoted *apache* used to follow him about Paris with a knife in his hand] I'm sure he had a fork in the other. [Attr.]

C. S. LEWIS

17 There is wishful thinking in Hell as well as on earth. [*The Screwtape Letters*, Preface]

18 I have known a human defended from strong temptations to social ambition by a still stronger taste for tripe and onions. [*Ib.* 13]

19 Gratitude looks to the past and love to the present; fear, avarice, lust and ambition look ahead. [*Ib.* 15]

20 He's vulgar, Wormwood. He has a vulgar mind. [Of God. *Ib.* 22]

21 The Future is something which everyone reaches at the rate of sixty minutes an hour, whatever he does, whoever he is. [*Ib.* 25]

22 If people knew how much ill-feeling Unselfishness occasions, it would not be so often recommended from the pulpit. [*Ib.* 26]

23 She's the sort of woman who lives for others – you can always tell the others by their hunted expression. [*Ib.*]

24 The long, dull, monotonous years of middle-aged prosperity or middle-aged adversity are excellent campaigning weather [for the Devil]. [*Ib.* 27]

25 Fatigue makes women talk more and men less. [*Ib.* 30]

26 Humanity does not pass through phases as a train passes through stations: being alive, it has the privilege of always moving yet never leaving anything behind. [*The Allegory of Love*, Ch. 1]

27 We can never know that a piece of writing is bad unless we have begun by trying to read it as if it was very good and ended

by discovering that we were paying the author an undeserved compliment. [*An Experiment in Criticism*, Ch. 4]

28 Friendship is unnecessary, like philosophy, like art.... It has no survival value; rather it is one of those things that give value to survival. [*The Four Loves*, 'Friendship']

29 The coarse joke proclaims that we have here an animal which finds its own animality either objectionable or funny. [*Miracles*]

30 Shall we perhaps, in Purgatory, see our own faces and hear our own voices as they really were? [*Reflections on the Psalms*, Ch. 1]

SIR GEORGE CORNEWALL LEWIS

31 Life would be tolerable, were it not for its amusements. [Quoted in Sagittarius and George, *The Perpetual Pessimist*]

JOHN L. LEWIS

32 I'm not interested in classes. ... Far be it from me to foster inferiority complexes among the workers by trying to make them think they belong to some special class. That has happened in Europe but it hasn't happened here yet. [Quoted in A. M. Schlesinger Jr, *The Coming of the New Deal*, Pt 7, Ch. 25, sect. viii]

SINCLAIR LEWIS

33 He was nimble in the calling of selling houses for more than people could afford to pay. [*Babbitt*, Ch. 1]

34 In fact there was but one thing wrong with the Babbitt house: it was not a home. [*Ib.* 2]

35 The first thing you got to understand is that all this uplift and flipflop and settlement-work and recreation is nothing on God's world but the entering wedge for socialism. [*Ib.*]

36 To George F. Babbitt ... his motor-car was poetry and tragedy, love and heroism. The office was his pirate ship, but the car his perilous excursion ashore. [*Ib.* 3]

37 A thing called Ethics, whose nature was confusing, but if you had it you were a

High-class Realtor, and if you hadn't you were a shyster, a piker, and a fly-by-night. [*Ib.* 4]

38 In other countries, art and literature are left to a lot of shabby bums living in attics and feeding on booze and spaghetti, but in America the successful writer or picture-painter is indistinguishable from any other decent business man. [*Ib.* 14]

39 She did her work with the thoroughness of a mind that reveres details and never quite understands them. [*Ib.* 18]

40 Our American professors like their literature clear and cold and pure and very dead. [Address on *The American Fear of Literature*, given in Stockholm on receiving the Nobel Prize, 12 Dec. 1930]

D. B. WYNDHAM LEWIS

41 Now welcomed, now expelled with angry shrieks, / Plied with champagne, or gnawed by wayward Pekes: / Be this their guerdon in a glorious cause – / They loved the Rich, whom all the world abhors. [*Paean*]

42 I am one of those unfortunates to whom death is less hideous than explanations. [*Welcome to All This*]

PERCY WYNDHAM LEWIS

43 The Vorticist does not suck up to Life. He lets Life know its place in a Vorticist universe. [*Blast*, 'Vorticist Manifesto']

44 *Where any sex-nuisance is concerned, the Greek indifference is the best specific.* For with regard to anything that is likely to obsess a society, it is of importance not to give it too much advertisement. [*Time and Western Man*, Pt I, Ch. 3]

45 Fundamentally all the tide of thought today, however broken up into a confusing network of channels, is setting towards the pole of Sensation. [*Ib.* Bk I, Ch. 1]

46 The revolutionary simpleton is everywhere. [*Ib.* Bk I, Ch. VI]

47 People are so overwhelmed with the prestige of their instruments that they consider their personal judgement of hardly any account. [*Ib.* Bk II, Pt I, Ch. 1]

48 If you want to know what is actually occurring *inside*, underneath, at the centre, at any given moment, art is a truer guide than 'politics', more often than not. [*Ib.* Appendix]

49 I ... believe ... that people should be compelled to be freer and more 'individualistic' than they naturally desire to be. ... I believe they could with advantage be compelled to remain absolutely alone for several hours every day; and a week's solitary confinement ... every two months, would be an excellent provision. [*Ib.*]

50 You persisted for a certain number of years like a stammer. You were a *stammer*, if you like, of Space-Time. [*The Human Age*, Bk I: *The Childermass*]

51 If you must go nowhere, step out. [*Ib.* closing words]

52 The British bar-shrimp was brought upon its finger of damp toast, from its circular glasscase. [*The Apes of God*, Pt II]

53 It is to what I have called the Apes of God that I am drawing your attention – *those prosperous mountebanks who alternately imitate and mock at and traduce those figures they at once admire and hate.* [*Ib.* III]

54 The SPLIT-MAN ... went on croaking harshly and merrily. His countenance was lighted with the sultry covetousness of the dung-fly. [*Ib.* XI]

55 She's an old heiress and has married *herself*, as it were – she's a bachelor-bride. From birth she has been lesbian. [*Ib.* XII]

56 Dozens of Americans do time as a matter of course now – they won't let them into America when they want to go back if they haven't! – I mean won't let them into the best literocriminal New York circles. The ticket-of-leave is as important as the passport. [*Ib.*]

57 The soul started at the knee-cap and ended at the navel. [*Ib.*]

58 This is God's own Peterpaniest family! [*Ib.*]

59 Oh yes Colonel – *do* tell us how you were killed at Colense again! [*Ib.*]

60 The ossature is my favourite part of a living animal organism, not its intestines. [*Men Without Art*]

61 I said (and I always say these things with the same voice) / 'Say it with locomotives ...' [*One-Way Song*]

62 I am rather like what Mr Shaw would have been like if he had been an artist. ... (He said he was a finer fellow than Shakespeare. I merely prefer myself to Mr Shaw.) [*Blasting and Bombardiering*]

63 The revolutionary state of mind is then, today, instinctive: the *all that is is bad, and to be superseded by a better* attitude. [*The Art of Being Ruled*, Pt I, Ch. 1]

64 'Dying for an idea,' again, sounds well enough, but why not let the idea die instead of you? [*Ib.*]

65 The delusion of impersonality could best be defined as the mistake by virtue of which persons are enabled to masquerade as *things*. [*Ib.* I. 6]

66 I believe that (in one form or another) castration may be the solution. And the feminization of the white European and American is already far advanced, coming in the wake of the war. [*Ib.* II. 2]

67 Sadistic excess attempts to reach roughly and by harshness what art reaches by fineness. [*Ib.* II. 4]

68 Absence of responsibility, an automatic and stereotyped rhythm, is what men most desire for themselves. All struggle has for its end relief or repose. [*Ib.* V. 2]

69 The *refusal to grow up* of Peter Pan was the specific found by the narquois mind of the Zeitgeist for the increasing difficulties connected *with* growing up. [*Ib.* VI. 4]

70 The 'homo' is the legitimate child of the 'suffragette'. [*Ib.* VIII. 4]

71 Try as women will to *engarçonner* themselves, to 'reduce' and 'reduce' till they can pass as a diminutive male adolescent, they cannot entirely banish the reflection, in those for whom they perform these feats, that they are nature's agents imitating their betters by a sleight of hand. [*Ib.* IX. 1]

72 There was a Greek proverb to the effect that *it was easier to hide five elephants under one's arm than one pathic.* [*Ib.* IX. 7]

73 The goitrous torpid and squinting husks provided by Matisse in his sculpture are worthless except as tactful decorations for a mental home. [*Ib.* XII. 7]

74 It is easy to understand how a machine which has taken to thinking, like Man, should develop hysteria in contemplating itself, and have a laughing fit about its hearing holes, its smelling and breathing holes, its intestinal barrel on legs. [On 'Calder's Mobiles' in the *Listener*, 18 Jan. 1951]

TRYGVE LEE
[Secretary of United Nations]

75 Now we are in a period which I can characterize as a period of cold peace. [*Observer*, 'Sayings of the Week', 21 Aug. 1949]

MAX LIEBERMANN

76 [To a portrait-painter who complained that he could not draw von Hindenburg's features] *Ich kann den Alten in den Schnee pissen.* – I can piss the old boy in the snow. [Quoted in Igor Stravinsky and Robert Craft, *Conversations with Stravinsky*]

KARL LIEBNECHT

77 We are fighting for the gates of heaven. [In the abortive German revolution, 1918–19. Quoted in Albert Camus, *The Rebel*, Ch. 3]

A. J. LIEBLING

78 Summer clothes in the North are make-shifts, like seasonal slipcovers on furniture, and look it. [*The Earl of Louisiana*]

N. VACHEL LINDSAY

79 It is portentous, and a thing of state / That here at midnight, in our little town / A mourning figure walks, and will not rest, / Near the old courthouse pacing up and down. [*Abraham Lincoln Walks at Midnight*]

80 And who will bring white peace / That he may sleep upon his hill again? [*Ib.*]

81 Fat black bucks in a wine-barrel room, / Barrel-house kings with feet unstable, / Sagged and reeled and pounded on the table. [*The Congo*]

82 Booth died blind and still by faith he trod, / Eyes still dazzled by the ways of God. [*General William Booth enters Heaven*]

ERIC LINKLATER

83 With a heavy step Sir Matthew left the room and spent the morning designing mausoleums for his enemies. [*Juan in America*, Prologue]

84 He preferred the lady to cricket – though he was an accomplished bat and, like his father, fielded boldly at cover-point; and she found him more comforting than cards – though she played very good bridge indeed. [*Ib.*]

85 It is notorious that we speak no more than half-truths in our ordinary conversation, and even a soliloquy is likely to be affected by the apprehension that walls have ears. [Bk II, Ch. 4]

86 I've been married six months. She looks like a million dollars, but she only knows a hundred and twenty words and she's only got two ideas in her head. The other one's hats. [*Ib.* II. 5]

87 There was ... a historian interested in British Colonial Administration. His advisers had instructed him to begin at the beginning, and he had therefore commenced a study of the duties of the Officers of the Household in the court of King Alfred the Great. [*Ib.* II. 9]

88 Buddy Hambone conducted after an epileptic fashion. His feet shuffled, his knees bent and straightened, his body writhed, his arms flapped widely, and his head jerked backwards and forwards like a vulture tearing gobbets from a carrion carcass. [*Ib.* III. 2]

89 I hear other professional men complaining, but I assure you there is no sign of depression among us morticians. Our parlours, I'm thankful to say, are never empty. [*Ib.* V. 1]

90 I was always fond of flowers. . . . I guess that influenced me in the choice of a profession, for a mortician's life is full of flowers. Flowers and beauty. [*Ib.*]

1 'There won't be any revolution in America,' said Isadore. Nikitin agreed. 'The people are too clean. They spend all their time changing their shirts and wash-

ing themselves. You can't feel fierce and revolutionary in a bathroom.' [*Ib*. V. 3]

2 'I dislike burdens,' said Juan, 'and at my back I often hear Time's winged chariot changing gear.' [*Juan in China*]

3 Here, with foul shirts and fouler breath, were Mars' heroes. Kings had fallen and nations perished, armies had withered and cities been ruined for this and this alone: that poor men in stinking pubs might have great wealth of memory. [*Magnus Merriman*]

4 As the father of seven sons he had insisted on the youngest being christened Saturday. [*Poet's Pub*, Ch. I]

5 Feng was the most fascinating person I ever painted. . . . He made improper proposals to me through an interpreter. They called him the Christian general. [*Ib.*]

6 All I've got against it [golf] is that it takes you so far from the club house. [*Ib.* 3]

7 Helen discovered that she was almost alone, among all her other friends, in never having been married or never having written a book. She decided that the second choice would probably have less permanent consequences. [*Ib.* 13]

8 He had all the confidence which an American motorist in England naturally has, and which comes from the knowledge that England is only a little island where one cannot go seriously out of one's way. [*Ib.* 22]

9 Authors and uncaptured criminals . . . are the only people free from routine. [*Ib.* 23]

10 'My dear,' said Saturday. 'My dear,' she answered; Venus's birds being parrots as often as doves. [*Ib.* 25]

LORD LLOYD

11 There never has been a British refugee. [1939. *Observer*, 'Sayings of Our Times', 31 May 1953]

DAVID, EARL LLOYD GEORGE

12 You cannot feed the hungry on statistics. [Speech, 1904, on Tariff Reform, quoted in Malcolm Thomson, *David Lloyd George*, Ch. 8]

13 A fully equipped Duke costs as much to keep up as two Dreadnoughts, and Dukes are just as great a terror, and they last longer. [Speech on the Budget of 1909]

14 You cannot trust the interests of any class entirely to another class; and you cannot trust the interests of any sex entirely to another sex. [Speech on Women's Suffrage, 1911, quoted in Thomson, op. cit., 9]

15 Every man has a House of Lords in his own head. Fears, prejudices, misconceptions – those are the peers, and they are hereditary. [Speech at Cambridge, 1927]

16 The world is becoming like a lunatic asylum run by lunatics. [1933. *Observer*, 'Sayings of Our Times', 31 May 1953]

17 If we are going in without the help of Russia we are walking into a trap. [Speech in House of Commons, 3 Apr. 1939]

18 Without Russia these three guarantees to Poland, to Roumania and to Greece are the most reckless commitments that any country has ever entered. [Speech, May 1939]

19 Poor Bonar can't bear being called a liar. Now I don't mind. [Quoted in G. M. Young, *Baldwin*]

20 He [Neville Chamberlain] saw foreign policy through the wrong end of a municipal drainpipe. [Quoted in Harris, *The Fine Art of Political Wit*, Ch. 6]

21 The Right Hon. gentleman [Sir John Simon] has sat so long on the fence that the iron has entered his soul. [Attr. in speech in House of Commons]

22 Doctrinaires are the vultures of principle. They feed upon principle after it is dead. [Quoted by Dingle Foot in *Guardian*, 17 Jan. 1963]

23 I am opposed to Titanic seamanship in politics and as an old mariner I would not drive the ship on to the ice floes that have drifted into our seas from the frozen wastes of the Tory past. [Quoted in *ib.*]

24 May I ask of Protestants and Catholics alike that in these days of rejoicing [Christmas] we shall not forget the pitiful Madonna of the Slums with her pallid children. [Speech in London, 18 Dec. 1925]

SIR OLIVER LODGE

25 This Universe must not fail. [Attr.]

CHRISTOPHER LOGUE

26 Nothing was left of Hector's raid except / Loose smoke-swaths drifting over the Aegean like dark hair, / And the ditch stained perfect crimson where / Some outraged god, five miles tall, had stamped on glass. [*Patrocleia*]

27 He speared the boy, and with his hip as pivot / Prised Thestor out of the chariot's basket / As easily as lesser men / Detach a sardine from an open tin. [*Ib.*]

28 For example, he [Brecht] composed / Plays that staged by us promote / All the values he opposed. [*Christopher Logue's ABC*, 'B']

29 I was among two thousand million. I read amusing books, / When nine-tenths of the rest had not been taught to read. [*Ib.* 'I']

30 Said Marx: 'Don't be snobbish, we seek to abolish / The 3rd Class, not the 1st.' [*Ib.* 'M']

A. LOISY

31 I am glad I was able to keep my vow of celibacy [after his excommunication]; otherwise it might have been used as an argument for the apostolic authorship of the Fourth Gospel or the Mosaic authorship of the Pentateuch. [Quoted in H. P. V. Nunn, *What is Modernism?*]

GINA LOLLOBRIGIDA

32 Glamour is when a man knows a woman is a woman. [*Observer*, 'Sayings of the Week', 15 July 1956]

JACK LONDON

33 The certain weak and delicate prettiness which characterizes the cockney lasses, a prettiness which is no more than a promise with no grip on time, and doomed to fade quickly away like the colour from a sunset sky. [*The People of the Abyss*, Ch. 2]

34 In an English ship, they say, it is poor grub, poor pay, and easy work; in an American ship, good grub, good pay, and hard work. And this is applicable to the working populations of both countries. [*Ib.* 20]

HUEY LONG

35 I looked around at the little fishes present, and said 'I'm the Kingfish.' [Quoted in A. M. Schlesinger Jr, *The Politics of Upheaval*, Bk I, Ch. 4, sect. v]

LORD LONGFORD

36 The male sex still constitute in many ways the most obstinate vested interest one can find. [Speech in House of Lords, 23 June 1963]

37 On the whole I would not say that our Press is obscene. I would say that it trembles on the brink of obscenity. [*Observer*, 'Sayings of the Year', 1963]

38 No sex without responsibility. [*Observer*, 'Sayings of the Week', 3 May 1964]

ANITA LOOS

39 Gentlemen always seem to remember blondes. [*Gentlemen Prefer Blondes*, Ch. 1]

40 So this gentleman said a girl with brains ought to do something else with them besides think. [*Ib.*]

41 Paris is devine. I mean Dorothy and I got to Paris yesterday, and it really is devine. Because the French are devine. [*Ib.*]

42 I think money is on the way out. [*Observer*, 'Sayings of the Week' 24 June 1956]

LYDIA LOPOKOVA
[LADY KEYNES]

43 I dislike being in the country in August, because my legs get so bitten by barristers. [Attr. Quoted in Robert L. Heilbroner, *The Worldly Philosophers*, Ch. 9]

LORD LOTHIAN

44 After all they are only going into their own back garden. [Comment on Hitler's military reoccupation of the Rhineland, 1936. Quoted in Winston S. Churchill, *The Gathering Storm*, Ch. 11]

ROBERT LOWELL

45 Yours the lawlessness / of something simple that has lost its law. [*Caligula*]

46 The man is killing time – there's nothing else. [*The Drinker*]

47 Terrible that old life of decency / without unseemly intimacy / or quarrels, when the unemancipated woman / still had her Freudian papa and maids! [*During Fever*]

48 This is death / To die and know it. This is the Black Widow, death. [*Mr Edwards and the Spider*]

49 They died / When time was open-eyed, / Wooden and childish; only bones abide / There, in the nowhere, where their boats were tossed / Sky-high, where mariners had fabled news / of IS, the whited monster. [*The Quaker Graveyard in Nantucket*]

50 The Lord survives the rainbow of His will. [*Ib.*]

51 Gored by the climacteric of his want, / he stalls above me like an elephant. [*To Speak of the Woe that is in Marriage*]

MALCOLM LOWRY

52 How many patterns of life were based on kindred misconceptions, how many wolves do we feel on our heels, while our real enemies go in sheepskin by. [*Under the Volcano*, Ch. 7]

53 Where are the children I might have had? You may suppose I might have wanted them. Drowned to the accompaniment of the rattling of a thousand douche bags. [*Ib.* 10]

54 How alike are the groans of love to those of the dying. [*Ib.* 12]

F. L. LUCAS

55 Human temperaments are too diverse; we can never agree how drunk we like our art to be. [*Literature and Psychology*, Ch. 10]

56 Soul is more than syntax. If your readers dislike you, they will dislike what you say. Indeed, such is human nature, unless they like you they will mostly deny you even human justice. [*Style*, Ch. 2]

57 In some modern literature there has appeared a tendency to replace communication by a private maundering to oneself which shall inspire one's audience to maunder privately to *themselves* – rather as if the author handed round a box of drugged cigarettes. [*Ib.*]

DOCTOR KARL LUEGER
[Mayor of Vienna]

58 *Wissenschaft is' wos a Jud' vom andern anschreibt.* – Science is what one Jew copies from another. [Quoted *Sunday Times*, 12 June 1966]

59 I decide who is a Jew. [Quoted in Alan Bullock, *Hitler*, Ch. 1, sect. i]

SIR EDWIN LUTYENS

60 The answer is in the plural and they bounce. [Before a Royal Commission. Attr.]

61 This piece of cod passes all understanding. [Attr. remark in restaurant]

LADY LYTTON

62 The first time you meet Winston [Churchill] you see all his faults and the rest of your life you spend in discovering his virtues. [Quoted in Christopher Hassall, *Edward Marsh*, Ch. 7]

M

GENERAL MacARTHUR

1 I shall return. [On leaving the Philippines, 11 March 1942]

ROSE MACAULAY

2 Poem me no poems. [*Poetry Review*, Autumn 1963]

3 Here is one of the points about this planet which should be remembered; into every penetrable corner of it, and into most of the impenetrable corners, the English will penetrate. [*Crewe Train*, Pt I, Ch. 1]

4 Gentlemen know that fresh air should be kept in its proper place – out of doors – and that, God having given us indoors and out-of-doors, we should not attempt to do away with this distinction. [*Ib.* I. 5]

5 Aunt Evelyn's cheek was colossal. She probably laboured under the common delusion that you made things better by talking about them. [*Ib.* I. 12]

6 Love's a disease. But curable. ... Did you ever look through a microscope at a drop of pond water? You see plenty of love there. All the amoebae getting married. I presume they think it very exciting and important. We don't. [*Ib.* I. 13]

7 The more intelligent a woman is, the more brains she ought to bring to bear on her home. The Oxford and Cambridge colleges are excellent training schools for housewives. [*Ib.* II. 6]

A. C. McAULIFFE

8 Nuts! [Reply to German demand to surrender Bastogne, 22 Dec. 1944]

GEORGE MacBETH

9 To leave great themes unfinished is / Perhaps the most satisfying exercise / Of power. [*The Spider's Nest*]

DESMOND MacCARTHY

10 When I meet those remarkable people whose company is coveted, I often wish they would show off a little more. [*Theatre*, 'Good Talk']

11 You understand *Epipsychidion* best when you are in love; *Don Juan* when anger is subsiding into indifference. Why not Strindberg when you have a temperature? [*Ib.* 'Miss Julie and The Pariah']

12 Your sensations during fever are nearly indistinguishable from pleasant ones, and yet there is a mockery about them all. ... You are consumed with the most promising thirst; there at your elbow stands the long, cool drink. You drink. What an uncanny and distressing disproportion appears between the glorious magnitude of that craving and the tiny satisfaction it brings! [*Ib.*]

13 The whole of art is an appeal to a reality which is not without us but in our minds. [*Ib.* 'Modern Drama']

14 It [Post-Impressionist painting] may ... appear ridiculous to those who do not recall the fact that a good rocking-horse has often more of the true horse about it than an instantaneous photograph of a Derby winner. [Introduction to exhibition, *Manet and His Contemporaries*, 1910]

MARY McCARTHY

15 God is less like air in the lungs, in Graham Greene, than like a depressing smog that hangs over an industrial city. ... He soaks up the smell of his surroundings – bad cooking and mildew and dirty sheets and stale alcohol. [*Nights and Spectacles*, 'Sheep in Wolves' Clothing']

16 Stepping into his new Buick convertible he [the American] knows that he would gladly do without it, but imagines that to his neighbour, who is just backing *his* out

of the driveway, this car is the motor of life. [*On the Contrary*, 'America the Beautiful']

17 Who are these advertising men kidding, besides the European tourist? Between the tired, sad, gentle faces of the subway riders and the grinning Holy Families of the Ad-Mass, there exists no possibility of even a wishful identification. [*Ib.*]

18 When an American heiress wants to buy a man, she at once crosses the Atlantic. The only really materialistic people I have ever met have been Europeans. [*Ib.*]

19 American life, in large cities at any rate, is a perpetual assault on the senses and the nerves; it is out of asceticism, out of unworldliness, precisely, that we bear it. [*Ib.*]

20 The American character looks always as if it had just had a rather bad haircut, which gives it, in our eyes at any rate, a greater humanity than the European, which even among its beggars has an all too professional air. [*Ib.*]

21 An interviewer asked me what book I thought best represented the modern American woman. All I could think of to answer was: *Madame Bovary*. [*Ib.* 'Characters in Fiction']

22 There are no new truths, but only truths that have not been recognized by those who have perceived them without noticing. A truth is something that everyone can be shown to know and to have known, as people say, all along. [*Ib.* 'The *Vita activa*']

W. D. H. McCULLOUGH and 'FOUGASSE'

23 A professor of anatomy once declared that there are only fourteen types of women – young women, women who are really wonderful all things considered, and the twelve most famous women in history – and the same applies to Bridge partners. Over and above this, they are usually either so good that you lose all your self-confidence, or so bad that you lose all your money. [*Aces Made Easy*]

24 '... that driving by the people through the people and over the people may shortly perish from the earth' – '*Straight-Eight*' *Lincoln* [Epigraph to *You Have Been Warned*]

25 Since the early days of motoring there have been many changes in the apparatus designed to keep drivers posted as to any sensational developments under the bonnet. In the first cars there was little or none of this form of affectation. ... Steam coming out of the radiator, or elsewhere, indicated that the water was boiling, and a radiator that slowly became incandescent showed that it had finished doing so. This was all there was to go on. ... In those days motorists *were* motorists. [*Ib.* Sec. vi]

HUGH McDIARMID

26 Our principal writers have nearly all been fortunate in escaping regular education. [*Observer*, 'Sayings of the Week', 29 Mar. 1953]

BETTY MacDONALD

27 I can feel for her because, although I have never been an Alaskan prostitute dancing on the bar in a spangled dress, I still get very bored with washing and ironing and dishwashing and cooking day after relentless day. [*The Egg and I*, Ch. 1]

28 In high school and college my sister Mary was very popular with the boys, but I had braces on my teeth and got high marks. [*Ib.* 2]

29 I knew how to make mayonnaise and mitre sheet corners and light candles for dinner, so, chickens or insurance, I could hold my end up. [*Ib.*]

30 The days slipped down like junket, leaving no taste on the tongue. [*Ib.* 4]

31 A woman wants her friends to be perfect. She sets a pattern, usually a reasonable facsimile of herself, lays a friend out on this pattern and worries and prods at any little qualities which do not coincide with her own image. [*Ib.* 16]

RAMSAY MacDONALD

32 [On forming the National Government] Tomorrow every Duchess in London will be wanting to kiss me! [Quoted in Viscount Snowden, *Autobiography*]

33 Society goes on and on and on. It is the same with ideas. [Speech, 1935. Quoted in Robert Graves and Alan Hodge, *The Long Weekend*]

34 Let them [France and Germany] especially put their demands in such a way that Great Britain could say that she supported both sides. [Quoted in A. J. P. Taylor, *The Origins of the Second World War*, Ch. 3]

WILLIAM C. MacDONALD

35 It took God longer to write the Bible than it has taken Him to build the British Empire. [*Modern Evangelism*, quoted in M. Bateman, *This England*, selections from the *New Statesman*, Pt I]

J. P. McEVOY

36 I've been in too many taxis not to know that a girl is lots safer with an orchestra between her and the tired business man, who don't act nearly as tired as you'd think. [*Show Girl*, Ch. 1]

37 It's been so long since he read anything except the *Graphic* that he can't even dial his own telephone numbers now. We're going to have little pictures put there instead of figures. [*Ib.*]

38 Say, for the last six weeks I've been busier than a one legged man in a forest fire. [*Ib.* 9]

ARTHUR MacEWEN

39 News is anything that makes a reader say 'Gee whiz!' ... News is whatever a good editor chooses to print. [Quoted in Daniel Boorstin, *The Image*, Ch. 1]

PHYLLIS McGINLEY

40 I'm happy the great ones are thriving, / But what puzzles my head / Is the thought that they needed reviving. / I had never been told they were dead. [*On the Prevalence of Literary Revivals*]

FELIX McGLENNON

41 They may build their ships, my lads, and think they know the game, / But they can't build boys of the bulldog breed / Who made old England's name. [*Sons of the Sea*]

COLIN MacINNES

42 The Wiz has for the oldies just the same kind of hatred psychos have for Jews or foreigners or coloureds. ... The Wiz just does not like the population outside the teenage bracket, and takes every chance he gets to make the oldies conscious of their hair-root dyes, and sing out aloud the anthem of the teenage triumph. [*Absolute Beginners*]

43 In England, pop art and fine art stand resolutely back to back. [*England, Half English*, 'Pop Songs and Teenagers']

44 In this decade we witness the second Children's Crusade, armed with strength and booty, against all 'squares', all adult nay-sayers. [*Ib.*]

45 England is, and always has been, a country infested with people who love to tell us what to do, but who very rarely seem to know what's going on. [*Ib.*]

46 They [pubs] make you as drunk as they can as soon as they can, and turn nasty when they succeed. [*Ib.* 'See you at Mabel's']

47 The decorations are like those of the embassy of a nation about to go into voluntary liquidation. [*Ib.*]

48 A coloured man can tell, in five seconds dead, whether a white man likes him or not. If the white man *says* he does, he is instantly – and usually quite rightly – mistrusted. [*Ib.* 'A Short Guide for Jumbles']

49 Car owners of the world, unite: you have nothing to lose but your manners and someone else's life. [*Ib.* 'Welcome, Beauty Walk']

50 He [Tommy Steele] is Pan, he is Puck, he is every nice young girl's boy, every kid's favourite elder brother, every mother's cherished adolescent son. [*Ib.* 'Young England, Half English']

DENIS MACKAIL

51 A first night was notoriously distracting owing to the large number of people who stand about looking famous. [*How Amusing*]

SIR COMPTON MACKENZIE

52 Women do not find it difficult nowadays to behave like men; but they often find it extremely difficult to behave like gentlemen. [*On Moral Courage*]

53 Everybody boasted aloud that they fed you really well on the *Murmania*, and hoped silently that perhaps the sense of being imprisoned in a decaying hot-water-bottle ... would pass away in the fresh Atlantic breezes. [*Poor Relations*, Ch. 1]

54 The selection of presents for children is never easy, because in order to extract real pleasure from the purchase it is necessary to find something that excites the donor as much as it is likely to excite the recipient. [*Ib.* 3]

55 There was a tradition among the novelists admired by Beatrice that well-bred people left out the final 'g's'; so she saved on these consonants what was squandered on aspirates. [*Ib.* 6]

56 The houses ... looked like an overcrowded row of tall thin men watching a football-match on a cold day; each red-faced house had a tree in front of it like an umbrella and trim white steps like spats. [*Ib.* 8]

57 She was a well preserved woman and reminded John of a crystallized pear; her frosted transformation glistened like encrusted sugar round the stalk, which was represented by a tubular head-ornament on the apex of the carefully tended pyramid; her greeting was sticky. [*Ib.*]

58 Modernity here wore a figleaf; wax candles were burnt instead of gas or electric light; and even the telephone was enshrined in a Florentine casket. [*Ib.* 9]

59 The present school is not fit for children at all ... 'How many water-closets have you?' one of these wise men from the East ... was asking me at the last meeting ... 'How many water closets, General? The whole island is a water closet,' I said. [*Whisky Galore*, Ch. 3]

H. S. MACKINTOSH

60 Give me that song of Picardy: / 'He has been duped – the station-master!' [*Ballades and Other Verse*, 'Il est cocu – le chef de gare!']

IAIN MACLEOD

61 History is too serious to be left to historians. [*Observer*, 'Sayings of the Week', 16 July 1961]

MARSHALL McLUHAN

62 If the nineteenth century was the age of the editorial chair, ours is the century of the psychiatrist's couch. [*Understanding Media*, Introduction]

HAROLD MACMILLAN

63 You've never had it so good. [Speech on financial situation, 20 July 1957 (originally U.S. presidential election slogan, 1952)]

64 When you're abroad you're a statesman: when you're at home you're just a politician. [Speech, 1958. Quoted in *Observer*, 28 July 1963]

65 The wind of change is blowing through the continent. [Speech, Capetown, 3 Feb. 1960]

66 Fifteen fingers on the safety catch. [Speech in House of Commons, 31 May 1960, on breakdown of summit conference on nuclear disarmament]

67 It is the duty of Her Majesty's government ... neither to flap nor to falter. [*Observer*, 'Sayings of the Week', 19 Nov. 1961]

68 I have never found in a long experience of politics, that criticism is ever inhibited by ignorance. [*Observer*, 'Sayings of the Year', 29 Dec. 1963]

JOHN MACMURRAY

69 He [Jesus] is not an idealist – for the same reason that he is not a materialist – because the distinction between the ideal and the material does not arise for him. [*The Clue to History*]

LOUIS MacNEICE

70 Conferences, adjournments, ultimatums, / Flights in the air, castles in the air, / The autopsy of treaties, dynamite under the bridges, / The end of *laissez faire*. [*Autumn Journal*, VII]

71 And we who have been brought up to think of 'Gallant Belgium' / As so much blague / Are now prepared again to essay good through evil / For the sake of Prague. [*Ib.*]

72 A howling radio for our paraclete. [*Ib.*]

73 It's no go the picture palace, it's no go the stadium, / It's no go the country cot with a pot of pink geraniums, / It's no go the Government grants, it's no go the elections, / Sit on your arse for fifty years and hang your hat on a pension. [*Bagpipe Music*]

74 Ordinary men ... / Put up a barrage of common sense to baulk / Intimacy but by mistake interpolate / Swear-words like roses in their talk. [*Conversation*]

75 Crumbling between the fingers, under the feet, / Crumbling behind the eyes, / Their world gives way and dies / And something twangs and breaks at the end of the street. [*Débâcle*]

76 Time was away and somewhere else, / There were two glasses and two chairs / And two people with one pulse. [*Meeting Point*]

77 In the beginning and in the end the only decent / Definition is tautology: man is man, / Woman woman, and tree tree. [*Plain Speaking*]

78 He can discover / A selfish motive for anything – and collect / His royalties as recording angel. [*The Satirist*]

SALVADOR DE MADARIAGA

79 First the sweetheart of the nation, then the aunt, woman governs America because America is a land of boys who refuse to grow up. [Quoted in Sagittarius and George, *The Perpetual Pessimist*]

BERNARD MALAMUD

80 Levin wanted friendship and got friendliness; he wanted steak and they offered spam. [*A New Life*, Sect. vi]

MANCHESTER GUARDIAN

81 If Mr Eliot had been pleased to write in demotic English, *The Wasteland* might not have been, as it just is to all but anthropologists and literati, so much wastepaper. [Quoted in Virginia Woolf, *The Common Reader* (First Series), 'How it Strikes a Contemporary']

LORD MANCROFT

82 We don't even talk of an escape from Bristol [prison]. The word is dematerialization. [*Observer*, 'Sayings of the Week', 5 Aug. 1956]

RUBY MANIKAN

[Indian Church Leader]

83 If you educate a man you educate a person, but if you educate a woman you educate a family. [*Observer*, 'Sayings of the Week', 30 Mar. 1947]

THOMAS MANN

84 Our capacity for disgust, let me observe, is in proportion to our desires; that is in proportion to the intensity of our attachment to the things of this world. [*The Confessions of Felix Krull*, Pt I, Ch. 5]

KATHERINE MANSFIELD

85 If there was one thing he hated more than another it was the way she had of waking him in the morning. .... It was her way of establishing her grievance for the day. [*Bliss*, 'Mr Reginald Peacock's Day']

86 He stands, smiling encouragement, like a clumsy dentist. [*The Garden Party*, 'Bank Holiday']

87 That evening for the first time in his life ... old Mr Neave felt he was too old for the spring. [*Ib.* 'An Ideal Family']

88 Nothing made little Lennie put it on. Taking him to the cemetery, even, never gave him a colour; a nice shake-up in the bus never improved his appetite. [*Ib.* 'Life of Ma Parker']

89 She couldn't possibly go back to the gentleman's flat; she had no right to cry in strangers' houses. [*Ib.*]

90 Whenever I prepare for a journey I prepare as though for death. Should I never return, all is in order. This is what life has taught me. [*Journal*, 1922]

MAO TSE-TUNG

1 The atom bomb is a paper tiger which the United States reactionaries use to scare people. [Interview, Aug. 1946]

2 All reactionaries are paper tigers. [*Quotations from Chairman Mao Tse-Tung*, sect. vi]

3 Letting a hundred flowers blossom and a hundred schools of thought contend is the policy for promoting the progress of the arts and the sciences. [*Ib.* sect. xxxii]

DON MARQUIS

4 but wotthehell wotthehell / oh i should worry and fret / death and I will coquette / there s a dance in the old dame yet / toujours gai toujours gai [*archy and mehitabel*, III 'the song of mehitabel']

5 a / whole scuttleful of chef douvres what / you mean is hors douvres mehitabel i / told her what i mean is grub [*Ib.* XI, 'why mehitabel jumped']

6 live so that you / can stick out your tongue / at the insurance / doctor [*Ib.* XII, 'certain maxims of archy']

7 procrastination is the / art of keeping / up with yesterday [*Ib.*]

8 i do not care / what a dogs / pedigree may be ... / millionaires and / bums taste / about alike to me [*Ib.*]

9 its cheerio / my deerio that / pulls a lady through [*Ib.* XXIV, 'cheerio my deerio']

10 always being / misunderstood by some / strait laced / prune faced bunch / of prissy mouthed / sisters of uncharity [*Ib.*]

11 and before i could argue him / out of his philosophy / he went and immolated himself on a patent cigar lighter [*Ib.* XX, 'the lesson of the moth']

12 one of my elizabethan / forebears was plucked from / a can of ale by / will shakespeare and / put down kit marlowe s back / what subtle wits they were in / those days [*Ib.* XXI, 'a roach of the taverns']

13 archy she told me / it is merely a plutonic / attachment / and the thing can be / believed for the tom / looks like one of pluto s demons [*Ib.* XXX, 'the old trouper']

14 the stage is not what it / used to be tom says / they don't have it any more / they don t have it here / the old troupers are gone [*Ib.*]

15 he had a voice / that used to shake / the ferryboats / on the north river [*Ib.*]

16 once he lost his beard / and my grandfather / dropped from the / fly gallery and landed / under his chin / and played his beard / for the rest of the act [*Ib.*]

17 mehitabel he says / both our professions / are being ruined / by amatours [*Ib.*]

18 you want to know / whether i believe in ghosts / of course i do not believe in them / if you had known / as many of them as i have / you would not / believe in them either [*Ib.* XXXIII, 'ghosts']

19 the quite irrational ichneumon is such a fool its almost human [*Ib.* XXXVI, 'archy at the zoo']

20 one of the most pathetic / sights however / is to see the ghost of queen / victoria going out every / evening with the ghost / of a sceptre in her hand / to find mr lytton strachey / and bean him [*Ib.* XLIII, 'archy goes abroad']

21 i ll tell the world i am a hard boiled œuf / i rend the clouds when i let off steam / to the orderly life i cry pouf pouf / it is worth far less than the bourgeois deem [*Ib.* XLV, 'mehitabel meets an affinity']

22 jamais triste archy jamais triste / that is my motto [*Ib.* XLVI, 'mehitabel sees paris']

23 there is always / a comforting thought / in time of trouble when / it is not our trouble. [*archy does his part*]

24 To stroke a platitude until it purrs like an epigram. [*The Sun Dial*]

25 An idea isn't responsible for the people who believe in it. [*Ib.*]

26 Poetry is what Milton saw when he went blind. [*Ib.*]

EDWARD MARSH

27 How I dislike 'Technicolour', which suffuses everything with stale mustard. [*Ambrosia and Small Beer*, Ch. 3]

28 *Dialogue between an M.O. and a recruit:*
M.O.: How are your bowels working?
R.: Haven't been issued with any, sir.
M.O.: I mean, are you constipated?
R.: No sir, I volunteered.
M.O.: Heavens man, don't you know the King's English?
R.: No sir, is he? [*Ib.* 4]

29 Why is it that the sudden mention of an aunt is so deflating to a poem? [*Ib.* 5]

30 If you call Le Gallienne a minor poet you might just as well call a street lamp a minor planet. [Letter, quoted in Christopher Hassall, *Edward Marsh*, Ch. 6]

31 He told me his object in life is to influence people for good, but he can't make up his mind whether to spread out his influence thin over 'millions' or give it in strong doses to a small circle of intimates. [*Ib.* 7]

32 The food is simple and extremely unwholesome. [Of the Brookes' home in Granchester, quoted in *ib.* 8]

33 Dear Roger Fry whom I love as a man but detest as a movement. [Quoted in *ib.* 11]

34 Praise of one's friends is always more unmixed pleasure than of oneself, because there isn't the slightest discomfort of doubting inwardly whether it is deserved. [Letter to Henry James, Spring 1915]

ARTHUR MARSHALL

35 Luncheon will be congealing on the table with Irene still staring, her eyes popping from her head, trying to discover just who it was who garotted Mademoiselle, set fire to the chapel and tarred and feathered Miss Parkinson's bust. ['Books for Girls', reprinted in V. S. Pritchett (ed.), *Turnstile One*]

36 There's nougat at the Hendersons, the Hopes have got some fudge, / And Pam has popped the pralines in the tool-bag of her Rudge. / Voluptuous and tarmacborne, she free-wheels through East Cheam, / My caramelly angel girl, my luscious sweet-meat dream. [*New Statesman* competition, parody of John Betjeman]

SYBIL MARSHALL

37 Education must have an end in view, for it is not an end in itself. [*An Experiment in Education*, Ch. 4]

CHICO MARX

38 Mustard's no good without roast beef. [In film, *Monkey Business*]

GROUCHO MARX

39 Do you think I could buy back my introduction to you. [In film, *Monkey Business*]

40 I've worked myself up from nothing to a state of extreme poverty. [*Ib.*]

41 Come back next Thursday with a specimen of your money. [Chapter heading in autobiography *Groucho and Me*]

42 My name is Captain Spaulding, / The African explorer – / Did anyone say *schnorrer*? [In film, *Animal Crackers*]

43 Didn't I tell you not to go over Australia? / Didn't I tell you Australia was up? [*Ib.*]

44 What's a thousand dollars? Mere chicken feed. A poultry matter. [In film, *Cocoanuts*]

45 GROUCHO: We're going to have an auction.
CHICO: I came over here on the Atlantic auction. [*Ib.*]

46 [As auctioneer]: Now, here's a lot! O, I know it doesn't look very big on top, but it goes down as far as you want to go. [*Ib.*]

47 Better rusty than missin'. [On throwing his wrist watch into the handbasin before conducting an operation. In film, *A Day at the Races*]

48 In my day a college widow stood for something. She stood for plenty. [*Ib.*]

49 A child of five would understand this. Send somebody to fetch a child of five. [In film, *Duck Soup*]

50 Send two dozen roses to Room 424 and put 'Emily, I love you' on the back of the bill. [In film, *A Night in Casablanca*]

51 I don't have a photograph, but you can have my footprints. They're upstairs in my socks. [In film, *A Night at the Opera*]

52 The strains of Verdi will come back to you tonight, and Mrs Claypool's cheque will come back to you in the morning. [*Ib.*]

53 I never forget a face, but I'll make an exception in your case. [Quoted in *Guardian*, 18 June 1965]

54 No, Groucho is not my real name. I'm breaking it in for a friend. [Attr.]

55 Please accept my resignation. I don't want to belong to any club that will accept me as a member. [Attr. telegram]

56 He's the best adjusted man in the world. If a flood comes, he'll be riding a house as if he had never done anything else but ride houses. When the bombs fall, he'll start fixing his chimney without even looking up to see what hit him. [Quoted in Kyle Crichton, *The Marx Brothers*, Ch. 22]

HARPO MARX

57 My God, there he is on the dock, waving good-bye, and there he is on the *ship*, waving good-bye to himself on the dock. [When his father played as an 'extra' in *A Night at the Opera*. Quoted in Kyle Crichton, *The Marx Brothers*, Ch. 22]

58 If you see me in the station at Moscow tomorrow morning, remind me I'm alive. [After having some trouble with Russian customs officials. Quoted in *ib.*]

ZEPPO MARX

59 You ever see me act? You could give me every good line since Chaucer, and I'd ruin it. [Quoted in Kyle Crichton, *The Marx Brothers*, Ch. 22]

ERIC MASCHWITZ

60 A Nightingale Sang in Berkeley Square. [Title of song]

JOHN MASEFIELD

61 How still this quiet cornfield is to-night! / By an intenser glow the evening falls, / Bringing, not darkness, but a deeper light. [*August, 1914*]

62 The moonlight runs / Over the grasses of the ancient way / Rutted this morning by the passing guns. [*Ib.*]

63 Best trust the happy moments. What they gave / Makes man less fearful of the certain grave, / And gives his work compassion and new eyes. / The days that make us happy make us wise. [*Biography*]

64 O grave, keep shut lest I be shamed. [*C.L.M.*]

65 Out into street I ran uproarious, / The devil dancing in me glorious. [*The Everlasting Mercy*]

66 'Saul Kane', she said, 'when next you drink, / Do me the gentleness to think / That every drop of drink accursed / Makes Christ within you die of thirst, / That every dirty word you say / Is one more flint upon His way.' [*Ib.*]

67 I did not shrink, I did not strive, / The deep peace burnt my me alive. [*Ib.*]

68 Life's battle is a conquest for the strong; / The meaning shows in the defeated thing. [*The 'Wanderer'*]

69 From the Gallows Hill to the Tineton Copse / There were ten ploughed fields, like ten full-stops. [*Reynard the Fox*]

70 The stars grew bright in the winter sky, / The wind came keen with a tang of frost, / The brook was troubled for new things lost, / The copse was happy for old things found, / The fox came home and he went to ground. [*Ib.*]

71 What am I, Life? A thing of watery salt / Held in cohesion by unresting cells, / Which work they know not why, which never halt, / Myself unwitting where their master dwells? [*Lollingdon Downs*, Sonnet 37]

72 In those days, as a little child, I was living in Paradise, and had no need of the arts, that at best are only a shadow of Paradise. [*So Long to Learn*]

73 In happiest childhood I could at once, without effort, imagine any needed scene with the brightness and detail of what is called 'vision'. [*Ib.*]

74 The Fifth-Act-Actor, my friend explained, is one who can be charming, attractive, startling and surprising through the fortunes of four acts, and yet be shattering and triumphant in the fifth. [*Ib.*]

75 Some day, in this England that has so often borne beauty, her genius will again move, in the unexpected ways of insight. Man will re-create the arts, or die. [*Ib.*]

76 The Englishman is naturally wasteful, especially of public money. It is a question of a blunted sense of life, a dullness towards a bright design, an apathy. Let us blame the climate for it: we pass, but the climate stays. [*Ib.*]

JOHN MASTERS

77 Join a Highland regiment, me boy. The kilt is an unrivalled garment for fornication and diarrhoea. [A major of Highlanders, quoted in *Bugles and a Tiger*]

GEORGE MATHEW

78 We cannot help the birds of sadness flying over our heads, / But we need not let them build their nests in our hair. [Alleged Chinese saying. Quoted in James Agate, *Ego 1*, 1933]

TOM MATHEWS

79 Why did you keep me on tiptoe so long if you weren't going to kiss me? [When Henry Luce eventually decided against a British Edition of *Time*. Quoted in *Observer*, 19 May 1963]

HENRI MATISSE

80 I don't know whether I believe in God or not. I think, really, I'm some sort of Buddhist. But the essential thing is to put oneself in a frame of mind which is close to that of prayer. [Quoted in Françoise Gilot and Carlton Lake, *Life with Picasso*, Part VI]

W. SOMERSET MAUGHAM

81 People are always rather bored with their parents. That's human nature. [*The Bread-Winner*, Act 2]

82 I don't think you want too much sincerity in society. It would be like an iron girder in a house of cards. [*The Circle*, Act 1]

83 You can't learn too soon that the most useful thing about a principle is that it can always be sacrificed to expediency. [*Ib.* 3]

84 I was brought up by a very strict mother to believe that men were naturally wicked. [*The Constant Wife*, I]

85 It's not the seven deadly virtues that make a man a good husband, but the three hundred pleasing amiabilities. [*Ib.*]

86 She's too crafty a woman to invent a new lie when an old one will serve. [*Ib.* II]

87 The only places John likes on the Continent are those in which it's only by an effort of the imagination that you can tell you're not in England. [*Ib.* III]

88 Some women can't see a telephone without taking the receiver off. [*Ib.*]

89 We have long passed the Victorian Era when asterisks were followed after a certain interval by a baby. [*Ib.*]

90 JOHN: Do you think I can't be a lover as well as a husband?
CONSTANCE: My dear, no one can make yesterday's cold mutton into tomorrow's lamb cutlets. [*Ib.*]

1 The right people *are* rude. They can afford to be. [*Our Betters*, II]

2 It was such a lovely day I thought it was a pity to get up. [*Ib.*]

3 My dear, she's been my greatest friend for fifteen years. I know her through and through, and I tell you that she hasn't got a single redeeming quality. [*Ib.* III]

4 She felt vaguely the pity of that child deprived of the only love in the world [parental] that is quite unselfish. [*Of Human Bondage*, Ch. 2]

5 Like all weak men he laid an exaggerated stress on not changing one's mind. [*Ib.* 37]

6 Money is like a sixth sense without which you cannot make a complete use of the other five. [*Ib.* 51]

7 The aesthetic sense ... is akin to the sexual instinct, and shares its barbarity. [*The Moon and Sixpence*, Ch. 1]

8 I forget who it was that recommended men for their soul's good to do each day two things they disliked ... it is a precept that I have followed scrupulously; for every day I have got up and I have gone to bed. [*Ib.* 2]

9 The Army and Navy Stores are a bond of union between all who dwell between the river and St James's Park. [*Ib.* 4]

151

10 It is not true that suffering ennobles the character; happiness does that sometimes, but suffering, for the most part, makes men petty and vindictive. [*Ib.* 17]

11 A woman can forgive a man for the harm he does her . . . but she can never forgive him for the sacrifices he makes on her account. [*Ib.* 41]

12 Because women can do nothing except love, they've given it a ridiculous importance. [*Ib.*]

13 She could not help saying beastly things about even her intimate friends, but she did this because she was a stupid woman and knew no other way to make herself interesting. [*The Razor's Edge*, Pt V, Ch. 7]

14 I could think of no one among my contemporaries who had achieved so considerable a position on so little talent. [*Cakes and Ale*, Ch. 1]

15 Hypocrisy is the most difficult and nerve-racking vice that any man can pursue; it needs an unceasing vigilance and a rare detachment of spirit. It cannot, like adultery or gluttony, be practised at spare moments; it is a whole-time job. [*Ib.*]

16 The Americans, who are the most efficient people on earth . . . have invented so wide a range of pithy and hackneyed phrases that they can carry on an amusing and animated conversation without giving a moment's reflection to what they are saying and so leave their minds free to consider the more important matters of big business and fornication. [*Ib.* 2]

17 Poor Henry [James], he's spending eternity wandering round and round a stately park and the fence is just too high for him to peep over and they're having tea just too far away for him to hear what the Countess is saying. [*Ib.* 9]

18 'But I can do nothing unless I am in complete possession of the facts.' 'Obviously you can't cook them unless you have them.' [*Ib.*]

19 From the earliest times the old have rubbed it into the young that they are wiser than they, and before the young had discovered what nonsense this was they were old too, and it profited them to carry on the imposture. [*Ib.*]

20 For to write good prose is an affair of good manners. It is, unlike verse, a civil art. . . . Poetry is baroque. [*The Summing Up*, Ch. 12]

21 Most people have a furious itch to talk about themselves and are restrained only by the disinclination of others to listen. Reserve is an artificial quality that is developed in most of us as the result of innumerable rebuffs. [*Ib.* 19]

22 It is dangerous to let the public behind the scenes. They are easily disillusioned and then they are angry with you, for it was the illusion they loved. [*Ib.* 23]

23 I thought to myself: Thank God, I can look at a sunset now without having to think how to describe it. I meant then never to write another book. [*Ib.* 33]

24 How can you write a play of which the ideas are so significant that they will make the critic of *The Times* sit up in his stall and at the same time induce the shop-girl in the gallery to forget the young man who is holding her hand? [*Ib.* 37]

25 Women will write novels to while away their pregnancies; bored noblemen, axed officers, retired civil servants fly to the pen as one might fly to the bottle. There is an impression abroad that everyone has it in him to write one book; but if by this is implied a good book the impression is false. [*Ib.* 47]

26 I'll give you my opinion of the human race in a nutshell. . . . Their heart's in the right place, but their head is a thoroughly inefficient organ. [*Ib.* 55]

27 The artist's egoism is outrageous; it must be; he is by nature a solipsist and the world exists only for him to exercise upon it his powers of creation. [*Ib.* 61]

28 It is a great nuisance that knowledge can only be acquired by hard work. It would be fine if we could swallow the powder of profitable information made palatable by the jam of fiction. [*10 Novels and Their Authors*, Ch. 1, sect. i]

29 Casting my mind's eye over the whole of fiction, the only absolutely original creation I can think of is Don Quixote. [*Ib.*]

30 I've always been interested in people, but I've never liked them. [*Observer*, 'Sayings of the Week', 28 Aug. 1949]

31 The trouble with our younger authors is that they are all in the sixties. [*Observer*, 'Sayings of the Week', 14 Oct. 1951]

'BILL' MAULDIN

32 'He's right, Joe, when we ain't fightin' we should ack like sojers.' [*Up Front*, cartoon caption]

ANDRÉ MAUROIS

33 In England there is only silence or scandal. [Attr.]

JAMES MAXTON

34 Sit down, man. You're a bloody tragedy. [To Ramsay MacDonald on the occasion of the last speech he made in the House of Commons. Attr.]

VLADIMIR MAYAKOVSKY

35 Oh for just / one / more conference / regarding the eradication of all conferences! [*In re Conferences*, trans. Herbert Marshall]

36 Always to shine, / and everywhere to shine, / and, to the very last, / to shine, – / thus runs / my motto / and the sun's. [*A Most Extraordinary Adventure*, trans. *ib.*]

37 Our planet / is poorly equipped / for delight / One must snatch / gladness / from the days that are / In this life / it's not difficult to die. / To make life / is more difficult by far. [*Sergei Yessenin*, trans. *ib.*]

LOUIS B. MAYER

38 Throw the little old lady down the stairs! Throw the mother's good, home-made chicken soup in the mother's face! *Step* on the mother! *Kick* her! That is *art*, they say. Art! [Quoted in Lillian Ross, *Picture*, 'Throw the Little Old Lady Down the Stairs!']

ANDREW MELLON

39 A nation is not in danger of financial disaster merely because it owes itself money. [1933. *Observer*, 'Sayings of Our Times', 31 May 1953]

H. L. MENCKEN

40 Nevada has no intellectual life. The members of the divorce colony occupy themselves by playing golf, watching the calendar, and practising adultery. [*Americana, 1925*, 'Notes for Foreign Students']

41 I can't remember a single masculine figure created by a woman who is not, at bottom, a booby. [*In Defence of Women*, Ch. 1, sect. i]

42 The average male gets his living by such depressing devices that boredom becomes a sort of natural state to him. [*Ib.* 3. xxviii]

43 We must respect the other fellow's religion, but only in the sense and to the extent that we respect his theory that his wife is beautiful and his children smart. [Notebooks, *Minority Report*, 1]

44 The United States has not only failed to produce a genuine aristocracy; it has also failed to produce an indigenous intelligentsia. The so-called intellectuals of the country are simply weather-vanes blown constantly by foreign winds, usually but not always English. [*Ib.* 38]

45 The scientist who yields anything to theology, however slight, is yielding to ignorance and false pretences, and as certainly as if he granted that a horse-hair put into a bottle of water will turn into a snake. [*Ib.* 45]

46 Men always try to make virtues of their weaknesses. Fear of death and fear of life both become piety. [*Ib.* 54]

47 It is now quite lawful for a Catholic woman to avoid pregnancy by a resort to mathematics, though she is still forbidden to resort to physics and chemistry. [*Ib.* 62]

48 The capacity of human beings to bore one another seems to be vastly greater than that of any other animals. Some of their most esteemed inventions have no other apparent purpose, for example, the dinner party of more than two, the epic poem, and the science of metaphysics. [*Ib.* 67]

49 Men are the only animals who devote themselves assiduously to making one another unhappy. It is, I suppose, one of their godlike qualities. Jahweh, as the Old Testament shows, spends a large part

of His time trying to ruin the business and comfort of all other gods. [*Ib.* 98]

50 A show of altruism is respected in the world chiefly for selfish motives. . . . Everyone figures himself profiting by it tomorrow. [*Ib.* 126]

51 War will never cease until babies begin to come into the world with larger cerebrums and smaller adrenal glands. [*Ib.* 164]

52 A nun, at best, is only half a woman, just as a priest is only half a man. [*Ib.* 221]

53 Whenever one comes to close grips with so-called idealism, as in war time, one is shocked by its rascality. [*Ib.* 223]

54 One of the things that makes a Negro unpleasant to white folk is the fact that he suffers from their injustice. He is thus a standing rebuke to them. [*Ib.* 272]

55 Why assume so glibly that the God who presumably created the universe is still running it? It is certainly perfectly conceivable that He may have finished it and then turned it over to lesser gods to operate. [*Ib.* 298]

56 The chief contribution of Protestantism to human thought is its massive proof that God is a bore. [*Ib.* 309]

57 The worst government is the most moral. One composed of cynics is often very tolerant and humane. But when fanatics are on top there is no limit to oppression. [*Ib.* 327]

58 Science, at bottom, is really anti-intellectual. It always distrusts pure reason, and demands the production of objective fact. [*Ib.* 412]

59 The great artists of the world are never Puritans, and seldom even ordinarily respectable. [*Prejudices*, First Series, 16]

60 Thousands of American women know far more about the Subconscious than they know about plain sewing. The pungency of myrrh and frankincense is mingled with *odeur de femme*. Physiology is formally repealed and repudiated; its laws are all lies. [*Ib.* 20]

61 When one hears of a Conservative man who has a Liberal wife, or *vice versa*, it is always safe to assume that she has her eye on a handsomer, richer or more docile fellow, and is thinking of calling on a solicitor. [*Prejudices*, Second Series 'On a Tender Theme']

62 To sum up: 1. The cosmos is a gigantic fly-wheel making 10,000 revolutions a minute. 2. Man is a sick fly taking a dizzy ride on it. 3. Religion is the theory that the wheel was designed and set spinning to give him the ride. [*Prejudices*, Third Series, '*Ad Imaginem dei creavit illum*', Coda]

63 When one hears of a poet past thirty-five, he seems somehow unnatural and even a trifle obscene; it is as if one encountered a greying man who still played the Chopin waltzes and believed in elective affinities. [*Ib.*, 'The Poet and his Art']

64 Poetry is a comforting piece of fiction set to more or less lascivious music. [*Ib.*]

65 Is it a well-known fact that love is an emotion that is almost as perishable as eggs – that it is biologically impossible for a given male to yearn for a given female for more than a few brief years? Then the poet disposes of it by assuring his girl that he will nevertheless love her for ever. [*Ib.*]

66 Faith may be defined briefly as an illogical belief in the occurrence of the improbable. [*Ib.* 'Types of Men']

67 Hygiene is the corruption of medicine by morality. It is impossible to find a hygienist who does not debase his theory of the healthful with a theory of the virtuous. [*Ib.*]

68 He [the businessman] is the only man who is for ever apologizing for his occupation. [*Ib.*]

69 The man who boasts that he habitually tells the truth is simply a man with no respect for it. It is not a thing to be thrown about loosely, like small change; it is something to be cherished and hoarded, and disbursed only when absolutely necessary. [*Ib.*]

70 Every man sees in his relatives, and especially in his cousins, a series of grotesque caricatures of himself. [*Ib.*]

71 The notion that a true and loving . . . wife inspires a man to high endeavour is largely illusory. Every sane woman knows instinctively, as a matter of fact, that the highest aspirations of her

husband are fundamentally inimical to her, and that their realization is apt to cost her her possession of him. [*Prejudices*, Fourth Series, 'Reflections on Monogamy', 4]

72 No healthy male ever really thinks or talks of anything save himself. [*Ib.* 8]

73 No man is genuinely happy, married, who has to drink worse gin than he used to drink when he was single. [*Ib.* 14]

74 Ah, that the eugenists would breed a woman as capable of laughter as the girl of twenty and as adept at knowing when not to laugh as the woman of thirty-nine! [*Ib.* 15]

PIERRE MENDÈS-FRANCE

75 To govern is to choose. [Attr.]

E. H. W. MEYERSTEIN

76 It seems to me the real attractions of varsity life are reserved for the sportsman and the loafer. [Letter, to his Mother, 21 Oct. 1908]

77 It [the last movement of Beethoven's Ninth Symphony] is the song of the angels sung by earth spirits. [*Ib.*]

78 It is bad enough to have a mother who believes in one, but a wife! The devotion of a wife is admirable – from the spectator's point of view. [Letter to John Freeman, May 1925]

79 It is pre-Whitman, and therefore pre-Pound and pre-Eliot, but not pre-possessing. [Describing poem by Clough, to R. N. Green-Armitage, 2 Sept. 1940]

SIR FRANCIS MEYNELL

80 So conscious he how short time was / For all he planned to do within it / He nothing did at all, alas, / Save note the hour – and file the minute. [*For a Functionary*]

JAMES MICHIE

81 Up in the heavenly saloon / Sheriff sun and rustler moon / Gamble, stuck in the sheriff's mouth / The fag end of an afternoon. [*Arizona Nature Myth*]

RICHARD MIDDLETON

82 It is impossible to speak of sodomy in any detail in polite society nowadays. [Letter, 1907]

GEORGE MIKES

83 It's not enough to sleep – sleep must be organized! [*Down with Everybody*]

84 London is chaos incorporated. [*Ib.*]

85 One of the most popular American entertainments is kissing. Young men and young girls pull up on the highways and kiss each other between 6.30 and 10.30 p.m. This kind of amusement is considered perfectly decent, probably because it keeps you from going to a cinema. [*Ib.*]

86 The Swiss managed to build a lovely country around their hotels. [*Ib.*]

87 The trouble with tea is that originally it was quite a good drink. [*How to be an Alien*]

88 In England it is bad manners to be clever, to assert something confidently. It may be your personal view that two and two make four, but you must not state it in a self-assured way, because this is a democratic country and others may be of a different opinion. [*Ib.*]

89 To employ an English charwoman is a compromise between having a dirty house and cleaning it yourself. [*Ib.*]

90 Taxis are . . . a Christian institution. They are here to teach drivers modesty and humility. They teach us never to be over-confident. [*Ib.*]

1 It was twenty-one years ago that England and I first set foot on each other. I came for a fortnight; I have stayed ever since. [*How to be Inimitable*]

2 The New Poor of yester-year are fighting a losing battle. To remain poor needs the utmost skill and ingenuity. [*Ib.*]

3 The one class you do *not* belong to and are not proud of at all is the lower-middle class. No one ever describes himself as belonging to the lower-middle class. [*Ib.*]

4 The place of the upstart is being taken by the downstart. I know people who secretly visit evening elocution classes in order to pick up a cockney accent. [*Ib.*]

5 A man in a queue is as much the image of a true Briton as a man in a bull-ring is the image of a Spaniard or a man with a two-foot cigar of an American. [*Ib.*]

6 All English shop assistants are Miltonists. A Miltonist firmly believes that 'they also serve who only stand and wait'. [*Ib.*]

GENERAL MILLÁN ASTRAY

7 *¡Viva la muerte! ¡Abajo la inteligencia!* – Long live death! Down with intelligence! [Slogan in Spanish Civil War]

EDNA ST VINCENT MILLAY

8 Euclid alone / Has looked on Beauty bare, Fortunate they / Who, though once only and then but far away, / Have heard her massive sandal set on stone. [*Euclid alone has looked on Beauty bare*]

9 I came upon no wine / So wonderful as thirst. [*Feast*]

10 Blessed be death that cuts in marble / What would have sunk in dust. [*Keen*]

11 Who builds her a house with love for timber, / Builds her a house of foam; / And I'd rather be bride to a lad gone down / Than widow to one safe home. [*Ib.*]

12 All I could see from where I stood / Was three long mountains and a wood. [*Renascence*]

ALICE DUER MILLER

13 In a world where England is finished and dead; / I do not wish to live. [*The White Cliffs*]

ARTHUR MILLER

14 A good newspaper, I suppose, is a nation talking to itself. [*Observer*, 'Sayings of the Week', 26 Nov. 1961]

15 All organization is and must be grounded on the idea of exclusion and prohibition just as two objects cannot occupy the same space. [*The Crucible*, I]

16 I have a sense for heat, John, and yours has drawn me to my window, and I have seen you looking up, burning in your loneliness. [*Ib.*]

17 A child's spirit is like a child, you can never catch it by running after it; you must stand still, and, for love, it will soon itself come back. [*Ib.*]

18 There are many who stay away from church these days because you hardly ever mention God any more. [*Ib.*]

19 The concept of unity, in which positive and negative are attributes of the same force, in which good and evil are relative, ever-changing and always joined to the same phenomenon – such a concept is still reserved to the physical sciences and to the few who have grasped the history of ideas. [*Ib.*]

20 I have not moved from there to there without I think to please you, and still an everlasting funeral marches round your heart. [*Ib.* II]

21 Oh, Elizabeth, your justice would freeze beer! [*Ib.*]

22 He's liked, but he's not well liked. [*Death of a Salesman*, I]

23 The world is an oyster, but you don't crack it open on a mattress. [*Ib.*]

24 Never fight fair with a stranger boy. You'll never get out of the jungle that way. [*Ib.*]

25 I still feel – kind of temporary about myself. [*Ib.*]

26 Willy Loman never made a lot of money. His name was never in the paper. He's not the finest character that ever lived. But he's a human being, and a terrible thing is happening to him. So attention must be paid. [*Ib.*]

27 A small man can be just as exhausted as a great man. [*Ib.*]

28 Everybody likes a kidder, but nobody lends him money. [*Ib.*]

29 I only wish during the war they'd a took me in the Army. I coulda been dead by now. [*Ib.* II]

30 He's a man way out there in the blue, riding on a smile and a shoeshine. And when they start not smiling back – that's an earthquake. .... A salesman is got to dream, boy. It comes with the territory. [*Ib.* Death Requiem]

31 I am inclined to notice the ruin in things, perhaps because I was born in Italy. [*A View from the Bridge*, I]

32 A man comes into a great hotel and says, I am a messenger. Who is this man? He disappears walking, there is no noise, nothing. Maybe he will never come back, maybe he will never deliver the message. But a man who rides up on a great machine, this man exists. He will be given messages. [*Ib.*]

33 I just hope that's his regular hair, that's all I hope. [*Ib.*]

34 My first thought was that he had committed a crime, but soon I saw it was only a passion that had moved into his body like a stranger. [*Ib.*]

35 The law is nature. The law is only a word for what has a right to happen. [*Ib.*]

HENRY MILLER

36 The world does seem to become one, however much its component elements may resist. Indeed, the stronger the resistance the more certain is the outcome. *We resist only what is inevitable.* [*Big Sur and the Oranges of Hieronymus Bosch*]

37 Sex is one of the nine reasons for reincarnation. . . . The other eight are unimportant. [*Ib.*]

38 Napoleon is nothing to me in comparison with Eddie Carney who gave me my first black eye. [*Black Spring*, 'The 14th Ward']

39 All my good reading, you might say, was done in the toilet. . . . There are passages of *Ulysses* which can be read only in the toilet – if one wants to extract the full flavour of their content. [*Ib.* 'Paris and its Suburbs']

40 Though I've never read a line of Homer I believe the Greek of today is essentially unchanged. If anything he is more Greek than he ever was. [*The Colossus of Maroussi*, Ch. 1]

41 In this life I am God, and like God / I am indifferent to my own fate. [*The Cosmological Eye*]

42 Every man with a belly full of the classics is an enemy of the human race. [*Tropic of Cancer*, 'Dijon']

HENRY MILLER

43 A Boy's Best Friend is His Mother [Title of song]

JONATHAN MILLER

44 I'm not really a Jew; just Jew-ish, not the whole hog. [*Beyond the Fringe*]

45 They do those little personal things people sometimes do when they think they are alone in railway carriages: things like smelling their own armpits. [*Ib.*]

WALTER M. MILLER JNR

46 Someone was smiling. It was only a small smile but in the midst of a sea of grave faces it stood out like a dead fly in a bowl of cream. [*A Canticle for Leibowitz*, 'Fiat Voluntas Tua']

SPIKE MILLIGAN

47 I said to the First Officer, 'Gad, that sun's hot,' to which he replied, 'Well, you shouldn't touch it.' [*A Dustbin of Milligan*, 'Letters to Harry Secombe', I]

48 I shook hands with a friendly Arab. . . . I still have my right hand to prove it. [*Ib.*]

49 At dinner a gentleman's shirt front exploded when he saw a lady in a low-cut evening gown. Mind you, my front looked as if it had exploded earlier with a wider area of devastation. [*Ib.* II]

50 He told me he had the sea in his blood, and believe me you can see where it gets in. [*Ib.*]

51 What a beautiful morning it's been out on deck. . . . Only on the third class tourist class passengers' deck was it a sultry overcast dull morning, but then if you do things on the cheap you must expect these things. [*Ib.*]

52 I have for instance among my purchases . . . several original Mona Lisas and all painted (according to the Signature) by the great artist Kodak. [*Ib.* III]

53 By Midday in Colombo, the heat is so unbearable that the streets are empty save for thousands of Englishmen taking mad dogs for walks. [*Ib.*]

54 Nowadays, the old prison has been turned into a first-class hotel with a service that any Michelin guide would be only too pleased to condemn. [*Ib.* V]

55 He walked with a pronounced limp, L-I-M-P, pronounced 'limp'. [*Ib.* 'The Great Man']

56 His thoughts, few that they were, lay silent in the privacy of his head. [*Puckoon*, Ch. 1]

57 Tank heaven the ground broke me fall. [*Ib.* 2]

58 I'm a hero wid coward's legs, I'm a hero from the waist up. [*Ib.*]

59 There coming up the drive was the worst Catholic since Genghis Khan. [*Ib.*]

60 When she saw a sign 'Members only' she thought of him. [*Ib.* 3]

61 Money can't buy friends, but you can get a better class of enemy. [*Ib.* 6]

62 PETER SELLERS: In South America. HARRY SECOMBE: That's abroad, isn't it? P.S.: It all depends on where you're standing. [B.B.C. comedy series, *The Goon Show*, 'The Affair of the Lone Banana']

63 H.S.: Whose side are you on? P.S.: There are no sides. We're all in this together. [*Ib.*]

64 Not so loud, you fool – remember – even people have ears. [*Ib.* 'The Marie Celeste']

65 H.S.: Gad, Bloodnok, I admire your guts. BLOODNOK: What, are they showing? [*Ib.* Variations in other instalments]

66 Ohhh – my nut – oh – I have been nutted on my bonce – oh I have been nutted! [*Ib.* Variations in other instalments]

67 The court will now stand for Judge Schnorrer – and if you'll stand for him you'll stand for anything. [*Ib.* 'Dishonoured']

68 MORIARTY: How are you at Mathematics? H.S.: I speak it like a native. [*Ib.*]

69 You silly twisted boy! [*Ib.* and other instalments]

70 BLUEBOTTLE: Enter Bluebottle – where's the sausinges? [*Ib.* and other instalments]

71 Points cardboard finger at thousands of savage naughty men with Indian-type bare chests. [*Ib.* Variations in other instalments]

72 BLUEBOTTLE: What do you want, my Capitain – as if I didn't know! [*Ib.* 'The Great Bank of England Robbery', and repeated elsewhere]

73 Are you going to come quietly or do I have to use earplugs? [*Ib.* 'The Great Mustard and Cress Shortage']

74 I'm walking backwards till Christmas. [Remarks by any character in *The Goon Show*]

75 Don't you think it's going to be rather wet for the horses? [On having the Boat Race course described to him. Attr.]

SPIKE MILLIGAN and ERIC SYKES

76 A floor so cunningly laid that no matter where you stood it was always under your feet. [*The Goon Show*, 'The China Story']

77 HENRY CRUN: You can't get the wood, you know! [*Ib.* 'The Siege of Fort Night', repeated in various forms]

78 To conserve energy we marched lying down and only stood up to sleep. [*Ib.*]

79 It's only 80 miles as the crow flies – and our crow is a sick man. [*Ib.*]

W. HASLAM MILLS

80 There was always a secular draught blowing through the railway station. I did not myself use the railway station on Sunday for departure or arrival, but several times I have been there to meet those who came on evangelical affairs and, while waiting, I have observed the measured pacing and inhaled the cigars of those who did not excessively fear the Lord. [*Grey Pastures*]

HUGH MILLS

81 Nothing unites the English like war. Nothing divides them like Picasso. [*Prudence and the Pill*, Ch. 4]

A. A. MILNE

82 The average man finds life very uninteresting as it is. And I think that the reason why ... is that he is always waiting for something to happen to him instead of

setting to work to make things happen. For one person who dreams of making fifty thousand pounds, a hundred people dream of being left fifty thousand pounds. [*If I May*, 'The Future']

83 It is only the very young girl at her first dinner-party whom it is difficult to entertain. At her second dinner-party, and thereafter, she knows the whole art of being amusing. All she has to do is to listen; all we men have to do is to tell her about ourselves. [*Ib.* 'Going out to Dinner']

84 If I walk through any of the big stores with a parcel in my hand I expect to hear a voice whispering in my ear, 'The manager would like to see you quietly in his office' ... When I settle a bill by cheque, my 'face-of-a-man-whose-account-is-already-overdrawn' can be read across the whole length of the shop as soon as I enter the door. [*Ib.* 'Not Guilty']

85 Two inches to the north-west is written a word full of meaning – the most purposeful word that can be written on a map. 'Inn' [*Ib.* 'An Ordnance Map']

86 I wrote somewhere once that the third rate mind was only happy when it was thinking with the majority, the second rate mind was only happy when it was thinking with the minority, and the first rate mind was only happy when it was thinking. [*War with Honour*]

87 I am old enough to be – in fact am – your mother. [*Belinda*]

88 And nobody knows (Tiddely Pom) / How cold my toes (Tiddely Pom) / How cold my toes (Tiddely Pom) / Are growing. [*The House at Pooh Corner*, Ch. 1]

EWART MILNE

89 I ween it is between those twain / That once is seen: that twice is not seen! [*Once More to Tourney*, 'Grandmer's Busy Day']

D. MIRSKY

90 Freud has been accepted as the consecration of all desires and all lusts, a sort of free pass to every kind of freedom or looseness, a complete liberation from all discipline. He has become the Bible of this intelligentsia. [*The Intelligentsia of Great Britain*, Ch. 1, sect. 5]

JULIAN MITCHELL

1 Freud is all nonsense; the secret of neurosis is to be found in the family battle of wills to see who can refuse longest to help with the dishes. The sink is the great symbol of the bloodiness of family life. All life is bad, but family life is worse. [*As Far as You Can Go*, Ch. 1]

2 At Oxford he had been deliberately Byronic, and the Don Juan attitude was still there in emergencies. An enemy had once told him to his face that he needed more buckle and less swash. [*Ib.* I. 2]

3 Helen Gallagher was a short girl, and her shortness was emphasized by curly brown hair that looked ... like a mop with a permanent wave. [*Ib.* I. 3]

SUSAN MITCHELL

4 Some men kiss and do not tell, some kiss and tell; but George Moore told and did not kiss. [Quoted in O. St John Gogarty, *As I was Going Down Sackville Street*, Ch. 5]

JESSICA MITFORD

5 Knowing few children of my own age, I envied the children of literature to whom interesting things were always happening: 'Oliver Twist was so *lucky* to live in a fascinating orphanage!' [*Hons and Rebels*, Ch. 3]

6 I have nothing against undertakers personally. It's just that I wouldn't want one to bury my sister. [Attr. *Saturday Review*, 1 Feb. 1964]

NANCY MITFORD

7 Aunt Sadie ... so much disliked hearing about health that people often took her for a Christian Scientist, which, indeed, she might have become had she not disliked hearing about religion even more. [*The Pursuit of Love*, Ch. 4]

8 I was always led to suppose that no educated person ever spoke of notepaper. [*Ib.*]

9 I have only read one book in my life, and that is *White Fang*. It's so frightfully good I've never bothered to read another. [*Ib.*]

10 The high spirits, which ... he had seemed to possess, must have been due to youth, drink and good health. Now that he was grown up and married he put all three resolutely behind him. [*Ib.* 10]

HENRY MOAT

11 Poor Sir George, he really is an hero for his bed. I have known him often being *tired* of laying in bed, get up to have a rest, and after he had rested get back again into bed like a martyr. [Quoted in Sir Osbert Sitwell, *The Scarlet Tree*, Bk 3, Ch. 3]

GENERAL SIR JOHN MONASH

12 I don't care a damn for your loyal service when you think I am right; when I really want it most is when you think I am *wrong*. [Attr. in Colin MacInnes, *England, Half English*, 'Joshua Reborn']

HAROLD MONRO

13 That star-enchanted song falls through the air / From lawn to lawn down terraces of sound, / Darts in white arrows on the shadowed ground; / While all the night you sing. [*The Nightingale near the House*]

14 Now is your voice a marble high and white, / Then like a mist in fields of paradise; / Now is a raging fire, then is like ice, / Then breaks and it is dawn. [*Ib.*]

C. E. MONTAGUE

15 War hath no fury like a non-combatant. [*Disenchantment*, Ch. 15]

16 A gifted small girl has explained that pins are a great means of saving life, 'by not swallowing them'. [*Dramatic Values*]

VISCOUNT MONTGOMERY

17 This sort of thing may be tolerated by the French, but we are British – thank God. [On Homosexuality Bill, quoted *Daily Mail*, 27 May 1965]

HENRI DE MONTHERLANT

18 *L'homme qui se marie fait toujours un cadeau à la femme parce qu'elle a besoin du marriage et lui n'en a pas besoin. ... La femme est faite pour l'homme, l'homme est fait pour la vie.* – The man who marries always makes the woman a present because she needs marriage and he does not. ... Woman is made for man, man is made for life. [*Les Jeunes Filles*]

DORIS LANGLEY MOORE

19 The Churches grow old but do not grow up. [*The Vulgar Heart*, Ch. 2]

GEORGE MOORE

20 The best prose is usually written by poets – Shakespeare wrote the best seventeenth century, and Shelley the best nineteenth; and I don't think I'm going too far when I say that Mr Hardy has written the worst. [*Conversations in Ebury Street*, Ch. 5]

21 I have searched modern life for the best substitute for the knight and have discovered nothing better than a King's Messenger. [*Ib.* 12]

22 Mr Conrad has paid us a pretty compliment by learning to write the English language correctly, and the journalists are so pleased that they have assigned him a place in our literature. [*Ib.* 19]

23 We can dispense with sex only when we are among three or four intelligences. [*Hail and Farewell*, 'Ave']

24 I had to keep you waiting till the strain of composition had worn off my face. [Quoted in O. St John Gogarty, *As I was Going Down Sackville Street*, Ch. 17]

25 To be aristocratic in Art one must avoid polite society. [Quoted in Cyril Connolly, *Enemies of Promise*, Ch. 15]

G. E. MOORE

26 The beautiful should be defined as that of which the admiring contemplation is good in itself. [*Principia Ethica*, VI]

MARIANNE MOORE

27 Openly, yes, / with the naturalness / of the hippopotamus or the alligator / when it climbs out on the bank to / experience the / sun, I do these / things which I do, which please / no one but myself. [*Black Earth*]

28 My father used to say, / 'Superior people never make long visits.' [*Silence*]

29 Nor was he insincere in saying, 'Make my house / your inn.' / Inns are not residences. [*Ib.*]

30 If 'compression is the first grace of style,' / you have it. [*To a Snail*]

T. STURGE MOORE

31 Two buttocks of one bum. [Of Belloc and Chesterton. Quoted in Stephen Potter, *Sense of Humour*, Ch. 1]

PROFESSOR J. H. MORGAN

32 We sigh for Mr Bradley's inimitable riot of playful metaphors when criticizing a certain metaphysical theory of how a baby comes to know a lump of sugar. [In article, *Quarterly Review*, Jan. 1929]

CHRISTIAN MORGENSTERN

33 *Ein Knie geht einsam durch die Welt. Es ist ein Knie, sonst nichts.* – There wanders through the world a knee, / A knee and nothing more. [*Galgenlieder*, '*Das Knie*', trans. R. F. C. Hull]

34 *Im Winkel König Fahrenheit / hat still sein Mus gegessen. / – 'Ach Gott, sie war doch schön, die Zeit, / da man nach mir gemessen!'* – In the corner King Fahrenheit / quietly ate his pap. / 'Oh God, those / were fine times / when they measured by me.' [*Ib.* '*Kronprätendenten*']

35 *Es war einmal ein Lattenzaun, / mit Zwischenraum, hindurchzuschaun. / Ein Architekt, der dieses sah, / stand eines Abends plötzlich da – / und nahm den Zwischenraum heraus / und baute draus ein groszes Haus.* – There was a fence with spaces you / Could look through if you wanted to. / An architect who saw this thing / Stood there one summer evening, / Took out the spaces with great care / And built a castle in the air. [*Ib.* '*Der Lattenzaun*']

36 *Die Möwen sehen alle aus / als ob sie Emma hieszen.* – The seagulls all look / as if they were called Emma. [*Ib.* '*Möwenlied*']

37 *Wenn ich sitze, will ich nicht / sitzen, wie mein Sitz-Fleisch möchte, / sondern wie mein Sitz-Geist sich, / säsze er, den Stuhl sich flöchte.* – When I sit I don't like to / sit the way my fleshly bottom wants to, / but in the way that my spiritual bottom would, if it sat, / intertwine itself with the chair. [*Der Gingganz*, '*Der Aesthet*']

38 *Es gibt ein Gespenst / das friszt Taschentücher; / es begleitet dich / auf deiner Reise.* – There is a ghost / That eats handkerchiefs; / It keeps you company / On all your travels. [*Ib.* '*Gespenst*']

39 *Korf erwidert darauf kurz und rund: / 'Einer hohen Direktion / stellt sich, laut persönlichen Befund, / untig angefertigte Person / als nichtexistent im Eigen-Sinn / bürgerlicher Konvention / vor und aus. –'* Korf sent an answer mild and bland: / 'Your letter of the 10th to hand. / The undersigned herewith presents / His most obsequious compliments. / But would apprise you of the fact / That, in the strict sense of the Act / As touching personal matters, he / Is a complete nonentity.' [*Palmström*, '*Die Behörde*']

40 *Palmström baut sich eine Geruchs-Orgel / und spielt darauf v. Korfs Nieswurz-Sonate.* – Palmström builds himself a Smell-organ/ and plays von Korf's sneeze-wort [hellebore] sonata on it. [*Ib.* '*Die Geruchs-Orgel*']

41 *Zwar ein Werk, wie allerwärts, / doch zugleich ein Werk – mit Herz.* – Though clockwork in its outward part / It hides within – a tender heart. [*Ib.*]

42 *Und er kommt zu dem Ergebnis: / 'Nur ein Traum war das Erlebnis. / Weil,' so schliiszt er messerscharf, / 'nicht sein kann, was nicht sein darf.'* – And so he comes to the conclusion / The whole affair was an illusion. / 'For look,' he cries triumphantly, / 'What's not permitted CANNOT be!' [*Ib.* '*Die unmögliche Tatsache*']

CHRISTOPHER MORLEY

43 There are three ingredients in the good life: learning, earning and yearning. [*Parnassus on Wheels*, Ch. 10]

44 A human being: an ingenious assembly of portable plumbing. [*Human Being*, Ch. 11]

45 He is too experienced a parent ever to make positive promises. [*Thunder on the Left*, Ch. 5]

46 Life is a foreign language: all men mispronounce it. [*Ib.* 14]

47 Prophets were twice stoned – first in anger; then, after their death, with a handsome slab in the graveyard. [*Where the Blue Begins*, Ch. 11]

ROBERT MORLEY

48 The British tourist is always happy abroad so long as the natives are waiters. [*Observer*, 'Sayings of the Week', 20 Apr. 1958]

49 Beware of the conversationalist who adds 'in other words'. He is merely starting afresh. [*Observer*, 'Sayings of the Week', 6 Dec. 1964]

J. E. MORPURGO

50 Every Englishman has to survive one insult the moment he lands on foreign soil: he is called an 'alien'. [*American Excursion*]

51 No matter what evidence may be cited as a proof of American crowd-mindedness, it is significant to note that the single most popular form of recreation in the United States is Walton's lonely sport of fishing. [R. B. Nye and J. E. Morpugo, *A History of the United States*]

52 Teachers regard tails as more important than heads for the inculcation of knowledge. [*The Road to Athens*]

53 God would not have invented the automobile if he had intended me to walk. [*Ib.*]

54 Austria is Switzerland, speaking pure German and with history added. [*Ib.*]

DESMOND MORRIS

55 There are one hundred and ninety-three living species of monkeys and apes. One hundred and ninety-two of them are covered with hair. The exception is a naked ape self-named *Homo sapiens*. [*The Naked Ape*, Introduction]

56 He [*Homo sapiens*] is proud that he has the biggest brain of all the primates, but attempts to conceal the fact that he also has the biggest penis. [*Ib.*]

57 Clearly, then, the city is not a concrete jungle, it is a human zoo. [*The Human Zoo*, Introduction]

JAMES MORRIS

58 The master illusion of Spain is the conviction that the Spaniards are a people different, when they are only a people separate. [*The Presence of Spain*]

JOHN MORTIMER

59 And what've I achieved? Three women in my life and one of *them* turned out to be a chartered accountant over thirty! [*Two Stars for Comfort*, I. ii]

60 Eddy was a tremendously tolerant person, but he wouldn't put up with the Welsh. He always said, surely there's enough English to go round. [*Ib.*]

J. B. MORTON
['BEACHCOMBER']

61 Dr Strabismus (Whom God Preserve) of Utrecht is carrying out research work with a view to crossing salmon with mosquitoes. He says it will mean a bite every time for fishermen. [*By the Way*, January Tail-piece]

62 Already the stream side is dotted with clusters of upadiddle and old man's foot and the curious may find in crannies of old walls the lovely bedsoxia, with its trailing stamen and its inverted corolla. [*Ib.* 7 February, 'Alone with Nature']

63 I hear that Lady Cabstanleigh has definitely 'taken up' Mrs Wretch, the novelist. They lunch frequently together at the Hibiscus, and Lady Cabstanleigh has two of Mrs Wretch's novels, expensively bound, lying on her drawing-room mantelpiece. [*Ib.* 10 February, 'Social Jottings']

64 Vegetarians have wicked, shifty eyes, and laugh in a cold and calculating manner. They pinch little children, steal stamps, drink water, favour beards ... wheeze, squeak, drawl and maunder. [*Ib.* 4 June]

65 Ilion is safe, and Agamemnon's fleet / Lies beached: Achilles yawns upon his bed, / Paris lies dreaming at Oenone's feet; / Helen is shingled, and the epic's dead. [*Ib.* June, Tail-piece]

66 I used to be able to shoot the rind off an apple stored in a loft at the top of a cast-iron lighthouse. [*Ib.* 13 August, 'On the Moors: Social Jottings']

67 One disadvantage of being a hog is that at any moment some blundering fool may try to make a silk purse out of your wife's ear. [*Ib.* September, Tail-piece]

68 Hush, hush, / Nobody cares! / Christopher Robin / Has / Fallen / Down- / Stairs. [*Ib.* 18 December, 'Now We are Sick']

69 A Mrs Tasker is accused of continually ringing the doorbell of a Mrs Renton, and then, when the door is opened, pushing a dozen red-bearded dwarfs into the hall and leaving them there. [*The Best of Beachcomber*, 1, 'The Case of the Twelve Red-bearded Dwarfs']

70 The Doctor is said to have invented an extraordinary weapon which will make war less brutal. It is described as a very powerful liquid which rots braces at a distance of a mile. [*Ib.* 5, 'Bracerot']

71 If perishable goods are used to wrap the tails of rocking-horses they become, by mansuetude, imperishable, because the tail of a rocking-horse, of which the wrapping is an integral part, is a structure and not a moving fixture. [*Ib.* 7, 'Cocklecarrot's Next Case']

72 He [Dr Smart-Allick of Narkover] said it was not always the timid fellow, with four conventional aces in his hand, who won the highest honours. 'It is often,' he said, 'the fifth ace that makes all the difference between success and failure.' [*Ib.* 8, 'The Drama at Badger's Earth']

73 She has a Rolls body and a Balham mind. [*Ib.* 9, 'A Foul Innuendo']

74 KEEPING THEIR END UP
Not many of our old families can boast that a Savile Row tailor calls four times a year at their country estates to measure the scarecrows in the fields for new suits. [*Ib.*]

75 He got the O.B.E. later for wearing an opera hat during a night attack on a mutinous tribe. [*Ib.*]

76 Behind every beetle you will find a good mother-beetle. [*Ib.* 10, 'Open Letter to Sir James Barrie']

77 'Mummy, who's that gentleman on the top of the column?' 'Hush, dear, that's Mr Victor Gollancz.' [*Ib.* 10, 'Overheard in Trafalgar Square']

78 I shall never forget my mother's horror and my father's cry of joy when, for the first time in my life, I said angrily to my father, 'That's not the hand I dealt you, Dad.' [*Ib.* 11, 'The Life and Times of Captain de Courcy Foulenough']

79 To fairy flutes, / As the light advances, / In square black boots / The cabman dances. [*Ib.* 12, 'The Saga of the Saucy Mrs Flobster: The Dancing Cabman']

80 SIXTY HORSES WEDGED IN A CHIMNEY
The story to fit this sensational headline has not turned up yet. [*Ib.* 13, 'Mr Justice Cocklecarrot: Home Life']

81 An hour later Jack Malpractice was doing ninety-four along the Great West Road in his long, low Sports Thanatos Six. [*Ib.* 15, 'Dead Man's Alibi']

82 'Does it occur to you,' asked a voice, 'that the absence of a dead body from a room does not necessarily prove that someone is dead? Your dead body is not in the kitchen, but you are not dead.' [*Ib.*]

83 All over England loving hands are packing trunks for the young gentlemen of Narkover, who reassemble today. [*Ib.* 16, 'The New Boy at Narkover']

84 Doctor Smart-Allick replied gravely, assuring the widow that an unarmed baby could carry the Crown Jewels openly down the High Street without being molested by anyone except the boys and masters. [*Ib.*]

85 Miss Boubou Flaring's reading of Agatha, the wronged rocking-horse maker's daughter, left nothing to be desired except death. [*Ib.* 17, 'If so be That']

86 Last night Cocklecarrot exclaimed, with his customary lucidity, that if a cow with handlebars is a bicycle, within the meaning of the Act, then a bicycle with four legs instead of two wheels is a cow. [*Ib.*]

87 Wagner is the Puccini of music. [Attr.]

SIR OSWALD MOSLEY

88 I am not, and never have been, a man of the right. My position was on the left and is now in the centre of politics. [Letter to *The Times*, 26 Apr. 1968]

89 Before the organization of the Blackshirt movement free speech did not exist in this country. [Quoted in M. Bateman, selections from the *New Statesman*, *This England*, Pt I]

STIRLING MOSS

90 It has taken thirty-three years and a bang on the head to get my values right. [*Observer*, 'Sayings of the Week', 23 Sept. 1962]

MALCOLM MUGGERIDGE

1 He [Sir Anthony Eden] is not only a bore but he bores for England. ['Boring for England', reprinted in Edward Hyams, *Newstatesmanship*]

2 They asked for a leader and were given a public relations officer; here is the news, and this is Anthony Eden reading it. [*Ib.*]

3 His [Eden's] writings are the same. There is nothing wrong with them except that they are unreadable. One has to fight one's way through them; only dogged determination and a series of pauses to get one's breath for a fresh assault will carry one on to the end. [*Ib.*]

4 Never forget that only dead fish swim with the stream. [Reported as said to him in Manchester, *Radio Times*, 9 July 1964]

5 California, where the twentieth century is a burning and a shining neon light, and where, anyway, cows are rarely seen out-of-doors nowadays. [*Observer*, 11 Apr. 1965]

EDWIN MUIR

6 These words rang in their ears as if they had said, / 'There was another road you did not see.' [*The Road*]

7 The House with the Seven Gables is gone, consumed by fire, / And in the evenings businessmen from Boston / Sit in the beautiful houses, mobbed by cars. [*Salem, Massachusetts*]

FRANK MUIR and DENNIS NORDEN

8 What are you – a sorcerer? / Only at home. In company I drink out of the cup. [BBC comedy series, *Take It from Here*, No. 216]

HERBERT J. MULLER

9 Few have heard of Fra Luca Parioli, the inventor of double entry book-keeping; but he has probably had much more influence on human life than has Dante or Michelangelo. [*The Uses of the Past*, Ch. 8]

LEWIS MUMFORD

10 Today, the notion of progress in a single line without goal or limit seems perhaps the most parochial notion of a very parochial century. [*Technics and Civilization*, Ch. 8, sect. xii]

11 However far modern science and technics have fallen short of their inherent possibilities, they have taught mankind at least one lesson: Nothing is impossible. [*Ib.* 8. xiii]

IRIS MURDOCH

12 'We aren't getting anywhere. You know that as well as I do.' 'One doesn't have to get anywhere in a marriage. It's not a public conveyance.' [*A Severed Head*, Ch. 3]

FRED MURRAY

13 When she play'd for Mister Gee, / She could always find the key, / Tho' she'd never had a lesson in her life. [*She'd Never Had a Lesson . . .*]

14 . . . 'Ginger, you're barmy! / Get your hair cut!' they all began to cry. [*Ginger, You're Barmy!*]

FRED MURRAY and GEO EVERARD

15 And it's all right in the summer time, / In the summer time it's lovely! / While my old man's painting hard, / I'm posing in the old back yard. / But oh, oh! In the winter-time / It's another thing you

know, / With a little red nose, / And very little clothes, / And the stormy winds do blow. [Song: *It's All Right in the Summer Time*]

GILBERT MURRAY

16 Experience dulls the edges of all our dogmas. [Attr.]

ROBERT MUSIL

17 Progress would be wonderful – if only it would stop. [Attr.]

BENITO MUSSOLINI

18 CURZON: What is your foreign programme?
MUSSOLINI: My foreign policy is 'Nothing for Nothing'. [Quoted in George Seldes, *Sawdust Caesar*, Ch. 12]

19 Fascism is a religion; the twentieth century will be known in history as the century of Fascism. [On Hitler's seizure of power, quoted in *ib.* 24]

20 Fascism is not an article for export. [German press report, 1932, quoted in *ib.* 24]

21 Between 1935 and 1940 we shall have reached a point that I should call crucial in European history. [Speech, May 1927]

22 I should be pleased, I suppose, that Hitler has carried out a revolution on our lines. But they are Germans. So they will end by ruining our idea. [Quoted in Christopher Hibbert, *Benito Mussolini*, Pt II, Ch. 1]

23 Yes, I have a tremendous admiration for Caesar. Still . . . I myself belong rather to the class of the Bismarcks. [*Conversations with Emil Ludwig*]

24 *Credere! Obbedire! Combattere!* – Believe! Obey! Fight! [Fascist slogan]

25 The Italians will laugh at me; every time Hitler occupies a country he sends me a message. [Remark to Ciano, quoted in Alan Bullock, *Hitler*, Ch. 8, sect. xii]

26 We cannot change our policy now. After all, we are not political whores. [Quoted in *ib.*]

F. W. H. MYERS

27 If our first clear facts about the Unseen World seem small and trivial, should that deter us from the quest? As well might Columbus have sailed home again, with America in the offing, on the ground that it was not worth while to discover a continent which manifested itself only by dead logs. [*Human Personality*]

28 Do you mean to tell me that you seriously believe in the possibility of the Lesbian vice between the ghost of a governess and a little girl of six? [Of *The Turn of the Screw*, quoted in Christopher Hassall, *Edward Marsh*]

N

VLADIMIR NABOKOV

1 She [went on] with her psychodramatics
and her lyrical ovipositing, laying all over
the place like an Easter rabbit, and in
those green and mauve poems – about the
child she wanted to bear and the lovers
she wanted to have ... every intonation,
every image, every simile had been used
before by other rhyming rabbits. [*Pnin*,
Ch. 2, sect. v]

2 Like so many ageing college people, Pnin
had long ceased to notice the existence of
students on the campus. [*Ib.* 3. vi]

3 Sterile instructors successfully endeavoured to 'produce' by reviewing the books
of more fertile colleagues. [*Ib.* 6. i]

4 Discussion in class, which means letting
twenty young blockheads and two cocky
neurotics discuss something that neither
their teacher nor they know. [*Ib.* 6. x]

5 Poor Knight! he really had two periods,
the first – a dull man writing broken
English, the second – a broken man writing dull English. [*The Real Life of
Sebastian Knight*, Ch. 1]

6 Spring and summer did happen in
Cambridge almost every year. [*Ib.* 5]

7 I am sufficiently proud of my knowing
something to be modest about my not
knowing all. [*Lolita*]

8 Literature and butterflies are the two
sweetest passions known to man. [Quoted
in *Radio Times*, Oct. 1962]

V. S. NAIPAUL

9 'But the man is a BA!' 'And LLB. I
know. I wouldn't trust an Aryan with my
great-grandmother.' [*A House for Mr
Biswas*, Ch. 3]

10 I think, then, that we should pass a
resolution to the effect that peaceful
persuasion should be followed by militant conversion. All right? [*Ib.*]

FRIDTJOF NANSEN

11 The difficult is what takes a little time;
the impossible is what takes a little
longer. [Attr.]

OGDEN NASH

12 Women would rather be right than
reasonable. [*Frailty, Thy Name Is a
Misnomer*]

13 Oh, what a tangled web do parents
weave / When they think that their
children are naïve. [*Baby, What Makes
the Sky Blue?*]

14 Sophisticated parents live agog in a
world that to them is enchanted; /
Ingenuous children just naïvely take it for
granted. [*Ib.*]

15 The camel has a single hump; / The
dromedary, two; / Or else the other
way around. / I'm never sure. Are you?
[*The Camel*]

16 The cow is of the bovine ilk; / One end
is moo, the other, milk. [*The Cow*]

17 The trouble with a kitten is / THAT /
Eventually it becomes a / CAT. [*The
Kitten*]

18 Beneath this slab / John Brown is
stowed. / He watched the ads, / And
not the road. [*Lather as You Go*]

19 Do you think my mind is maturing late, /
Or simply rotted early? [*Lines on Facing
Forty*]

20 Do you know my friend Mr Betts? /
I wish I could remember as accurately as
he forgets. [*Mr Betts's Mind a Kingdom
Is*]

21 Tell me, O Octopus, I begs, / Is those
things arms, or is they legs? / I marvel
at thee, Octopus; / If I were thou, I'd
call me Us. [*The Octopus*]

22 I prefer to forget both pairs of glasses and
pass my declining years saluting strange
women and grandfather clocks. [*Peeka-
boo, I Almost See You*]

23 He tells you when you've got on / too much lipstick, / And helps you with your girdle / when your hips stick. [*The Perfect Husband*]

24 She left stuff to be posted or expressed, / Hecate Hopper, the Polterguest. [*Polterguest, My Polterguest*]

25 The turtle lives 'twixt plated decks / Which practically conceal its sex. / I think it clever of the turtle / In such a fix to be so fertile. [*The Turtle*]

26 Plus ça change, plus c'est la memsahib. [Attr.]

SHRI JAWAHARLAL NEHRU

27 The only alternative to co-existence is co-destruction. [*Observer*, 'Sayings of the Week', 29 Aug. 1954]

W. D. NESBIT

28 *Let's keep the glow in old glory and the free in freedom too.* [Title of song]

H. W. NEVINSON

29 He [H. Scott Holland] used to run as if the Holy Grail were just round the corner, and he might catch it if only he could run fast enough. [*In the Dark Backward*]

BERNARD NEWMAN

30 Surely this is not cricket, even in Bulgaria. [When, told to ride straight on, he rode into the Danube. Attr.]

NEWS OF THE WORLD

31 'I have no doubt that this man deliberately took poison and he appears to have done so in a most cold-blooded and heartless way,' the coroner remarked in summing up. [Quoted in *New Statesman*, 'This England', 1937]

SIR JOHN NEWSOM

32 *All* education is, in a sense, vocational, vocational for living. ['The Education Women Need', *Observer*, 6 Sept. 1964]

BEVERLEY NICHOLS

33 Herr Hitler has one of the endearing characteristics of Ferdinand the Bull. Just when the crowds expect him to be most violent he stops and smells the flowers. I have a feeling, and I hope I am right, that for the next month or so Herr Hitler is going to take things a little easier and smell the flowers and listen to the nightingales. [From the *Sunday Graphic*, quoted in M. Bateman, *This England*, selections from the *New Statesman*, Pt I]

ROBERT NICHOLS

34 The sound of my own voice. [When asked what music he liked best. Quoted in Edward Marsh, *Ambrosia and Small Beer*, Ch. 5, sect. i]

BASIL NICHOLSON

35 There's enough acid in your stomach to burn a hole in the carpet. [Advertisement headline for digestive tablet]

BASIL NICHOLSON (or another member of the firm of J. Walter Thomson)

36 Horlicks guards against Night Starvation. [Advertising slogan]

HAROLD NICOLSON

37 How narrow is the line which separates an adventure from an ordeal, and escape from exile. [*Small Talk*, On Byron's Last Journey]

38 I do not consider that efficiency need be mated to extreme delicacy or precision of touch. . . . It should possess a sweeping gesture – even if that gesture may at moments sweep the ornaments from the mantelpiece. [*Ib.* 'On Being Efficient']

CARL NIELSEN

39 The right of life is stronger than the most sublime art, and even if we reached agreement on the fact that now the best and most beautiful has been achieved, mankind, thirsting more for life and adventure than perfection, would rise and shout in one voice: Give us something else, give us something new, indeed for

Heaven's sake give us rather the bad, and let us feel that we are still alive, instead of constantly going around in deedless admiration for *the conventional*. [*My Childhood*]

PRESIDENT RICHARD NIXON

40 This is the greatest week in the history of the world since the creation. [Of man's first moon-landing, said on board the *Hornet*, 24 July 1969]

FRANK NORMAN

41 Fings Ain't Wot They Used T'Be. [Title of play]

LORD NORTHCLIFFE

42 It is hard news that catches readers. Features hold them. [Quoted in T. Clarke, *My Northcliffe Diary*]

43 When I want a peerage, I shall buy one like an honest man. [Attr.]

44 It was necessary to get a paper talked about before the public would take any interest in it. There were only two reasons, I saw, for the purchase of papers. One was Curiosity, the other Habit. [Quoted in Hamilton Fyfe, *Northcliffe, an Intimate Biography*, Ch. 3]

45 [To Stewart Hamilton] I'm sure you must be a Jew; you've got such a Scotch name. [Quoted in *ib.* 10]

46 Six hundred years ago, there was near the site of *The Times* office a monastery, the home of the Blackfriars, recluses who lived remote from the world. The same kind of men inhabit Printing House Square today. [Quoted in *ib.* 14]

47 They are only ten. [Said to have been written up in his offices to remind the staff of their public's mental age]

MARY NORTON

48 They imagined they had their own names – quite different from human names – but with half an ear you could tell they were borrowed.... Everything they had was borrowed; they had nothing of their own at all. [*The Borrowers*, Ch. 1]

49 We don't talk fancy grammar and eat anchovy toast. But to live under the kitchen doesn't say we aren't educated. [*Ib.* 5]

50 If you're born in India, you're bilingual. And if you're bilingual, you can't read. Not so well. [*Ib.* 9]

51 But we *are* Borrowers ... like you're a – a Human Bean or whatever it's called. [*Ib.* 10]

52 'But I had me feeling. I had it bad.' 'What's that?' asked Arrietty. 'His feeling?' 'Up the back of his head and in his fingers,' said Homily. 'It's a feeling your father gets when' – she dropped her voice – 'there's someone about.' [*Ib.* 11]

53 She came to bed at last, looking spiky, like a washed-out golliwog. [*Ib.* 15]

GILBERT NORWOOD

54 It would be an uplifting sight when some grey-haired fanatic passed into the Beyond crying, 'Long live "Butterflies of North-East Bucks".' [*Too Many Books*]

JACK NORWORTH

55 Sister Susie's Sewing Shirts for Soldiers. [Title of First World War song]

IVOR NOVELLO

56 There's something Vichy about the French. [Quoted in Edward Marsh, *Ambrosia and Small Beer*, Ch. 4]

57 And Her Mother Came Too. [Title of song]

O

JOHN OATES

1 I am just going outside, and may be some time. [Last words, 16 Mar. 1912, quoted in Scott's diary, *Scott's Last Expedition*]

CONOR CRUISE O'BRIEN

2 It [Dublin] is a city where you can see a sparrow fall to the ground, and God watching it. [Attr.]

EDNA O'BRIEN

3 To Crystal, hair was the most important thing on earth. She would never get married because you couldn't wear curlers in bed. [*Winter's Tales*, 8: 'Come into the Drawing Room, Doris']

SEAN O'CASEY

4 I killin' meself workin', an' he sthruttin' about from mornin' till night like a paycock! [*Juno and the Paycock*, I]

5 He's an oul' butty o' mine – oh, he's a darlin' man, a daarlin' man. [*Ib.*]

6 It's only a little cold I have; there's nothing derogatory wrong with me. [*The Plough and the Stars*, I]

7 There's no reason to bring religion into it. I think we ought to have as great a regard for religion as we can, so as to keep it out of as many things as possible. [*Ib.*]

8 I've something else to do besides shinan-nickin' after Judies! [*Ib.* II]

9 English literature's performing flea. [Of P. G. Wodehouse, quoted in P. G. Wodehouse, *Performing Flea*]

CLIFFORD ODETS

10 Go out and fight so life shouldn't be printed on dollar bills. [*Awake and Sing*, I]

R. M. OGILVIE

11 He [Livy] had no wish to spend long years burrowing for irrefutable but trivial facts and to secure himself against criticism by burying them again in unreadable monographs. [Talk on Sir Walter Scott and Livy, *Listener*, 8 Nov. 1960]

DAVID OGILVY

12 At 60 miles an hour the loudest noise in this new Rolls-Royce comes from the electric clock. [Advertisement]

13 *Tout soldat porte dans sa giberne le bâton de maréchal*. Yes, but don't let it stick out. [*Confessions of an Advertising Man*, Ch. 10]

OKAKURA KAKUZO

14 He [the average Westerner] was wont to regard Japan as barbarous while she indulged in the gentle arts of peace: he calls her civilized since she began to commit wholesale slaughter on Manchurian battlefields. [*The Book of Tea*, Ch. 1]

OLE-LUK-OIE [pseudonym of Sir Ernest Swinton]

15 Evidently not well off – probably a charwoman. I caught a look at her gloves as she loosened her bonnet-strings, and the finger-tips were like a split bud of a black fuchsia just about to bloom. [*The Great Tab Dope*, 'The Sense of Touch']

EUGENE O'NEILL

16 For de little stealin' dey gits you in jail soon or late. For de big stealin' dey makes you emperor and puts you in de Hall o' Fame when you croaks. [*The Emperor Jones*]

J. ROBERT OPPENHEIMER

17 We knew the world would not be the same. [After first atomic test. *The Decision to Drop the Bomb*]

18 The physicists have known sin; and this is a knowledge which they cannot lose. [Lecture at Massachusetts Institute of Technology, 25 Nov. 1947]

JOSÉ ORTEGA Y GASSET

19 The epoch of the masses is the epoch of the colossal. We are living . . . under the brutal empire of the masses. [*The Revolt of the Masses*, Ch. 2]

20 The uprising of the masses implies a fabulous increase of vital possibilities; quite the contrary of what we hear so often about the decadence of Europe. [*Ib.*]

21 The world is the sum-total of our vital possibilities. [*Ib.* 4]

22 Revolution is not the uprising against pre-existing order, but the setting-up of a new order contradictory to the traditional one. [*Ib.* 6]

23 Civilization consists in the attempt to reduce violence to the *ultima ratio*, the final argument. [*Ib.* 8]

JOE ORTON

24 I'd the upbringing a nun would envy and that's the truth. Until I was fifteen I was more familiar with Africa than my own body. [*Entertaining Mr Sloane*, Act 1]

25 Persuade her. Cut her throat but persuade her! [*Ib.* III]

26 It's all any reasonable child can expect if the dad is present at the conception. [*Ib.*]

27 FAY: Have you known him long?
   HAL: We shared the same cradle.
   FAY: Was that economy or malpractice? [*Loot*, Act 1]

28 Every luxury was lavished on you – atheism, breast-feeding, circumcision. I had to make my own way. [*Ib.*]

29 Policemen, like red squirrels, must be protected. [*Ib.*]

30 Reading isn't an occupation we encourage among police officers. We try to keep the paper work down to a minimum. [*Ib.* II]

31 God is a gentleman. He prefers blondes. [*Ib.*]

GEORGE ORWELL

32 A person of bourgeois origin goes through life with some expectation of getting what he wants, within reasonable limits. Hence the fact that in times of stress 'educated' people tend to come to the front. [*The Road to Wigan Pier*, Ch. 3]

33 We may find in the long run that tinned food is a deadlier weapon than the machine-gun. [*Ib.* 6]

34 Sheffield, I suppose, could justly claim to be called the ugliest town in the Old World: its inhabitants, who want it to be pre-eminent in everything, very likely do make that claim for it. [*Ib.* 7]

35 There can hardly be a town in the South of England where you could throw a brick without hitting the niece of a bishop. [*Ib.*]

36 You can have an affection for a murderer or a sodomite, but you cannot have an affection for a man whose breath stinks – habitually stinks, I mean. [*Ib.* 8]

37 Comrade X, it so happens, is an old Etonian. He would be ready to die on the barricades, in theory anyway, but you notice that he still leaves his bottom waistcoat button undone. [*Ib.*]

38 The typical socialist . . . a prim little man with a white-collar job, usually a secret teetotaller and often with vegetarian leanings. [*Ib.* 11]

39 To the ordinary working man, the sort you would meet in any pub on Saturday night, Socialism does not mean much more than better wages and shorter hours and nobody bossing you about. [*Ib.*]

40 One of the analogies between Communism and Roman Catholicism is that only the 'educated' are completely orthodox. [*Ib.*]

41 It is only the 'educated' man, especially the literary man, who knows how to be a bigot. And, *mutatis mutandis*, it is the same with Communism. The creed is never found in its pure form in a genuine proletarian. [*Ib.*]

42 The underlying motive of many Socialists, I believe, is simply a hypertrophied sense of order. The present state of affairs offends them not because it causes misery, still less because it makes freedom impossible, but because it is untidy; what they desire, basically, is to reduce the world to something resembling a chessboard. [*Ib.*]

43 Queer that Comrade Mirsky's spiritual brother should be Father —! The Communist and the Catholic are not saying the same thing, in a sense they are even saying opposite things, and each would gladly boil the other in oil if circumstances permitted; but from the point of view of an outsider they are very much alike. [*Ib.*]

44 The foaming denouncers of the bourgeoisie, and the more-water-in-your-beer reformers of whom Shaw is the prototype, and the astute young social-literary climbers who are Communists now, as they will be Fascists five years hence, because it is all the go. [*Ib.*]

45 The higher-water mark, so to speak, of Socialist literature is W. H. Auden, a sort of gutless Kipling. [*Ib.*]

46 Man is not, as the vulgarer hedonists seem to suppose, a kind of walking stomach; he has also got a hand, an eye, and a brain. Cease to use your hands, and you have lopped off a huge chunk of your consciousness. [*Ib.* 12]

47 It is usual to speak of the Fascist objective as the 'beehive state', which does a grave injustice to bees. A world of rabbits ruled by stoats would be nearer the mark. [*Ib.*]

48 We of the sinking middle class ... may sink without further struggles into the working class where we belong, and probably when we get there it will not be so dreadful as we feared, for, after all, we have nothing to lose but our aitches. [*Ib.* 13]

49 Gordon averted his eyes from a beastly Rackhamesque dust-jacket; elvish children tripping Wendily through a bluebell glade. [*Keep the Aspidistra Flying*, Ch. 1]

50 In every one of those little stucco boxes there's some poor bastard who's *never* free except when he's fast asleep and dreaming that he's got the boss down the bottom of a well and is bunging lumps of coal at him. [*Coming Up for Air*, Pt I, Ch. 2]

51 Is it gone for ever? I'm not certain. But I tell you it was a good world to live in. I belong to it. So do you. [*Ib.* I, 4]

52 Before the war, and especially before the Boer War, it was summer all the year round. [*Ib.* II. 1]

53 If the war didn't happen to kill you it was bound to start you thinking. After that unspeakable idiotic mess you couldn't go on regarding society as something eternal and unquestionable, like a pyramid. You knew it was just a balls-up. [*Ib.* II. 8]

54 The novel is practically a Protestant form of art; it is a product of the free mind, of the autonomous individual. [*Inside the Whale*, II]

55 Probably the Battle of Waterloo *was* won on the playing-fields of Eton, but the opening battles of all subsequent wars have been lost there. [*The Lion and the Unicorn*, 'England, Your England']

56 Public life in England has never been *openly* scandalous. It has not reached the pitch of disintegration at which humbug can be dropped. [*Ib.* 'The Ruling Class']

57 A family with the wrong members in control – that, perhaps, is as near as one can come to describing England in a phrase. [*Ib.*]

58 Whatever goes upon two legs is an enemy. Whatever goes upon four legs, or has wings, is a friend. [*Animal Farm*, Ch. 1]

59 War is war. The only good human being is a dead one. [*Ib.* 4]

60 You would often hear one hen remark to another, 'Under the guidance of our Leader, Comrade Napoleon, I have laid five eggs in six days.' [*Ib.* 8]

61 Squealer always spoke of it as a 'readjustment', never as a 'reduction'. [*Ib.* 9]

62 Napoleon had commanded that once a week there should be held something called a Spontaneous Demonstration. [*Ib.*]

63 He intended, he said, to devote the rest of his life to learning the remaining twenty-two letters of the alphabet. [*Ib.*]

64 In reality there is no kind of evidence or argument by which one can show that Shakespeare, or any other writer, is 'good'. .... Ultimately there is no test of literary merit except survival, which is itself an index to majority opinion. [*Selected Essays*, 'Lear, Tolstoy and the Fool']

65 Creeds like pacifism and anarchism, which seem on the surface to imply a complete renunciation of power, rather encourage this habit of mind. For if you have embraced a creed which appears to be free from the ordinary dirtiness of politics – a creed from which you yourself cannot expect to draw any material advantage – surely that proves that you are in the right? And the more you are in the right, the more natural that everyone else should be bullied into thinking likewise. [*Ib.*]

66 Objective consideration of contemporary phenomena compels the conclusion that success or failure in competitive activities exhibits no tendency to be commensurate with innate capacity, but that a considerable element of the unpredictable must invariably be taken into account. Paraphrase of Ecclesiastes, Ch. 9, 11 [*Ib.* in *Politics and the English Language*]

67 The inflated style is itself a kind of euphemism. A mass of Latin words falls upon the facts like soft snow, blurring the outlines and covering up the details. The great enemy of clear language is insincerity. [*Ib.*]

68 The Catholic and the Communist are alike in assuming that an opponent cannot be both honest and intelligent. [*Ib.* 'The Prevention of Literature']

R. OSBORN

69 What religion not only promises a better life hereafter, but also organizes a series of five-year plans to realize that better life here and now? [*Freud and Marx*, Ch. 8]

JOHN OSBORNE

70 Never believe in mirrors or newspapers. [*The Hotel in Amsterdam*, Act I]

71 She's like the old line about justice – not only must be done but must be seen to be done. [*Time Present*, Act I]

CARL VON OSSIETSKY
(German pacifist)

72 Nothing that produced this war has been changed by it. [Said in 1919. Quoted in Erwin Leiser, *A Pictorial History of Nazi Germany*]

FRANK OTTER

73 I am of the opinion that had your father spent more of your mother's immoral earnings on your education you would not even then have been a gentleman. [Seymour Hicks, *Vintage Years*]

P. D. OUSPENSKY

74 Truths that become old become decrepit and unreliable; sometimes they may be kept going artificially for a certain time, but there is no life in them. ... Ideas can be too old. [*A New Model of the Universe*, Preface to Second Edition]

75 Man, as he is, is not a genuine article. He is an imitation of something, and a very bad imitation. [*The Psychology of Man's Possible Evolution*, Ch. 2]

76 The idea that man is a machine is not a new one. [*Ib.* 3]

77 What would happen to all our life, without negative emotions? What would happen to what we call art, to the theatre, to drama, to most novels? [*Ib.* 4]

78 Osokin looks round, and suddenly an extraordinarily vivid sensation sweeps over him that, if he were not there, everything would be exactly the same. [*Strange Life of Ivan Osokin*]

WILFRED OWEN

79 And in the happy no-time of his sleeping/ Death took him by the heart. [*Asleep*]

80 The old Lie: *Dulce et decorum est / Pro patria mori*. [*Dulce et decorum est*]

81 Whatever mourns when many leave these shores; / Whatever shares / The eternal reciprocity of tears. [*Insensibility*]

82 So secretly, like wrongs hushed-up, they went. / They were not ours: / We never heard to which front these were sent. [*The Send-off*]

83 My soul looked down from a vague height with Death, / As unremembering how I rose or why, / And saw a sad land, weak with sweats of dearth. [*The Show*]

P

LORD CHIEF JUSTICE PARKER

1 A judge is not supposed to know anything about the facts of life until they have been presented in evidence and explained to him at least three times. [*Observer*, 'Sayings of the Week', 12 Mar. 1961]

DOROTHY PARKER

2 He's really awfully fond of coloured people. Well, he says himself, he wouldn't have white servants. [*Arrangement in Black and White*]

3 Why, after all, should readers never be harrowed? Surely there is enough happiness in life without having to go to books for it. [Attr.]

4 All I say is, nobody has any business to go around looking like a horse and behaving as if it were all right. You don't catch horses going around looking like people, do you? [*The Best of Dorothy Parker*, 'Horsie']

5 I bet you could get into the subway without using anybody's name. [*Ib.* 'Just a Little One']

6 Three highballs, and I think I'm St Francis of Assisi. [*Ib.*]

7 And I'll stay off Verlaine too; he was always chasing Rimbauds. [*The Little Hours*]

8 I really can't be expected to drop everything and start counting sheep at my age. I hate sheep. [*Ib.*]

9 How do people go to sleep? I'm afraid I've lost the knack. I might try busting myself smartly over the temple with the nightlight. I might repeat to myself, slowly and soothingly, a list of quotations beautiful from minds profound; if I can remember any of the damn things. [*Ib.*]

10 I'm never going to be famous. My name will never be writ large on the roster of Those Who Do Things. I don't do anything. Not a single thing. I used to bite my nails, but I don't even do that any more. [*Ib.*]

11 Sorrow is tranquillity remembered in emotion. [*Sentiment*]

12 'Dinner,' she murmured bashfully, as if it were not quite a nice word for a young woman to use, and vanished. [*Too Bad*]

13 How do you do, Mr Jukes? And how is that dear little brother of yours, with the two heads? [*The Waltz*]

14 There was I, trapped. Trapped like a trap in a trap. [*Ib.*]

15 You can lead a whore to culture but you can't make her think. [Speech to American Horticultural Society]

16 If, with the literate, I am / Impelled to try an epigram, / I never seek to take the credit; / We all assume that Oscar said it. [*Oscar Wilde*]

17 You will be frail and musty / With peering, furtive head, / While I am young and lusty / Among the roaring dead. [*Braggart*]

18 Whose love is given over-well / Shall look on Helen's face in hell, / Whilst they whose love is thin and wise / May view John Knox in paradise. [*Partial Comfort*]

19 Here's my strength and my weakness, gents, / I loved them until they loved me. [*Ballade at Thirty-Five*]

20 The sweeter the apple, the blacker the core – / Scratch a lover and find a foe! [*Ballade of a Great Weariness*]

21 His voice was intimate as the rustle of sheets, and he kissed easily. [*Dusk before Fireworks*]

22 He lies below, correct in cypress wood, / And entertains the most exclusive worms. [*Epitaph for a Very Rich Man*]

23 Some men break your heart in two, / Some men fawn and flatter, / Some men never look at you; / And that cleans up the matter. [*Experience*]

24 That thing he wrote, the time the sparrow died – / (Oh, most unpleasant – gloomy, tedious words!) / I called it sweet, and made believe I cried; / The stupid fool! I've always hated birds. [*From a Letter from Lesbia*]

25 Four be the things I'd been better without: / Love, curiosity, freckles, and doubt. [*Inventory*]

26 There was nothing more fun than a man. [*The Little Old Lady in Lavender Silk*]

27 But I, despite expert advice, / Keep doing things I think are nice, / And though to good I never come – / Inseparable my nose and thumb! [*Neither Bloody nor Bowed*]

28 Why is it no one ever sent me yet / One perfect limousine, do you suppose? / Ah no, it's always just my luck to get / One perfect rose. [*One Perfect Rose*]

29 Accursed from their birth they be / Who seek to find monogamy, / Pursuing it from bed to bed – / I think they would be better dead. [*Reuben's Children*]

30 Lady, Lady, should you meet / One whose ways are all discreet, / One who murmurs that his wife / Is the lodestar of his life, / One who keeps assuring you / That he never was untrue, / Never loved another one ... / Lady, lady, better run! [*Social Note*]

31 'And if he never came,' said she, / 'Now what on earth is that to me? / I wouldn't have him back!' / I hope / Her mother washed her mouth with soap. [*Story*]

32 The man she had was kind and clean / And well enough for every day, / But oh, dear friends, you should have seen / The one that got away! [*Tombstones in the Starlight*, 'The Fisherwoman']

33 By the time you swear you're his, / Shivering and sighing, / And he vows his passion is / Infinite, undying – / Lady, make a note of this: / One of you is lying. [*Unfortunate Coincidence*]

34 Wit's End. [Nickname for Alexander Woollcott's New York apartment. Quoted in James Thurber, *The Years with Ross*]

35 If all the young ladies who attended the Yale promenade dance were laid end to end, no one would be the least surprised. [Quoted in Alexander Woollcott, *While Rome Burns*]

36 The affair between Margot Asquith and Margot Asquith will live as one of the prettiest love stories in all literature. [Reviewing Margot Asquith, *Autobiography*, in *New Yorker*]

37 Congratulations: we all knew you had it in you. [Telegram to friend who retired to the country to have a baby. Attr.]

38 Why, I never even knew that he was alive. [On being told that ex-President Coolidge had died. Attr.]

C. NORTHCOTE PARKINSON

39 Work expands so as to fill the time available for its completion. General recognition of this fact is shown in the proverbial phrase 'It is the busiest man who has time to spare.' [*Parkinson's Law*, Ch. 1]

40 The rise in the total of those employed is governed by Parkinson's Law and would be much the same whether the volume of work were to increase, diminish or even disappear. [*Ib.*]

41 For this real or imagined overwork there are, broadly speaking, three possible remedies. He [A] may resign; he may ask to halve the work with a colleague called B; he may demand the assistance of two subordinates, to be called C and D. There is probably no instance in history, however, of A choosing any but the third alternative. [*Ib.*]

42 Seven officials are now doing what one did before. This is where Factor 2 comes into operation. For these seven make so much work for each other that all are fully occupied and A is actually working harder than ever. [*Ib.*]

43 It is not the business of the botanist to eradicate the weeds. Enough for him if he can tell us just how fast they grow. [*Ib.*]

44 The British, being brought up on team games, enter their House of Commons in the spirit of those who would rather be doing something else. If they cannot be playing golf or tennis, they can at least pretend that politics is a game with very similar rules. [*Ib.* 2]

45 The result is a phenomenon that has often been observed but never yet investigated. It might be termed the Law of Triviality. Briefly stated, it means that the time spent on any item of the agenda will be in inverse proportion to the sum involved. [*Ib*. 3]

46 The defect in the intelligence test is that high marks are gained by those who subsequently prove to be practically illiterate. So much time has been spent in studying the art of being tested that the candidate has rarely had time for anything else. [*Ib*. 5]

47 Let us suppose that the post to be filled is that of Prime Minister. The modern method is to trust in various methods of election, with results that are almost invariably disastrous. [*Ib*.]

48 While the British Empire was mostly acquired at a period when the Colonial Office (in so far as there was one) occupied haphazard premises in Downing Street, a new phase of colonial policy began when the department moved into buildings actually designed for the purpose. This was in 1875 and the structure was well designed as a background for the disasters of the Boer War. [*Ib*. 6]

49 The age of Frustration will not always be the same in years ... but its symptoms are easy to recognize. The man who is denied the opportunity of taking decisions of importance begins to regard as important the decisions he is allowed to take. He becomes fussy about filing, keen on seeing that pencils are sharpened, eager to ensure that the windows are open (or shut) and apt to use two or three different-coloured inks. [*Ib*. 10]

50 It is now known ... that men enter local politics solely as a result of being unhappily married. [*Ib*.]

51 It will be observed that air travel, considered as a retirement-accelerator, has the advantage of including a fair amount of form-filling. [*Ib*.]

52 We knew how to make our predecessors retire. When it comes to forcing our own retirement, our successors must find some method of their own. [*Ib*.]

BORIS PASTERNAK

53 Gardens, ponds, palings, the creation, / foamed with the purity of tears, / are only categories of passion, / hoarded by the human heart. [*Definition of the Creative Power*, trans. J. M. Cohen]

54 And yet the order of the acts is planned, / The way's end destinate and unconcealed. / Alone. Now is the time of Pharisees. / To *live is not like walking through a field*. [*Hamlet*, trans. Henry Kamen]

55 When the heart dictates the line / it sends a slave on to the stage / and there's an end of art and there's / a breath of earth and destiny. [*Oh, had I known*, trans. J. M. Cohen]

56 No bad man can be a good poet. [Quoted in Ilya Ehrenburg, *Truce*]

CHARLES PÉGUY

57 The Social Revolution will be moral, or it will not be. [*Basic Verities*]

58 He who does not bellow the truth when he knows the truth makes himself the accomplice of liars and forgers. [Attr.]

THE PEOPLE

59 Sherry, pet cat of the Bishop of Colchester, has been renamed Shandy. 'One of my clergy suggested Sherry was a little too strong,' explained the Bishop. [Quoted in M. Bateman, *This England*, selections from the *New Statesman*, Pt III]

S. J. PERELMAN

60 The greatest naturalist I know lives in a penthouse overlooking Central Park. He hasn't raised his window shades in twenty years. [*Acres and Pains*, Ch. 1]

61 No country home is complete without a surly figure seated in the kitchen like Rodin's Thinker, wishing she was back in a hot little room under the Third Avenue Elevated. [*Ib*. 11]

62 If anyone wants to trade a couple of centrally located, well-cushioned showgirls for an eroded slope ninety minutes from Broadway, I'll be on this corner tomorrow at eleven with my tongue hanging out. [*Ib*. 18]

63 He takes her to a concert, where Tchaikovsky's Fifth Symphony makes them kinspirits, and, swept away by the bassoons, kisses her. [*Cloudland Revisited*, 'Sodom in the Suburbs']

64 Crazy Like a Fox [Title of book]

65 I guess I'm just an old mad scientist at bottom. Give me an underground laboratory, half a dozen atomsmashers, and a beautiful girl in a diaphanous veil waiting to be turned into a chimpanzee, and I care not who writes the nation's laws. [*Crazy Like a Fox*, 'Captain Future, Block that Kick']

66 You'll know me right away because my eyes will be so radiant; and, besides, I'll have a fresh mauve orchid in my hair – to say nothing of *Mademoiselle*, *Vogue* and *House and Garden*. [*Ib.* 'Hold that Christmas Tiger!']

67 By now my shabby old reflexes would tell me it was time to buy an evening paper and bury my head in it. A little whim of my wife's; she liked to dig it up, as a puppy does a bone, while I was sipping my cocktail. [*Ib.* 'Is there an Osteosynchrondroitrician in the House?']

68 Take a small boy smeared with honey and lower him between the walls. The bees will fasten themselves to him by the hundreds and can be scraped off when he is pulled up, after which the boy can be thrown away. If no small boy smeared with honey can be found, it may be necessary to take an ordinary small boy and smear him, which should be a pleasure. [*Ib.* 'Beauty and the Bee']

69 A feeling of emulsion swept over me. [*Ib.* 'The Love Decoy']

70 I tried to resist his overtures, but he plied me with symphonies, quartettes, chamber music and cantatas. [*Ib.*]

71 He bit his lip in a manner which immediately awakened my maternal sympathy, and I helped him bite it. [*Ib.*]

72 There had been a heavy fall of talcum several hours before and as far as the ground could see the eye was white. [*Ib.*]

73 Philomène was a dainty thing, built somewhat on the order of Lois de Fee, the lady bouncer. She had the rippling muscles of a panther, the stolidity of a water buffalo, and the lazy insolence of a shoe salesman. [*Ib.* 'Kitchen Bouquet']

74 For years I have let dentists ride roughshod over my teeth; I have been sawed, hacked, chopped, whittled, bewitched, bewildered, tatooed, and signed on again; but this is cuspid's last stand. [*Ib.* 'Nothing but the Tooth']

75 I'll dispose of my teeth as I see fit, and after they've gone, I'll get along. I started off living on gruel, and by God, I can always go back to it again. [*Ib.*]

76 Every now and then, when business slackens up in the bowling alley and the other pin boys are hunched over their game of bezique, I like to exchange my sweat shirt for a crisp white surgical tunic, polish up my optical mirror, and examine the corset advertisements in the New York *Herald Tribune* rotogravure section and the various women's magazines. [*Ib.* 'Sauce for the Gander']

77 You've a sharp tongue in your head, Mr Essick. Look out it doesn't cut your throat. [*The Rising Gorge*, 'All Out . . .']

78 Ostensibly the pair are engaged in running a cosmetic laboratory; actually, they seem to spend the business day mousing around each other, trading molten kisses and generally over-heating themselves. [*Keep it Crisp*, 'Amo, amas, amat . . .']

79 Her bosom was heaving and it looked even better that way. [*Ib.* 'Farewell, my lovely Appetiser']

80 Do young men nowadays still become hopelessly enamoured of married women easily ten years their senior who have mocking, humorous mouths, eyes filled with tender raillery, and indulgent husbands? Back in the twenties, when it was a lot easier for a woman to be ten years my senior than it is now, I was privileged to know one who fitted these specifications. [*Ib.* 'The Longer the Lip, the Smoother the Grift']

81 Hats, shoes and clothes off to Manuel Dexterides, a rugged, unaffected American . . . a man whose single-mindedness of purpose takes your breath away and points toward the dawn of a new tomorrow. [*Ib.* 'Nothing could be Finer']

82 Then he got to his feet, bowed formally, and went into the Pig 'n Whistle for an atomburger and a frosted mango. [*Ib.* 'Physician, Steel Thyself']

JUAN PERÓN

83 If I had not been born Perón, I would have liked to be Perón. [*Observer*, 'Sayings of the Week', 21 Feb. 1960]

MARSHAL PÉTAIN

84 Nobody was better placed than the President [Poincaré] to be aware that France was neither led nor governed. [On Poincaré's handling of the war. Quoted in Alistair Horne, *The Price of Glory*, Ch. 26]

85 One does not fight with men against material; it is with material served by men that one makes war. [Quoted in *ib.* 27]

86 To make a union with Great Britain would be fusion with a corpse. [On Churchill's proposal for Anglo-French union, 1940. Quoted in Winston S. Churchill, *Their Finest Hour*, Ch. 10]

DR LAURENCE J. PETER and RAYMOND HULL

87 *The Peter Principle:* In a Hierarchy Every Employee Tends to Rise to his Level of Incompetence. [*The Peter Principle*, Ch. 1]

88 Work is accomplished by those employees who have not yet reached their level of incompetence. [*Ib.*]

89 Competence, like truth, beauty and contact lenses, is in the eye of the beholder. [*Ib.* 3]

90 The watchword for Side-Issue Specialists is *Look after the molehills and the mountains will look after themselves.* [*Ib.* 13]

1 If you don't know where you are going, you will probably end up somewhere else. [*Ib.* 15]

2 *Lateral Arabesque* – a pseudo-promotion consisting of a new title and a new work place. [*Ib.* Glossary]

3 *Papyromania* – compulsive accumulation of papers. . . .
Papyrophobia – abnormal desire for 'a clean desk'. [*Ib.*]

SIR W. M. FLINDERS PETRIE

4 Instead of a five years sentence for bigamy, let us exile a man to a Muhammedan country. [*Janus in Modern Life*, Ch. 5]

NIKOLAUS PEVSNER

5 To fight against the shoddy design of those goods by which our fellow-men are surrounded becomes a moral duty. [*Industrial Art in England*]

6 Of park furnishings the most notable are the FOUNTAIN given by Baroness Burdett-Coutts in 1861, an elephantine polygonal structure with oversized putti and dolphins in niches, the whole in a Gothic-cum-Moorish style. [*London, except the Cities of London and Westminster*]

7 Hearty, robust and revolting. [Of a church. *Ib.*]

8 No part of the walls is left undecorated. From everywhere the praise of the Lord is drummed into you. [*Ib.*]

9 Seated also and steadily looking W. the bronze statue of Mr Peabody who established the Peabody Trust, by W. W. Story, 1868. [*London, the Cities of London and Westminster*]

PIERRE PFLIMLIN

10 The Channel really is not much wider than the Rhine. [*Observer*, 'Sayings of the Week', 20 Jan. 1963]

EDEN PHILPOTTS

11 Beer drinking don't do half the harm of lovemaking. [*The Farmer's Wife*, Ch. 1]

PABLO PICASSO

12 The beautiful doesn't matter to me. [Attr. Quoted in Murray Schafer, *British Composers in Interview*]

13 God is really only another artist. He invented the giraffe, the elephant and the cat. He has no real style, He just goes on trying other things. [Quoted in Françoise Gilot and Carlton Lake, *Life with Picasso*, Ch. 1]

14 Every positive value has its price in negative terms, and you never see anything very great which is not, at the same time, horrible in some respect. The genius of Einstein leads to Hiroshima. [Quoted in *ib*. 2]

15 I hate that aesthetic game of the eye and the mind, played by these connoisseurs, these mandarins who 'appreciate' beauty. What *is* beauty, anyway? There's no such thing. I never 'appreciate', any more than I 'like'. I love or I hate. [Quoted in *ib*.]

16 Age only matters when one is ageing. Now that I have arrived at a great age, I might just as well be twenty. [Quoted in John Richardson, 'Picasso in Private', reprinted in 'Shouts and Murmurs' from the *Observer*]

17 Painting is a blind man's profession. He paints not what he sees, but what he feels, what he tells himself about what he has seen. [Quoted in Jean Cocteau, *Journals*, 'Childhood']

18 I do not seek, I find. [Attr.]

WILFRED PICKLES

19 In Cornwall it's Saturday before you realize it's Thursday. [In BBC programme, *Have a Go*]

HAROLD PINTER

20 Fortnight after I married her, no, not so much as that, no more than a week, I took the lid off a saucepan, you know what was in it? A pile of her underclothing, unwashed. The pan for vegetables it was. The vegetable pan. That's when I left her and I haven't seen her since. [*The Caretaker*, I]

21 I got this mate in Shepherd's Bush. In the convenience. Well, he was in the convenience. Run about the best convenience they had. [*Ib*.]

22 I said to this monk, here, I said, . . . you haven't got a pair of shoes, have you, a pair of shoes, I said, enough to keep me on my way. . . . Piss off, he said to me. [*Ib*.]

23 I can't drink Guinness from a thick mug. I only like it out of a thin glass. [*Ib*.]

24 If only I could get down to Sidcup! I've been waiting for the weather to break. He's got my papers, this man I left them with, it's got it all down there, I could prove everything. [*Ib*.]

25 Shirts like these don't go far in the winter-time. I mean that's one thing I know for a fact. No, what I need, is a kind of a shirt with stripes, a good solid shirt, with stripes going down. [*Ib*. II]

26 I mean, don't forget the earth's about five thousand million years old, at least. Who can afford to live in the past? [*The Homecoming*, Act II]

27 In other words, apart from the known and the unknown, what else is there? [*Ib*.]

28 He's had more dolly than you've had cream cakes. [*Ib*.]

29 I've been the whole hog plenty of times. sometimes . . . you can be happy . . . and not go the whole hog. Now and again . . . you can be happy . . . without going any hog. [*Ib*.]

DAVID PIPER

30 A magnanimous tribute by Imperial England to a gallant if muddle-headed girl. [On the statue of Joan of Arc at Stanhope Gate, Hyde Park. *The Companion Guide to London*]

RUTH PITTER

31 The seldom female in a world of males! [*The Kitten's Eclogue*, IV]

WILLIAM PITTS

32 It is the overtakers who keep the undertakers busy. [*Observer*, 'Sayings of the Week', 22 Dec. 1963]

MAX PLANCK

33 I regard consciousness as fundamental. I regard matter as derivative from consciousness. We cannot get behind consciousness. [In an interview with J. W. N. Sullivan, quoted in Kenneth Walker, *The Circle of Life*, Pt 2, Ch. 3]

WILLIAM PLOMER

34 The whip-crack of a Union Jack / In a stiff breeze. [*The Boer War*]

35 Out of that bungled, unwise war / An alp of unforgiveness grew. [*Ib.*]

36 A pleasant old buffer, nephew to a lord, / Who believed that the bank was mightier than the sword, / And that an umbrella might pacify barbarians abroad: / Just like an old liberal / Between the wars. [*Father and Son: 1939*]

37 With first-rate sherry flowing into second-rate whores, / And third-rate conversation without one single pause: / Just like a couple / Between the wars. [*Ib.*]

38 Who strolls so late, for mugs a bait, / In the mists of Maida Vale, / Sauntering past a stucco gate / Fallen, but hardly frail? [*French Lisette*]

39 On a sofa upholstered in panther skin / Mona did researches in original sin. [*Mews Flat Mona*]

40 A rose-red cissy half as old as time. [*The Playboy of the Demi-World: 1938*]

41 There you'll encounter aunts of either sex, / Their jokes equivocal or over-ripe, / Ambiguous couples wearing slacks and specs / And the stout Lesbian knocking out her pipe. [*Ib.*]

42 'Look who's here! / Do come and help us fiddle while Rome burns!' [*Ib.*]

43 The eyes of some old saurian in decay / That asks no questions and is told no lies. [*Ib.*]

44 So never say to D'Arcy, 'Be your age!' – / He'd shrivel up at once or turn to stone. [*Ib.*]

45 It's so utterly out of the world! / So fearfully wide of the mark! / A Robinson Crusoe existence will pall / On that unexplored side of the Park – / Not a soul will be likely to call! [*A Shot in the Park*]

46 No, officer, it's something less. / It's justifiable matricide. [*The Widow's Plot*]

HENRI POINCARÉ

47 Thought is only a flash between two long nights, but this flash is everything. [Quoted in H. L. Mencken, *A New Dictionary of Quotations*]

DEPUTY POLIVANOV

48 I place my trust in the impenetrable spaces, impassable mud, and the mercy of Saint Nicholas Mirlikisky, Protector of Holy Russia. [Speech in the Duma, 4 Aug. 1915, quoted in Leon Trotsky, *History of the Russian Revolution*, Vol. II]

MICHAEL POPE

49 A fire has destroyed the Chameleon at Strood, / Which makes me exceedingly glad; / For the waitresses there were disgustingly rude / And the food was incredibly bad. [*Capital Levities*, 'Epitaph on a Country Inn Destroyed by Fire']

COLE PORTER

50 My Heart Belongs to Daddy. [Title of song]

51 Miss Otis regrets she's unable to lunch today. [Song: *Miss Otis Regrets*]

52 It's not 'cause I shouldn't, / It's not 'cause I wouldn't. / And you know, it's not 'cause I couldn't. / It's simply because I'm the laziest gal in town [Song: *Laziest Gal in Town*]

53 Let's Do It; Let's Fall in Love. [Title of song]

PETER PORTER

54 London is full of chickens on electric spits, / Cooking in windows where the public pass. / This, say the chickens, is their Auschwitz, / And all poultry eaters are psychopaths. [*Annotations of Auschwitz*]

55 Who would be loved / If he could be feared and hated, yet still / Enjoy his lust, eat well and play the flute? [*Soliloquy at Potsdam*]

BEATRIX POTTER

56 I shall tell you a tale of four little rabbits whose names were Flopsy, Mopsy, Cottontail and Peter. [*The Tale of Peter Rabbit*]

57 You may go into the field or down the lane, but don't go into Mr McGregor's garden. [*Ib.*]

58 I am worn to a ravelling. [*The Tailor of Gloucester*]

59 I am undone and worn to a thread-paper for I have NO MORE TWIST. [*Ib.*]

60 It is said that the effect of eating too much lettuce is 'soporific'. [*The Tale of the Flopsy Bunnies*]

STEPHEN POTTER

61 It was only by his *opening remarks*, his power of creating a sense of dis-ease, that one realized, as one used to say of him, that Gattling was *always in play*. [*Lifemanship*, Ch. 1]

62 It is an *important general rule* always to refer to your friend's country establishment as a 'cottage'. [*Ib.* 2]

63 To 'language up' an opponent is, according to Symes' *Dictionary of Lifemanship and Gameswords*, 'to confuse, irritate and depress by the use of foreign words, fictitious or otherwise, either singly or in groups'. [*Ib.*]

64 There is no doubt that basic weekendmanship should contain some reference to Important Person Play. [*Ib.*]

65 If you have nothing to say, or, rather, something extremely stupid and obvious, say it, but in a 'plonking' tone of voice – i.e. roundly, but hollowly and dogmatically. [*Ib.* 3]

66 In Newstatesmaning the critic must always be on top of, or better than, the person criticized. [*Ib.* 5]

67 Donsmanship he defines as 'the art of criticizing without actually listening'. [*Ib.* 6]

68 Lumer likes to be called 'The Guv'nor', but likes it to be thought that he likes to be called 'Bert'. [*One-Upmanship*, Ch. 3]

69 If your man says of some picture, 'Yes, but what does it mean?' ask him, and keep on asking him, what his carpet means, or the circular patterns on his rubber shoe-soles. Make him lift up his foot to look at them. [*Ib.* 4]

70 Basic Birdsmanship is of course to have the best pair of field-glasses in any group. [*Ib.* 10]

71 It is WRONG to do what everyone else does – namely, to hold the wine list just out of sight, look for the second cheapest claret on the list, and say, 'Number 22, please'. [*Ib.* 14]

72 A good general rule is to state that the bouquet is better than the taste, and vice versa. [*Ib.*]

EZRA POUND

73 Great Literature is simply language charged with meaning to the utmost possible degree. [*How to Read*]

74 I once told Fordie [Ford Madox Ford] that if he were placed naked and alone in a room without furniture, I would come back in an hour and find total confusion. [Quoted in V. S. Pritchett, *The Working Novelist*]

75 His true Penelope was Flaubert. [*Hugh Selwyn Mauberley*, 'E. P. Ode Pour L'Élection de son Sepulcre', I]

76 Observed the elegance of Circe's hair / Rather than the mottoes on sundials. [*Ib.*]

77 Caliban casts out Ariel. [*Ib.* III]

78 Walked eye-deep in hell / believing in old men's lies, then unbelieving / came home, home to a lie. [*Ib.* IV]

79 There died a myriad, / And of the best, among them, / For an old bitch gone in the teeth, / For a botched civilization. [*Ib.* V]

80 Dowson found harlots cheaper than hotels. [*Ib.* 'Siena mi fe; disfecemi Maremma']

81 And give up verse, my boy, / there's nothing in it. [*Ib.* 'Mr Nixon']

82 And we have heard the fauns chiding Proteus / in the smell of hay under the olive-trees, / And the frogs singing against the fauns / in the half-light. [*Cantos*, II]

83 And the life goes on, mooning upon bare hills; / Flame leaps from the hand, the rain is listless, / Yet drinks the thirst from our lips, / solid as echo. [*Ib.* VII]

84 Go to hell Apovitch. Chicago aint the whole punkin. [*Ib.* XII]

85 'I am not your fader but your moder,' quod he. / 'Your father was a rich merchant in Stambouli.' [*Ib.*]

86 The blossoms of the apricot / blow from the east to the west, / And I have tried to keep them from / falling. [*Ib.* XIII]

87 And old T.E.H. went to it, / With a lot of books from the library, / London Library, and a shell buried 'em in a dug-out, / And the Library expressed its annoyance. [*Ib.* XVI]

88 To the beat of the measure / From star-up to the half-dark / From half-dark to half-dark / Unceasing the measure. [*Ib.* XXXIX]

89 Said Paterson: / Hath benefit of interest in all / the moneys which it, the bank, creates out of / nothing. [*Ib.* XLVI]

90 Pull down thy vanity / Thou art a beaten dog beneath the hail, / A swollen magpie in a fitful sun, / Half black half white / Nor knowst'ou wing from tail / Pull down thy vanity. [*Ib.* LXXXI]

1 Of all those young women / not one has enquired the cause of the world / Nor the modus of lunar eclipses / Nor whether there be any patch left of us / After we cross the infernal ripples. [*Homage to Sextus Propertius*]

2 She is dying piece-meal / of a sort of emotional anaemia. / And round about there is a rabble / of the filthy, sturdy, unkillable infants / of the very poor. [*Lustra*]

3 Real education must ultimately be limited to men who insist on knowing; the rest is mere sheep-herding. [*ABC of Reading*]

COURTICE POUNDS

4 Alas, they are Bovril now! [Gag in *The Cherry Girl*, 1904]

ANTHONY POWELL

5 'He fell in love with himself at first sight and it is a passion to which he has always remained faithful. Self-love seems so often unrequited.' [*The Acceptance World*, Ch. 1]

6 Dinner at the Huntercombe's possessed 'only two dramatic features – the wine was a farce and the food a tragedy'. [*Ib.* 4]

7 Her carriage suggested that she was unable to decide whether she wanted to be taken for a discontented tragedy queen on a holiday or a careless tomboy caught up through no fault of her own in serious bohemian life. [*Agents and Patients*, Ch. 1]

JACQUES PRÉVERT

8 *La mère fait du tricot / Le fils fait la guerre / Elle trouve ça tout naturel la mère / Et le père qu'est-ce qu'il faite le père?* – The mother is knitting / The son is fighting in the war. / The mother finds this quite natural, and what's the father up to? [*Familiale*]

9 *Notre Père qui êtes aux cieux / Restez-y / Et nous resterons sur la terre.* – Our Father that art in heaven, stay there and we will stay on earth. [*Pater Noster*]

FRANK PREWETT

10 Know you not, fool, we are the mock / Of gods, time, clothes, and priests? / But come, there is no time for talk. [*Come Girl and Embrace*]

11 Alas, no maid shall get him / For all her love, / Where he sleeps a million strong. [*Voices of Women*]

J. B. PRIESTLEY

12 There's a good reason why the distillers are working at full blast. They're busy giving Old Highland Blended Courage by the case. Faith and Hope at twelve-and-six a bottle. Love seven years in bond. [*I Have Been Here Before*, Ch. 1]

13 I can't help feeling wary when I hear anything said about the masses. First you take their faces from 'em by calling 'em the masses, and then you accuse 'em of not having any faces. [*Saturn Over the Water*, Ch. 2]

14 Comedy, we may say, is society protecting itself – with a smile. [*George Meredith*]

15 We swing up the dizzy arpeggios as a hunted mountaineer might leap from crag to crag; we come down a run of demi-semi-quavers with the blind confidence of men trying to shoot the rapids of Niagara. Only the stout-hearted and great of soul can undertake these perilous but magnificent ventures. [*Self-Selected Essays*, 'An Apology for Bad Pianists']

16 I never walk into my own tailor's without feeling apologetic. I know I am unworthy of their efforts. It is as if a man without an ear for music should be invited to spend an evening with the Lener Quartet. [*Ib.* 'At the Tailor's']

181

17 When I first entered adult life I imagined, like the young idiot I then was, that I had complete control of my face. . . . As I never saw myself, it was some time before I was disillusioned. [*Ib*. 'Different Inside']

18 If there was a little room somewhere in the British Museum that contained only about twenty exhibits and good lighting, easy chairs, and a notice imploring you to smoke, I believe I should become a museum man. [*Ib*. 'In the British Museum']

19 I fancy that the Hell of Too Many People would occupy a respectable place in the hierarchy of infernal regions. [*Ib*. 'Too Many People']

20 Our great-grandchildren, when they learn how we began this war by snatching glory out of defeat . . . may also learn how the little holiday steamers made an excursion to hell and came back glorious. [On Dunkirk. Broadcast, 5 June 1940]

21 Our trouble is that we drink too much tea. I see in this the slow revenge of the Orient, which has diverted the Yellow River down our throats. [*Observer*, 'Sayings of the Week', 15 May 1949]

22 It is hard to tell where MCC ends and the Church of England begins. ['Topside Schools', *New Statesman*, 20 July 1962]

23 God can stand being told by Professor Ayer and Marghanita Laski that He doesn't exist. ['The B.B.C.'s Duty to Society', *Listener*, 1 July 1965]

V. S. PRITCHETT

24 Dickens was not the first or the last novelist to find virtue more difficult to portray than the wish for it. [*Books in General*, 'Oliver Twist']

25 The detective novel is the art-for-art's sake of yawning Philistinism. [*Ib*. 'The Roots of Detection']

26 Smollett's temper was, in some respects, a new, frost-bitten bud of civilization, of which sick, divided and impossible men are frequently the growing point. [*Ib*. 'The Unhappy Traveller']

MARCEL PROUST

27 Everything great in the world is done by neurotics; they alone founded our religions and created our masterpieces. [Quoted in Sagittarius and George, *The Perpetual Pessimist*]

28 The taste was that of the little crumb of madeleine which on Sunday mornings at Combray . . ., when I used to say good-day to her in her bedroom, my aunt Léonie used to give me, dipping it first in her own cup of real or of limeflower tea. [*Remembrance of Things Past: Swann's Way*, 'Overture', trans. R. Scott Moncrieff]

29 Once we believe that a fellow-creature has a share in some unknown existence to which that creature's love for ourselves can win us admission, that is, of all the preliminary conditions which love exacts, the one to which he attaches most importance, the one which makes him generous or indifferent as to the rest. [*Ib*. 'Combray']

30 That was not to say that M. Legrandin was anything but sincere when he inveighed against snobs. He could not (from his own knowledge, at least) be aware that he was one also, since it is only with the passions of others that we are ever really familiar, and what we come to find out about our own can be no more than what other people have shown us. [*Ib*.]

31 It was in vain that I lingered before the hawthorns, to breathe in, to marshal before my mind . . . to lose in order to rediscover their invisible and unchanging odour. [*Ib*.]

32 And so was wafted to my ears the name of Gilberte, bestowed on me like a talisman which might, perhaps, enable me some day to rediscover her whom its syllables had just endowed with a definite personality. [*Ib*.]

33 Bodily passion, which has been so unjustly decried, compels its victims to display every vestige that is in them of unselfishness and generosity, and so effectively that they shine resplendent in the eyes of all beholders. [*Ib*.]

34 Swann, who behaved quite simply and was at his ease when with a duchess, would tremble, for fear of being despised, and would instantly begin to pose, were he to meet her grace's maid. [*Ib*. 'Swann in Love']

35 Among all the methods by which love is brought into being, among all the agents which disseminate that blessed bane, there are few so efficacious as the great gust of agitation which now and then sweeps over the human spirit. [*Ib.*]

36 Examining his complaint with as much scientific detachment as if he had inoculated himself with it in order to study its effects, he told himself that, when he was cured of it, what Odette might or might not do would be indifferent to him. But in his morbid state, to tell the truth, he feared death itself no more than such a recovery, which would, in fact, amount to the death of all that he then was. [*Ib.*]

37 People often say that, by pointing out to a man the faults of his mistress, you succeed only in strengthening his attachment to her, because he does not believe you; yet how much more so if he does! [*Ib.*]

38 What we suppose to be our love, our jealousy, are neither of them, single, continuous and individual passions. They are composed of an infinity of successive loves, of different jealousies, each of which is ephemeral, although by their uninterrupted multitude they give us the impression of continuity, the illusion of unity. [*Ib.*]

39 To think that I have wasted years of my life, that I have longed for death, that the greatest love that I have ever known has been for a woman who did not please me, who was not in my style! [*Ib.*]

40 The places that we have known belong now only to the little world of space on which we map them for our own convenience. None of them was ever more than a thin slice, held between the contiguous impressions that composed our life at that time; remembrance of a particular form is but regret for a particular moment; and houses, roads, avenues are as fugitive, alas, as the years. [*Ib.* 'Place Names']

41 The applause ... was mechanically produced by the effect of the applause that had gone before, just as in a storm, once the sea is sufficiently disturbed, it will continue to swell, even after the wind has begun to subside. [*Ib. Within a Budding Grove*, 'Madame Swann at Home']

42 The bonds that unite us to another creature receive their consecration when that creature adopts the same point of view as ourself in judging one of our imperfections. [*Ib.*]

43 In theory one is aware that the earth revolves, but in practice one does not perceive it, the ground upon which one treads seems not to move, and one can live undisturbed. So it is with Time in one's life. [*Ib.*]

44 Neurotic subjects are perhaps less addicted than any, despite the time-honoured phrase, to 'listening to their insides': they can hear so many things going on inside themselves, by which they realize later that they did wrong to let themselves be alarmed, that they end by paying no attention to any of them. [*Ib.*]

45 The man of genius, to shelter himself from the ignorant contempt of the world, may say to himself that, since one's contemporaries are incapable of the necessary detachment, works written for posterity should be read by posterity alone, like certain pictures which one cannot appreciate when one stands too close to them. [*Ib.*]

46 We alone can, by a belief that they have an existence of their own, give to certain of the things that we see a soul, which they afterwards keep, which they develop in our minds. [*Ib.*]

47 A powerful idea communicates some of its strength to him who challenges it. [*Ib.*]

48 There can be no peace of mind in love, since the advantage one has secured is never anything but a fresh starting-point for further desires. [*Ib.*]

49 As soon as one is unhappy one becomes moral. [*Ib.*]

50 It is our noticing them that puts things in a room, our growing used to them that takes them away again and clears a space for us. [*Ib.* 'Place Names']

51 As to the pretty girls who went past, from the day on which I had first known that their cheeks could be kissed, I had become curious about their souls. [*Ib.*]

52 Beauty is a sequence of hypotheses which ugliness cuts short when it bars the way that we could already see opening into the unknown. [*Ib.*]

53 He strode rapidly across the hotel, seeming to be in pursuit of his monocle, which kept darting away in front of him like a butterfly. [*Ib.*]

54 To strip our pleasures of imagination is to reduce them to their own dimensions, that is to say to nothing. [*Ib.* 'Bloch']

55 Artistic genius in its reactions is like those extremely high temperatures which have the power to disintegrate combinations of atoms which they proceed to combine afresh in a diametrically opposite order, following another type. [*Ib.* 'Elstir']

56 We have only to see, by the side of any of those girls, her mother or her aunt, to realize the distance over which, obeying the gravitation of a type that is, generally speaking, deplorable, her features will have travelled in less than thirty years. [*Ib.*]

57 A certain similarity exists, although the type evolves, between all the women we love, a similarity that is due to the fixity of our temperament, which it is that chooses them, eliminating all those who would not be at once our opposite and our complement, fitted that is to say to gratify our senses and to wring our heart. [*Ib.*]

58 We understand the characters of people who do not interest us; how can we ever grasp that of a person who is an intimate part of our existence ... whose motives provide us with an inexhaustible supply of anxious hypotheses which we perpetually reconstruct? [*Ib.*]

59 The human face is indeed, like the face of the God of some Oriental theogony, a whole cluster of faces, crowded together but on different surfaces so that one does not see them all at once. [*Ib.*]

60 The other person is destroyed when we cease to see him; after which his next appearance means a fresh creation of him, different from that which immediately preceded it, if not from them all. [*Ib.*]

61 Berma's interpretation was, around Racine's work, a second work, quickened also by the breath of genius. [*Ib.* The Guermantes Way, Vol. I]

62 The ever infuriated servants of the Mystery, the umbrageous priestesses of the Invisible, the Young Ladies of the Telephone. [*Ib.*]

63 She's the sort of woman who does a tremendous lot for her old governesses. [*Ib.*]

64 I realized that many women for the sake of whom men live, suffer, take their lives, may be in themselves or for other people what Rachel was for me. The idea that anyone could be tormented by curiosity with regard to her life stupefied me. [*Ib.*]

65 It was not 'Rachel when from the Lord' – who seemed to me a small matter – it was the power of the human imagination, the illusion on which were based the pains of love; these I felt to be vast. [*Ib.*]

66 She had one of those faces to which distance – and not necessarily that between stalls and stage, the world being in this respect only a larger theatre – gives form and outline and which, seen close at hand, dissolve back into dust. [*Ib.*]

67 I knew, of course, that idealism, even subjective idealism, did not prevent great philosophers from still having hearty appetites or from presenting themselves with untiring perseverance for election to the Academy. [*Ib.*]

68 As soon as he ceased to be mad he became merely stupid. There are maladies we must not seek to cure because they alone protect us from others that are more serious. [*Ib.*]

69 Certainly it is more reasonable to devote one's life to women than to postage-stamps or old snuffboxes, even to pictures or statues. Only the example of other collectors should be a warning to us to make changes, to have not one woman only but several. [*Ib.* Vol. II, Ch. 1]

70 There is nothing like desire for preventing the thing one says from bearing any resemblance to what one has in mind. [*Ib.* 2]

71 It has been said that the highest praise of God consists in the denial of Him by the atheist, who finds creation so perfect that he can dispense with a creator. [*Ib.*]

72 There was nothing else in the picture, a bundle of asparagus exactly like what you're eating now. But I must say I declined to swallow M. Elstir's asparagus. He asked three hundred francs for them. [*Ib.*]

73 His hatred of snobs was a derivative of his snobbishness, but made the simpletons (in other words, everyone) believe that he was immune from snobbishness. [*Ib.*]

74 She was already one of those sacred monsters before whom I refused to bow the knee when I made my first appearance in society. I thought she had been dead for years; which for that matter would be the only possible explanation of the spectacle she presents. [*Ib. Cities of the Plain*, Vol. II, Ch. 1]

75 Illness is the doctor to whom we pay most heed: to kindness, to knowledge we make promises only; pain we obey. [*Ib.*]

76 I have a horror of sunsets, they're so romantic, so operatic. [*Ib.* 2]

77 'Of course I do!' was what she said; but 'I haven't the faintest idea' was the message proclaimed by her voice and features which did not mould themselves to the shape of any recollection and by a smile that floated without support, in the air. [*Ib.*]

78 Since railways came into existence, the necessity of not missing the train has taught us to take account of minutes whereas among the ancient Romans, who had not only a more cursory science of astronomy but led less hurried lives, the notion not of minutes but even of fixed hours barely existed. [*Ib.*]

79 One would have thought that it was Mme de Marsantes who was entering the room, so prominent at that moment was the woman whom a mistake on the part of Nature had enshrined in the body of M. de Charlus. [*Ib.*]

80 Distances are only the relation of space to time and vary with that relation. [*Ib.* 3]

81 The conversation of a woman one loves is like the soil that covers a subterranean and dangerous water; one feels at every moment beneath the words the presence, the penetrating chill of an invisible pool; one perceives here and there its treacherous percolation, but the water itself remains hidden. [*Ib.*]

82 Albertine never related facts that were capable of injuring her, but always other facts which could be explained only by them, the truth being rather a current which flows from what people say to us and which we apprehend, invisible as it may be, than the actual thing that they say. [*Ib.*]

83 'He lives at Balbec?' intoned the Baron, with an air so far from questioning that it is a nuisance that the written language does not possess a sign other than the mark of interrogation with which to end these speeches that are apparently so little interrogative. [*Ib.*]

J. W. PRUITT

84 An' the Devil says, 'Boys, the next stop's Hell' / An' all the passengers yelled with pain / An' begged the Devil to stop the train. [Song, *The Hell-bound Train*]

85 You paid the fare with the rest of my load / An' you got to ride to the end of the road. [*Ib.*]

DAVID PRYCE-JONES

86 A bit of experience is excellent: a man must knock around the world, or the West End of London. [*Owls and Satyrs*, Pt I]

87 When you're bored with yourself, marry and be bored with someone else. [*Ib.*]

88 Down the winding Surrey lanes, past the decorated pubs, and houses set back from the road, with a Bentley instead of a garden in front. [*Ib.* III]

PUNCH

89 Darling only one more instalment and Baby will be *ours*. [Quoted in Robert Graves and Alan Hodge, *The Long Weekend*, Ch. 11]

COMMANDER PURSEY, M.P.

90 There we were, one foot on a bar of soap and the other in the gutter. [Attr.]

SIR ARTHUR QUILLER-COUCH

1 When a man talks of a 'home' and I discover him to mean a house of detention, I judge that he is trying to deceive. [*Open Letter to the Bishop of Exeter*]

R

RADIO TIMES

1 To me Thursday evening has always been pale pink with a faint green stripe growing broader towards nine o'clock. I am sure that all your readers will be thrilled to know this. [Letter quoted in *New Statesman*, 'This England', 1937]

JOHN RAE

2 His zeal was hollow; his sermons were like students' songs imperfectly recalled by a senile don. [*The Custard Boys*, Ch. 6]

3 A mother has an innate ability for aggravating the wounds of her offspring's pride. This is inevitable since the relationship between mother and child is a most unnatural one; other species have the good sense to banish their young at an early age. [*Ib.* 13]

4 War is, after all, the universal perversion. We are all tainted: if we cannot experience our perversion at first hand we spend our time reading war stories, the pornography of war; or seeing war films, the blue films of war; or titillating our senses with the imagination of great deeds, the masturbation of war. [*Ib.*]

ADMIRAL RAEDER

5 The C.-in-C. Navy [Raeder] cannot . . . advocate an invasion of Britain as he did in the case of Norway. [Quoted in W. L. Shirer, *The Rise and Fall of the Third Reich*, Ch. 2]

SIR WALTER RALEIGH

6 On leaving the Exhibition at the Royal Academy in company with his friend Mr Bell, the Author expressed his conviction that it is better, after all, to be a Human Being. Speaking of the writings of William Morris, Olive Schreiner and Andrew Lang, the Author remarked that they were very like the Bible, only sillier. [*Laughter from a Cloud*, 'Remarks']

7 We could not lead a pleasant life, / And 'twould be finished soon, / If peas were eaten with the knife, / And gravy with the spoon. / Eat slowly: only men in rags / And gluttons old in sin / Mistake themselves for carpet bags / And tumble victuals in. [*Ib.* 'Stans puer ad mensam']

8 An anthology is like all the plums and orange peel picked out of a cake. [Letter to Mrs Robert Bridges, 15 Jan. 1915, *Letters*, Vol. II]

9 There is no one thing to be found in books which it is a disgrace not to know. [Attr.]

JOHN CROWE RANSOM

10 And if no Lethe flows beneath your casement, / and when ten years have not brought full effacement, / Philosophy was wrong, and you may meet. [*Parting at Dawn*]

11 Here lies a lady of beauty and high degree. / Of chills and fevers she died, of fever and chills. [*Here lies a Lady*]

TERENCE RATTIGAN

12 The headmaster said you ruled with a rod of iron. He called you the Himmler of the lower fifth. [*The Browning Version*]

13 She has ideas above her station. . . . How would you say that in French? . . . You can't say au-dessus de sa gare. It isn't that sort of station. [*French without Tears*, I]

14 ROGER: Well, of course, there was only one thing to do. So I gave the order – all hands on deck—
ALAN: And did they come? [*Ib.*]

15 You can be in the Horse Guards and still be common, dear. [*Separate Tables*: 'Table Number Seven']

16 In future I trust that a son of mine will at least show enough sense to come in out of the rain. [*The Winslow Boy*, I]

17 A nice, respectable, middle-class, middle-aged maiden lady, with time on her hands and the money to help her pass it. . . . Let us call her Aunt Edna. . . . Aunt Edna is universal, and to those who may feel that all the problems of the modern theatre might be solved by her liquidation, let me add that . . . she is also immortal. [*Collected Plays*, Vol. II, Preface]

GWEN RAVERAT

18 But she never, never missed the train. I think she felt that it would not have been sporting to start in time; it would not have given the train a fair chance of getting away without her. [*Period Piece*, Ch. 5]

19 I have defined Ladies as people who did not do things themselves. [*Ib.* 7]

E. T. RAYMOND

20 During the Spring [of 1918] it seemed possible that the Japanese would, in quite a friendly way, invade Siberia, and that Britain would smile approval. [*Mr Balfour*, Ch. 20]

HERBERT READ

21 I saw him stab / And stab again / A well-killed Boche. / This is the happy warrior. / This is he . . . [*The Happy Warrior*]

PETER REDGROVE

22 He sighs, and the waves are a city of doors slamming; / God's arm englobes this tree and brandishes it. [*The Affianced*]

23 Love pines loudly to go out where / It need not spend itself on fancy and the empty air. [*Bedtime Story for My Son*]

24 I am a man that sits on benches. / My back is crossed and warranted by planks. / I accept beech-mast in payment. / The children take my conkers for their pleasantries. [*Genius Loci*]

25 For sixpence he can get drunk / And be a torero, the government, or a saint. [*Malagueño*]

HENRY REED

26 The wind within a wind, unable to speak for wind. [*A Map of Verona*, 'Chard Whitlow' (Mr Eliot's Sunday Evening Postscript)]

27 It is, we believe, / Idle to hope that the simple stirrup-pump / Can extinguish hell. [*Ib.*]

28 Oh, listeners, / And you especially who have switched off the wireless, / And sit in Stoke or Basingstoke, listening / appreciatively to the silence / (which is also the silence of hell), pray / not for yourselves but your souls. [*Ib.*]

29 To-day we have naming of parts. Yesterday / We had daily cleaning. And to-morrow morning, / We shall have what to do after firing. But to-day, / To-day we have naming of parts. [*Ib.* 'Lessons of the War', I]

30 They call it easing the Spring: it is perfectly easy / If you have any strength in your thumb: like the bolt, / And the breech, and the cocking-piece, and the point of balance, / Which in our case we have not got. [*Ib.*]

31 You must never be over-sure. You must say, when reporting: / At five o'clock in the central sector is a dozen / Of what appear to be animals; whatever you do, / Don't call the bleeders *sheep*. [*Ib.*]

32 Perhaps between me and the apparent lovers, / (who, incidentally, appear by now to have finished,) / At seven o'clock from the houses, is roughly a distance / Of about one year and a half. [*Ib.*]

33 And the various holds and rolls and throws and breakfalls / Somehow or other I always seemed to put / In the wrong place. And as for war, my wars / Were global from the start. [*Ib.* III]

34 We must learn the lesson / Of the ever important question of human balance. / It is courage that counts. [*Ib.*]

35 I think it may justly be said that English women in general are very common diatonic little numbers. They differ greatly in this from the women of, say, North Africa. [Radio drama, *Emily Butter*]

36 Take, for example, the passage in Act Seven when Emily gets herself locked into the lift. Here we have a series of frag-

mentary utterances, pathetic, wistful and disjointed, which suddenly melt into a heavenly curve of melody. [*Ib.*]

37 Henry has always led what could be called a sedentary life, if only he'd ever got as far as actually sitting up. [Radio drama, *Not a Drum was Heard: The War Memoirs of General Gland*]

38 It was, I think, a *good* war, one of the best there have so far been. I've often advanced the view that it was a war deserving of better generalship than it received on either side. [*Ib.*]

39 It's a life-mask of myself wearing an army respirator. Rather an experimental piece, of course. I did it myself. [*Ib.*]

40 A charming, simple, extremely virile race ... barely touched by civilization, their only garb a small loin-cloth, loosely slung over the right shoulder. [*Ib.*]

41 She's invented a new religion. Called 'Creative Sleep'. [*Ib.*]

42 In a civil war, a general must know – and I'm afraid it's a thing rather of instinct than of practice – he must know exactly when to move over to the other side. [*Ib.*]

43 We spent one whole evening a few weeks ago recording a very loud and beautiful chromium-plated bicycle bell. I bought it specially. Dreadfully tiring to the thumb, of course, but oh, it was worth it! [Radio drama, *The Primal Scene, as it were*]

44 GLAND: I would say it's somehow redolent, and full of vitality.
HILDA: Well, I would say it's got about as much life in it as a potted shrimp.
GLAND: Well, I think we're probably both trying to say the same thing in different words. [*Ib.*]

45 Anyone else in my position would have been riddled with internal persecutors, *riddled* with them; but my internal persecutors are all external ones, as you have only to look around you to see. [*Ib.*]

46 I dream quite a bit, myself. Only when I'm asleep, of course. Curious thing is it's always the same dream. ... Not that I mind, of course, I'm not one to hanker after change the whole time. [*Ib.*]

47 If one doesn't get birthday presents it can remobilize very painfully the persecutory anxiety which usually follows birth. [*Ib.*]

48 HILDA: This dance is absolutely authentic.
GLAND: No, no. It's just a debased copy of the things Sister Martin and the two nurses used to do in the jungle on their afternoon off. [*Ib.*]

49 Throw your voice *at* the note, by all means; but for God's sake remember to miss it. [Radio drama, *The Private Life of Hilda Tablet*]

50 Richard Sherwin is the only man, alive or dead, who can ever have been said to have interfered with ... my basic tone-row. [*Ib.*]

51 The sooner the tea's out of the way, the sooner we can get out the gin, eh? [*Ib.*]

52 Very few of our meetings with Miss Tablet were destined to be short ones. ... It was only when we came to say good-bye that we realized Miss Tablet had kindly accorded us nine-and-a-half hours of her illuminating company. [*Ib.*]

53 HILDA: Have you ever heard of a couple of chaps called Faber and Faber?
REEVE: Oh, of course, I ...
HILDA: Good. Right. Well, they're both after my life. [*Ib.*]

54 The original idea was that it should take place in the sixteenth century on a boat anchored off Rimini; it's Hilda who's altered it to a mutiny in the bargain basement of a drapery store. [*Ib.*]

55 Of course, we've all dreamed of reviving the castrati; but it's needed Hilda to take the first practical steps towards making them a reality. ... She's drawn up a list of well-known singers who she thinks would benefit from ... treatment. ... It's only a question of getting them to agree. [*Ib.*]

56 The work I refer to is my recent Quintet for eight instruments. [*Ib.*]

57 I know when Richard tickles me / Or bites me on the calf / It isn't for any subconscious reasons: / He does it to make me laugh. [Radio drama, *A Very Great Man Indeed*]

58 BETTY: Modest? My word, no. Nobody could say that. He was an all-the-lights-on man, Dicky Sherwin was.
ADELA: And a looking-glass too. [*Ib.*]

59 She's really quite playful sometimes. I know you wouldn't think it, but really I

189

have known her pass the whole evening without mentioning a single book, or *in fact anything unpleasant* at all. [*Ib.*]

60 It's the last scene from that final exquisite study in the ambiguity that attends all human relationships, *The Arse and the Elbow*. [*Ib.*]

JOHN REED

61 Ten Days that Shook the World [Title of book on Russian Revolution]

LEONARD REES

62 Damn it, man, I could cut the Lord's Prayer! [Quoted in James Agate, *Ego 1*]

REV. JAMES REID

63 'What's the good?' expresses the most characteristic mood of the modern mind. [1932. *Observer*, 'Sayings of Our Times', 31 May 1953]

GOTTFRIED REINHARDT

64 Hollywood people are afraid to leave Hollywood. Out in the world, they are frightened. ... Sam Hoffenstein used to say we are the croupiers in a crooked gambling house. And it's true. Everyone of us thinks, You know, I really don't deserve a swimming pool. [Quoted in Lillian Ross, *Picture*, 'Throw the Little Old Lady Down the Stairs!']

65 It reminds me of the time Sam Hoffenstein was given a Tarzan picture to rewrite. He was told to give it a new twist. He rewrote it – he put it all into Yiddish. [Quoted in *ib.* 'Everything has just gone Zoom']

66 You know, there are three kinds of intelligence – the intelligence of man, the intelligence of the animal, and the intelligence of the military. In that order. [Quoted in *ib.* 'Piccolos under Your Name, Strings under Mine']

67 Money is good for bribing yourself through the inconveniences of life. [Quoted in *ib.* 'Looks Like We're Still in Business']

LORD REITH

68 You can't think rationally on an empty stomach, and a whole lot of people can't do it on a full one either. [Attr.]

MANDY RICE-DAVIES

69 I am notorious. I will go down in history as another Lady Hamilton. [Apropos the Profumo scandal, 1963]

FRANK RICHARDS

70 'My esteemed chums,' murmured Hurree Jamset Ram Singh. 'This is not an occasion for looking the gift horse in the mouthfulness.' [*Bunter's Last Fling*, Ch. 5]

I. A. RICHARDS

71 Anything is valuable that will satisfy an appetency without involving the frustration of some equal or *more important* appetency. [*Principles*]

72 It [poetry] is a perfectly possible means of overcoming chaos. [*Science and Poetry*]

JOHN RICHARDSON

73 Picasso has a whim of iron. ['Shouts and Murmurs', from the *Observer*, 'Picasso in Private']

RALPH RICHARDSON

74 The most precious things in speech are pauses. [Attr.]

WILLIAM J. RICHARDSON

75 Do you want your philosophy straight or with a dash of Legerdemain? [*Heidegger*]

DONALD RICHBERG

76 In the first months of N.R.A. [National Recovery Administration] it seemed as though a great part of the business world had 'got religion'. [Quoted in A. M. Schlesinger Jr, *The Coming of the New Deal*, Pt 7, Ch. 25, sect. ii]

MORDECAI RICHLER

77 Remember this, Griffin. The revolution eats its own, Capitalism re-creates itself. [*Cocksure*, Ch. 22]

78 And furthermore did you know that behind the discovery of America there was a Jewish financier? [*Ib.* 24]

EDGELL RICKWORD

79 My soul's a trampled duelling ground where Sade, / the gallant marquis, fences for his life / against the invulnerable retrograde / Masoch, his shade, more constant than a wife. [*Chronique Scandaleuse*]

80 Twittingpan preached the marriage of true friends / when blessed parthenogenesis arrives / and he-uranians can turn honest wives. [*The Encounter*]

81 They flaunted gay shirts and a grand old vice. [*Ib.*]

82 Those censers of impurity / infect the air with banal dreams / of lovers by exclusive streams / and plages of dear fatuity. [*Provincial Nightmare*]

83 The oldest griefs of summer seem less sad / than drone of mowers on suburban lawns / and girls' thin laughter, to the ears that hear / the soft rain falling of the failing stars. [*Regrets*, II]

W. PETT RIDGE

84 The street in which she lived had started with the idea of going somewhere, but being discouraged had come to a definite stop as at the bottom of a sack. [*Lost Property*, Pt I, Ch. 5]

85 He took her up in his arms in the way of a bachelor who in his time has had amateur experience of the carrying of nieces. [*Ib.* 8]

86 She had once met a most gentlemanly lad about five feet in height on the pier at Southend, who had told her in confidence that he was an officer in the Life Guards, and whom she had afterwards seen riding a fishmonger's cycle cart down Tottenham Court Road. [*Ib.* II. 13]

87 Got looped up now with a publican's widow. . . . It's a funny thing she can't see a tumbler without wiping it with her handkercher. Still I don't blame her for giving up public life. [*Ib.* 20]

88 Horses is my occupation, but the ocean's my hobby. [*Love at Paddington*, Ch. 1]

89 When you take the bull by the horns . . . what happens is a toss up. [*Ib.* 4]

90 Gertie recommended her to adopt the habit of not magnifying grievances; if you wanted to view trouble, you could take opera-glasses, but you should be careful to hold them the wrong way round. [*Ib.*]

1 'How did you think I managed at dinner, Clarence?' 'Capitally!' 'I had a knife and two forks left at the end,' she said regretfully. [*Ib.* 6]

2 Gertie thanked him with a glance that, at any honestly managed exchange office, could be converted into bank notes. [*Ib.* 11]

3 We always call our maids Laura. . . . It's a tradition in the family. [*Mord Em'ly*, Ch. 2]

4 'Always a pleasant smile.' 'Steps off the pavement rather than run up against you.' 'Seldom without a cigar stuck in his face.' 'Gets shaved every day.' 'Never counts his change.' 'And with all that,' remarked the hostess, 'with all that, never letting anybody think that he's superior to those round about him.' [*Mrs Galer's Business*, Ch. 5]

5 No one knew what was happening, but every one bore a hopeful look as though wishful for the sight of disaster or entertainment of some kind. [*Ib.* 6]

6 Ballard admitted he was no hand at giving descriptions; the man was apparently a gentleman and the woman – well, not exactly a lady, although she had a very fine flow of language. [*Ib.*]

RAINER MARIA RILKE

7 *O Bäume Lebens, o wann winterlich? / Wir sind nicht einig. Sind nicht wie die Zug- / vögel verständigt. Überholt und spät, / so drängen wir uns plötzlich Winden auf / und fallen ein auf teilnahmslosen Teich.* – O trees of life, when will it be winter for you? We are not at one. We are not of one mind like the migratory birds. Overtaken and late, we suddenly hurry up-wind and fall on the indifferent pond. [*Duineser Elegien*, IV]

8 *Uns aber, wo wir Eines meinen, ganz, / ist schon des andern Aufwand fühlbar. Feindschaft ist uns das Nächste.* But we, when we are entirely intent on one thing, can feel the pull of another. Hostility comes easiest to us. [*Ib.*]

9 *Wer zeigt ein Kind, so wie es steht? Wer stellt | es ins Gestirn und gibt das Masz des Abstands | ihm in die Hand?* – Who will show a child, as it really is? Who will place it in its constellation and put the measure of distance in its hand? [*Ib.*]

10 *den ganzen Tod, noch vor dem Leben so | sanft zu enthalten und nicht bös zu sein, | ist unbeschreiblich.* – To contain the whole of death so gently even before life has begun, and not to be angry – this is beyond description. [*Ib.*]

11 *Plätze, o Platz in Paris, unendlicher Schauplatz, | wo die Modistin, Madame Lamort, | die ruhlosen Wege der Erde, endlose Bänder, | schlingt und windet –* Squares, O square in Paris, endless showplace where the modiste, Madame Lamort, loops and winds endless ribbons, the restless roads of the world. [*Ib. V*]

12 *ihre Türme aus Lust, ihre | längst, wo Boden nie war, nur aneinander | lehnenden Leitern, bebend.* – Their towers of pleasure, their ladders that have for so long now leaned against each other, where there was no ground, trembling. [*Ib.*]

13 *Feigenbaum, seit wie lange schon ist mir bedeutend | wie du die Blüte beinah ganz überschlägst | und hinein in die zeitig entschlossene Frucht, | ungerühmt, drängst dein reines Geheimnis.* – Fig-tree, for a long time now I have found meaning in the way you almost entirely overleap the stage of blossom and thrust your pure mystery, unsung, into the early set fruit. [*Ib. VI*]

14 *Wunderlich nah ist der Held doch den jugendlich Toten.* – The hero is strangely akin to those who die young. [*Ib.*]

15 *War er nicht Held schon in dir, O Mutter, begann nicht | dort schon, in dir, seine herrische Auswahl?* – Was he not already a hero inside you, O mother? Did not his imperious choice already begin there, in you? [*Ib.*]

16 *abgewendet schon, stand er am Ende der Lächeln, anders.* – But already withdrawn, he stood at the end of smiles, different. [*Ib.*]

17 *Unser | Leben geht hin mit Verwandlung.* – Our life passes in transformation. [*Ib. VII*]

18 *Wo einmal ein dauerndes Haus war, | schlägt sich erdachtes Gebild vor, quer, zu Erdenklichem | völlig gehörig.* – Where once a lasting house was, obliquely an invented picture starts up, which belongs entirely to the imaginary. [*Ib.*]

19 *o Glück der Mücke, die noch innen hüpft, | selbst wenn sie Hochzeit hat: denn Schoosz ist alles.* – O joy of the gnat, that still leaps inwards even in the act of wedding; for womb is all! [*Ib. VIII*]

20 *so leben wir und nehmen immer Abschied.* – Thus we live, for ever taking leave. [*Ib.*]

21 *Hier ist des Säglichen Zeit, hier seine Heimat. Sprich und bekenn.* – Here is the time of the tellable, here is its home. Speak and proclaim. [*Ib. IX*]

22 *Preise dem Engel die Welt, nicht die unsägliche, ihm | kannst du nicht grosztun mit herrlich Erfühltem; im Weltall, | wo er fühlender fühlt, bist du ein Neuling. Drum zeig ihm das Einfache.* – Praise the world to the angel, not the untellable. You cannot impress him with the splendour you have felt; in the cosmos where he feels with greater feeling you are a novice. So show him the simple thing. [*Ib.*]

23 *beklebt mit Plakaten des 'Todlos', | jenes bitteren Biers, das den Trinkenden süsz scheint.* – Stuck with placard for 'Deathless', that bitter beer that tastes sweet to its drinkers. [*Ib. X*]

24 *Das war der Seelen wunderliches Bergwerk.* – That was the wonderful mine of souls. [*Orpheus, Eurydike, Hermes*]

25 *Sie war schon aufgelöst wie langes Haar | und hingegeben wie gefallner Regen | und ausgeteilt wie hundertfacher Vorrat.* – She was already loosened like long hair, given up like fallen rain, and divided like a hundredfold store. [*Ib.*]

26 *Ist er ein Hiesiger? Nein, aus beiden | Reichen erwuchs seine weite Natur.* – Is he a man of this side? No, his broad nature grew from both realms. [*Die Sonette an Orpheus*, I, vi]

27 *Nicht sind die Leiden erkannt, | nicht ist die Liebe gelernt, | und was im Tod uns entfernt, | ist nicht entschleiert.* – Sorrows are not known, love is not learnt, and what removes us in death is not revealed. [*Ib. xix*]

28 *Frühling ist wiedergekommen. Die Erde |
ist wie ein Kind, das Gedichte weisz. –*
Spring has returned. The earth is like a
child that knows poems. [*Ib.* xxi]

29 *Alles das Eilende | wird schon vorüber
sein; | denn das Verweilende | erst weiht
uns ein. –* All that is hurrying will soon be
past; for that which stays gives us our
first initiation. [*Ib.* xxiii]

30 *O du verlorener Gott! Du unendliche
Spur! | Nur weil dich reiszend zuletzt die
Feindschaft verteilte, | sind wir die Hören-
den jetzt und ein Mund der Natur. –* O
thou lost God! O endless trace! Only
because hostility finally tore you to
pieces are we now the listeners and a
mouthpiece of Nature. [*Ib.* xxvi]

31 *O dieses ist das Tier, das es nicht gibt. –*
O this is the animal that does not exist.
[*Ib.* II. iv]

32 *Alles Erworbene bedroht die Maschine. –*
The machine threatens all achievement.
[*Ib.* x]

33 *Sei allem Abschied voran, als wäre er
hinter | dir, wie der Winter der eben geht. –*
Be ahead of all farewells, as if they were
behind you, like the winter that is just
departing. [*Ib.* xiii]

34 *Alle die dich suchen, versuchen dich. |
Und die, so dich finden, binden dich | an
Bild und Gebärde. –* All who seek you
tempt you, and as soon as they find you,
bind you to an image and a posture.
[*Das Stundenbuch, 'Alle welche dich
suchen'*]

35 *Die Könige der Welt sind alt | und
werden keine Erben haben. –* The kings of
the earth are old and will have no heirs.
[*Ib. 'Die Könige der Welt sind alt'*]

36 *Was wirst du tun, Gott, wenn ich sterbe? |
Ich bin dein Krug (wenn ich zerscherbe?) –*
What will you do, God, if I die? I am
your pitcher (if I break?). [*Ib. 'Was
wirst du tun, Gott'*]

NIKOLAI RIMSKY-KORSAKOV

37 I have already heard it [Debussy's music].
I had better not go: I will start to get
accustomed to it and finally like it.
[Quoted in Robert Craft and Igor
Stravinsky, *Conversations with Stravin-
sky*]

MICHAEL ROBERTS

38 More often than prose or mathematics,
poetry is received in a hostile spirit, as if
its publication were an affront to the
reader. [*The Faber Book of Modern
Verse*, Introduction]

GEORGE ROBEY

39 Desist! [Said with raised eyebrows and
lifted hand to quell applause. Quoted in
A. E. Wilson, *The Prime Minister of
Mirth*, Ch. 3]

40 The inmate of a lunatic asylum was
writing a letter. A man looked over his
shoulder and asked: "To whom are you
writing?' The inmate replied: 'I am
writing to myself.' 'What are you saying?' asked the other man. 'Oh, I shan't
know till I get it tomorrow,' said the
inmate. [Quoted in *ib.* 12]

41 The Prime Minister of Mirth. [Sobriquet
of unknown origin]

42 I said 'Archibald, certainly not'. [Song
refrain]

43 I stopped, I looked and I listened. [Song
in *The Bing Boys*; words by Clifford
Grey]

44 The pleasantry of the Music Hall is to
show Father bathing the twins, not
seducing the typist. [*Looking Back on
Life*, Ch. 14]

45 I am satiated with fishing stories – there's
no truth in them! The man who caught
that fish [stuffed in a glass case] is a
blasted liar! [Reported conversation after
Piscatorial Society dinner. *Ib.* 26]

46 *Complaints* should be made to the
management in writing and placed in the
receptacle installed for that purpose at
the Entrance, which is cleared twice
weekly by the Dustman. [*George Robey's
Advertiser*]

EDWIN ARLINGTON
ROBINSON

47 Friends / To borrow my books and set
wet glasses on them. [*Captain Craig*, II]

48 I shall have more to say when I am dead.
[*John Brown*]

49 Miniver loved the Medici, / Albeit he had never seen one; / He would have sinned incessantly / Could he have been one. [*Miniver Cheevy*]

JAMES HARVEY ROBINSON

50 Partisanship is our great curse. We too readily assume that everything has two sides and that it is our duty to be on one or the other. [*The Mind in the Making*]

ANDRÉ ROCHE

51 Mount Everest is very easy to climb, only just a little too high. [*Observer*, 'Sayings of the Week', 25 Jan. 1953]

JOSÉ RODÓ

52 Democratic equality is the most efficacious instrument of spiritual selection. [*Ariel*]

THEODORE ROETHKE

53 Over this damp grave I speak the words of my love: / I, with no rights in this matter, / Neither father nor lover. [*Elegy for Jane*]

54 I wake to sleep, and take my waking slow. / I learn by going where I have to go. [*The Waking*]

WILL ROGERS

55 We know lots of things we used to dident know but we don't know any way to prevent em happening. [In letter to Will Durant, on eve of the New Deal, 1931]

56 A comedian can only last till he either takes himself serious or his audience takes him serious. [Newspaper article, 1931]

57 I was born because it was a habit in those days, people dident know anything else. [*Autobiography*, Ch. 1]

58 I was not a Child Prodigy, because a Child Prodigy is a child who knows as much when it is a child as it does when it grows up. [*Ib.*]

59 You know these American and Australian horses killed and crippled more soldiers than the Boers. (In the Boer War.) [*Ib.* 2]

60 Course, we don't get meat as often as our forefathers, but we have our peanut butter and radio. [*Ib.* 12]

61 You see a Conservative in Russia is a fellow that thinks you only ought to divide with him what you have, while a real communist believes that you ought to give it all to him, in exchange get you calling him Comrade. [*Ib.*]

62 Communism is like prohibition, it's a good idea but it won't work. [*Ib.* Nov. 1927]

63 I never was much on this Book reading, for it takes em too long to describe the color of the eyes of all the Characters. [*Ib.* 14]

64 England elects a Labor Government. When a man goes in for politics over here, he has no time to labor, and any man that labors has no time to fool with politics. Over there politics is an obligation; over here it's a business. [*Ib.*]

65 The tariff is an instrument invented for the benefit of those who make against those who buy. [*Ib.*]

66 You can't say civilization don't advance, however, for in every war they kill you a new way. [*Ib.*]

67 It's great to be great but it's greater to be human. [*Ib.* 15]

68 Half our life is spent trying to find something to do with the time we have rushed through life trying to save. [*Ib.*]

69 The movies are the only business where you can go out front and applaud yourself. [Quoted in Daniel Boorstin, *The Image*, Ch. 1]

70 See what'll happen to you if you don't stop biting your finger-nails. [On the Venus de Milo, quoted in Bennett Cerf, *Shake Well Before Using*]

71 Any nation is heathen that ain't strong enough to punch you in the jaw. . . . Missionaries teach em not only to serve the Lord but run a Ford car . . . then the American agent sells em one. . . . You take religion backed up by Commerce and it's awful hard for a heathen to overcome. [From 'A Rogers Thesaurus', *Saturday Review*, 25 Aug. 1962]

72 Being a hero is about the shortest-lived profession on earth. [*Ib.*]

73 Coolidge is a better example of evolution than either Bryan or Darrow, for he knows when not to talk, which is the biggest asset the monkey possesses over the human. [*Ib.*]

74 I don't make jokes – I just watch the government and report the facts. [*Ib.*]

75 I had just enough white in me to make my honesty questionable. [*Ib.*]

76 In the early days of the Indian Territory, there were no such things as birth certificates. You being there was certificate enough. [*Ib.*]

77 It [Income Tax] has made more liars out of the American people than Golf. [*Ib.*]

78 Now you won't catch these old boys dying so promiscuously like they did. This bill [the Inheritance Tax] makes patriots out of everybody. [*Ib.*]

79 Once you are a showman you are plum ruined for manual labour again. [*Ib.*]

80 The more you read about politics, you got to admit that each party is worse than the other. [*Ib.*]

81 They got him [Pancho Villa] in the morning editions, but the afternoon ones let him get away. [*Ib.*]

82 The United States never lost a war or won a conference. [*Ib.*]

83 Everybody is ignorant, only on different subjects. [*The Illiterate Digest*]

84 Everything is funny, as long as it's happening to somebody else. [*Ib.*]

85 My folks didn't come over on the *Mayflower*, but they were there to meet the boat. [Quoted in *Treasury of Humorous Quotations*]

86 Our country has plenty of good five-cent cigars, but the trouble is they charge fifteen cents for them. [Quoted in *ib.*]

87 So live that you wouldn't be ashamed to sell the family parrot to the town gossip. [Quoted in *ib.*]

MIES VAN DER ROHE

88 Less is more. [Architectural axiom. Quoted in obituary notice, *The Times*, 19 Aug. 1969]

ROMAIN ROLLAND

89 *C'est le rôle de l'artiste de créer le soleil, lorsqu'il n'y en a pas* – It's the artist's job to create sunshine when there isn't any. [*Jean Christophe: La Foire sur la Place*]

SIR HUMPHREY ROLLESTON

90 First they [physicians] get *on*, then they get *honour*, then they get *honest*. [Quoted in David Ogilvy, *Confessions of an Advertising Man*]

FRANKLIN D. ROOSEVELT

1 This generation of Americans has a rendezvous with destiny. [Speech accepting renomination, 27 June 1936]

2 We have always known that heedless self-interest was bad morals; we know now that it is bad economics. [*Second Inaugural Address*, 20 Jan. 1937]

3 The change in the moral climate of America. [*Ib.*]

4 Quarantine the aggressors. [Speech at Chicago, 5 Oct. 1937]

5 I have told you once and I will tell you again – your boys will not be sent into any foreign wars. [Election Speech, 1940]

6 The best immediate defence of the United States is the success of Great Britain defending itself. [At press conference, 17 Dec. 1940. Quoted in Winston S. Churchill, *Their Finest Hour*, Ch. 28]

7 It is fun to be in the same decade with you. [To Churchill, in answer to congratulations on his 60th birthday. Quoted in Winston S. Churchill, *The Hinge of Fate*, Ch. 4]

8 Stalin hates the guts of all your top people. He thinks he likes me better, and I hope he will continue to do so. [Quoted in *ib.* II]

9 Defeat of Germany means the defeat of Japan, probably without firing a shot or losing a life. [Quoted in *ib.* 25]

10 Never before have we had so little time in which to do so much. [Radio address, 23 Feb. 1942]

11 The only limit to our realization of tomorrow will be our doubts of today.

[Address written for Jefferson Day dinner to have been given 13 Apr. 1945. He died on the 12th]

THEODORE ROOSEVELT

12 Kings and such like are just as funny as politicians. [Quoted in John dos Passos, *Mr Wilson's War*, Ch. 1, sect. i]

BILLY ROSE

13 Does the Spearmint Lose Its Flavour on the Bedpost Overnight? [Title of song]

ISAAC ROSENBERG

14 The darkness crumbles away – / It is the same old druid Time as ever. [*Break of Day in the Trenches*]

15 Droll rat, they would shoot you if they knew / Your cosmopolitan sympathies / (And God knows what antipathies). [*Ib.*]

16 Earth has waited for them, / All the time of their growth / Fretting for their decay: / Now she has them at last. [*Dead Man's Dump*]

17 Death could drop from the dark / As easily as song. [*Returning, We hear the Larks*]

M. L. ROSENTHAL

18 He twirled a gay guitar / He smoked the sweetest cigar. / He lay on the grass / With the head of the class / And left her all ajar. [*Blue Boy on Skates*]

AMANDA ROSS

19 I don't believe in publishers who wish to butter their bannocks on both sides while they'll hardly allow an author to smell treacle. I consider they are too grabby together and like Methodists they love to keep the Sabbath and everything else they can lay their hands on. [Letter to Lord Ponsonby, 1910]

HAROLD W. ROSS

20 You can exclude noise by soundproofing your mind. [Quoted in James Thurber, *The Years with Ross*]

21 Is Moby Dick the whale or the man? [Quoted in *ib.*]

22 I don't want you to think I'm not incoherent. [Quoted in *ib.*]

23 Thurber is the greatest unlistener I know. [Quoted in *ib.*]

24 WOMAN AT ZOO: Is that a male or a female hippopotamus?
KEEPER: Madam, I don't see how that could interest anybody except another hippopotamus. [Tale of unknown origin, told by H. R., quoted in *ib.*]

25 I understand the hero keeps getting in bed with women, and the war wasn't fought that way. [Comment on Hemingway's *A Farewell to Arms*, quoted in *ib.*]

26 I've never been in there [the Louvre] ... but there are only three things to see, and I've seen colour reproductions of all of them. [Quoted in *ib.*]

LILLIAN ROSS

27 He was almost the only man in Chasen's [restaurant] who was not at that moment looking around at someone other than the person he was talking to. [*Picture*, 'Throw the Little Old Lady Down the Stairs!']

28 'The music isn't right,' he says. 'It's a picture about France,' he said, 'so I want a lot of French horns.' [*Ib.*]

PHILIP ROTH

29 Since I was a little girl I always wanted to be Very Decent to People. Other little girls wanted to be nurses and pianists. They were less dissembling. [*Letting Go*, Pt I, Ch. 1]

30 My first impression of her had been clear and sharp: profession – student; inclinations – neurotic. [*Ib.*]

31 It's the little questions from women about tappets that finally push men over the edge. [*Ib.*]

32 It's a family joke that when I was a tiny child I turned from the window out of which I was watching a snowstorm, and hopefully asked, 'Momma, do we believe in winter?' [*Portnoy's Complaint*]

33 Doctor, my doctor, what do you say – let's put the id back in yid! [*Ib.*]

LORD ROTHERMERE

34 Hats off to France. [Title of article in the *Daily Mail*, 1923, supporting French occupation of the Ruhr]

RICHARD H. ROVERE

35 Gullibility may be an amiable failing in some departments of life. The sucker may be afflicted by nothing but an excess of faith, hope, and charity. [*The American Establishment*, 'On Political Sophistication']

A. L. ROWSE

36 Burnings of people and (what was more valuable) works of art. [Quoted in H. R. Trevor Roper, *Historical Essays*]

PAUL RUBENS

37 She was a miller's daughter, / And lived beside the mill; / Yes, there were flies on the water / But she was flier still! [Song from *Three Little Maids*]

38 *We don't want to lose you but we think you ought to go.* [Title of song]

SIR STEVEN RUNCIMAN

39 Unlike Christianity, which preached a peace that it never achieved, Islam unashamedly came with a sword. [*A History of the Crusades*, 'The First Crusade']

DAMON RUNYON

40 Little Isadore reaches out and spears himself a big hunk of my gefillte fish with his fingers, but I overlook this, as I am using the only knife at the table. [*Furthermore*, 'Butch Minds the Baby']

41 Sonny tells him to be sure and be at the track this day to bet on a certain horse in the fifth race, because it is nothing but a boat race, and everything in it is as stiff as a plank, except this certain horse. [*Ib*. 'The Lemon Drop Kid']

42 Now of course this is strictly the old ackamarackus, as the Lemon Drop Kid cannot even spell arthritis, let alone have it. [*Ib*.]

43 Any time you see him he is generally by himself because being by himself is not apt to cost him anything. [*Ib*. 'Little Miss Marker']

44 If this little doll is sitting in your joint all afternoon ... the best thing to do right now is to throw a feed into her as the chances are her stomach thinks her throat is cut. [*Ib*.]

45 Personally, I consider a taxicab much more convenient and less expensive than an old fashioned victoria if you wish to get to some place, but of course guys and dolls engaged in a little off-hand guzzling never wish to get any place in particular, or at least not soon. [*Ib*. 'Princess O'Hara']

46 The way you give a hot foot is to sneak up behind some guy who is standing around thinking of not much, and stick a paper match in his shoe between the sole and the upper along about where his little toe ought to be, and then light the match. [*Ib*. 'Sense of Humour']

47 My boy ... always try to rub up against money, for if you rub up against money long enough, some of it may rub off on you. [*Ib*. 'A Very Honourable Guy']

48 All she has to do is to walk around and about Georgie White's stage with only a few light bandages on, and everybody considers her very beautiful, especially from the neck down. [*Ib*.]

49 Even Mr Justin Veezee is not so old-fashioned as to believe any doll will go to his apartment just to look at etchings nowadays. [*Ib*. 'What, No Butler?']

50 Solid John, the doorman ... opens up very quick indeed, and gives us a big castor-oil smile, for nobody in this town is keeping doors shut on Rusty Charley very long. [*More than Somewhat*, 'Blood Pressure']

51 Charlotte is not such a doll as cares to spend more than one or two years looking at the pictures on the wall. [*Ib*. 'The Brain Goes Home']

52 This Izzy Cheesecake has another name, which is Morris something, and he is slightly Jewish, and has a large beezer, and is considered a handy man in many respects. [*Ib*. 'Gentlemen, the King!']

53 Sam the Gonoph is by no means a college guy. In fact, the nearest Sam ever came to college is once when he was passing through the yard belonging to the Princetons, but Sam is on the fly at the time as a gendarme is after him, so he does not really see much of the college. [*Ib.* 'Hold 'em, Yale!']

54 'In fact,' Sam the Gonoph says, 'I long ago came to the conclusion that all life is six to five against.' [*Ib.* 'A Nice Price']

55 Angie the Ox is an importer himself, besides enjoying a splendid trade in other lines, including artichokes and extortion. [*Ib.* 'The Old Doll's House']

56 And you cannot tell by the way a party looks or how he lives in this town, if he has any scratch, because many a party who is around in automobiles, and wearing good clothes, and chucking quite a swell is nothing but a phonus bolonus and does not have any real scratch whatever. [*Ib.* 'The Snatching of Bookie Bob']

57 If I have all the tears that are shed on Broadway by guys in love, I will have enough salt water to start an opposition to the Atlantic and Pacific, with enough left over to run the Great Salt Lake out of business. [*Ib.* 'Tobias the Terrible']

58 I judge from the sound that he gets his kiss, and it is a very large kiss, indeed, with the cut-out open. [*Ib.* 'Breach of Promise']

59 She is a smart old broad. It is a pity she is so nefarious. [*Runyon à la carte*, 'Broadway Incident']

60 At such an hour the sinners are still in bed resting up from their sinning of the night before, so they will be in good shape for more sinning a little later on. [*Ib.* 'The Idyll of Miss Sarah Brown']

61 I quietly give Girondel a boff over his pimple with a blackjack and flatten him like a welcome mat. [*Ib.* 'A Light in France']

62 I step over to his table and give him a medium hello, and he looks up and gives me a medium hello right back, for, to tell the truth, Maury and I are never bosom friends. [*Ib.*]

63 If I am interested in the kissing and hugging business, I will most certainly take my business to Marie, especially as

she speaks English, and you will not have to waste time with the sign language. [*Ib.*

64 He is up in the paint-cards on age when I meet him, being maybe close on seventy, and he is a fashion-plate of the fashion of about 1922. [*Ib.*]

65 I remarked that his eyes were open so he must be awake. 'The one on your side is,' said a backer, 'but the one on the other side is closed. He is sleeping one-eyed.' [*Short Takes*, 'Bed-Warmers']

66 I once knew a chap who had a system of just hanging the baby on the clothes line to dry and he was greatly admired by his fellow citizens for having discovered a wonderful innovation on changing a diaper. [*Ib.* 'Diaper Dexterity']

67 A free-loader is a confirmed guest. He is the man who is always willing to come to dinner. [*Ib.* 'Free-Loading Ethics']

68 The man in evening clothes dining with the napkin in his lap will eat only half as much food as a diner in evening clothes with his napkin in his collar. The former will not only be worrying about spotting his shirt bosom but about the remarks his wife will make if he does. [*Ib.* 'Napkin Techniques']

69 I do not approve of guys using false pretences on dolls, except, of course, when nothing else will do. [*Take it Easy*, 'It comes up Mud']

70 These citizens are always willing to bet that what Nicely-Nicely dies of will be over-feeding and never anything small like pneumonia, for Nicely-Nicely is known far and wide as a character who dearly loves to commit eating. [*Ib.* 'Lonely Heart']

71 He is without strict doubt a Hoorah Henry, and he is generally figured as nothing but a lob as far as doing anything useful in this world is concerned. [*Ib.* 'Tight Shoes']

72 Much as he is opposed to lawbreaking, he is not bigoted about it. [Attr.]

BERTRAND RUSSELL

73 One of the symptoms of approaching nervous breakdown is the belief that one's work is terribly important. If I were a medical man, I should prescribe a holiday to any patient who considered his work important. [*Ib.* 5]

74 Of all forms of caution, caution in love is perhaps the most fatal to true happiness. [*Ib.* 12]

75 One of the great drawbacks to self-centred passions is that they afford so little variety in life. The man who loves only himself cannot, it is true, be accused of promiscuity in his affections, but he is bound in the end to suffer intolerable boredom from the inevitable sameness of the object of his devotion. [*Ib.* 17]

76 Man is not a solitary animal, and so long as social life survives, self-realization cannot be the supreme principle of ethics. [*History of Western Philosophy*, 'Romanticism']

77 Mathematics, rightly viewed, possesses not only truth, but supreme beauty – a beauty cold and austere, like that of sculpture. [*Mysticism and Logic*, Ch. 4]

78 The solution of the difficulties which formerly surrounded the mathematical infinite is probably the greatest achievement of which our age can boast. [*Ib.*]

79 Mathematics may be defined as the subject in which we never know what we are talking about, nor whether what we are saying is true. [*Ib.* 4]

80 Pure mathematics consists entirely of assertions to the effect that, if such and such a proposition is true of *anything*, then such and such another proposition is true of that thing. It is essential not to discuss whether the first proposition is really true, and not to mention what the anything is, of which it is supposed to be true. [*Ib.* 5]

81 Organic life, we are told, has developed gradually from the protozoon to the philosopher, and this development, we are assured, is indubitably an advance. Unfortunately it is the philosopher, not the protozoon, who gives us this assurance. [*Ib.* 6]

82 Better the world should perish than that I or any other human being should believe a lie ... that is the religion of thought, in whose scorching flames the dross of the world is being burnt away. [*Ib.* 10]

83 The place of the father in the modern suburban family is a very small one – particularly if he plays golf, which he usually does. [*Why I am not a Christian*]

84 Only on the firm foundation of unyielding despair can the soul's edifice henceforth be built. [Quoted in Sagittarius and George, *The Perpetual Pessimist*]

85 Patriots always talk of dying for their country, and never of killing for their country. [Attr.]

86 Matter ... a convenient formula for describing what happens where it isn't. [*An Outline of Philosophy*]

87 I was not born happy. As a child, my favourite hymn was: 'Weary of earth and laden with my sin.' [*The Conquest of Happiness*, Ch. 1]

88 Interest in oneself, on the contrary, leads to no activity of a progressive kind. It may lead to the keeping of a diary, to getting psycho-analysed, or perhaps to becoming a monk. [*Ib.*]

89 The megalomaniac differs from the narcissist by the fact that he wishes to be powerful rather than charming, and seeks to be feared rather than loved. To this type belong many lunatics and most of the great men of history. [*Ib.*]

90 Suspicion of one's own motives is especially necessary for the philanthropist and the executive. [*Ib.* 8]

1 Those who try to make you uneasy by talk about atom bombs are regarded as trouble-makers, as people to be avoided, as people who spoil the pleasure of a fine day by foolish prospects of impossible rain. [*Autobiography*, Vol. III, Ch. 1]

2 I think that bad philosophers may have a certain influence, good philosophers, never. [*Observer*, 'Sayings of the Week', 24 Apr. 1955]

3 The collection of prejudices which is called political philosophy is useful provided that it is not called philosophy. [*Observer*, 'Sayings of the Year', 1962]

4 What men really want is not knowledge but certainty. [Quoted in G. M. Carstairs, *Listener*, 30 July 1964]

5 The nuns who never take a bath without wearing a bathrobe all the time. When asked why, since no man can see them, they reply 'Oh, but you forget the good God.' [The Basic Writings Pt. II, Ch. 7]

6 The average man's opinions are much less foolish than they would be if he thought for himself. [Attr.]

7 Few people can be happy unless they hate some other person, nation or creed. [Attr.]

LORD RUTHERFORD

8 Well, I made the wave, didn't I? [In answer to the jibe: 'Lucky fellow, Rutherford, always on the crest of the wave.' Quoted in C. P. Snow, *The Two Cultures and the Scientific Revolution*]

GENERAL N. V. RUZSKY

9 Generals also are proletarian. [Quoted in Leon Trotsky, *History of the Russian Revolution*, Vol. II, Ch. 5]

GILBERT RYLE

10 So too Plato was, in my view, a very unreliable Platonist. He was too much of a philosopher to think that anything he had said was the last word. It was left to his disciples to identify his footmarks with his destination. [*Dilemmas*, Ch. 1]

11 Philosophy is the replacement of category habits by category-disciplines. [*The Concept of Mind*, Introduction]

S

VICTORIA SACKVILLE-WEST

1 They had a passion for getting something for nothing. Every blackberry in the hedgerow was an agony to Lavinia until she had bottled it. [*All Passion Spent*, Ch. 1]

2 It was chance which had made men turn gold into their symbol, rather than stones; it was chance which had made men turn strife into their principle, rather than amity. That the planet might have got on better with stones and amity – a simple solution – had apparently never occurred to its inhabitants. [*Ib.*]

3 The country habit has me by the heart, / For he's bewitched for ever who has seen, / Not with his eyes but with his vision, Spring / Flow down the woods and stipple leaves with sun. [*The Land*, 'Winter']

4 Forget not bees in winter, though they sleep, / For winter's big with summer in her womb. [*Ib.* 'Spring']

5 Only the moon shall look behind the hedge, / Confederate of youth. [*Ib.* 'Summer']

6 Birds moult, and in the leafy copses hide, / And summer makes a silence after spring. [*Ib.*]

7 All craftsmen share a knowledge. They have held / Reality down fluttering to a bench. [*Ib.*]

8 I saw the round moon rise above the pines, / One quiet planet prick the greening west, / As goats came leaping up the stony crest / And the crook'd goatherd moved between the rocks. [*Ib.* 'Autumn']

ANTOINE DE SAINT-EXUPÉRY

9 Grown-ups never understand anything for themselves, and it is tiresome for children to be always and forever explaining things to them. [*The Little Prince* Ch. 1]

10 On the morning of his departure he put his planet in perfect order. He carefully cleaned out his active volcanoes. He possessed two active volcanoes, and they were very convenient for heating his breakfast in the morning. [*Ib.* 9]

11 It is much more difficult to judge oneself than to judge others. [*Ib.* 10]

'SAKI' (H. H. MUNRO) and CHARLES MAUDE

12 My father believed in smiting sin wherever he found it; what I complained of was that he always seemed to find it in the same place. [*The Watched Pot*, Ch. 1]

13 Woman is a belated survival from a primeval age of struggle and competition; that is why, the world over, you find all the superfluous dust and worry being made by the gentler sex. [*Ib.* 3]

'SAKI' (H. H. MUNRO)

14 I believe I once considerably scandalized her by declaring that clear soup was a more important factor in life than a clear conscience. [*The Blind Spot*]

15 A little inaccuracy sometimes saves tons of explanation. [*The Comments of Moung Ka*]

16 His hair and forehead furnished a recessional note in a personality that was in all other respects obtrusive and assertive. [*Cousin Teresa*]

17 Children may sometimes be time-servers, but they do not encourage long accounts. [*The Easter Egg*]

18 One of those strapping florid girls that go so well with autumn scenery or Christmas decorations in church. [*Esmé*]

19 Waldo is one of those people who would be enormously improved by death. [*The Feast of Nemesis*]

20 Whenever a massacre of Armenians is reported from Asia Minor, everyone assumes that it has been carried out 'under orders' from somewhere or another; no one seems to think that there are people who might *like* to kill their neighbours now and then. [*Filboid Studge*]

21 To say that anything was a quotation was an excellent method, in Eleanor's eyes, for withdrawing it from discussion. [*The Jesting of Arlington Stringham*]

22 The censorious said that she slept in a hammock and understood Yeats's poems, but her family denied both stories. [*Ib.*]

23 The people of Crete unfortunately make more history than they can consume locally. [*Ib.*]

24 All decent people live beyond their incomes nowadays, and those who aren't respectable live beyond other people's. A few gifted individuals manage to do both. [*The Match-Maker*]

25 His socks compelled one's attention without losing one's respect. [*Ministers of Grace*]

26 Scandal is merely the compassionate allowance which the gay make to the humdrum. [*Reginald at the Carlton*]

27 The young have aspirations that never come to pass, the old have reminiscences of what never happened. [*Ib.*]

28 There may have been disillusionments in the lives of the medieval saints, but they would scarcely have been better pleased if they could have foreseen that their names would be associated nowadays chiefly with racehorses and the cheaper clarets. [*Ib.*]

29 Every reformation must have its victims. You can't expect the fatted calf to share the enthusiasm of the angels over the prodigal's return. [*Reginald on the Academy*]

30 She took to telling the truth; she said she was forty-two and five months. It may have been pleasing to the angels, but her elder sister was not gratified. [*Reginald on Besetting Sins*]

31 People may say what they like about the decay of Christianity; the religious system that produced green Chartreuse can never really die. [*Reginald on Christmas Presents*]

32 A woman who leaves her cook never wholly recovers her position in Society. [*Reginald on House-Parties*]

33 Even the Hooligan was probably invented in China centuries before we thought of him. [*Ib.*]

34 I think she must have been very strictly brought up, she's so desperately anxious to do the wrong thing correctly. [*Reginald on Worries*]

35 Her frocks are built in Paris, but she wears them with a strong English accent. [*Ib.*]

36 I always say beauty is only sin deep. [*Reginald's Choir Treat*]

37 The aunt of Clovis . . . churned away like a Nile steamer, with a long brown ripple of Pekingese spaniel trailing in her wake. [*The Talking-out of Tarrington*]

38 The woman who can sacrifice a clean unspoiled penny stamp is probably unborn. [*The Unbearable Bassington*]

39 To see her standing at the top of an expensively horticultured staircase receiving her husband's guests was rather like watching an animal performing on a music-hall stage. One always tells oneself that the animal likes it, and one always knows that it doesn't. [*Ib.*]

40 The English have a proverb: 'Conscience makes cowboys of us all.' [*Wratislav*]

J. D. SALINGER

41 Sex is something I really don't understand too hot. You never know *where* the hell you are. I keep making up these sex rules for myself, and then I break them right away. [*The Catcher in the Rye*, Ch. 9]

42 I was about half in love with her by the time we sat down. That's the thing about girls. Every time they do something pretty, even if they're not much to look at, or even if they're sort of stupid, you fall half in love with them, and then you never know *where* the hell you are. [*Ib.* 10]

43 He looked like the kind of a guy that wouldn't talk to you much unless he wanted something off you. He had a lousy personality. [*Ib.* 11]

44 The thing is, it's really hard to be room-mates with people if your suitcases are much better than theirs – if yours are really good ones and theirs aren't. You think if they're intelligent and all, the other person, and have a good sense of humour, that they don't give a damn whose suitcases are better, but they do. [*Ib.* 15]

45 They didn't act like people and they didn't act like actors. It's hard to explain. They acted more like they knew they were celebrities and all. I mean they were good, but they were *too* good. [*Ib.* 17]

46 He was the kind of phoney that have to give themselves *room* when they answer somebody's question. He stepped back, and stepped right on the lady's foot behind him. [*Ib.*]

47 Take most people, they're crazy about cars ... and it they get a brand-new car already they start thinking about trading it in for one that's even newer. I don't even like *old* cars. I mean they don't even interest me. I d rather have a god-dam horse. A horse is at least *human*, for God's sake. [*Ib.*]

48 The trouble with girls is, if they like a boy, no matter how big a bastard he is, they'll say he has an inferiority complex, and if they *don't* like him, no matter how nice a guy he is, or how big an inferiority complex he has, they'll say he's conceited. Even smart girls do it. [*Ib.* 18]

49 Sally said I was a sacrilegious atheist. I probably am. The thing Jesus *really* would've liked would be the guy that plays the kettle drums in the orchestra. [*Ib.*]

50 Old Luce. He was strictly a pain in the ass, but he certainly had a good vocabu-lary. He had the largest vocabulary of any boy at Whooton. They gave us a test. [*Ib.* 19]

51 For Esmé, With Love and Squalor. [Title of Story]

52 Poetry, surely, is a crisis, perhaps the only actionable one we can call our own. [*Seymour: An Introduction*]

53 Probably passed on, these many years, of an overdose of garlic, the way all New York barbers eventually go. [*Ib.*]

54 A confessional passage has probably never been written that didn't stink a little bit of the writer's pride in having given up his pride. [*Ib.*]

55 One of the thousand reasons I quit going to the theater when I was about twenty was that I resented like hell filing out of the theater just because some playwright was forever slamming down his silly curtain. [*Ib.*]

ANTHONY SAMPSON

56 Members rise from CMG (known some-times in Whitehall as 'Call me God') to the KCMG ('Kindly Call me God') to ... the GCMG ('God Calls me God') [*Anatomy of Britain*, Ch. 18]

GEORGE SAMPSON

57 The well-meaning people who talk about education as if it were a substance dis-tributable by coupon in large or small quantities never exhibit any understand-ing of the truth that you cannot teach any-body anything that he does not want to learn. [*Seven Essays*]

LORD SAMUEL

58 To expect us to feel 'humble' in the presence of astronomical dimensions merely because they are big, is a kind of cosmic snobbery ... what is significant is mind. [*Belief and Action*]

59 Without doubt the greatest injury ... was done by basing morals on myth, for sooner or later myth is recognized for what it is, and disappears. Then morality loses the foundation on which it has been built. [*Romanes Lecture*, 1947]

60 Hansard is history's ear, already listening. [*Observer*, 'Sayings of the Week', 18 Dec. 1949]

61 A library is thought in cold storage. [In his *A Book of Quotations*]

62 I didn't know the Tories ate their prisoners. [Comment on abandonment of Free Trade by the National Government, 1931. Attr.]

63 A difficulty for every solution. [Of the Civil Service. Attr.]

CARL SANDBURG

64 The people will live on. / The learning and blundering people will live on. / They will be tricked and sold and again sold / And go back to the nourishing earth for rootholds. [*The People, Yes*]

65 Hog Butcher for the World. [Of Chicago in *Chicago*]

GEORGE SANTAYANA

66 The young man who has not wept is a savage, and the old man who will not laugh is a fool. [*Dialogues in Limbo*, Ch. 3]

67 The barbarian is the man who regards his passions as their own excuse for being; who does not domesticate them either by understanding their cause or by conceiving their ideal goal. [*Egotism in German Philosophy*]

68 As the Latin languages are not composed of two diverse elements, as English is of Latin and German, so the Latin mind does not have two spheres of sentiment, one vulgar and the other sublime. All changes are variations on a single key, which is the key of intelligence. [*Interpretations of Poetry and Religion*]

69 English genius is anti-professional; its affinities are with amateurs. [Quoted in Rayne Kruger, *Good-bye Dolly Gray*, Postscript]

70 Life is not a spectacle or a feast; it is a predicament. [Quoted in Sagittarius and George, *The Perpetual Pessimist*]

71 Let a man once overcome his selfish terror at his own finitude, and his finitude itself is, in one sense, overcome. A part of his soul, in sympathy with the infinite, has accepted the natural status of all the rest of his being. Perhaps the only true dignity of man is his capacity to despise himself. [Introduction to Spinoza's *Ethics*]

72 The truth is cruel, but it can be loved, and it makes free those who have loved it. [*Ib.*]

73 Those who cannot remember the past are condemned to repeat it. [*The Life of Reason*, Vol. I, Ch. 12]

74 Happiness is the only sanction of life; where happiness fails, existence remains a mad and lamentable experiment. [*Ib.*]

75 Art supplies constantly to contemplation what nature seldom affords in concrete experience – the union of life and peace. [*Ib.* 4]

76 Trust the man who hesitates in his speech and is quick and steady in action, but beware of long arguments and long beards. [*Soliloquies in England*, 'The British Character']

77 The truth, which is a standard for the naturalist, for the poet is only a stimulus. [*Ib.* 'Ideas']

78 My atheism, like that of Spinoza, is true piety towards the universe and denies only gods made men in their own image, to be servants of their human interests. [*Ib.* 'On My Friendly Critics']

79 Nothing you can lose by dying is half so precious as the readiness to die, which is man's charter of nobility. [*Ib.* 'Tipperary']

80 My instinct is to go and stand under the cross, with the monks and crusaders, far away from these Jews and Protestants who adore the world and who govern it. [*Ib.* 'War Shrines']

81 The working of great institutions is mainly the result of a vast mass of routine, petty malice, self interest, carelessness, and sheer mistake. Only a residual fraction is thought. [*The Crime of Galileo*]

JEAN-PAUL SARTRE

82 I hate victims who respect their executioners. [*Altona*, I]

83 There are two ways of destroying a people. Either condemn them *en bloc* or force them to repudiate the leaders they adopted. The second is the worse. [*Ib.*]

84 When one does nothing, one believes oneself responsible for everything. [*Ib.*]

85 An American is either a Jew, or an anti-Semite, unless he is both at the same time. [*Ib.*]

86 I don't think the profession of historian fits a man for psychological analysis. In our work, we have to deal only with simple feelings to which we give generic names such as Ambition and Interest. [*Nausea*, Monday, 29 Jan. 1932. Trans. by Robert Baldick]

87 Three o'clock is always too late or too early for anything you want to do. [*Ib.* Friday]

88 I think they do that to pass the time, nothing more. But time is too large, it refuses to let itself be filled up. [*Ib.* 5.30]

89 A man is always a teller of tales, he lives surrounded by his stories and the stories of others, he sees everything that happens to him through them; and he tries to live his life as if he were recounting it. [*Ib.* Saturday, noon]

90 You get the impression that their normal condition is silence and that speech is a slight fever which attacks them now and then. [*Ib.* Sunday]

1 Doctors, priests, magistrates, and officers know men as thoroughly as if they had made them. [*Ib.* Shrove Tuesday]

2 Things are entirely what they appear to be and *behind them* . . . there is nothing. [*Ib.* Monday]

3 My thought is *me*: that is why I can't stop. I exist by what I think . . . and I can't prevent myself from thinking. [*Ib.*]

4 Existence is a repletion which man can never abandon. [*Ib.* Six o'clock in the evening]

5 At the same time, I learnt that you always lose. Only the bastards think they win. [*Ib.* Tuesday at Bouville]

6 They think about Tomorrow, in other words simply about another today; towns have only one day at their disposal which comes back exactly the same every morning. [*Ib.*]

7 I know perfectly well that I don't want to do anything; to do something is to create existence – and there's quite enough existence as it is. [*Ib.* One hour later]

8 I am not fond of the word psychological. There is no such thing as psychological. Let us say that one can improve the biography of the person. [Quoted in R. D. Laing, *The Divided Self*, Ch. 8]

SIEGFRIED SASSOON

9 If I were fierce and bald and short of breath, / I'd live with scarlet Majors at the Base, / And speed glum heroes up the line to death. [*Base Details*]

10 And there'd be no more jokes in Music-halls / To mock the riddled corpses round Bapaume. [*Blighters*]

11 'He's a cheery old card,' grunted Harry to Jack / As they slogged up to Arras with rifle and pack. . . / But he did for them both by his plan of attack. [*The General*]

12 Here was the world's worst wound. And here with pride / 'Their name liveth for ever,' the Gateway claims. / Was ever an immolation so belied / As these intolerably nameless names? [*On Passing the New Menin Gate*]

13 Safe with his wound, a citizen of life, / He hobbled blithely through the garden gate, / And thought: 'Thank God they had to amputate!' [*The One-Legged Man*]

14 There must be crowds of ghosts among the trees, – / Not people killed in battle – they're in France / But horrible shapes – old men who died / Slow natural deaths – old men with ugly souls, / Who wore their bodies out with nasty sins. [*Repression of War Experience*]

15 He spoke with homicidal eloquence, keeping the game alive with genial and well-judged jokes. . . . Man, it seemed, had been created to jab the life out of Germans. [*Memoirs of an Infantry Officer*, Pt. I, Ch. 1]

16 Allgood said that the French Generals looked much brainier than the British ones; but I told him that they must be cleverer than they looked, and anyhow, they'd all got plenty of medal-ribbons. [*Ib.* I. 2]

17 My stretcher was popped into an ambulance which took me to a big hospital at Denmark Hill. At Charing Cross a woman handed me a bunch of flowers and a leaflet by the Bishop of London who earnestly advised me to lead a clean life and attend Holy Communion. [*Ib.* VIII. 4]

18 I am making this statement as a wilful defiance of military authority because I believe that the War is being deliberately prolonged by those who have the power to end it. [Letter quoted in *ib.* X. 3]

'DOCTOR SAWBONES'

19 In the best American clinics the patients as well as the doctors are professionals. [Attr.]

DOROTHY L. SAYERS

20 I can't see that she could have found anything nastier to say if she'd thought it out with both hands for a fortnight. [*Busman's Holiday*, 'Prothalamion']

SENATOR SCHALL (of Minnesota)

21 To hell with Europe! [1935. *Observer*, 'Sayings of Our Times', 31 May 1953]

ARNOLD SCHOENBERG

22 Very well, I can wait. [When told that his Violin Concerto required a soloist with six fingers. Attr.]

FIELD MARSHAL VON SCHLIEFFEN

23 When you march into France, let the last man on the right brush the Channel with his sleeve. [Of the Schlieffen plan. Quoted in B. Tuchman, *The Guns of August*, Ch. 2]

24 Only make the right wing strong. [*Ib.*]

ALBERT SCHWEITZER

25 I too had thoughts once of being an intellectual, but I found it too difficult. [To an African who refused to perform some humdrum duty on the grounds that he was an intellectual. Attr.]

C. P. SCOTT

26 Television? No good will come of this device. The word is half Greek and half Latin. [Attr.]

ROBERT FALCON SCOTT

27 What lots and lots I could tell you of this journey. How much better has it been than lounging in too great comfort at home. [Extract from letter quoted in Apsley Cherry-Garrard, *The Worst Journey in the World*]

RONALD SEARLE and TIMOTHY SHY (D. B. Wyndham Lewis)

28 During her first year at Somerville, a Fellow of Judas, having essayed a private pinch in the Bodleian Lounge, described her as physically a *fausse maigre*. [*The Terror of St Trinian's*, Ch. 3]

29 A well-flung lacrosse stick caught Matron on the ear as she scurried frantically from her sanctum round the corner and doubled downstairs to the Infirmary. [*Ib.*]

30 Though loaded firearms were strictly forbidden at St Trinian's to all but Sixth-Formers ... one or two of them carried automatics acquired in the holidays, generally the gift of some indulgent relative. [*Ib.*]

31 Gentlemen from the Board of Education may like a bit of devil with their culture. He certainly gave me a *very* agreeable look – practically a leer. [*Ib.*]

32 It was at this precise moment that a brilliant idea recurred to Angela Menace. That very night she would set fire to the School. [*Ib.* 6]

33 In the spring ... your lovely Chloë lightly turns to one mass of spots. [*Ib.* 7]

34 At the beginning of every summer holidays since the age of fourteen Angela had brought home to The Pines, Godalming, for tea and tennis a succession of speechless, pimply, and lovesick youths, to each of whom she had subsequently become engaged for life in turn. [*Ib.* 9]

35 His strong red face resembled something terrible out of Easter Island. [*Ib.*]

36 Chloë married a rather scrubby biologist, lost her looks almost immediately, and is now received nowhere, since her husband smells strongly of hydrocyanic acid. [*Ib.* 11]

HARRY SECOMBE

37 My advice if you insist on slimming: Eat as much as you like – just don't swallow it. [Quoted in *Daily Herald*, 5 Oct. 1962]

GEORGE SELDES

38 Sawdust Caesar. [Title of biography of Benito Mussolini]

H. GORDON SELFRIDGE

39 The Great Principles on which we will build this Business are as everlasting as the Pyramids. [Preliminary announcement on Selfridge's store]

W. C. SELLAR and R. J. YEATMAN

40 To confess that you are totally Ignorant about the Horse, is social suicide: you will be despised by everybody, especially the horse. [*Horse Nonsense*]

41 America became top nation and history came to a full stop. [*1066 and All That*]

42 For every person wishing to teach there are thirty not wanting to be taught. [*And Now All This*]

ROBERT SERVICE

43 Ah! the clock is always slow; / It is later than you think. [*It is Later than You Think*]

GEORGE BERNARD SHAW

44 Why, how is it that you've just beaten us? Sheer ignorance of the art of war, nothing else. [*Indignantly*] I never saw anything so unprofessional. [*Arms and the Man*, I]

45 My father is a very hospitable man: he keeps six hotels. [*Ib.*]

46 Bulgarians of really good standing – people in our position – wash their hands nearly every day. So you see I can appreciate your delicacy. [*Ib.*]

47 A man ought to be able to be fond of his wife without making a fool of himself about her. [*Candida*, I]

48 So long as you come here honestly as a self-respecting, thorough, convinced scoundrel, justifying your scoundrelism and proud of it, you are welcome. [*Ib.*]

49 Love is assumed to be the only theme that touches all your audience infallibly. ... And yet love is the one subject that the drawing room drama dare not present. [*Three Plays for Puritans*, Preface]

50 I have a technical objection to making sexual infatuation a tragic theme. Experience proves that it is only effective in the comic spirit. [*Ib.*]

51 So much for Bardolatry! [*Ib.*]

52 It does not follow ... that the right to criticize Shakespear involves the power of writing better plays. And in fact ... I do not profess to write better plays. [*Ib.*]

53 BETTER THAN SHAKESPEAR? [*Ib.* crossheading]

54 This is Britannus, my secretary. He is an islander from the western end of the world, a day's voyage from Gaul. [*Caesar and Cleopatra*, II]

55 He is a barbarian, and thinks that the customs of his tribe and island are the laws of nature. [*Ib.*]

56 When a stupid man is doing something he is ashamed of, he always declares that it is his duty. [*Ib.* III]

57 Give women the vote, and in five years there will be a crushing tax on bachelors. [*Man and Superman*, Preface]

58 Effectiveness of assertion is the alpha and omega of style. [*Ib.*]

59 Beware of the man whose god is in the skies. [*Man and Superman*, 'Maxims for Revolutionists']

60 Do not love your neighbour as yourself. If you are on good terms with yourself, it is an impertinence; if on bad, an injury. [*Ib.*]

61 He who slays a king and he who dies for him are alike idolaters. [*Ib.*]

62 The maternal instinct leads a woman to prefer a tenth share in a first rate man to the exclusive possession of a third rate one. [*Ib.*]

63 Titles distinguish the mediocre, embarrass the superior, and are disgraced by the inferior. [*Ib.*]

64 Self-denial is not a virtue; it is only the effect of prudence on rascality. [*Ib.*]

65 The most intolerable pain is produced by prolonging the keenest pleasure. [*Ib.*]

66 She'll commit every crime a respectable woman can; and she'll justify every one of them by saying that it was the wish of her guardians. [*Man and Superman*, I]

67 The more things a man is ashamed of, the more respectable he is. [*Ib.*]

68 Vitality in a woman is a blind fury of creation. She sacrifices herself to it. [*Ib.*]

69 Of all human struggles there is none so treacherous and remorseless as that between the artist man and the mother woman. [*Ib.*]

70 Your pious English habit of regarding the world as a moral gymnasium built expressly to strengthen your character in. [*Ib.*]

71 Very nice sort of place, Oxford, I should think, for people that like that sort of place. [*Ib.* II]

72 ... Never noticing the advent of the New Man. Straker's the New Man. [*Ib.*]

73 As a rule there is only one person an English girl hates more than she hates her eldest sister; and thats her mother. [*Ib.*]

74 Lying hardly describes it. I overdo it. I get carried away in an ecstasy of mendacity. [*Ib.*]

75 ... any port from which we can sail to a Mahometan country where men are protected from women. [*Ib.*]

76 I am a gentleman: I live by robbing the poor. [*Ib.* III]

77 Until a movement shews itself capable of spreading among brigands, it can never hope for a political majority. [*Ib.*]

78 We are dregs and scum, sir: the dregs very filthy, the scum very superior. [*Ib.*]

79 There is plenty of humbug in hell. [*Ib.*]

80 If you go to Heaven without being naturally qualified for it, you will not enjoy yourself there. [*Ib.*]

81 In the arts of peace Man is a bungler. [*Ib.*]

82 As an old soldier I admit the cowardice: it's as universal as sea sickness, and matters just as little. [*Ib.*]

83 What is virtue but the Trade Unionism of the married? [*Ib.*]

84 Marriage is a mantrap baited with simulated accomplishments and delusive idealizations. [*Ib.*]

85 Those who talk most about the blessings of marriage and the constancy of its vows are the very people who declare that if the chain were broken and the prisoners left free to choose, the whole social

fabric would fly asunder. You cannot have the argument both ways. If the prisoner is happy, why lock him in? If he is not, why pretend that he is? [*Ib.*]

86 Hot water is the revolutionist's element. You clean men as you clean milk-pails, by scalding them. [*Ib.* IV]

87 We're from Madeira, but perfectly respectable, so far. [*You Never Can Tell*, I]

88 Well, sir, you never can tell. Thats a principle in life with me, sir, if youll excuse my having such a thing, sir. [*Ib.* II]

89 To ask him his intentions? What a violation of Twentieth Century principles! [*Ib.* III]

90 He's the very incarnation of intellect. You can hear his mind working. [*Ib.* IV]

1 My speciality is being right when other people are wrong. [*Ib.*]

2 All matches are unwise. It's unwise to be born; it's unwise to be married; it's unwise to live; and it's wise to die. [*Ib.*]

3 My way of joking is to tell the truth. It's the funniest joke in the world. [*John Bull's Other Island*, II]

4 He's not an Irishman. He'll never know theyre laughing at him; and while theyre laughing he'll win the seat. [*Ib.* IV]

5 I am somewhat surprised to hear a member of your Church quote so essentially a Protestant document as the Bible. [*Ib.*]

6 We must be thoroughly democratic, and patronize everybody without distinction of class. [*Ib.*]

7 What really flatters a man is that you think him worth flattering. [*Ib.*]

8 You will comfort me with ... the sight of the little children carrying the golf clubs of your tourists as a preparation for the life to come. [*Ib.*]

9 For four wicked centuries the world has dreamed this foolish dream of efficiency; and the end is not yet. [*Ib.*]

10 That is sound Crosstianity. But this Crosstianity has got entangled with something that Barbara calls Christianity and which unexpectedly causes her to refuse to play the hangman's game of Satan casting out Satan. [*Major Barbara*, Preface]

11 Nobody can say a word against Greek: it stamps a man at once as an educated gentleman. [*Major Barbara*, I]

12 He is always breaking the law. He broke the law when he was born: his parents were not married. [*Ib.*]

13 I am a sort of collector of religions; and the curious thing is that I find I can believe in them all. [*Ib.* II]

14 The love of the common people may please an earl's granddaughter and a university professor; but I have been a common man and a poor man; and it has no romance for me. [*Ib.*]

15 I cant talk religion to a man with bodily hunger in his eyes. [*Ib.*]

16 CUSINS: Do you call poverty a crime? UNDERSHAFT: The worst of all crimes. All the other crimes are virtues beside it. [*Ib.* IV]

17 Whatever can blow men up can blow society up. The history of the world is the history of those who had courage enough to embrace this truth. [*Ib.*]

18 Like all young men, you greatly exaggerate the difference between one young woman and another. [*Ib.*]

19 I now want to give the common man weapons against the intellectual man. I love the common people. I want to arm them against the lawyers, the doctors, the priests ... who, once in authority, are more disastrous and tyrannical than all the fools, rascals and impostors. [*Ib.*]

20 It's easier to replace a dead man than a good picture. [*The Doctor's Dilemma*, II]

21 Morality consists in suspecting other people of not being legally married. [*Ib.* III]

22 I don't believe in morality. I'm a disciple of Bernard Shaw. [*Ib.*]

23 Martyrdom is the only way in which a man can become famous without ability. [Quoted in Preface to 1908 Reprint of *Fabian Essays*]

24 The injury to the child would be far less if the voluptuary said frankly: 'I beat you because I like beating you; and I shall do it whenever I can contrive an excuse for it.' [*Misalliance*, Preface]

25 Heaven, as conventionally conceived, is a place so inane, so dull, so useless, so miserable, that nobody has ever ventured to describe a whole day in heaven, though plenty of people have described a day at the seaside. [*Ib.*]

26 The secret of being miserable is to have leisure to bother about whether you are happy or not. [*Ib.*]

27 Children must be taught some sort of religion. Secular education is an impossibility. Secular education comes to this: that the only reason for ceasing to do evil and learning to do well is that if you do not you will be caned. This is worse than being taught in a church school that if you become a dissenter you will go to hell; for hell is presented as the instrument of something eternal, divine and inevitable; you cannot evade it the moment the schoolmaster's back is turned. [*Ib.*]

28 Assassination is the extreme form of censorship. [*The Shewing-Up of Blanco Posnet*, 'The Limits of Toleration']

29 John the Baptist may have been a Keir Hardie; but Jesus of Matthew is of the Ruskin–Morris class. [*Androcles and the Lion*, Preface]

30 Years ago I said that the conversion of a savage to Christianity is the conversion of Christianity to savagery. [*Ib.*]

31 When Jesus called Peter from his boat, he spoiled an honest fisherman, and made nothing better out of the wreck than a salvation monger. [*Ib.*]

32 Whether you think Jesus was God or not, you must admit that he was a first-rate political economist. [*Ib.* Preface, 'Jesus as Economist']

33 I dont want to talk grammar. I want to talk like a lady. [*Pygmalion*, II]

34 No: I don't want no gold and no diamonds. I'm a good girl, I am. [*Ib.*]

35 My needs is as great as the most deserving widow's that ever got money out of six different charities in one week for the death of the same husband. [*Ib.*]

36 Undeserving poverty is my line. Taking one station in society with another, it's – it's – well, it's the only one that has any ginger in it, to my taste. [*Ib.*]

37 They all thought she was dead; but my father he kept ladling gin down her throat till she came to so sudden that she bit the bowl off the spoon. [*Ib.* III]

38 Gin was mother's milk to her. [*Ib.*]

39 Tied me up and delivered me into the hands of middle class morality. [*Ib.* V]

40 All great truths begin as blasphemies. [*Annajanska*]

41 When I meet a man who makes a hundred thousand a year, I take off my hat to that man ... and call him brother. [*Heartbreak House*, I]

42 You want to rest your wounded bosom against a grindstone. Well ... here is the grindstone. [*Ib.* II]

43 The very burglars cant behave naturally in this house. [*Ib.*]

44 Go anywhere in England where there are natural, wholesome, contented, and really nice English people: and what do you always find? That the stables are the real centre of the household. [*Ib.* III]

45 The captain is in his bunk, drinking bottled ditchwater; and the crew is gambling in the forecastle. ... Do you think the laws of God will be suspended in favor of England because you were born in it? [*Ib.*]

46 God's trustiest lieutenants often lack official credentials. They may be professed atheists who are also men of honor and high public spirit. [*Back to Methuselah*, Preface]

47 Every genuine scientist must be ... a metaphysician. [*Ib.*]

48 Make me a beautiful word for doing things tomorrow, for that surely is a great and blessed invention. [*Back to Methuselah*, Pt I, I]

49 Well, as the serpent used to say, why not? [*Ib.* II]

50 The He-Ancient. [Character in *ib.* Pt V]

51 It is the only remaining fragment of a lost scripture called The Confessions of St Augustin, the English Opium Eater. [*Ib.*]

52 If ever I utter an oath again may my soul be blasted to eternal damnation! [*St Joan*, sc. ii]

53 We were not fairly beaten, my lord. No Englishman is ever fairly beaten. [*Ib.* iv]

54 Take Gateshead and Middlesbrough alone! ... their daily output of chocolate creams totals up to twenty thousand tons. [*The Apple Cart*, I]

55 I never resist temptation, because I have found that things that are bad for me do not tempt me. [*Ib.* II]

56 No woman can shake off her mother. There should be no mothers, only women. [*Too Good to be True*]

57 Half the young ladies in London spend their evenings making their father take them to plays that are not fit for elderly people to see. [*Fanny's First Play*, Introduction]

58 It's all that the young can do for the old, to shock them and keep them up to date. [*Ib.*]

59 You don't expect me to know what to say about a play when I don't know who the author is, do you? [*Ib.* Epilogue]

60 All Shaw's characters are himself: mere puppets stuck up to spout Shaw. [*Ib.*]

61 The one point on which all women are in furious secret rebellion against the existing law is the saddling of the right to a child with the obligation to become the servant of a man. [*Getting Married*, Preface]

62 There are couples who dislike one another furiously for several hours at a time; there are couples who dislike one another permanently; and there are couples who never dislike one another; but these last are people who are incapable of disliking anybody. [*Ib.*]

63 In the middle classes, where the segregation of the artificially limited family in its little brick box is horribly complete, bad manners, ugly dresses, awkwardness, cowardice, peevishness and all the petty vices of unsociability flourish like mushrooms in a cellar. [*Ib.*]

64 Physically there is nothing to distinguish human society from the farm-yard except that children are more troublesome and costly than chickens and women are not so completely enslaved as farm stock. [*Ib.*]

65 What God hath joined together no man shall ever put asunder: God will take care of that. [*Getting Married*]

66 Very few books of any nationality are worth reading. People read to kill time; consequently it is no more objection to a book that it is not worth reading than it is to a pack of cards that it does not pile up treasures in heaven. [*Table-Talk of G.B.S*]

67 It is the sexless novel that should be distinguished: the sex novel is now normal. [*Ib.*]

68 I could not write the words Mr Joyce uses: my prudish hand would refuse to form the letters. [*Ib.*]

69 Look after the limelight; and the play will look after itself. [Letter to Herbert Samuel on Censorship controversy, quoted in J. Bowle, *Viscount Samuel*, Ch. 5, sect. ii]

70 No, he isn't dancing. That's the Ethical Movement. [On seeing Dr Stanton Coit dancing. Quoted in C. E. Bechofer Roberts 'Ephesian', *Philip Snowden*, Ch. 6]

71 LORD NORTHCLIFFE: The trouble with you, Shaw, is that you look as if there were a famine in the land.
G.B.S.: The trouble with you, Northcliffe, is that you look as if you were the cause of it. [Attr.]

72 A coquette is a woman who rouses passions she has no intentions of gratifying. [Attr.]

73 If all economists were laid end to end, they would not reach a conclusion. [Attr.]

74 Like fingerprints, all marriages are different. [Quoted in Pulling, *They Were Singing*, Ch. 5]

75 We are a nation of governesses. [*New Statesman*, 12 Apr. 1913]

76 If he [T. E. Lawrence] hides in a quarry he puts red flags all round. [Quoted in the *Guardian*, 22 Jan. 1963]

PATRICK SHAW-STEWART

77 I saw a man this morning / Who did not wish to die: / I ask, and cannot answer, / If otherwise would I. [Quoted in Evelyn Waugh, *Ronald Knox*, Pt I, Ch. 4]

SIR JOHN SHEPPARD

78 He knew Greek. [Slight tittering.] Well, some of them don't, you know! [Estimating in a Cambridge lecture the merits of an editor of Aeschylus. Attr.]

MARK SHERIDAN

79 Belgium Put the Kibosh on the Kaiser. [Title of song; words by Alf Ellerton]

80 Here We Are! Here We Are!! / Here We Are Again!!! [Title of song; words by Charles Knight and Kenneth Lyle]

ROBERT SHIELDS

81 A well-preserved virginity *may* signify a limited capacity for love. [*Observer*, 13 June 1965]

JEAN SIBELIUS

82 Pay no attention to what the critics say; no statue has ever been put up to a critic. [Attr.]

HERBERT SIDEBOTHAM

83 The old Labour Party were taught to speak Marxism; then Keir Hardie taught them to speak Scots; but Philip Snowden has rendered a great service by teaching them to speak English. [Speech at dinner to Snowden. Quoted in C. E. Bechofer Roberts, *Philip Snowden*, Ch. 2, 'Ephesian']

H. R. SIDEY

84 The heights by great men reached and kept / Were not attained without exertion / But they, while their companions worked, / Were contacting the proper person. [*Spectator*, competition, 20 Aug. 1955]

N. F. SIMPSON

85 There's somebody at the door wanting you to form a government. [*A Resounding Tinkle*, I. i]

86 If he's a criminal, he's in plain clothes – that's all I can say. [*Ib.*]

87 The small of my back is too big, doctor. [*Ib.*]

88 And suppose we solve all the problems it presents? What happens? We end up with more problems than we started with. Because that's the way problems propagate their species. A problem left to itself dries up or goes rotten. But fertilize a problem with a solution – you'll hatch out dozens. [*Ib.*]

89 She says they ordered a snake and they've got one that's too short. [*Ib.* II]

90 I don't want to get mixed up in a lot of rain. I haven't got a hat for that sort of thing. [*Ib.*]

1 We lent him a couple of lampshades Myrtle has grown out of for his little boy. [*Ib.*]

2 Don! Why, you've changed your sex! [*Ib.*]

3 I sometimes envy the man in the street who's never learned to drink for himself at all. [*Ib.*]

4 The best that can be hoped for from the ending is that sooner or later it will arrive. [*Ib.*]

5 I eat merely to put food out of my mind. [*The Hole*]

6 MRS EDO: Sid just had another bad night worrying about being so different from the people he sees round him.

MRS MESO: Has he tried resembling anybody? [*Ib.*]

7 He went to Dr Bunch – he's been going to him for years — and complained about his ribs, and told him they seemed to be giving him claustrophobia. [*Ib.*]

8 He's out of step with it – he's breathing in all the time when he should be breathing out and that puts him out all the way along. He can't get back into phase with it except by breathing in twice running. [*Ib.*]

9 I personally am a firm believer in live and let live and always have been, but all the same there are a good few people who'd be better out of the way in my opinion. [*Ib.*]

10 If we've got to *have* five hundred weighing machines in the house, I'd just as soon they did sing. [*One Way Pendulum*, I]

11 Knocked down a doctor? With an ambulance? How could she? It's a contradiction in terms. [*Ib.*]

12 It'll do him good to lie there unconscious for a bit. Give his brain a rest. [*Ib.*]

13 You should have thought of all this before you were born. [*Ib.*]

14 We've got nothing against apes, Sylvia. As such. [*Ib.*]

15 [*Holding up a copy of 'Uncle Tom's Cabin'*] I swear, by Harriet Beecher Stowe, that the evidence I shall give shall be the truth, the whole truth, and nothing but the truth. [*Ib.* II]

16 She said she had a string of pearls in the form of a necklace but she wore it round her waist for the tightness. [*Ib.*]

17 On the last occasion on which he took a life he was warned by Detective Sergeant Barnes that complaints had been lodged and that action would be taken against him if he failed to conform to the law. [*Ib.*]

18 Someone's been messing about with my death's head. It wasn't working when you gave it to me. [*Ib.*]

19 We got it all planned before he was born that if we had a white baby we were going to dress him in black – or her in black if it had been a girl – and if either of them were black we'd have everything white, so as to make a contrast. But when he came he was white, so we had the black. [*Ib.*]

20 In sentencing a man for one crime, we may well be putting him beyond the reach of the law in respect of those crimes which he has not yet had an opportunity to commit. The law, however, is not to be cheated in this way. I shall therefore discharge you. [*Ib.*]

EDITH SITWELL

21 The fire was furry as a bear. [*Dark Song*]

22 Jumbo asleep! / Grey leaves thick-furred / As his ears, keep / Conversations blurred. [*Lullaby for Jumbo*]

23 Do not take a bath in Jordan, / Gordon, / On the holy Sabbath, on the peaceful day! [*Scotch Rhapsody*]

24 I have often wished I had time to cultivate modesty. . . . But I am too busy thinking about myself. [*Observer*, 'Sayings of the Week', 30 Apr. 1950]

SIR OSBERT SITWELL

25 Too fond of Moping / And of Reading Books – / Charges synonymous / And polyonymous, / Almost as serious / As Breaking Down the Palings and Stealing Property. [*In a Nutshell*]

26 Chrysanthemums, which in their art shades of mauve, and terra-cotta and russet, smell of moths, camphorball, and drowned sailors. [*Essay on Gardening*]

27 Now the nimble fingers are no more nimble, / And the silver thimble lies cold and tarnished black. [*Miss Mew's Window-Box*]

28 In reality, *killing time* / Is only the name for another of the multifarious ways / By which Time kills us. [*Milordo Inglese*]

29 Sworn foe / Of every cobweb, mouse and Roman Catholic. [*Mrs Nutch*]

30 On the coast of Coromandel / Dance they to the tunes of Handel. [*On the Coast of Coromandel*]

31 But He was never, well, / What I call / A Sportsman; / For forty days / He went out into the desert / – And never shot anything. [*Old Fashioned Sportsmen*]

32 When Doctor Dougall attended a funeral, / The horse would gallop, as if in eagerness, / As if his master had at last / Been granted his reward. [*The Two Doctors*]

33 Our poverty, then, signified chiefly that we were no longer allowed to throw down pennies, done up in screws of paper, to the conductors of German bands. [*The Scarlet Tree*, Bk III, Ch. 1]

34 When younger he [Sir George Sitwell] had invented many other things; at Eton, for example, a musical toothbrush which played 'Annie Laurie' as you brushed your teeth, and a small revolver for killing wasps. [*Ib.* Bk IV, Ch. 1]

35 The men of the Golden Horde were almost as kind to children as to horses and dogs – though, naturally, they regarded them with less reverence. [*Ib.* 2]

36 The artist, like the idiot or clown, sits on the edge of the world, and a push may send him over it. [*Ib.*]

37 The fun brigade. [*Ib.*]

38 We attended stables, as we attended church, in our best clothes, thereby no doubt showing the degree of respect due to horses, no less than to the deity. [*Ib.*]

39 That particular carriage of the head, poised midway between stiff-neck and goitre, which is yet a spiritual more than a physical attribute, associated with the desire for independence and a resolve to get the best of a bargain; an aspect to which Modigliani, alone of portraitists, has done justice. [*Ib.*]

40 The terrible, newly-imported American doctrine that everyone ought to do something. [*Ib.*]

41 Everywhere in England and America, statesmen were already preparing their triumphs of 1914 and '39 by spending long days on the golf-course and long nights at the bridge-table. [*Great Morning*, Bk V, Ch. 2]

42 [Sir George Sitwell] would omnisciently reply, with an air of final and absolute authority, and without deeming it necessary to offer proof or divulge the source of such, no doubt, mystical awareness, '*We happen to know.*' [*Ib.*]

43 She belonged to the super-annuated dairy-maid type, and possessed a voice that, like a mill, ground silence into its component parts. [*Ib.*]

LORD SHAWCROSS

44 The so-called new morality is too often the old immorality condoned. [*Observer*, 'Sayings of the Week', 17 Nov. 1963]

CORNELIA OTIS SKINNER

45 Woman's virtue is man's greatest invention. [Attr.]

PROFESSOR B. F. SKINNER

46 Education is what survives when what has been learnt has been forgotten. [*New Scientist*, 21 May 1964]

GEORGE SLOCOMBE

47 He [Woodrow Wilson] was the Messiah of the new age, and his crucifixion was yet to come. [On Wilson's visit to Europe for the Versailles conference. *Mirror to Geneva*]

GEORGE JOSEPH SMITH
(murderer of the Brides in the Bath)

48 Sir – In answer to your application regarding my parentage, my mother was a bus-horse, my father a cab-driver, my sister a rough-rider over the Arctic regions. My brothers were all gallant sailors on a steam-roller. [Letter to father-in-law produced at trial, quoted in Edward Marjoribanks, *Life of Sir Edward Marshall Hall*, Ch. 10]

LOGAN PEARSALL SMITH

49 How awful to reflect that what people say of us is true! [*All Trivia*]

50 I might give my life for my friend, but he had better not ask me to do up a parcel. [*Ib.*]

51 I am one of the unpraised, unrewarded millions without whom Statistics would be a bankrupt science. It is we who are born, who marry, who die, in constant ratios. [*Ib.*]

52 I cannot forgive my friends for dying: I do not find these vanishing acts of theirs at all amusing. [*Ib.*]

53 Is it seemly that I, at my age, should be hurled with my books of reference, and bed-clothes, and hot-water bottle, across the sky at the unthinkable rate of nineteen miles a second? As I say, I don't like it at all. [*Ib.*]

54 It is the wretchedness of being rich that you have to live with rich people. [*Ib.*]

55 Nay, in His confabulations with His chosen people, does not the Creator of the Universe Himself make the most astounding efforts to impress upon those Hebrews His importance, His power, His glory? Wasn't I made in His image? [*Ib.*]

56 O Plato, O Shelley, O Angels of Heaven, what scrapes, what scrapes you do get us into! [*Ib.*]

57 Solvency is entirely a matter of temperament and not of income. [*Ib.*]

58 That Stonehenge circle of elderly disapproving faces – Faces of the Uncles, and Schoolmasters and the Tutors who frowned on my youth. [*Ib.*]

59 There is more felicity on the far side of baldness than young men can possibly imagine. [*Ib.*]

60 These pieces of moral prose have been written, dear Reader, by a large Carnivorous Mammal, belonging to that sub-order of the Animal Kingdom which includes also the Orang-outang, the tusked Gorilla, the Baboon with his bright blue and scarlet bottom, and the gentle Chimpanzee. [*Ib.*]

61 The thought that my mind is really nothing but an empty sieve – often this, too, disconcerts me. [*Ib.*]

62 We need two kinds of acquaintances, one to complain to, while we boast to the others. [*Ib.*]

63 What I like in a good author is not what he says, but what he whispers. [*Ib.*]

64 What is more enchanting than the voices of young people, when you can't hear what they say? [*Ib.*]

65 Yes, there it still was, the old External World, still apparently quite unaware of its own non-existence. [*Ib.*]

66 A friend who loved perfection would be the perfect friend, did not that love shut his door on me. [Last Words in *Great Turnstile*, ed. V. S. Pritchett]

STEVIE SMITH

67 Shall I tell you the signs of a New Age coming? / It is a sound of drubbing and sobbing / Of people crying, We are old, we are old / And the sun is going down and becoming cold. [*The New Age*]

68 I was much too far out all my life. / And not waving but drowning. [*Not Waving But Drowning*]

69 Oh to become sensible about social advance at seventeen is to be lost. [*Parents*]

70 It [my poetry] does as well for telling atom secrets as for knowing whatever Mabel's been up to lately. [Quoted in *Observer*, 9 Nov. 1969]

71 I do really think that death will be marvellous. . . . If there wasn't death, I think you couldn't go on. [Quoted in *ib.*]

THORNE SMITH

72 He was an institutional sort of animal, but not morbid. Not apparently. So completely and successfully had he

inhibited himself that he veritably believed he was the freest person in the world. [*The Jovial Ghosts*, Ch. 1]

73 To Mrs Topper it was an endless source of comfort to be able to trace all mystifying cases of conduct, even her own, to such a tangible and well-established institution as a stomach. [*Ib.* 2]

74 He never loitered to pluck forbidden flowers beside the marital path, but had mechanically kept to his schedule with Mrs Topper at one end and the office at the other. [*Ib.*]

75 'I knew you would like it,' said Mrs Topper as though she were addressing a sceptical cannibal who had just made a meal of a questionable victim. 'I've always said you liked lamb.' [*Ib.* 4]

76 Stevens' mind was so tolerant that he could have attended a lynching every day without becoming critical. [*Ib.* 11]

77 His secretary was a middle-aged woman who valiantly strove to draw attention from that depressing fact by decorating various parts of her body with the tender ribbons of infancy. [*Ib.*]

78 'My first husband always wore slippers – the cutest things – plush. We could never hear him coming.' 'Who's "we"?' demanded the Colonel. 'None of your business,' replied Mrs Hart. 'Those slippers cost me a comfortable home. Ask the waiter to pour.' [*Topper Takes a Trip*, Ch. 14]

79 'I find it rather sad. Mrs Hart had a hard life.' 'You mean she led a hard life,' declared Marion. 'She was a trull before she could toddle.' [*Ib.*]

WALLACE SMITH

80 The gulls began a new chorus of sick-cat calls. [*The Captain Hates the Sea*, Ch. 1]

81 That concern's about as square as a new-laid egg. They been mixed up in so many shady deals it takes a sleight-of-hand artist to keep their books. [*Ib.* 7]

82 Mildred's always managed to confuse the duties of matrimony with its pleasures. [*Ib.* 9]

83 'The major probably guessed,' said Mister Layton, 'that you're one of these hot-pants athletes whenever you get shore-leave.' [*Ib.* 20]

C. P. SNOW

84 *The Two Cultures* [Title of article in *New Statesman*, 6 Oct. 1956]

85 I am today, and men aren't at their most exciting: I am tomorrow and one often sees them at their noblest. [*The Two Cultures and the Scientific Revolution*]

86 When scientists are faced with an expression of the traditional culture it tends ... to make their feet ache. [*Ib.*]

87 'I grant you that he's not two-faced,' I said. 'But what's the use of that when the one face he has got is so peculiarly unpleasant?' [*The Affair*, Ch. 4]

PHILIP SNOWDEN

88 It would be desirable if every Government, when it comes into power, should have its old speeches burned. [Quoted in C. E. Bechofer Roberts 'Ephesian', *Philip Snowden*, Ch. 12]

A. SOLZHENITSYN

89 Prayers are like those appeals of ours. Either they don't get through or they're returned with 'rejected' scrawled across 'em. [*One Day in the Life of Ivan Denisovich*]

E. E. SOMERVILLE and MARTIN ROSS

90 Neither principalities nor powers should force me into the drawing-room, where sat the three unhappy women of my party, being entertained within an inch of their lives by Mrs McRory. [*Further Experiences of an Irish R.M.*, 'Sharper than a Ferret's Tooth']

CHARLES SORLEY

1 Give them not praise. For, deaf, how should they know / It is not curses heaped on each gashed head? [*When you see Millions of the Mouthless Dead*]

MURIEL SPARK

2 On another occasion he had said, 'My sympathies are not entirely with Patrick. He may be a good medium, but as a citizen—' 'It is time spiritualism was recognized as a mark of good citizenship,' Marlene said. [*The Bachelors*]

3 Nelly Mahone, who had lapsed from her native religion on religious grounds. [*The Ballad of Peckham Rye*, Ch. 1]

4 She doesn't have anything to do with youth clubs. There are classes within classes in Peckham. [*Ib.* 3]

5 Of course this choreographer is a projection of me. I was at the University of Edinburgh myself, but in the dream I'm the Devil and Cambridge. [*Ib.*]

6 There are four types of morality in Peckham. [*Ib.* 6]

7 A short neck denotes a good mind. . . . You see, the messages go quicker to the brain because they've shorter to go. [*Ib.* 7]

8 My God, he's supposed to be a professional man, . . . and he opens his mouth and whistles at a girl. [*Ib.*]

9 The one certain way for a woman to hold a man is to leave him for religion. [*The Comforters*, Ch. 1]

10 Parents learn a lot from their children about coping with life. [*Ib.* 6]

11 All the nice people were poor; at least, that was a general axiom, the best of the rich being poor in spirit. [*The Girls of Slender Means*, Ch. 1]

12 Every communist has a fascist frown, every fascist a communist smile. [*Ib.* 4]

13 With the impurity of those to whom all things pertaining to themselves are pure. [*The Go-Away Bird*, 'Daisy Overend']

14 One day in my young youth at high summer, lolling with my lively companions upon a haystack I found a needle. [*Ib.* 'The Portobello Road']

15 Selwyn Macgregor, the nicest boy who ever committed the sin of whisky. [*Ib.* 'A Sad Tale's Best for Winter']

16 But I did not remove my glasses, for I had not asked for her company in the first place, and there is a limit to what one can listen to with the naked eye. [*Voices at Play*, 'The Dark Glasses']

FRED SPARKS

17 The man who is always the life of the party will be the death of his wife. [*Saturday Review*, 5 Dec. 1964, 'As it Happens']

ROBERT SPEAIGHT

18 If you dislike Mr Lloyd George or Sir Alfred Mond as much as Belloc disliked them, it is much better not to think about them too much. But Belloc thought about them incessantly. [*Life of Hilaire Belloc*, Ch. 14, sect. i]

BERNARD SPENCER

19 Love detonates like sap / Up into the limbs of men and bears all the seasons / And the starving and the cutting and hunts terribly through lives / To find its peace. [*Allotments; April*]

STANLEY SPENCER

20 I no more like people personally than I like dogs. When I meet them I am only apprehensive whether they will bite me, which is reasonable and sensible. [Quoted in Maurice Collis, *Stanley Spencer, a Biography*, Ch. 17]

21 Beautifully done. [Last words, to the nurse who had given him his injection. Quoted in *ib.* 19]

STEPHEN SPENDER

22 Different living is not living in different places / But creating in the mind a map. [*Different Living*]

23 But let the wrong cry out as raw as wounds / This Time forgets and never heals, far less transcends. [*In Railway Halls*]

24 Born of the sun, they travelled a short while towards the sun / And left the vivid air signed with their honour. [*I Think Continually*]

25 Our single purpose was to walk through snow / With faces swung to their prodigious North / Like compass needles. [*Polar Exploration*]

26 Pylons, those pillars / Bare like nude giant girls that have no secret. [*The Pylons*]

27 Only the lucid friend to aerial raiders / The brilliant pilot moon, stares down / Upon this plain she makes a shining bone. [*Two Armies*]

28 Who live under the shadow of a war, / What can I do that matters? [*Who live under the Shadow*]

HILDE SPIEL

29 Malice is like a game of poker or tennis; you don't play it with anyone who is manifestly inferior to you. [*The Darkened Room*]

LAURENCE P. SPINGARN

30 When I said that mercy stood / Within the borders of the wood, / I meant the lenient beast with claws / And bloody swift despatching jaws. [*The Lost River*, 'Definition']

DR BENJAMIN SPOCK

31 How to fold a diaper depends on the size of the baby and the diaper. [*Baby and Child Care*, § 261]

32 To win in Vietnam, we will have to exterminate a nation. [*Dr Spock on Vietnam*, Ch. 7]

SIR JOHN SQUIRE

33 But Shelley had a hyper-thyroid face. [*Ballade of the Glandular Hypothesis*]

34 Full many a vice is born to blush unseen, / Full many a crime the world does not discuss, / Full many a pervert lives to reach a green / Replete old age, and so it was with us. [*If Gray had had to write his Elegy in the Cemetery of Spoon River*]

35 When I leapt over Tower Bridge / There were three that watched below, / A bald man and a hairy man, / And a man like Ikey Mo. [*Parody of G. K. Chesterton*]

36 To a land where the sky is as red as the grass / And the sun as green as the rain. [*Ib.*]

HENRY DE VERE STACPOLE

37 In home-sickness you must keep moving – it is the only disease that does not require rest. [*The Bourgeois*]

MR JUSTICE STABLER

38 I cannot imagine a worse cure for psycho-neurosis than safe-blowing with gelignite. [*Observer*, 'Sayings of the Week', 21 Mar. 1954]

39 It would be much better if young women should stop being raped much earlier in the proceedings than some of them do. [*Observer*, 'Sayings of the Week', 8 Jan. 1961]

J. V. STALIN

40 The state is an instrument in the hands of the ruling class for suppressing the resistance of its class enemies. [On 'Proletarian democracy'. Quoted in *Stalin's Kampf*, ed. M. R. Werner]

41 The tasks of the party are ... to be cautious and not allow our country to be drawn into conflicts by warmongers who are accustomed to have others pull the chestnuts out of the fire for them. [Speech to the 8th Congress of the Communist Party, 6 Jan. 1941]

42 The party is the rallying-point for the best elements of the working class. [Attr.]

OLIVER STANLEY

43 You see, whether we win or lose, it will be the end of everything we stand for. [On 11 Sept. 1938. Quoted in Harold Nicolson, *Diaries and Letters, 1930–39, ed.* Nigel Nicolson]

COL. C. E. STANTON

44 Lafayette, we are here! [At Lafayette's grave, 1917. Attr.]

OLAF STAPLEDON

45 That strange blend of the commercial traveller, the missionary, and the barbarian conqueror, which was the American abroad. [*First and Last Man*, Ch. 3, sect. i]

THE STAR

46 On her 107th birthday, in August, she attributed her great age to a lifetime of hard work and the fact that she never had a boy friend. [Quoted in M. Bateman, *This England*, selections from the *New Statesman*, Pt III]

SUSAN STEBBING

47 It is not swinish to be happy unless one is happy in swinish ways. [*Ideals and Illusions*]

WICKHAM STEED

48 The famous 'A.E.I.O.U.' policy – *Austriae est imperare orbi universo* (to Austria belongs universal rule). [*The Hapsburg Monarchy*]

TOMMY STEELE

49 Normally, I read my Classics in strip form. [*Observer*, 'Sayings of the Week', 5 June 1960]

GERTRUDE STEIN

50 Two things are always the same the dance and war. One might say anything is the same but the dance and war are particularly the same because one can see them. That is what they are for. [*Everybody's Autobiography*, Ch. 5]

51 Pigeons on the grass alas. [*Four Saints in Three Acts*, III, ii]

52 Ida never sighed, she just rested. When she rested she turned a little and she said, yes dear. She said that very pleasantly. This was all of Ida's life just then. [*Ida*, Pt II]

53 Ida decided that she was just going to talk to herself. Anybody could stand around and listen but as for her she was just going to talk to herself. She no longer even needed a twin. [*Ib.*]

54 It is difficult never to have been younger but Ida almost she almost never had been younger. [*Ib.*]

55 Ida never spoke, she just said what she pleased. Dear Ida. [*Ib.*]

56 Ida returned more and more to be Ida. She even said she was Ida. [*Ib.*]

57 In the United States there is more space where nobody is than where anybody is. That is what makes America what it is. [*The Geographical History of America*]

58 Disillusionment in living is the finding out nobody agrees with you not those that are fighting for you. Complete disillusionment is when you realize that no one can for they can't change. [*The Making of Americans*]

59 Any one not coming to be a dead one before coming to be an old one comes to be an old one and comes then to be a dead one as any old one comes to be a dead one. [*Ib.*]

60 COLD CLIMATE A season in yellow sold extra strings makes lying places. [*Tender Buttons*]

61 Just before she died she asked, 'What *is* the answer?' No answer came. She laughed and said, 'In that case what is the question?' Then she died. [Last words recorded by Duncan Sutherland in *G.S., a Biography of her Work*]

JOHN STEINBECK

62 Man, unlike any other thing organic or inorganic in the universe, grows beyond his work, walks up the stairs of his concepts, emerges ahead of his accomplishments. [*The Grapes of Wrath*, Ch. 14]

63 Okie use' to mean you was from Oklahoma. Now it means you're scum. Don't mean nothing itself, it's the way they say it. [*Ib.* 18]

WILHELM STEKEL

64 The mark of the immature man is that he wants to die nobly for a cause, while the mark of the mature man is that he wants to live humbly for one. [Quoted in J. D. Salinger, *The Catcher in the Rye*, Ch. 24]

JAMES STEPHENS

65 Men come of age at sixty, women at fifteen. [*Observer*, 'Sayings of the Week', 1 Oct. 1944]

66 Finality is death. Perfection is finality. Nothing is perfect. There are lumps in it. [*The Crock of Gold*]

RICHARD G. STERN

67 Every man has a question which terrifies him, and to the avoidance of which he gives himself with an energy that helps shape his life. [*Golk*, Ch. 1, sect. i]

68 Inside the rose-tinted, air-conditioned, environment-proof bulk reigned the modern architectural trinity, cleanliness, spaciousness and luminosity. [*Ib.* 2. i]

69 When love gets to be important to some-one, it means that he hasn't been able to manage something else. Falling in love seems to me an almost sure sign of failure. Except for the very few who have a real talent for it. [*Ib*. 2. iii]

70 Anybody can shock a baby, or a tele-vision audience. But it's too easy, and the effect is disproportionate to the effort. [*Ib*. 4. iii]

WALLACE STEVENS

71 What counted was mythology of self, / Blotched out beyond unblotching. [*The Comedian as the Letter C*, I]

72 The only emperor is the emperor of ice-cream. [*The Emperor of Ice-Cream*]

73 Poetry is the supreme fiction, madame. / Take the moral law and make a nave of it / And from the nave build haunted heaven. [*A High-toned Old Christian Woman*]

74 In the high west there burns a furious star. / It is for fiery boys that star was set / And for sweet-smelling virgins close to them. [*Le Monocle de Mon Oncle*]

75 If sex were all, then every trembling hand / Could make us squeak, like dolls, the wished-for words. [*Ib*.]

76 She bathed in her still garden, while / The red-eyed elders watching, felt / The basses of their beings throb / In witching chords, and their thin blood / Pulse pizzicati of Hosanna. [*Peter Quince at the Clavier*]

77 Beauty is momentary in the mind – / The fitful tracing of a portal; / But in the flesh it is immortal. [*Ib*.]

78 I do not know which to prefer, / The beauty of inflections / Or the beauty of innuendoes, / The blackbird whistling / Or just after. [*Thirteen Ways of Looking at the Blackbird*]

79 I had as lief be embraced by the porter at the hotel / As to get no more from the moonlight / Than your moist hand. [*Two Figures in Dense Violet Night*]

ADLAI STEVENSON

80 Let's talk sense to the American people. Let's tell them the truth, that there are no gains without pains. [Speech in Chicago, 26 July 1952]

81 Your public servants serve you right. [Speech in Los Angeles, 11 Sept. 1952]

82 There is no evil in the atom; only in men's souls. [Speech in Hartford, Con-necticut, 18 Sept. 1952]

83 She [Eleanor Roosevelt] would rather light candles than curse the darkness, and her glow has warmed the world. [*Sunday Times*, 11 Nov. 1962]

84 Power corrupts, but lack of power corrupts absolutely. [Quoted in *Observer*, Jan. 1963]

85 My definition of a free society is a society where it is safe to be unpopular. [Speech in Detroit, Oct. 1952]

86 A politician is a statesman who ap-proaches every question with an open mouth. [Quoted in L. Harris, *The Fine Art of Political Wit*]

JOHN STILL

87 The memories of men are too frail a thread to hang history from. [*The Jungle Tide*, Ch. 5]

MERVYN STOCKWOOD, BISHOP OF SOUTHWARK

88 A psychiatrist is a man who goes to the Folies-Bergère and looks at the audience. [*Observer*, 'Sayings of the Week', 15 Oct. 1961]

LORD STONHAM

89 During a fairly active life, including 25 years playing team games, I have never encountered homosexuality. [Quoted in *Daily Mail*, 25 May, 1965]

G M STONIER [under pseudonym of FANFARLO]

90 It was on the forty-seventh day of the new razor-blade. Well, one must start somewhere. [*Shaving through the Blitz*, Ch. 1]

1 There it is, the Blitz, all night and half the day, coming and going, sniffing, grunting, throwing up showers of gravel against the windows, as though one had accommo-dated too big a dog in the garden. [*Ib*.]

2 Doors open to reveal a full carriage. A man in front of me leans back and then hurls himself against this living wall. I follow. The doors snap behind. I am caught, nose to nose, belly to belly, unwillingly, with a girl whose face is near enough for map-reading. [*Ib.* 2]

3 Lizzie, of course, at this moment is in the bathroom. A trunk call, in the circumstances, to a Channel swimmer would not be more impossible. [*Ib.* 3]

4 Mrs Greenbaum is the most persistent dreamer. At one time she seems to have been concerned with moving house in Poland, and when she wags her head from side to side, and struggles to speak, it is almost certain that the piano has stuck again while being lowered from the window in the snow. [*Ib.* 4]

5 I explain my theory of optimo-pessimism. [*Ib.* 5]

6 I have always felt a faint scepticism, a mild horror, about the country. One goes for quiet; and a gang of rooks is at work murderously tearing at the furrows. [*Ib.* 6]

7 Two more suicides at the Ministry of Babel. If this goes on we shall be able to reorganize on a basis of efficiency. [*Ib.* 9]

8 Without my teeth (my fine upper set from Islington) I am a different person, a sick man. I talk differently, with lewd grimaces and hissing sounds; I look, I ponder, I eat, I even walk differently. [*Ib.* 10]

REX STOUT

9 When the last trumpet sounds the *Times* [the *New York Times*] will want to check with Gabriel himself, and for the next edition will try to get it confirmed by even Higher Authority. [*Gambit*, Ch. 3]

10 He was born with the attitude toward all attractive women that a fisherman has toward all the trout in the stream, and has never seen any reason to change it. [*Ib.* 9]

11 Handshakes can be faked and usually are, but smiles can't. It isn't often that a man gets a natural, friendly, straightforward smile from a young woman, with no come on, no catch, and no dare, and the least he can do is return it if he has that kind in stock. [*Homicide Trinity*, 'Death of a Demon']

12 The U.N. is wonderful for broadening a man's outlook. For instance, Turkish girls have short legs and Indian girls have flat feet. [*A Right to Die*, Ch. 3]

13 'I'll discuss it with you,' she said, in a voice that could have been used to defrost her refrigerator. [*Three Witnesses*, 'Die like a Dog', III]

14 I like to walk around Manhattan, catching glimpses of its wild life, the pigeons and cats and girls. [*Ib.* 'When a Man Murders']

JOHN STRACHEY

15 The oldest and greatest monopolist of all, Holy Church herself, the monopolist in God, had to be assailed if the new middle men, the soldiers of the market, were to grow and prosper. [*The Coming Struggle for Power*, Pt I, Ch. 1]

16 While the other arts ... are the algebra of emotional expression, literature is the arithmetic. Music and the plastic arts seek to express the generalized essence of man's predicament in the universe. Literature, for the most part, attempts to illuminate some particular predicament of a particular man or a particular woman at a given time and place. [*Ib.* III. 10]

17 Becoming an Anglo-Catholic must surely be a sad business – rather like becoming an amateur conjurer. [*Ib.* III. 11]

18 Mr MacDonald has become ... an actor – and that type of actor which the cruel French call a '*m'as-tu vu?*' 'Have you seen me as the Prime Minister? – My greatest role, I assure you,' Mr MacDonald is anxiously asking the nation. Yes, we have seen him. [*Ib.* V. 17]

19 Fascism means war. [Slogan of the Thirties]

EUGENE STRATTON

20 Little Dolly Daydream, pride of Idaho. [Song: *Little Dolly Daydream*]

21 I know she likes me, / 'Cause she says so. [Song: *The Lily of Laguna*]

IGOR STRAVINSKY

22 It is not art that rains down upon us in the song of a bird; but the simplest

modulation, correctly executed is already art. [*Poetics of Music*, Ch. 2]

23 If melody were all of music, what could we prize in the various forces that make up the immense work of Beethoven, in which melody is assuredly the least? [*Ib.*]

24 Poussin said quite correctly that 'the goal of art is delectation'. He did not say that this delectation should be the goal of the artist who must always submit solely to the demands of the work to be done. [*Ib.* 4]

25 A renewal is fruitful only when it goes hand in hand with tradition. [*Ib.* 5]

26 Rachmaninov's immortalizing totality was his scowl. He was a six-and-a-half-foot-tall scowl. [Igor Stravinsky and Robert Craft, *Conversations with Igor Stravinsky*]

27 He [Rachmaninov] was the only pianist I have ever seen who did not grimace. That is a great deal. [*Ib.*]

28 It is interesting to note that conductors' careers are made for the most part with 'romantic' music. 'Classic' music eliminates the conductor; we do not remember him in it. [*Ib.*]

29 Nothing is likely about masterpieces, least of all whether there will be any. [*Ib.* 'The Future of Music']

30 The very people who have done the breaking through are themselves often the first to try to put a scab on their achievement. [*Ib.* 'Advice to Young Composers']

31 Academism results when the reasons for the rule change, but not the rule. [*Ib.* 'Some Musical Questions']

32 My music is best understood by children and animals. [*Observer*, 'Sayings of the Week', 8 Oct. 1961]

33 I had another dream the other day about music critics. They were small and rodent-like with padlocked ears, as if they had stepped out of a painting by Goya. [Quoted in *Evening Standard*, 29 Oct. 1969]

MR JUSTICE STREATFIELD

34 Facts speak louder than statistics. [*Observer*, 'Sayings of the Week', 19 Mar. 1950]

TERRY SULLIVAN

35 She sells sea-shells on the sea-shore. / The shells she sells are sea-shells, I'm sure. [Song, *She sells sea-shells*]

SUNDAY TIMES

36 When our sovereign [Edward VIII] was born he was given, among other qualities, the rare boon of youth. [*This England*, Anthology from *New Statesman*, 1937]

ITALO SVEVO

37 The really original woman is the one who first imitates a man. [*A Life*, Ch. 8]

38 In a theatre Annetta cared less about the performance on the stage than the audience. She said that she preferred watching people like herself rather than wretched creatures perform with other wretched creatures. [*Ib.* 9]

39 For a long time young Lanucci had ceased struggling against his own laziness, and to spare himself remorse elevated it to a theory. [*Ib.* 13]

40 Whenever I look at a mountain I always expect it to turn into a volcano. [*Confessions of Zeno*]

41 There are three things I always forget. Names, faces, and – the third I can't remember. [Attr.]

T

JOSEPH TABRAR

1 Daddy wouldn't buy me a bow-wow,
bow-wow. / I've got a little cat / And
I'm very fond of that. [Song: *Daddy
Wouldn't Buy Me A Bow-Bow*]

S G. TALLENTYRE

2 The crowning blessing of life – to be born
with a bias to some pursuit. [*The Friends
of Voltaire*]

BOOTH TARKINGTON

3 There are two things that will be believed
of any man whatsoever, and one of them
is that he has taken to drink. [*Penrod*,
Ch. 10]

ALLEN TATE

4 Row upon row with strict impunity /
The headstones yield their names to the
element. [*Ode to the Confederate Dead*]

5 Autumn is desolation in the plot / Of
a thousand acres, where these memories
grow / From the inexhaustible bodies
that are not / Dead, but feed the grass,
row after rich row. [*Ib.*]

6 The brute curiosity of an angel's stare /
Turns you like them to stone. [*Ib.*]

7 Those midnight restitutions of the blood.
[*Ib.*]

8 Now that the salt of their blood /
Stiffens the saltier oblivion of the sea.
[*Ib.*]

R. H. TAWNEY

9 As long as men are men, a poor society
cannot be too poor to find a right order
of life, nor a rich society too rich to have
need to seek it. [*The Acquisitive Society*]

A. J. P. TAYLOR

10 Communism continued to haunt Europe
as a spectre – a name men gave to their
own fears and blunders. But the crusade
against Communism was even more
imaginary than the spectre of Communism. [*The Origins of the Second
World War*, Ch. 2]

11 The systems are created by historians, as
happened with Napoleon; and the
systems attributed to Hitler are really
those of Hugh Trevor-Roper, Elizabeth
Wiskemann, and Alan Bullock. [*Ib.* 4]

12 Lenin was the first to discover that
capitalism 'inevitably' caused war; and
he discovered this only when the first
World war was already being fought. Of
course he was right. Since every great
state was capitalist in 1914, capitalism
obviously 'caused' the first World war;
but just as obviously it had 'caused' the
previous generation of Peace. [*Ib.* 6]

13 A racing tipster who only reached
Hitler's level of accuracy would not do
well for his clients. [*Ib.* 7]

14 Every visit from a well-meaning business-
man or representative of the Board of
Trade increased Hitler's belief in British
weakness. He was not to know that they
had merely been reading Left-wing
writers on the economic causes of war.
[*Ib.* 9]

15 But can dreams really come true? Or do
they remain dreams even if men enact
them in waking life? [On de Gaulle.
Observer, 27 Sept. 1959]

16 He [Napoleon III] was what I often think
is a dangerous thing for a statesman to
be – a student of history; and like most of
those who study history, he learned from
the mistakes of the past how to make new
ones. [*Listener*, 6 June 1963]

17 They say that men become attached even
to Widnes. [*Observer*, 15 Sept. 1963]

JOHN TAYLOR [Editor of *Tailor and Cutter*]

18 The only man who really needs a tail coat is a man with a hole in his trousers. [Remark quoted in *Shouts and Murmurs*, from the *Observer*]

PIERRE TEILHARD DE CHARDIN

19 *La Foi a besoin de toute la vérité* – Faith has need of the whole truth. [*The Appearance of Man*]

20 Individual human beings are so subtly developed through the centuries that it is strictly impermissible to compare any two men who are not contemporaries – that is to say are taken from two quite different times. [*Ib.* Ch. 17, sect. ii]

21 The past has revealed to me the structure of the future. [*Letters from a Traveller*]

22 The only universe capable of containing the human person is an irreversibly 'personalizing' universe. [*The Phenomenon of Man*, Bk IV, Ch. 3, sect. iii]

23 From an evolutionary point of view, man has stopped moving, if he ever did move. [*Ib.* Postscript]

WILLIAM TEMPLE, ARCHBISHOP OF CANTERBURY

24 If a man is going to be a villain, in heaven's name let him remain a fool. [*Mens Creatrix*]

25 Personally, I have always looked on cricket as organized loafing. [Remark to parents when Headmaster of Repton School]

26 It is not the ape, nor the tiger in man that I fear, it is the donkey. [Attr.]

27 The Church exists for the sake of those outside it. [Attr.]

28 I believe in the Church. One Holy, Catholic and Apostolic, and I regret that it nowhere exists. [Attr.]

29 Unless all existence is a medium of revelation, no particular revelation is possible. [Attr.]

SHERPA TENSING

30 We've done the bugger! [On climbing Everest. Attr.]

ELLEN TERRY

31 How Henry would have loved it! [At Sir Henry Irving's funeral. Quoted in Robert Hitchens, *Yesterdays*]

JOSEPHINE TEY

32 When she had gone creaking away, in a shoes-and-corset concerto, he went back to Mr Tanner and tried to improve his mind by acquiring some of Mr Tanner's interest in the human race. [*The Daughter of Time*, Ch. 4]

ALLEN D. THOMAS

33 Women add zest to the unlicensed hours. [Remark made in a pub, 1964]

DYLAN THOMAS

34 Before I knocked and flesh let enter, / With liquid hands tapped on the womb, / I who was shapeless as the water / That shaped the Jordan near my home / Was brother to Mnetha's daughter / And sister to the fathering worm. [*Before I Knocked*]

35 I, born of flesh and ghost, was neither / A ghost nor man, but mortal ghost. / And I was struck down by death's feather. [*Ib.*]

36 The conversation of prayers about to be said / Turns on the quick and the dead, and the man on the stairs / Tonight shall find no dying but alive and warm. [*The Conversation of Prayer*]

37 The world is half the devil's and my own, / Daft with the drug that's smoking in a girl / And curling round the bud that forks her eye. [*If I were Tickled by the Rub of Love*]

38 Man be my metaphor. [*Ib.*]

39 A process in the weather of the heart / Turns damp to dry; the golden shot / Storms in the freezing tomb. [*A Process in the Weather of the Heart*]

40 A process blows the moon into the sun, /
Pulls down the shabby curtains of the
skin; / And the heart gives up its dead.
[*Ib.*]

41 There shall be corals in your beds, /
There shall be serpents in your tides, /
Till all our sea-faiths die. [*Where once the
Waters of your Face*]

42 I read somewhere of a shepherd who,
when asked why he made, from within
fairy rings, ritual observances to the
moon to preserve his flocks, replied: 'I'd
be a damn fool if I didn't!' [*Note to
Collected Poems*]

43 I'm Jonah Jarvis, come to a bad end, very
enjoyable. [*Under Milk Wood*]

44 Chasing the naughty couples down the
grassgreen gooseberried double bed of the
wood. [*Ib.*]

45 Every night of her married life she has
been late for school. [*Ib.*]

46 . . . kissed her once by the pigsty when she
wasn't looking and never kissed her again
although she was looking all the time.
[*Ib.*]

47 Oh, isn't life a terrible thing, thank God?
[*Ib.*]

48 Oh I'm a martyr to music. [Mrs Organ
Morgan. *Ib.*]

49 I love you until Death do us part and then
we shall be together for ever and ever.
[*Ib.*]

50 . . . thinking of a woman soft as Eve and
sharp as sciatica to share his bread-
pudding bed. [*Ib.*]

51 . . . his nicotine eggyellow weeping
walrus Victorian moustache worn thick
and long in memory of Doctor Crippen.
[*Ib.*]

52 Portraits of famous bards and preachers,
all fur and wool from the squint to the
kneecaps. [*Ib.*]

53 I missed the chance of a lifetime, too.
Fifty lovelies in the rude and I'd left my
Bunsen burner home. [*Portrait of the
Artist as a Young Dog*, 'One Warm
Saturday']

54 The land of my fathers. My fathers can
have it. [Quoted in John Ackerman,
Dylan Thomas]

55 Too many of the artists of Wales spend
too much time about the position of the
artist of Wales. There is only one
position for an artist anywhere: and that
is, upright. [Quoted by Geoffrey Grigson
in *New Statesman*, 18 Dec. 1964]

EDWARD THOMAS

56 All are behind, the kind / And the un-
kind too, no more / To-night than a
dream. The stream / Runs softly and
drowns the Past, / The dark-lit stream
has drowned the Future and the Past.
[*The Bridge*]

57 There is not any book / Or face of
dearest look / That I would not turn
from now / To go into the unknown /
I must enter, and leave, alone, / I know
not how. [*Lights Out*]

58 Its silence I hear and obey / That I may
lose my way / And myself. [*Ib.*]

59 All was foretold me; naught / Could I
foresee; / But I learned how the wind
would sound / After these things should
be. [*The New House*]

60 The green elm with the one great bough
of gold / Lets leaves into the grass slip
[*October*]

61 But if this be not happiness – who
knows? / Some day I shall think this a
happy day, / And this mood by the
name of melancholy / Shall no more
blackened and obscurèd be. [*Ib.*]

62 How weak and little is the light, / All
the universe of sight, / Love and
delight, / Before the might, / If you
love it not, of night. [*Out in the Dark*]

63 Merrily / Answered staid drinkers, good
bedmen, and all bores: / 'At Mrs Green-
land's Hawthorn Bush,' said he / 'I
slept.' [*A Private*]

64 Now all roads lead to France / And
heavy is the tread / Of the living; but
the dead / Returning lightly dance.
[*Roads*]

65 I like the dust on the nettles, never lost /
Except to prove the sweetness of a
shower. [*Tall Nettles*]

66 Make me content / With some sweetness / From Wales / Whose nightingales / Have no wings. [*Words*]

GWYN THOMAS

67 I wanted a play that would paint the full face of sensuality, rebellion and revivalism. In South Wales these three phenomena have played second fiddle only to the Rugby Union which is a distillation of all three. [Introduction to *Jackie the Jumper, Plays and Players*, 19 Jan. 1963]

68 You are truly God's trumpet, Mr Rees. After a session on you he must feel whacked. [*Jackie the Jumper*, II]

69 There are still parts of Wales where the only concession to gaiety is a striped shroud. [*Punch*, 18 June 1958]

R. S. THOMAS

70 It is too late to start / For destinations not of the heart. / I must stay here with my hurt. [*Here*]

71 Shelley dreamt it. Now the dream decays. / The props crumble. [*Song at the Year's Turning*]

72 . . . an impotent people, / Sick with inbreeding, / Worrying the carcase of an old song. [*Welsh Landscape*]

H. W. THOMPSON

73 An old man marrying a young girl is like buying a book for some one else to read. [*Body, Boots and Britches*]

74 Never speak loudly to one another unless the house is on fire. [*Ib.*]

JAMES THURBER

75 She developed a persistent troubled frown which gave her the expression of someone who is trying to repair a watch with his gloves on. [*The Beast in Me and Other Animals*, 'Look Homeward, Jeannie']

76 Grandog. [*The Dogs*, Preface]

77 Charles Vayne, as regular and as futile as a clock in an empty house, showed up once a week. [*Alarms and Diversions*, 'A final note on Chanda Bell']

78 'I think this calls for a drink' has long been one of our national slogans. [*Ib.* 'Merry Christmas']

79 'Joe,' I said, 'was perhaps the first great nonstop literary drinker of the American nineteenth century. He made the indulgences of Coleridge and De Quincey seem like a bit of mischief in the kitchen with the cooking sherry.' [*Ib.* 'The Moribundant Life . . .']

80 I was seized by the stern hand of Compulsion, that dark, unseasonable Urge that impels women to clean house in the middle of the night. [*Ib.* 'There's a Time for Flags']

81 No man . . . who has wrestled with a self-adjusting card table can ever quite be the man he once was. [*Let Your Mind Alone*, 'Sex ex Machina']

82 Old Nat Burge sat on the rusted wreck of an ancient sewing machine in front of Hell Fire, which was what his shack was known as among the neighbours and to the police. He was chewing on a splinter of wood and watching the moon come up lazily out of the old cemetery in which nine of his daughters were lying, and only two of them were dead. [*Ib.* 'Bateman Comes Home']

83 I myself have accomplished nothing of excellence except a remarkable and, to some of my friends, unaccountable expertness in hitting empty ginger ale bottles with small rocks at a distance of thirty paces. [*My Life and Hard Times*, Preface]

84 They [humorists] lead, as a matter of fact, an existence of jumpiness and apprehension. They sit on the edge of the chair of Literature. In the house of Life they have the feeling that they have never taken off their overcoats. [*Ib.*]

85 Q. We have cats the way most people have mice. [Signed] Mrs C.L. FOOTLOOSE A. I see you have. I can't tell from your communication whether you wish advice or are just boasting. [*The Owl in the Attic*]

86 'We all have flaws,' he said, 'and mine is being wicked.' [*The 13 Clocks*, Ch. 8]

87 If he knew where he was going, it is not apparent from this distance. He fell down a great deal during this period, because of a trick he had of walking into himself. [On himself as a child. *The Thurber Carnival*, Preface]

88 If you don't pay no mind to diseases, they will go away. [*Ib.* 'Recollections of the Gas Buggy']

89 There is, of course, a certain amount of drudgery in newspaper work, just as there is in teaching classes, tunnelling into a bank, or being President of the United States. I suppose that even the most pleasurable of imaginable occupations, that of batting baseballs through the windows of the R.C.A. Building, would pall a little as the days ran on. [*Ib.* 'Memoirs of a Drudge']

90 You wait here and I'll bring the etchings down. [*Men, Women and Dogs,* cartoon caption]

1 I said the hounds of spring are on winter's traces – but let it pass, let it pass! [*Ib.* Cartoon caption]

2 Why don't you get dressed, then, and go to pieces like a man? [*Alarms and Diversions,* cartoon caption]

3 Ooooo, guesties! [*Ib.* Cartoon caption]

4 All right, have it your way – you heard a seal bark. [*The Seal in the Bedroom,* cartoon caption]

5 You might as well fall flat on your face as lean over too far backward. [*Fables for Our Time,* 'The Bear who let it alone']

6 Early to rise and early to bed makes a male healthy and wealthy and dead. [*Ib.,* 'The Shrike and the Chipmunks']

7 As difficult as getting a combative drunk man out of the night club in which he fancies he has been insulted. [*The Middle-Aged Man on the Flying Trapeze,* 'The Departure of Emma Inch']

8 In those days all the heads of business firms adopted a guarded kind of double talk, commonly expressed in low, muffled tones, because nobody knew what was going to happen and nobody understood what had. [*The Secret Life of James Thurber*]

9 Mosher came out into the reception room, looking like a professor of English literature who has not approved of the writings of anybody since Sir Thomas Browne. [*The Years with Ross,* Ch. 2]

10 It had only one fault. It was kind of lousy. [When asked his opinion of a play. Quoted in P. G. Wodehouse, *Performing Flea,* 1947–52]

11 Ashes to ashes and clay to clay, if the enemy don't get you, your own folks may. [*Observer,* 'Sayings of the Week', 1 July 1956]

12 The difference between our decadence and the Russians' is that while theirs is brutal, ours is apathetic. [*Observer,* 'Sayings of the Week', 5 Feb. 1961]

13 Why do you have to be a nonconformist like everybody else? [Attr. Thurber: actually cartoon caption by Stan Hunt in *New Yorker*]

THWACKHURST

14 'You have ruined all the graffiti. You can't find anything in a piss-house now but political remarks. . . . And just when the spread of popular education was bringing the graffiti lower on the walls.' 'Lower on the walls?' 'Sure. Don't you see the little children were beginning to add their quota, when all this damn politics comes along.' [Quoted in Oliver St John Gogarty, *As I Was Going Down Sackville Street,* Ch. 4]

PAUL TILLICH

15 Loneliness can be conquered only by those who can bear solitude. [*The Eternal Now,* Pt I, Ch. 3]

16 Life could not continue without throwing the past into the past, liberating the present from its burden. [*Ib.* II. i]

17 Neurosis is the way of avoiding non-being by avoiding being. [*The Courage to Be*]

THE TIMES

18 In my childhood it was said by all: 'A child of ten can go on the road of a town playing with a golden ball in perfect safety under British rule.' [Quoted in *The Times*]

J. R. R. TOLKIEN

19 Hobbits are an unobtrusive but very ancient people, more numerous formerly than they are today. [*The Lord of the Rings,* 'Prologue']

RUDOLPHE TOMASCHEK

20 Modern Physics is an instrument of [world] Jewry for the destruction of Nordic science. . . . True physics is the creation of the German spirit. [Quoted in W. L. Shirer, *The Rise and Fall of the Third Reich*, Ch. 8]

H. M. TOMLINSON

21 I will never believe again that the sea was ever loved by anyone whose life was married to it. [*The Sea and the Jungle*, Ch. 1]

22 Some men will touch their crowns to Carnegie in heaven. [*Ib.*]

ARNOLD TOYNBEE

23 No annihilation without representation. [Pressing for a greater British voice in the affairs of U.N.O., 1947]

24 The human race's prospects of survival were considerably better when we were defenceless against tigers than they are today when we have become defenceless against ourselves. [*Observer*, 'Sayings of the Year', 1963]

PHILIP TOYNBEE

25 What I mean by moral progress is an increasing and active recognition of the fact that other human beings are fully as human as oneself. ['Two Cheers for Moral Progress', reprinted in *Shouts and Murmurs* from the *Observer*]

SIR HERBERT BEERBOHM TREE

26 I was born old and get younger every day. At present I am sixty years young. [Quoted in Hesketh Pearson, *Beerbohm Tree*, Ch. 1]

27 And Sillabub, the son of Sillabub reigned in his stead. [Remark at his wedding breakfast. Quoted in *ib*. 4]

28 FELLOW-MEMBER [after a scene at the Garrick Club]: When I joined all the members were gentlemen.
TREE: I wonder why they left. [Quoted in *ib*. 5]

29 The only man who wasn't spoilt by being lionized was Daniel. [*Ib*. 12]

30 A whipper-snapper of criticism who quoted dead languages to hide his ignorance of life. [Of A. B. Walkley. Quoted in *ib*.]

31 The national sport of England is obstacle-racing. People fill their rooms with useless and cumbersome furniture, and spend the rest of their lives in trying to dodge it. [*Ib*.]

32 She has kissed her way into society. I don't like her. But don't misunderstand me: my dislike is purely platonic. [Of an actress who was better as a lover than on the stage. Quoted in *ib*.]

33 My poor fellow, why not carry a watch? [To a man who was staggering in the street under the weight of a grandfather clock. Quoted in *ib*.]

34 Oh my God! Remember you're in Egypt. The *skay* is only seen in Kensington. [To a leading lady. Quoted in *ib*. 16]

35 Sirs, I have tested your machine. It adds a new terror to life and makes death a long-felt want. [To a gramophone company who asked for a testimonial. Quoted in *ib*. 19]

36 When I pass my name in such large letters I blush, but at the same time instinctively raise my hat. [Quoted in *ib*.]

37 God is a sort of burglar. As a young man you knock him down; as an old man you try to conciliate him, because he may knock you down. [Quoted in *ib*. 21]

38 His face shining like Moses, his teeth like the Ten Commandments, all broken. [Of Israel Zangwill. Quoted in *ib*.]

39 He is an old bore; even the grave yawns for him. [*Ib*.]

40 TREE [in a post-office]: Do you sell postage-stamps?
GIRL: Yes, sir.
T.: Please show me some. [Then pointing to one in the middle of the sheet] I'll have that one, please. [Quoted in George Robey, *Looking Back on Life*, Ch. 27]

41 Ladies, just a little more virginity, if you don't mind. [To a 'collection of damsels that had been dragged into the theatre as ladies in waiting to the queen' in his production of *Henry VIII*. Quoted in Alexander Woollcott, *Shouts and Murmurs*, 'Capsule Criticism']

227

G. M. TREVELYAN

42 Socrates gave no diplomas or degrees, and would have subjected any disciple who demanded one to a disconcerting catechism on the nature of true knowledge. [*History of England*, Bk II, Ch. 4]

43 Walpole ... even when Prime Minister was said to open his gamekeeper's letters first of the batch. [*Ib*. V. 2]

44 Nelson, born in a fortunate hour for himself and for his country, was always in his element and always on his element. [*Ib*. V. 5]

H. R. TREVOR-ROPER

45 [James I] remained an omniscient umpire whom no one consulted. [*Archbishop Laud*]

LIONEL TRILLING

46 The diminution of the reality of class, however socially desirable in many respects, seems to have the practical effect of diminishing our ability to see people in their difference and specialness. [*The Liberal Imagination*, 'Art and Fortune']

47 The great psychological fact of our time which we all observe with baffled wonder and shame is that there is no possible way of responding to Belsen and Buchenwald. The activity of mind fails before the incommunicability of man's suffering. [*Ib*.]

48 We are all ill: but even a universal sickness implies an idea of health. [*Ib*. 'Art and Neurosis']

49 Our liberal ideology has produced a large literature of social and political protest, but not, for several decades, a single writer who commands our real literary admiration. [*Ib*. 'The Function of the Little Magazine']

50 There is no connexion between the political ideas of our educated class and the deep places of the imagination. [*Ib*.]

51 It would seem that Americans have a kind of resistance to looking closely at society. [*Ib*. 'Manners, Morals and the Novel']

TOMMY TRINDER

52 You lucky people! [Used throughout his BBC comedy programmes]

LEON TROTSKY

53 Revolution by its very nature is sometimes compelled to take in more territory than it is capable of holding. Retreats are possible – when there is territory to retreat from. [*Diary in Exile*, 15 Feb. 1935]

54 Nicholas II inherited from his ancestors not only a giant empire, but also a revolution. And they did not bequeath him one property that would have made him capable of governing an empire or even a province or a county. [*History of the Russian Revolution*, Pt I, Ch. 4]

55 The 23rd of February was International Woman's Day.... It had not occurred to anyone that it might become the first day of the revolution. [*Ib*. I. 7]

56 The revolution does not choose its paths: it made its first steps towards victory under the belly of a Cossack's horse. [*Ib*.]

57 The English and French bourgeoisie created a new society after their own image. The Germans came later, and they were compelled to live for a long time on the pale gruel of philosophy. [*Ib*. I. 10]

58 The most revolutionary party which human history until this time had ever known was nevertheless caught unawares by the events of history. [*Ib*. I. 21]

59 The slanders poured down like Niagara. If you take into consideration the setting – the war and the revolution – and the character of the accused – revolutionary leaders of millions who were conducting their party to the sovereign power – you can say without exaggeration that July 1917 was the month of the most gigantic slander in world history. [*Ib*. II. 5]

60 Revolutions are always verbose. [*Ib*. II. 12]

61 Civilization has made the peasantry its pack animal. [*Ib*. III. 1]

62 A civil war is inevitable. We have only to organize it as painlessly as possible. [Speech quoted in *ib*. III. 5]

63 In practice a reformist party considers unshakable the foundations of that which it intends to reform. [*Ib.*]

64 Insurrection is an art, and like all arts it has its laws. [*Ib.* III. 6]

65 The fundamental premise of a revolution is that the existing social structure has become incapable of solving the urgent problems of development of the nation. [*Ib.*]

66 There is a limit to the application of democratic methods. You can inquire of all the passengers as to what type of car they like to ride in, but it is impossible to question them as to whether to apply the brakes when the train is at full speed and accident threatens. [*Ib.*]

67 From being a patriotic myth, the Russian people have become an awful reality. [*Ib.* III. 7]

68 Armed insurrection stands in the same relation to revolution that revolution as a whole does to evolution. It is the critical point when accumulating quantity turns with an explosion into quality. [*Ib.* III. 9]

69 The historic ascent of humanity, taken as a whole, may be summarized as a succession of victories of consciousness over blind forces – in nature, in society, in man himself. [*Ib.* Conclusion]

70 For us, the tasks of education in socialism were closely integrated with those of fighting. Ideas that enter the mind under fire remain there securely and for ever. [*My Life*, Ch. 35]

71 Whatever opposition there might be was tested in action, on the very spot. . . . If we had had more time for discussion we should probably have made a great many more mistakes. [*Ib.* 36]

72 It was the supreme expression of the mediocrity of the apparatus that Stalin himself rose to his position. [*Ib.* 40]

PRESIDENT HARRY TRUMAN

73 The buck stops here. [Notice on his presidential desk]

74 It's a recession when your neighbour loses his job; it's a depression when you lose your own. [*Observer*, 'Sayings of the Week', 6 Apr. 1958]

75 The President spends most of his time kissing people on the cheek in order to get them to do what they ought to do without getting kissed. [*Observer*, 'Sayings of the Week', 6 Feb. 1949]

BARBARA W. TUCHMAN

76 Edward [VII], whose two passions in life were correct clothes and unorthodox company, overlooked the former, and admired M. Clemenceau. [*The Guns of August*, Ch. 1]

77 Nothing so comforts the military mind as the maxim of a great but dead general. [*Ib.* 2]

78 Dead battles, like dead generals, hold the military mind in their dead grip. [*Ib.*]

79 No more distressing moment can ever face a British government than that which requires it to come to a hard and fast and specific decision. [Of August 1914. *Ib.* 9]

A. W. TUER

80 English as She is Spoke. [Title of book of English-Portuguese conversation]

CHARLES TURLEY

81 Modesty can be cultivated until it becomes something very like a crime. [*A Band of Brothers*]

W. J. TURNER

82 You will have been told that men only become professors when they are dead, that only the dead can lecture, finally and most comprehensively, that only the dead can talk at all. It is a fact of far-reaching significance, whose implications very few among earth's profoundest scholars have begun as yet to suspect, that the living do not talk at all. [*Henry Airbubble*, Ch. 22]

83 There is virtue in recognizing that Bach had more intellectual and emotional power than an infinite number of Puccinis and Stravinskys. But Bach a great religious composer! Oh, dear no! [Review reprinted in V. S. Pritchett, *Turnstile One*]

JULIAN TUWIM

84 There are two kinds of blood, the blood that flows in the veins and the blood that flows out of them. [*We, the Polish Jews*]

MARK TWAIN

85 Soap and education are not as sudden as a massacre, but they are more deadly in the long run. [Quoted in Sagittarius and George, *The Perpetual Pessimist*]

86 It is by the goodness of God that we have in our country three unspeakably precious things: freedom of speech, freedom of conscience, and the prudence never to practise either. [Quoted in *ib.*]

87 Whoever has lived long enough to find out what life is knows how deep a debt of gratitude we owe to Adam, the first great benefactor of our race. He brought death into the world. [Quoted in *ib.*]

GEORGE TYRRELL

88 We do not need to prove religion to men but to prove to them that they are religious. [Attr.]

89 I never quite forgave Mahaffy for getting himself suspended from preaching in the College Chapel. Ever since his sermons were discontinued, I suffer from insomnia in church. [Quoted in Oliver St John Gogarty, *As I was Going Down Sackville Street*, Ch. 25]

90 'Are you coming to the picnic, Mrs Murphy?' 'Picnic, me neck! Look at Mary's belly since the last picnic.' [Quoted in *ib.*]

1 That's this country [Ireland] all over! Not content with a contradiction in terms, it must go on to an antithesis in ideas. 'Temperance Hotel'! You might as well speak of a celibate kip [brothel]! [Quoted in *ib.*]

KENNETH TYNAN

2 William Congreve is the only sophisticated playwright England has produced; and like Shaw, Sheridan, and Wilde, his nearest rivals, he was brought up in Ireland. [*Curtains*, 'The Way of the World']

3 A novel is a static thing that one moves through; a play is a dynamic thing that moves past one. [*Ib.* 'Cards of Identity']

4 What, when drunk, one sees in other women, one sees in Garbo sober. [Quoted in *Sunday Times*, 25 Aug. 1963]

U

MIGUEL DE UNAMUNO

1 *La vida es duda, / y la fe sin la duda es sólo muerte.* – Life is doubt, and faith without doubt is nothing but death. [*Poesías*, 1907]

2 All right, my lord creator, Don Miguel, you too will die and return to the nothing whence you came. God will cease to dream you! [*Mist*]

3 It is not usually our ideas that make us optimists or pessimists, but it is our optimism or pessimism, of physiological or pathological origin ... that makes our ideas. [*The Tragic Sense of Life*, Ch. 1]

4 My work ... is to shatter the faith of men here, there and everywhere, faith in affirmation, faith in negation, and faith in abstention from faith, and this for the sake of faith in faith itself. [*Ib.* Conclusion]

5 May God deny you peace but give you glory! [*Ib.* Closing words]

6 They [the Franc rebels] will conquer, but they will not convince. [Said at the end of his life]

UNKNOWN JUDGE

7 [Reprimanding prisoner before sentence] You have been found guilty of indulging in unnatural practices under one of London's most *beautiful* bridges. [Traditional at the Bar]

JOHN UPDIKE

8 Everybody who tells you how to act has whisky on their breath. [*Rabbit, Run*]

9 The difficulty with humorists is that they will mix what they believe with what they don't; whichever seems likelier to win an effect. [*Ib.*]

10 He is a man of brick. As if he was born as a baby literally of clay and decades of exposure have baked him to the colour and hardness of brick. [*Ib.*]

11 The founding fathers in their wisdom decided that children were an unnatural strain on parents. So they provided jails called schools, equipped with tortures called education. School is where you go between when your parents can't take you and industry can't take you. [*The Centaur*, Ch. 4]

RICHARD USBORNE

12 There is no suggestion that either club man or girl would recognize a double bed except as so much extra sweat to make an apple-pie of. [*Wodehouse at Work*, 'The Short Stories']

13 Definition of a slogan: a form of words for which memorability has been *bought*. [In letter to editors, 1964]

PETER USTINOV

14 Laughter would be bereaved if snobbery died. [*Observer*, 'Sayings of the Week', 13 Mar. 1955]

15 If Botticelli were alive today he'd be working for *Vogue*. [*Observer*, 'Sayings of the Week', 21 Oct. 1962]

V

HORACE ANNESLEY VACHELL

1 In nature there are no rewards or punishments; there are consequences. [*The Face of Clay*, Ch. 10]

AMANDA VAIL

2 But for some reason Amy's sense of shame stops above the waist. Vanity, I suppose, will overcome almost any other feeling. [*Love Me Little*, Ch. 3]

3 She will end up not only wanting marriage, but with invitations so deeply engraved they can be read with one's finger-tips. [*Ib.* 5]

4 Sometimes I think if there was a third sex men wouldn't get so much as a glance from me. [*Ib.* 6]

5 We talked a lot about life. There was nothing else to talk about. [*Ib.* 8]

6 'Parents are strange,' Amy said, 'for their age.' [*Ib.* 10]

7 'American girls do have regrets,' Amy said. 'That is what distinguishes them from French girls.' [*Ib.*]

R. VAUGHAN WILLIAMS

8 I realize now it [his London Symphony] is not as boring as I thought it was. [Quoted by Sir Adrian Boult in a broadcast, 1 Aug. 1965]

9 I don't know whether I like it [his Fourth Symphony], but it is what I meant. [Quoted in *Ib.*]

THORSTEN VEBLEN

10 All business sagacity reduces itself in the last analysis to a judicious use of sabotage. [*The Nature of Peace*]

11 That was *not* my niece. [Referring to a young lady staying in his house. Quoted in R. Heilbroner, *The Worldly Philosophers*, Ch. 8]

CARL VAN VECHTEN

12 There are, I have discovered, two kinds of people in this world, those who long to be understood and those who long to be misunderstood. It is the irony of life that neither is gratified. [*The Blind Bow-Boy*]

A. W. VERRALL

13 Arthur is a good boy; he doesn't say *them's grouses*, he says *them's grice*. [Said of himself as a child standing before a picture of partridges. Prefatory Memoir to *Collected Literary Essays*, ed. M. A. Bayfield]

14 Oh, quite easy! The Septuagint minus the Apostles. [To someone who said that 58 was a difficult number to remember. Attr.]

DR VERWOERD (Prime Minister of South Africa)

15 We did what God wanted us to do. [*Observer*, 'Sayings of the Week', 26 Mar. 1961]

COMMANDER ALAN VILLIERS

16 Only fools and passengers drink at sea. [*Observer*, 'Sayings of the Week', 28 Apr. 1957]

ANDREI VOZNESENSKY

17 it is time / For you to run out of me and I / Out of you. [*Autumn in Sigulda*, trans. W. H. Auden]

W

JOHN WAIN

1 The lesson is that dying men must groan; / And poets groan in rhymes that please the ear. / But still it comes expensive, you must own. [*Don't let's spoil it all, I thought we were going to be such good friends*]

ARTHUR WALEY

2 It is not difficult to censor foreign news, / What is hard today is to censor one's own thoughts, – / To sit by and see the blind man / On the sightless horse, riding into the bottomless abyss. [*Censorship*]

3 I therefore caution all wise men / That August visitors should not be admitted. [*Satire on Paying Calls in August* trans. from Chinese of Ch'eng Hsiao, *c.* A.D. 220–164]

4 In the early dusk, down an alley of green moss, / The garden-boy is leading the cranes home. [*The Cranes*, trans. from the Chinese of Po-Chü-I]

5 Keep off your thoughts from things that are past and done; / For thinking of the past wakes regret and pain. [*Resignation*, trans. from the Chinese of Po-Chü-I]

JAMES WALKER

6 Will you love me in December / As you did in May? [Song: *Will You Love Me in December?*]

JAMES J. WALKER

7 A reformer is a guy who rides through a sewer in a glass-bottomed boat. [Speech as Mayor of New York, 1928]

KENNETH WALKER

8 The patient has been so completely taken to pieces that nobody is able to look on him again as a whole being. He is no longer an individual man but a jumble of scientific data. [*The Circle of Life*, Pt I, Ch. 1]

EDGAR WALLACE

9 A writer of crook stories ought never to stop seeking new material. [On standing for Parliament. Quoted in Robert Graves and Alan Hodge, *The Long Weekend*]

10 He was a small man, painfully thin and bald; an irregular greying beard was a decoration to a face which badly needed assistance. [*Again Sanders*, 'Thy Neighbour as Thyself']

HENRY WALLACE

11 I doubt if even China can equal our record of soil destruction. [Quoted in A. M. Schlesinger Jr, *The Coming of the New Deal*, Pt V, Ch. 20, sect. iv]

GEORGE WARE

12 The boy I love is up in the gallery, / The boy I love is looking now at me. [Song: *The Boy in the Gallery*, sung by Marie Lloyd]

JACK WARNER

13 Mind my bike! [Repeated in *Garrison Theatre*, wartime broadcasts]

G. F. WATTS

14 I was so desirous of getting it right [a drawing] I did it with my shoes off. [Quoted in Christopher Hassall, *Edward Marsh*, Ch. 6]

EVELYN WAUGH

15 I expect you'll be becoming a schoolmaster sir. That's what most of the gentlemen does sir, that gets sent down for indecent behaviour. [*Decline and Fall*, Prelude]

16 We class schools, you see, into four grades: Leading School, First-rate School, Good School, and School. [*Ib.* I. 1]

17 Meanwhile you will write an essay on 'self-indulgence'. There will be a prize of half a crown for the longest essay, irrespective of any possible merit. [*Ib.* I. 5]

18 I can't quite explain it, but I don't believe one can ever be unhappy for long provided one does just exactly what one wants to and when one wants to. [*Ib.*]

19 For generations the British bourgeoisie have spoken of themselves as gentlemen, and by that they have meant, among other things, a self-respecting scorn of irregular perquisites. It is the quality that distinguishes the gentleman from both the artist and the aristocrat. [*Ib.* I. 6]

20 There aren't many left like him nowadays, what with education and whisky the price it is. [*Ib.* I. 7]

21 We can trace almost all the disasters of English history to the influence of Wales. [*Ib.* I. 8]

22 Nonconformity and lust stalking hand in hand through the country, wasting and ravaging. [*Ib.*]

23 'The Welsh,' said the Doctor, 'are the only nation in the world that has produced no graphic or plastic art, no architecture, no drama. They just sing,' he said with disgust, 'sing and blow down wind instruments of plated silver.' [*Ib.*]

24 If my brother had been alive he'd have licked all that out of the young cub. It takes a man to bring up a man. [*Ib.*]

25 I have noticed again and again since I have been in the Church that lay interest in ecclesiastical matters is often a prelude to insanity. [*Ib.*]

26 But no man can you ask against his Maker to blaspheme whatever unless him to pay more you were. Three pounds for the music is good and one for the blasphemy look you. [*Ib.* I. 9]

27 I have often observed in women of her type a tendency to regard all athletics as inferior forms of fox-hunting. [*Ib.* I. 10]

28 I haven't been to sleep for over a year. That's why I go to bed early. One needs more rest if one doesn't sleep. [*Ib.* II. 3]

29 There is a species of person called a 'Modern Churchman' who draws the full salary of a beneficed clergyman and need not commit himself to any religious belief. [*Ib.* II. 4]

30 'But you married?' 'Yes, mum, but it was in the war, and he was very drunk.' [*Ib.* II. 5]

31 Services are voluntary – that is to say, you must either attend all or none. [*Ib.* III. 1]

32 He stood twice for Parliament, but so diffidently that his candidature passed almost unnoticed. [*Ib.*]

33 I came to the conclusion many years ago that almost all crime is due to the repressed desire for aesthetic expression. [*Ib.*]

34 'How do you do?' said Paul politely. 'Are you here for long?' 'Life,' said the other. 'But it doesn't matter much. I look daily for the Second Coming.' [*Ib.* III. 3]

35 Anyone who has been to an English public school will always feel comparatively at home in prison. It is the people brought up in the gay intimacy of the slums, Paul learned, who find prison so soul-destroying. [*Ib.* III. 4]

36 He was greatly pained at how little he was pained by the events of the afternoon. [*Ib.* III. 4]

37 Instead of this absurd division into sexes they ought to class people as static and dynamic. [*Ib.* III. 7]

38 When the war broke out she took down the signed photograph of the Kaiser and with some solemnity, hung it in the men-servants' lavatory; it was her one combative action. [*Vile Bodies*, Ch. 3]

39 She had heard someone say something about an Independent Labour Party, and was furious that she had not been asked. [*Ib.* 4]

40 All this fuss about sleeping together. For physical pleasure I'd sooner go to my dentist any day. [*Ib.* 6]

41 Assistant masters came and went. . . . Some liked little boys too little and some too much. [*A Little Learning*]

42 That impersonal insensitive friendliness that takes the place of ceremony in that land [the U.S.A.] of waifs and strays. [*The Loved One*]

43 You never find an Englishman among the underdogs – except in England of course. [*Ib.*]

44 Most cemeteries, he says, provide a dog's toilet and a cat's motel. [*Ib.*]

45 I took Art at College as my second subject one semester. I'd have taken it as first subject only Dad lost his money in religion so I had to learn a trade. [*Ib.*]

46 In the dying world I come from quotation is a national vice. It used to be the classics, now it's lyric verse. [*Ib.*]

47 '*The Beast* stands for strong mutually antagonistic governments everywhere,' he said. 'Self-sufficiency at home, self-assertion abroad.' [*Scoop*, Bk I, Ch. 3]

48 Yes, cider and tinned salmon are the staple diet of the agricultural classes. [*Ib. I. 4*]

49 News is what a chap who doesn't care much about anything wants to read. And it's only news until he's read it. After that it's dead. [*Ib. I. 5*]

50 Personally I can't see that foreign stories are ever news – not *real* news. [*Ib.*]

51 Pappenhacker says that every time you are polite to a proletarian you are helping bolster up the capitalist system. [*Ib.*]

52 As there was no form of government common to the peoples thus segregated, nor tie of language, history, habit, or belief, they were called a Republic. [*Ib. II. 1*]

53 The better sort of Ishmaelites have been Christian for many centuries and will not publicly eat human flesh uncooked in Lent, without special and costly dispensation from their bishop. [*Ib.*]

54 'I will not stand for being called a woman in my own house,' she said. [*Ib.*]

55 Other nations use 'force'; we Britons alone use 'Might'. [*Ib. II. 5*]

56 Freddy was large, masculine, prematurely bald and superficially cheerful; at heart he was misanthropic and gifted with that sly, sharp instinct for self-preservation that passes for wisdom among the rich; his indolence was qualified with enough basic bad temper to ensure the respect of those about him. [*Put Out More Flags*]

57 Enclosing every thin man, there's a fat man demanding elbow-room. [*Officers and Gentlemen*, Interlude]

58 Manners are especially the need of the plain. The pretty can get away with anything. [*Observer*, 'Sayings of the Year', 1962]

59 No writer before the middle of the 19th century wrote about the working classes other than as grotesques or as pastoral decorations. Then when they were given the vote certain writers started to suck up to them. [Interview in *Paris Review*, 1963]

ANTON VON WEBERN

60 Music is natural law as related to the sense of hearing. [*The Path to the New Music*, two lectures trans. by Leo Black]

ANTHONY WEDGWOOD BENN

61 Britain today is suffering from galloping obsolescence. [*Observer*, 'Sayings of the Week', 2 Feb. 1963]

KURT WEILL

62 *Die Nachwelt ist mir gleichgültig – ich schreibe für heute –* I don't care about posterity. I'm writing for today. [Attr.]

C. F. VON WEIZSÄCKER

63 Body and soul are not two substances but one. They are man becoming aware of himself in two different ways. [*The History of Nature*]

MME WELLINGTON KOO

64 The air is thick with the wings of birds coming home to roost. [Remark after Munich Crisis. Attr.]

DEE WELLS

65 Maybe show-business people don't share our 20-years-of-Mortgage, 20-years-of-children, and Have-you-put-the-cat-out? view of marriage. [*Daily Herald*, 13 Feb. 1964]

H. G. WELLS

66 Rich men amenable to use are hard to find and often very intractable when found. [*The Autocracy of Mr Parham*]

67 It was a room to eat muffins in. [*Ib.*]

68 The cat is the offspring of a cat and the dog of a dog, but butlers and lady's maids do not reproduce their kind. They have other duties. [*Bealby*, Pt I, Ch. 1]

69 The life of breezy freedom resolves itself in practice chiefly into washing up and an anxious search for permission to camp. [*Ib*. III. 7]

70 He was quite sure that he had been wronged. Not to be wronged is to forgo the first privilege of goodness. [*Ib*. IV. 1]

71 Miss Madeleine Philips was making it very manifest to Captain Douglas that she herself was a career; that a lover with any other career in view need not – as the advertisements say – apply. [*Ib*. V. 5]

72 The uglier a man's legs are the better he plays golf. It's almost a law. [*Ib*. V. 8]

73 He began to think the tramp a fine, brotherly, generous fellow. He was also growing accustomed to something – shall I call it an olfactory bar – that had hitherto kept them apart. [*Ib*. VI. 3]

74 The army ages men sooner than the law and philosophy; it exposes them more freely to germs, which undermine and destroy, and it shelters them more completely from thought, which stimulates and preserves. [*Ib*. VIII. 1]

75 He had one peculiar weakness; he had faced death in many forms but he had never faced a dentist. The thought of dentists gave him just the same sick horror as the thought of Socialism. [*Ib*.]

76 Cossar was a large-bodied man with gaunt inelegant limbs casually placed at convenient corners of his body, and a face like a carving abandoned as altogether too unpromising for completion. [*The Food of the Gods*]

77 Mr Polly went into the National School at six, and he left the private school at fourteen, and by that time his mind was in much the same state that you would be in, dear reader, if you were operated on for appendicitis by a well-meaning, boldly enterprising, but rather overworked and underpaid butcher boy, who was superseded towards the climax of the operation by a left-handed clerk of high principles but intemperate habits – that is to say, it was in a thorough mess. [*The History of Mr Polly*, Pt I, Ch. 2]

78 '*Language*, man!' roared Parsons; 'why, it's LITERATURE!' [*Ib*. I. 3]

79 'Back to the collar, O' Man,' Parsons would say. There is no satisfactory plural to 'O' Man, so he always used it in the singular. [*Ib*. I. 4]

80 'The High Egrugious is fairly on,' he said, and dived down to return by devious subterranean routes to the outfitting department. [*Ib*. II. 2]

81 'Smart Juniors,' said Polly to himself, 'full of Smart Juniosity. The Shoveacious Cult.' [*Ib*. III. 1]

82 'You're a Christian?' 'Church of England,' said Mr Polly. 'Mm,' said the employer, a little checked. 'For good all round business work, I should have preferred a Baptist.' [*Ib*.]

83 We've no time for sideshows and second-rate stunts, Mamie. We want just the Big Simple Things of the place, just the Broad Elemental Canterbury Prahposition. What is it saying to us? [*Ib*. III. 2]

84 'He was really quite cheerful at the end,' she said several times, with congratulatory gusto; 'quite cheerful.' She made dying seem almost agreeable. [*Ib*. IV. 1]

85 Uncle Pentstemon was rather a shock. He was an aged rather than a venerable figure. Time had removed the hair from the top of his head and distributed a small dividend of the plunder in little bunches carelessly and impartially over the rest of his features. [*Ib*. IV. 3]

86 '*I* don't mind a squeeze,' said Mr Polly. He decided privately that the proper phrase for the result of that remark was 'Hysterial catechunations'. [*Ib*. IV. 4]

87 High old jawbacious argument we had, I tell you. [*Ib*. V. 2]

88 'Have to have a Tom-cat,' said Mr Polly, and paused for an expectant moment. 'Wouldn't do to open shop one morning, you know, and find the window full of kittens. Can't sell kittens. . . .' [*Ib*. VI. 1]

89 'They do say,' said Uncle Pentstemon, 'one funeral makes many. This time it's a wedding. But it's all very much of a muchness. . . .' [*Ib*. VI. 7]

90 Arson, after all, is an artificial crime. . . . A large number of houses deserve to be burnt. [*Ib*. X. 1]

1 Of course he had no desire to place himself on an equality in any way with Ibsen; still the fact remained that his own experience in England and America and the colonies was altogether more extensive than Ibsen could have had. Ibsen had probably never seen 'one decent bar scrap' in his life. [*Kipps*, Bk I, Ch. 4, Sect. iv]

2 'It's giving girls names like that [Euphemia],' said Buggins, 'that nine times out of ten makes 'em go wrong. It unsettles 'em. If ever I was to have a girl, if ever I was to have a dozen girls, I'd call 'em all Jane.' [*Ib*. I. 6. ii]

3 It's legitimate. Much more legitimate than the Wild Duck – where there isn't a duck! [*Ib*. II. 1. v]

4 Of course we can Learn even from Novels, Nace Novels that is, but it isn't the same thing as serious reading. [*Ib*. II. 2. i]

5 He felt like some lonely and righteous man dynamited into Bliss. [*Ib*. I. 2. ii]

6 She stamped Kipps so deeply with the hat-raising habit that he would uncover if he found himself in the same railway ticket office with a lady, and so stand ceremoniously until the difficulties of change drove him to an apologetic provisional oblique resumption of his headgear. [*Ib*. II. 5. ii]

7 He found that a fork in his inexperienced hand was an instrument of chase rather than capture. [*Ib*. II. 7. vi]

8 It's 'aving 'ouses built by men, I believe, makes all the work and trouble. [*Ib*. III. 1. ii]

9 Everybody hates house-agents because they have everybody at a disadvantage. All other callings have a certain amount of give and take; the house-agent simply takes. [*Ib*. III. 1. ii]

10 One book's very like another – after all what is it? Something to read and done with. It's not a thing that matters like print dresses or serviettes – where you either like 'em or don't, and people judge you by. [*Ib*. III. 3. iii]

11 Except that it failed, the Associated Booksellers' Trading Union had all the stigmata of success. Its fault perhaps was that it had them all instead of only one or two. [*Ib*. III. 3. iv]

12 Miss Heydinger sat in the room her younger sister called her 'Sanctum'. Her Sanctum was only too evidently an intellectualized bedroom. [*Love and Mr Lewisham*, Ch. 16]

13 The book from the Contemporary Science Series was Professor Letourneau's *Evolution of Marriage*. It was interesting certainly, but of little immediate use. [*Ib*. 20]

14 The Social Contract is nothing more nor less than a vast conspiracy of human beings to lie to and humbug themselves and one another for the general Good. Lies are the mortar that binds the savage individual man into the social masonry. [*Ib*. 23]

15 Notice the smug suppressions of his face. In his mouth are Lies in the shape of false teeth. [*Ib*.]

16 We were taught as the chief subjects of instruction Latin and Greek. We were taught very badly because the men who taught us did not habitually use either of these languages. [*The New Machiavelli*, Bk I, Ch. 3, sect. v]

17 I sometimes think that if Adam and Eve had been merely engaged, she would not have talked with the serpent; and the world had been saved an infinity of misery. [*Select Conversations with an Uncle*]

18 Now it is on the whole more convenient to keep history and theology apart. [*A Short History of the World*, Ch. 37]

19 Marx sought to replace national antagonism by class antagonisms. [*Ib*. 59]

20 'Clearly,' the Time Traveller proceeded, 'any real body must have extension in *four* directions; it must have Length, Breadth, Thickness, and Duration. [*The Time Machine*]

21 Their prose was convulsive, they foamed at the headline. . . . Before the week was out they were not so much published as carried screaming into the street. [*The War in the Air*, Ch. 1]

22 To Europe she was America, to America she was the gateway of the earth. But to tell the story of New York would be to write a social history of the world. [*Ib*. 6]

23 The third peculiarity of aerial warfare was that it was at once enormously destructive and entirely indecisive. [*Ib.* 8]

24 The coming of the aristocrat is fatal and assured. The end will be the Over-man – for all the mad protests of humanity. [*When the Sleeper Wakes*, Ch. 19]

25 The world is no place for the bad, the stupid, the enervated. Their duty – it's a fine duty too! – is to die. The death of the failure! That is the path by which the beast rose to manhood, by which man goes on to higher things. [*Ib.*]

26 So why should I not write and forget altogether that visible chill, that inky catarrh of a climate which is snivelling against the window-panes? [*The World of William Clissold*]

27 To him at least the Door in the Wall was a real door, leading through a real wall to immortal realities. [*Short Stories*, 'The Door in the Wall']

28 William was at first a rather shabby young man of the ready-made black coat school of costume. He had watery grey eyes, and a complexion appropriate to the brother of one in a Home for the Dying. [*Ib.* 'The Jilting of Jane']

29 'I'll call my article', meditated the war correspondent, '"Mankind *versus* Iron-mongery".' [*Ib.* 'The Land Ironclads']

30 He had the face of a saint, but he had rendered this generally acceptable by growing side-whiskers. [*Ib.* 'The Last Trump']

31 He was an enormous asset in the spiritual life of the metropolis – to give it no harsher name – and his fluent periods had restored faith and courage to many a poor soul hovering on the brink of the dark river of thought. [*Ib.*]

32 Cynicism is humour in ill-health. [*Ib.*]

33 He was a practical electrician but fond of whisky, a heavy red-haired brute with irregular teeth. He doubted the existence of the Deity but accepted Carnot's cycle, and he had read Shakespeare and found him weak in chemistry. [*Ib.* 'The Lord of the Dynamos']

34 At first the miracles worked by Mr Fotheringay were timid little miracles – little things with the cups and parlour fitments, as feeble as the miracles of Theosophists. [*Ib.* 'The Man who Worked Miracles']

35 Bricklayers kick their wives to death, and dukes betray theirs; but it is among the small clerks and shopkeepers nowadays that it comes most often to the cutting of throats. [*Ib.* 'The Purple Pileus']

36 Of one fact about professed atheists I am convinced; they may be – they usually are – fools, void of subtlety, revilers of holy institutions, brutal speakers, and mischievous knaves, but they lie with difficulty. [*Ib.* 'A Slip under the Microscope']

37 My dear fellow, half the great awks in the world are about as genuine as the handkerchief of Saint Veronica, as the Holy Coat of Trèves. [*Ib.* 'The Triumphs of a Taxidermist']

38 He behaved just as I should have expected a great, fat, self-indulgent man to behave under trying circumstances – that is to say, very badly. [*Ib.* 'The Truth about Pyecraft']

39 It seems to me that I am more to the left than you, Mr Stalin. [In an interview with Stalin, *New Statesman*, 27 Oct. 1934]

40 There is no reason whatever to believe that the order of nature has any greater bias in favour of man than it had in favour of the icthyosaur or the pterodactyl. [Quoted in Sagittarius and George, *The Perpetual Pessimist*]

ARNOLD WESKER

41 My name is Corporal Hill, I'm not a happy man. [*Chips with Everything*, I. i]

42 You breed babies and you eat chips with everything. [*Ib.* I. ii]

43 Every place I look at I work out the cubic feet, and I say it will make a good warehouse or it won't. Can't help myself. One of the best warehouses I ever see was the Vatican in Rome. [*Ib.* I. vi]

44 Don't you sit there and sigh gal like you was Lady Nevershit. [*Roots*, III]

45 There's nothing more pathetic than the laughter of people who have lost their pet faith. [*I'm Talking about Jerusalem*, II. i]

46 COLONEL: ... I believe each person has his place.
DAVE: You're decent like, but it's a favour like? [*Ib.* II. ii]

MAE WEST

47 'My goodness, those diamonds are lovely!'
M.W.: 'Goodness had nothing whatever to do with it.' [*Diamond Lil*]

48 Everything. [When asked what she wanted to be remembered for. Quoted in *Observer Weekend Review*, 30 Nov. 1969]

NATHANAEL WEST

49 Are-you-in-trouble? – Do-you-need-advice? – Write-to-Miss-Lonelyhearts-and-she-will-help-you. [*Miss Lonelyhearts*]

50 When they ask for bread don't give them crackers as does the Church, and don't, like the State, tell them to eat cake. Explain that man cannot live by bread alone, and give them stones. [*Ib.* 'Miss Lonelyhearts and the dead pan']

51 The Church is our only hope, the First Church of Christ Dentist, where He is worshipped as Preventer of Decay. [*Ib.* 'In the dismal swamp']

52 He could not go on finding the same joke funny thirty times a day for months on end. And on most days he received more than thirty letters, all of them alike, stamped from the dough of suffering with a heart-shaped cookie knife. [*Ib.*]

53 Prayers for the condemned man's soul will be offered on an adding machine. Numbers ... constitute the only universal language. [*Ib.*]

54 Goldsmith ... smiled, bunching his fat cheeks like twin rolls of smooth pink toilet paper. [*Ib.*]

55 Americans have dissipated their radical energy in an orgy of stone breaking. In their few years they have broken more stones than did centuries of Egyptians. And they have done their work hysterically, desperately, almost as if they knew that the stones would some day break them. [*Ib.*]

REBECCA WEST

56 Our four uncles. [Wells and Bennett, Shaw and Galsworthy. Quoted in Stephen Potter, *Sense of Humour*, Ch. 1]

GENERAL WEYGAND

57 In three weeks England will have her neck wrung like a chicken. [At the fall of France. Quoted in Winston S. Churchill, *Their Finest Hour*, Ch. 10; Churchill answered, 'Some chicken, some neck!']

EDITH WHARTON

58 Blessed are the pure in heart for they have so much more to talk about. [*John O'London's Weekly*, 10 Apr. 1932]

59 She keeps on being Queenly in her own room with the door shut. [*The House of Mirth*, Bk II, Ch. 1]

E B. WHITE

60 As in the sexual experience, there are never more than two persons present in the act of reading – the writer who is the impregnator, and the reader who is the respondent. [*The Second Tree from the Corner*]

61 The dream of the American male is for a female who has an essential languor which is not laziness, who is unaccompanied except by himself, and who does not let him down. He desires a beautiful, but comprehensible creature who does not destroy a perfect situation by forming a complete sentence. [*Ib.* 'Notes on our Time']

62 The city's effort to quell noise turned out to be loudly characteristic. To the existing din the city added a large yellow truck, filled with flashy newspaper reporters and decibel detectors, and hired two taxicabs to roar across its path, blowing their horns continuously. The heavens boomed with anti-sound. [*Ib.* 'Notes on the City']

63 To perceive Christmas through its wrapping becomes more difficult with every year. [*Ib.* 'Time Present']

64 All poets who, when reading from their own works, experience a choked feeling, are major. For that matter, all poets who read from their own works are major, whether they choke or not. [*How to Tell a Major Poet from a Minor Poet*]

65 It is easier for a man to be loyal to his club than to his planet; the by-laws are

shorter, and he is personally acquainted with the other members. [*One Man's Meat*]

66 MOTHER: It's broccoli, dear.
CHILD: I say it's spinach, and I say the hell with it. [Caption to cartoon by Carl Rose]

PATRICK WHITE

67 But bombs *are* unbelievable until they actually fall. [*Riders in the Chariot*, Pt I, Ch. 4]

68 It was perhaps doubtful if anyone would ever notice Mrs Poulter or Mrs Dun unless life took its cleaver to them. [*The Solid Mandala*, Ch. 1]

69 'I dunno,' Arthur said. 'I forget what I was taught. I only remember what I've learnt.' [*Ib.* 2]

T. H. WHITE

70 The Victorians had not been anxious to go away for the weekend. The Edwardians, on the contrary were nomadic. [*Farewell Victoria*, Ch. 4]

A. N. WHITEHEAD

71 Life is an offensive, directed against the repetitive mechanism of the Universe. [*Adventures of Ideas*, Pt I, Ch. 5]

72 Language is incomplete and fragmentary, and merely registers a stage in the average advance beyond ape-mentality. But all men enjoy flashes of insight beyond meanings already stabilized in etymology and grammar. [Ib. III. 15]

73 Philosophy is the product of wonder. [*Nature and Life*, Ch. 1]

74 A dead Nature aims at nothing. It is the essence of life that it exists for its own sake, as the intrinsic reaping of value. [*Ib.*]

75 Science can find no individual enjoyment in Nature: science can find no aim in Nature; science can find no creativity in Nature; it finds mere rules of succession. [*Ib.* 2]

76 The fact of the instability of evil is the moral order of the world. [Quoted in Victor Gollancz, *A Year of Grace*]

77 A science which hesitates to forget its founders is lost. [Attr.]

78 The history of Western philosophy is, after all, no more than a series of footnotes to Plato's philosophy. [Attr.]

KATHARINE WHITEHORN

79 Hats divide generally into three classes: offensive hats, defensive hats, and shrapnel. [*Shouts and Murmurs*, a selection from the *Observer* 1962–3, 'Hats']

80 It is a pity, as my husband says, that more politicians are not bastards by birth instead of vocation. [*Observer*, 12 Jan. 1964]

81 Have you ever taken anything out of the clothes basket because it had become, relatively, the cleaner thing? ['On Shirts', *Observer*, 1964]

82 In real life, women are always trying to mix something up with sex – religion or babies or hard cash; it is only men who long for sex separated out, without rings or strings. ['Man's Ideal Woman', *Observer*, 20 Dec. 1964]

83 We were discussing the possibility of making one of our cats Pope, recently, and we decided that the fact that she was not Italian, and was female, made the third point that she was a cat, quite irrelevant. ['Luciad', *Leicester University Magazine*, Jan. 1965]

84 In heaven they may bore you. In hell you will bore them. [Quoted in the *Observer*, 13 June 1965]

RICHARD WHITNEY

85 I claim that this country [the U.S.A.] has been built by speculation, and further progress must be made in that line. [Quoted in A. M. Schlesinger Jr, *The Coming of the New Deal*, Pt VII, Ch. 29, sect. iv]

WILLIAM H. WHYTE

86 This book is about the organization man. . . . I can think of no other way to describe the people I am talking about. They are not the workers, nor are they the white-collar people in the usual, clerk sense of the word. These people only work for the Organization. The ones I am talking about *belong* to it as well. [*The Organization Man*, Ch. 1]

GEORGE WIGG

87 For Hon. Members opposite the deterrent is a phallic symbol. It convinces them that they are men. [*Observer*, 'Sayings of the Week', 8 Mar. 1964]

THORNTON WILDER

88 For what human ill does not dawn seem to be an alleviation? [*The Bridge of San Luis Rey*, Ch. 3]

89 Music came into the world to give pleasure – Softer! Softer! Get it out of your heads that music's only good when it's loud. You leave loudness to the Methodists. [*Our Town*, I]

90 Most everybody in the world climbs into their graves married. [*Ib.* II]

1 My advice to you is not to inquire why or whither, but just enjoy your ice-cream while it's on your plate, – that's my philosophy. [*The Skin of our Teeth*, I]

2 It's girls like I who inspire the multiplication table! [*Ib.*]

3 That great fraternal order – the Ancient and Honourable Order of Mammals, Subdivision Humans. [*Ib.* II]

4 We'll trot down to the movies and see how girls with wax faces live. [*Ib.* III]

5 When you're at war you think about a better life; when you're at peace you think about a more comfortable one. [*Ib.*]

6 A living is made, Mr Kemper, by selling something that everybody needs at least once a year. Yes, sir! And a million is made by producing something that everybody needs every day. You artists produce something that nobody needs at any time. [*The Matchmaker*, I]

7 Ninety-nine per cent of the people in the world are fools and the rest of us are in great danger of contagion. [*Ib.*]

8 Marriage is a bribe to make a housekeeper think she's a householder. [*Ib.*]

9 The future is the most expensive luxury in the world. [*Ib.*]

10 Money should circulate like rainwater. [*Ib.*]

11 The best undertaker in Brooklyn, respected, esteemed. He knew all the best people – knew them well, even before they died. [*Ib.*]

12 Chief clerk! Promoted from chief clerk to chief clerk. [*Ib.*]

13 The best of all would be a person who has all the good things a poor person has, and all the good meals a rich person has, but that's never been known. [*Ib.*]

14 The best part of married life is the fights. The rest is merely so-so. [*Ib.* II]

15 Just keep telling yourself how pretty she is. Pretty girls have very little opportunity to improve their other advantages. [*Ib.* III]

16 AMBROSE: That old man with one foot in the grave!
MRS LEVI: And the other three in the cash box. [*Ib.*]

17 There's nothing like eavesdropping to show you that the world outside your head is different from the world inside your head. [*Ib.*]

18 That's not a friend, that's an employer I'm trying out for a few days. [*Ib.*]

19 Never support two weaknesses at the same time. It's your combination sinners – your lecherous liars and your miserly drunkards – who dishonor the vices and bring them into bad repute. [*Ib.*]

20 But there comes a moment in everybody's life when he must decide whether he'll live among human beings or not – a fool among fools or a fool alone. [*Ib.* IV]

21 Life is an unbroken succession of false situations. [*Observer*, 'Sayings of the Week', 28 Apr. 1957]

KAISER WILHELM II

22 I would have liked to go to Ireland, but my grandmother [Queen Victoria] would not let me. Perhaps she thought I wanted to take the little place. [Quoted in H. Montgomery Hyde, *Carson*, Ch. 9, sect. vi]

23 You will be home before the leaves have fallen from the trees. [To troops leaving for front, Aug. 1914. Quoted in B. Tuchman, *The Guns of August*, Ch. 9]

24 A contemptible little army. [Description of British Expeditionary Force, 1914. Attr.]

ELLEN WILKINSON

25 I should like to help Britain to become a Third Programme country. [*Observer*, 'Sayings of the Week', 2 Feb. 1947]

GEOFFREY WILLANS and RONALD SEARLE

26 Pater . . . can relax at week-ends and if it is a good skool Eustace will soon be strong and bonny ennuff to bring in the coal. [*How to be Topp*, Ch. 2]

27 Lately things are a bit different. The oiks have become v. well dressed certainly beter than pauncefootes pater and their skools are quite remarkable with all those windows to let the sunshine in. [*Ib.*]

28 Actually it is quite easy to be topp in lat. you just have to work chizz chizz chizz. [*Ib.*3]

29 Cads have always a grandmother who is the DUCHESS of BLANK hem hem. They are inclined to cheat at conkers having baked them for 300 years in the ancestral ovens. [*Ib.* 4]

30 fr. masters kno how to cope they unroll a huge pikture of a farmyard and point out a turkey. [*Ib.* 7]

31 Still xmas is a good time with all those presents and good food and i hope it will never die out or at any rate not until i am grown up and hav to pay for it all. [*Ib.* 11]

DR ERIC WILLIAMS

32 A small country like ours [Trinidad and Tobago] only has principles. [The *Observer*, 'Sayings of the Week', 27 June 1965]

RAYMOND WILLIAMS

33 A very large part of English middle-class education is devoted to the training of servants. . . . In so far as it is, by definition, the training of upper servants, it includes, of course, the instilling of that kind of confidence which will enable the upper servants to supervise and direct the lower servants. [*Culture and Society*, Ch. 3, Conclusion]

34 The human crisis is always a crisis of understanding: what we genuinely understand we can do. [*Ib.*]

TENNESSEE WILLIAMS

35 Why d'ya call Gooper's kiddies no-neck monsters? [*Cat on a Hot Tin Roof*, I]

36 It is a terrible thing for an old woman to outlive her dogs. [*Camino Real*, Prologue]

37 The most dangerous word in any human tongue is the word for brother. It's inflammatory. [*Ib.* Block 2]

38 My suit is pale yellow. My nationality is French, and my normality has been often subject to question. [*Ib.* Block 4]

39 Caged birds accept each other but flight is what they long for. [*Ib.* Block 7]

40 *Make voyages! – Attempt them!* there's nothing else. [*Ib.* Block 8]

41 But tenderness, the violets in the mountains – can't break the rocks! [*Ib.* Block 10]

42 Excuse the way I'm – not dressed . . . [*The Rose Tattoo*, II. i]

43 I can't stand a naked light bulb, any more than I can a rude remark or a vulgar action. [*A Streetcar Named Desire*, iii]

44 Poker shouldn't be played in a house with women. [*Ib.*]

45 If people behaved in the way nations do they would all be put in straitjackets. [In a B.B.C. interview]

WILLIAM CARLOS WILLIAMS

46 Obviously, in a plutocracy / the natural hero / is the man who robs a bank. [*Childe Harold to the Round Tower Came*]

47 Liquor and love / rescue the cloudy sense / banish its despair / give it a home. [*The World Narrowed to a Point*]

48 Minds like beds always made up, / (more stony than a shore) / unwilling or unable. [*Paterson*, I, Preface]

49 Divorce is / the sign of knowledge in our time. [*Ib.*]

50 so much depends / upon / a red wheel / barrow / glazed with rain / water / beside the white / chickens. [*Spring and Fall*, 21, 'The Red Wheelbarrow']

WENDELL WILLKIE

51 The constitution does not provide for first and second class citizens. [*An American Programme*, Ch. 2]

52 There exists in the world today a gigantic reservoir of good will toward us, the American people. [*One World*, Ch. 10]

53 Freedom is an indivisible word. If we want to enjoy it, and fight for it, we must be prepared to extend it to everyone, whether they are rich or poor, whether they agree with us or not, no matter what their race or the colour of their skin. [*Ib.* 13]

ANGUS WILSON

54 She was more than ever proud of the position of the bungalow, so almost in the country. [*A Bit Off the Map*, 'A Flat Country Christmas']

55 He would give them his every imitation from 'Eton and Oxford' to the flushing of the lavatory cistern, and so, perhaps, carry the evening through. [*Ib.*]

56 'God knows how you Protestants can be expected to have any sense of direction,' she said. 'It's different with us. I haven't been to mass for years, I've got every mortal sin on my conscience, but I know when I'm doing wrong. I'm still a Catholic.' [*The Wrong Set*, 'Significant Experience']

CHARLES E. WILSON

57 What is good for the country is good for General Motors, and what's good for General Motors is good for the country. [To a Congressional Committee, 1952]

HAROLD WILSON

58 There is something utterly nauseating about a system of society which pays a harlot 25 times as much as it pays its Prime Minister, 250 times as much as it pays its Members of Parliament, and 500 times as much as it pays some of its ministers of religion. [On the case of Christine Keeler. Speech in House of Commons, 1963]

59 Everybody should have an equal chance – but they shouldn't have a flying start. [*Observer*, 'Sayings of the Year', 1963]

JOSEPH RUGGLES WILSON

60 When you frame a sentence don't do it as if you were loading a shotgun but as if you were loading a rifle. Don't fire in such a way and with such a load that you will hit a lot of things in the neighbourhood besides, but shoot with a single bullet and hit that one thing alone. [Quoted in John Dos Passos, *Mr Wilson's War*, Ch. 1, sect. ii]

SANDY WILSON

61 She says it's nicer, much nicer in Nice. [*The Boy Friend*, II]

62 DULCIE: The modern buildings that you see / Are often most alarming.
LORD B.: But I am sure that you'll agree
DULCIE: A ruin
LORD B.: Can be charming. [*Ib.* III]

63 It's never too late to have a fling / For autumn is just as nice as spring, / And it's never too late to fall in love. [*Ib.*]

PRESIDENT WOODROW WILSON

64 I would never read a book if it were possible to talk half an hour with the man who wrote it. [Advice to his students at Princeton, 1900]

65 Business underlies everything in our national life, including our spiritual life. Witness the fact that in the Lord's Prayer the first petition is for daily bread. No one can worship God or love his neighbour on an empty stomach. [Speech, New York, 1912]

66 It [D. W. Griffiths's film *Birth of a Nation*] is like writing history with lightning. [Quoted in Daniel J. Boorstin, *The Image*, Ch. 4]

67 Right is more precious than peace. [Quoted in *Radio Times*, 10 Sept. 1964]

68 Never murder a man who is committing suicide. [Of Governor Hughes's election campaign. Quoted in John Dos Passos, *Mr Wilson's War*, Pt. 2, Ch. 10, sect. x]

69 Once lead this people into war and they'll forget there ever was such a thing as tolerance. [Quoted in *ib.* 3.2 xii]

70 America . . . is the prize amateur nation of the world. Germany is the prize professional nation. [Speech to officers of the fleet, Aug. 1917. Quoted in *ib.* Pt III, Ch. 13]

71 People will endure their tyrants for years, but they tear their deliverers to pieces if a millennium is not created immediately. [Said to George Creel. Quoted in *ib.*, heading to Pt V, Ch. 22]

72 Tell me what's right and I'll fight for it. [To his experts at the Peace Conference. Quoted in *ib.*]

73 The war we have just been through, though it was shot through with terror, is not to be compared with the war we would have to face next time. [Quoted in *ib.*]

A. WIMPERIS

74 O Hades! The ladies who leave their wooden huts / For Gilbert, the Filbert, the Col'nel of the Knuts. [Song: *Gilbert the Filbert*]

75 On Sunday I walk out with a soldier, / On Monday I'm taken by a tar, / On Tuesday I'm out with a baby Boy Scout, / On Wednesday an Hussar. [Song: *On Sunday*]

76 And on Saturday I'm willing, / If you'll only take the shilling, / To make a man of every one of you. [*Ib.*]

77 My dear fellow a unique evening! I wouldn't have left a turn unstoned. [On a vaudeville show. Quoted in E. Short, *Fifty Years of Vaudeville*]

MARTY WINCH

78 It's better to be wanted for murder than not to be wanted at all. [*Psychology in the Wry*]

GODFREY WINN

79 Praise be to God and to Mr Chamberlain. I find no sacrilege, no bathos, in coupling these two names. [*Daily Express*, Sept. 1938]

80 If you find that your own dog doesn't take to your boy and greet him with affection, you can make up your mind on the spot that there's a yellow streak in that young man's make-up somewhere. [*Woman's Own*, 1937]

LORD WINTERTON

81 The risk of anyone being lynched at Lord's is a very small one. [1950. *Observer*, 'Sayings of Our Times', 31 May 1953]

LUDWIG WITTGENSTEIN

82 All philosophy is 'Critique of language' . . . [*Tractatus Logico-Philosophicus* 4.0031]

83 Philosophy is not a theory but an activity. [*Ib.* 4.112]

84 Everything that can be said can be said clearly. [*Ib.* 4.116]

85 Whereof one cannot speak, thereof one must be silent. [*Ib.* 7]

WOBURN HOUSE (Seat of committees for relief of German refugees, 1933 onwards)

86 The Bei unsers. [German refugees who complained that in England there was no central heating, etc. From the phrase: '*Bei uns in Berlin* . . .']

87 Sein Emigranz. [Title for self-important German refugee]

P. G. WODEHOUSE

88 Chumps always make the best husbands. When you marry, Sally, grab a chump. Tap his forehead first, and if it rings solid, don't hesitate, All the unhappy marriages come from the husbands having brains. What good are brains to a man? They only unsettle him. [*The Adventures of Sally*]

89 'What ho!' I said. 'What ho!' said Motty. 'What ho! What ho!' 'What ho! What ho! What ho!' After that it seemed rather difficult to go on with the conversation. [*Carry On Jeeves*, 'Jeeves and the Unbidden Guest']

90 Aunt Agatha, who eats broken bottles and wears barbed wire next to the skin. [*The Code of the Woosters*, Ch. 1]

1 It is no use telling me that there are bad aunts and good aunts. At the core they are all alike. Sooner or later, out pops the cloven hoof. [*Ib.* 2]

2 Big chap with a small moustache and the sort of eye that can open an oyster at sixty paces. [*Ib.*]

3 'Oh Bertie,' she said in a low voice like beer trickling out of a jug, 'you ought not to be here!' [*Ib.* 3]

4 He paused, and swallowed convulsively, like a Pekingese taking a pill. [*Ib.*]

5 It was the look which caused her to be known in native bearer and halfcaste circles as 'Mgobi-'Mgumbi, which may be loosely translated as She On Whom It Is Unsafe To Try Any Oompus-Boompus. [*Money in the Bank*, Ch. 2]

6 'That,' I replied cordially, 'is what it doesn't do nothing else but.' [*Ukridge*, Ch. 6]

7 'Alf Todd,' said Ukridge, soaring to an impressive burst of imagery, 'has about as much chance as a one-armed blind man in a dark room trying to shove a pound of melted butter into a wild cat's left ear with a red-hot needle.' [*Ib.*]

8 I can honestly say that I always look on Pauline as one of the nicest girls I was ever engaged to. [*Thank You Jeeves*, Ch. 6]

9 One of the foulest cross-country runs that ever occurred outside Dante's *Inferno*. [*Mike*]

10 The stationmaster's whiskers are of a Victorian bushiness and give the impression of having been grown under glass. [Quoted in Usborne, *Wodehouse at Work*, Ch. 2]

11 Like so many substantial Americans, he had married young and kept on marrying, springing from blonde to blonde like the chamois of the Alps leaping from crag to crag. [Quoted in *ib.*]

12 He felt like a man who, chasing rainbows, has had one of them suddenly turn and bite him in the leg. [*Ib.* 4]

13 He was either a man of about a hundred and fifty who was rather young for his years or a man of about a hundred and ten who had been aged by trouble. [*Ib.* 6]

14 It is never difficult to distinguish between a Scotsman with a grievance and a ray of sunshine. [*Ib.* 8]

15 He groaned slightly and winced, like Prometheus watching his vulture dropping in for lunch. [*Ib.* 10]

16 She went out, breathing flame quietly through her nostrils. [*Ib.* Appendix 1]

17 Unlike the male codfish which, suddenly finding itself the parent of three-and-a-half million little codfish, cheerfully resolves to love them all, the British aristocracy is apt to look with a somewhat jaundiced eye on its younger sons. [Quoted in the *Listener*, 30 May 1963]

18 I turned to Aunt Agatha, whose demeanour was now rather like that of one who, picking daisies on the railway, has just caught the down express in the small of the back. [*The Inimitable Jeeves*, Ch. 4]

19 She had a penetrating sort of laugh. Rather like a train going into a tunnel. [*Ib.* 6]

20 Sir Roderick Glossop . . . is always called a nerve specialist, because it sounds better, but everybody knows that he's really a sort of janitor to the looney-bin. [*Ib.* 7]

21 He had a pair of shaggy eyebrows which gave his eyes a piercing look which was not at all the sort of thing a fellow wanted to encounter on an empty stomach. [*Ib.* 8]

22 I trickled out to the Lambs Club, where I had an appointment to feed the Wooster face with a cove of the name of Caffyn. [*Ib.* 9]

23 It was one of those cold, clammy, accusing sort of eyes – the kind that makes you reach up to see if your tie is straight: and he looked at me as I were some sort of unnecessary product which Cuthbert the Cat had brought in after a ramble among the local ash-cans. [*Ib.* 10]

24 Did you notice a fellow standing on my left in our little troupe yesterday? Small, shrivelled chap. Looks like a haddock with lung-trouble. [*Ib.* 11]

25 Jeeves coughed one soft, low, gentle cough like a sheep with a blade of grass stuck in its throat. [*Ib.* 13]

26 I found the proceedings about as scaly as I had expected. It was a warm day, and the hall grounds were a dense, almost liquid mass of peasantry. Kids seethed to and fro. [*Ib.* 14]

27 Mr Steggles offered to back his nominee in a weight-for-age eating contest against Master Burgess for a pound a side. [*Ib.* 15]

28 Even the Tough Eggs liked it. [*Ib.* 15]

29 I'm not lugged into Family Rows. On the occasions when Aunt is calling to Aunt like mastodons bellowing across primeval swamps and Uncle James's letter about Cousin Mabel's peculiar behaviour is being shot round the family circle ('Please read this carefully and send it on to Jane'), the clan has a tendency to ignore me. [*Ib.* 16]

30 It must have been about one in the afternoon when I woke. I was feeling more or less something the Pure Food Committee had rejected. [*Ib.*]

31 There's no doubt that Jeeves's pick-me-up will produce immediate results in anything short of an Egyptian mummy. [*Ib.*]

32 It was my Uncle George who discovered that alcohol was a food well in advance of modern medical thought. [*Ib.*]

33 She gave a sort of despairing gesture, like a vicar's daughter who has discovered Erastianism in the village. [*Laughing Gas*, Ch. 9]

34 It is a good rule in life never to apologize. The right sort of people do not want apologies, and the wrong sort take a mean advantage of them. [*The Man Upstairs*, title story]

35 Women with hair and chins like Mary's may be angels most of the time, but when they take off their wings for a bit, they aren't half-hearted about it. [*My Man Jeeves*, 'Absent Treatment']

36 I felt rather like Lot's friends must have done when they dropped in for a quiet chat and their genial host began to criticize the Cities of the Plain. [*Ib.* 'The Aunt and the Sluggard']

37 New York's a small place when it comes to the part of it that wakes up just as the rest is going to bed. [*Ib.*]

38 His ideas of first-aid stopped short at squirting soda-water. [*Ib.* 'Doing Clarence a Bit of Good']

39 I don't owe a penny to a single soul – not counting tradesmen, of course. [*Ib.* 'Jeeves and the Hard-Boiled Egg']

40 Dear old Bicky ... was in many ways one of the most pronounced fatheads that ever pulled on a suit of gent's underwear. [*Ib.*]

41 In this matter of shimmering into rooms the chappie [Jeeves] is rummy to a degree. [*Ib.*]

42 He moves from point to point with as little uproar as a jellyfish. [*Ib.*]

43 A very decent chappie, but rather inclined to collar the conversation and turn it in the direction of his home-town's new water-supply system. [*Ib.*]

44 She fitted into my biggest armchair as if it had been built round her by someone who knew they were wearing armchairs tight about the hips that season. [*Ib.* 'Jeeves and the Unbidden Guest']

45 His eyes bulged, too, but they weren't bright. They were a dull grey with pink rims. His chin gave up the struggle about half-way down, and he didn't appear to have any eyelashes. [*Ib.*]

46 I gave Motty the swift east-to-west. [*Ib.*]

47 What with excellent browsing and sluicing and cheery conversation and what-not, the afternoon passed quite happily. [*Ib.*]

48 I've got about a month of New York, and I mean to store up a few happy memories for the long winter evenings. This is my only chance to collect a past, and I'm going to do it. [*Ib.*]

49 And what with brooding on this prospect, and sitting up in the old flat waiting for the familiar footstep, and putting it to bed when it got there, and stealing into the sick-chamber next morning to contemplate the wreckage, I was beginning to lose weight. [*Ib.*]

50 Another slightly *frappé* silence. [*Ib.*]

51 As a rule, from what I've observed, the American captain of industry doesn't do anything out of business hours. When he has put the cat out and locked up the office for the night, he just relapses into a state of coma from which he emerges only to start being a captain of industry again. [*Ib.* 'Leave it to Jeeves']

52 I was so darned sorry for poor old Corky that I hadn't the heart to touch my breakfast. I told Jeeves to drink it himself. [*Ib.*]

53 She was rather like one of those innocent-tasting American drinks which creep imperceptibly into your system so that,

before you know what you're doing, you're starting out to reform the world by force if necessary, and pausing on your way to tell the large man in the corner that, if he looks at you like that, you will knock his head off. [*Ib.*]

54 I spent the afternoon musing on Life. If you come to think of it, what a queer thing Life is! So unlike anything else, don't you know, if you see what I mean. [*Ib.* 'Rallying Round Old George']

55 My record speaks for itself. Three times pinched, but never once sentenced under the correct label. [*Right Ho, Jeeves*, Ch. 15]

56 'I may as well inform you that it is not twenty-four hours since she turned me down.' 'Turned you down?' 'Like a bedspread. In this very garden.' [*Ib.*]

57 'How much gin did you put in the jug?' 'A liberal tumblerful, sir.' 'Would that be a normal dose for an adult defeatist, do you think?' [*Ib.* 16]

58 Bingo uttered a stricken woofle like a bull-dog that has been refused cake. [*Very Good, Jeeves!*, 'Jeeves and the Impending Doom']

59 The Right Hon. was a tubby little chap who looked as if he had been poured into his clothes and had forgotten to say 'When!' [*Ib.*]

60 Aunt Agatha, ... better known as the Pest of Pont Street, the human snapping-turtle. [*Ib.* 'Jeeves and the Kid Clementina']

61 I once got engaged to his daughter, Honoria, a ghastly dynamic exhibit who read Nietzsche and had a laugh like waves breaking on a stern and rock-bound coast. [*Ib.* 'Jeeves and the Yule-Tide Spirit']

62 She was as sore as a sunburnt neck because she had had her trip for nothing. [*Ib.* 'The Ordeal of Young Tuppy']

63 If I had had to choose between him and a cockroach as a companion for a walking-tour, the cockroach would have had it by a short head. [*Ib.* 'The Spot of Art']

64 And closing the door with the delicate caution of one brushing flies off a sleeping Venus, he passed out of my life. [*Ib.* 'Jeeves and the Old School Chum']

65 In my Rogues Gallery of repulsive small boys I suppose he would come about third. [*Thank You, Jeeves*, Ch. 3]

66 I did not quite slap him on the back, but I made a sort of back-slapping gesture. [*Ib.* 10]

HUMBERT WOLFE

67 You cannot hope / To bribe or twist / Thank God! The British journalist / But seeing what / That man will do / Unbribed, there's no occasion to. [Contribution to *Punch*]

THOMAS WOLFE

68 Most of the time we think we're sick, it's all in the mind. [*Look Homeward, Angel*, Pt I, Ch. 1]

69 Making the world safe for hypocrisy. [*Ib.* III. 36]

SIR DONALD WOLFIT

70 You are going to let me do what you want done in the way that I want to do it. [To BBC producer. Attr.]

LEONARD WOOLF

71 The grinding of the intellect is for most people as painful as a dentist's drill. [*Observer*, 'Sayings of the Week', 28 June 1959]

VIRGINIA WOOLF

72 Somewhere, everywhere, now hidden, now apparent in whatever is written down, is the form of a human being. If we seek to know him, are we idly occupied? [*The Captain's Death Bed*, 'Reading']

73 The poet gives us his essence, but prose takes the mould of the body and mind entire. [*Ib.*]

74 *Middlemarch*, the magnificent book which with all its imperfections is one of the few English novels for grown up people. [*The Common Reader*, 1st Series, 'George Eliot']

75 She [Charlotte Brontë] does not attempt to solve the problems of human life; she is even unaware that such problems exist; all her force, and it is the more tremendous for being constricted, goes into the assertion, 'I love', 'I hate', 'I suffer'. [*Ib.* 'Jane Eyre']

76 A good essay must have this permanent quality about it; it must draw its curtain round us, but it must be a curtain that shuts us in not out. [*Ib.* 'The Modern Essay']

77 Trivial personalities decomposing in the eternity of print. [*Ib.*]

78 Life is not a series of gig lamps symmetrically arranged; life is a luminous halo, a semi-transparent envelope surrounding us from the beginning of consciousness to the end. [*Ib.* 'Modern Fiction']

79 The interest in life does not lie in what people do, nor even in their relations to each other, but largely in the power to communicate with a third party, antagonistic, enigmatic, yet perhaps persuadable, which one may call life in general. [*The Common Reader*, 'On Not Knowing Greek']

80 A man or woman of thoroughbred intelligence galloping across open country in pursuit of an idea. [Definition of a highbrow. Quoted in Kenneth Tynan, *Curtains*]

81 At Mudie's corner in Oxford Street all the red and blue beads had run together on the string. The motor omnibuses were locked. [*Jacob's Room*, Ch. 5]

82 Each had his past shut in him like the leaves of a book known to him by heart; and his friends could only read the title. [*Ib.*]

83 She first washed her head; then ate chocolate creams; then opened Shelley. [*Ib.*]

84 It's not catastrophes, murders, deaths, diseases, that age and kill us; it's the way people look and laugh, and run up the steps of omnibuses. [*Ib.* 6]

85 The lamps of London uphold the dark as upon the points of burning bayonets. [*Ib.* 8]

86 Fraser ... left his children unbaptized – his wife did it secretly in the washing basin. [*Ib.* 9]

87 There is in the British Museum an enormous mind. Consider that Plato is there cheek by jowl with Aristotle; and Shakespeare with Marlowe. This great mind is hoarded beyond the power of any single mind to possess it. [*Ib.*]

88 'The guns?' said Betty Flanders, half asleep. . . . Again, far away, she heard the dull sound, as if nocturnal women were beating great carpets. [*Ib.* 13]

89 Life itself, every moment of it, every drop of it, here, this instant, now, in the sun, in Regent's Park, was enough. Too much, indeed. [*Mrs Dalloway*]

90 Women have served all these centuries as looking-glasses possessing the magic and delicious power of reflecting the figure of man at twice its natural size. [*A Room of One's Own*]

1 So that is marriage, Lily thought, a man and a woman looking at a girl throwing a ball. [*To the Lighthouse*, Ch. 13]

2 I have lost friends, some by death ... others through sheer inability to cross the street. [*The Waves*]

3 Let a man get up and say, 'Behold, this is the truth,' and instantly I perceive a sandy cat filching a piece of fish in the background. Look, you have forgotten the cat, I say. [*Ib.*]

4 On the outskirts of every agony sits some observant fellow who points. [*Ib.*]

ALEXANDER WOOLLCOTT

5 The chair ... was upholstered in one of those flagrant chintzes, designed, apparently, by the art editor of a seed catalogue. [*While Rome Burns*, 'The Editor's Easy Chair']

6 Subjunctive to the last, he preferred to ask, 'And that, sir, would be the Hippodrome?' [*Ib.* 'Our Mrs Parker']

7 The most beautiful thing ever fashioned by the hand of man on this continent marks the nameless grave of a woman who is not mentioned in her husband's autobiography. [*Ib.* 'The Wife of Henry Adams']

8 I am in no need of your God damned sympathy. I ask only to be entertained by some of your grosser reminiscences. [*Letter to a Friend*, 1942]

9 Ross, a man who knew nothing ... and had contempt for anything he didn't understand, which was practically everything. [Quoted in James Thurber, *The Years with Ross*]

10 You are the only artist that should be permitted to draw hooded figures. [To James Thurber. Quoted in *ib.*]

MRS WRIGHT

11 Eh! but it would make a grand Co-op! [Of All Souls College, Oxford. Quoted in E. M. Wright's biography of Prof. J. Wright]

FRANK LLOYD WRIGHT

12 The physician can bury his mistakes, but the architect can only advise his client to plant vines. [*New York Times Magazine*, 4 Oct. 1953]

ESME WYNNE-TYSON

13 Scheherazade is the classical example of a woman saving her head by using it. [Attr.]

JON WYNNE-TYSON

14 The wrong sort of people are always in power because they would not be in power if they were not the wrong sort of people. [Book review in *Times Literary Supplement*]

Y

JUDGE LÉON R. YANKWICH

1 There are no illegitimate children – only illegitimate parents. [Decision in State District Court for the Southern District of California, June 1928]

W. B. YEATS

2 Nothing can stay my glance / Until that glance run in the world's despite / To where the damned have howled away their hearts, / And where the blessed dance. [*All Souls' Night*]

3 Bring the balloon of the mind / That bellies and drags in the wind / Into its narrow shed. [*The Balloon of the Mind*]

4 That dolphin-torn, that gong-tormented sea. [*Byzantium*]

5 Suddenly I saw the cold and rook-delighting heaven / That seemed as though ice burned and was but the more ice. [*The Cold Heaven*]

6 I would be ignorant as the dawn / That has looked down / On that old queen measuring a town / With the pin of a brooch. [*The Dawn*]

7 Yet always when I look death in the face, / When I clamber to the heights of sleep, / Or when I grow excited with wine, / Suddenly I meet your face. [*A Deep-Sworn Vow*]

8 The fascination of what's difficult / Has dried the sap out of my veins, and rent / Spontaneous joy and natural content / Out of my heart. [*The Fascination of What's Difficult*]

9 I swear before the dawn comes round again / I'll find the stable and pull out the bolt. [*Ib.*]

10 What tumbling cloud did you cleave, / Yellow-eyed hawk of the mind, / Last evening? that I, who had sat / Dumb-founded before a knave, / Should give to my friend / A pretence of wit. [*The Hawk*]

11 Processions that lack stilts have nothing that catches the eye. [*High Talk*]

12 I have drunk ale from the Country of the Young / And weep because I know all things now. [*He Thinks of his Past Greatness*]

13 I shudder and I sigh to think / That even Cicero / And many minded Homer were / Mad as the mist and snow. [*Mad as the Mist and Snow*]

14 We had fed our hearts on fantasies, / The heart's grown brutal from the fare. [*Meditations in Time of Civil War*. VI]

15 An intellectual hatred is the worst. [*A Prayer for My Daughter*]

16 Soul clap its hands and louder sing / For every tatter in its mortal dress. [*Sailing to Byzantium*]

17 A Roman Caesar is held down / Under this hump. [*The Saint and the Hunchback*]

18 We have gone round and round / In the narrow theme of love / Like an old horse in a pound. [*Solomon to Sheba*]

19 He that crowed out eternity / Thought to have crowed it in again. [*Solomon and the Witch*]

20 It seems that I must bid the Muse go pack, / Choose Plato and Plotinus for a friend / Until imagination, ear and eye, / Can be content with argument and deal / In abstract things; or be derided by / A sort of battered kettle at the heel. [*The Tower*, I]

21 Unwearied still, lover by lover, / They paddle in the cold / Companionable streams or climb the air ... [*The Wild Swans at Coole*]

22 It is so many years before one can believe enough in what one feels even to know what the feeling is. [*Autobiographies*]

23 O'CONNOR: How are you?
W.B.Y.: Not very well, I can only write prose today. [Attr.]

250

24 The young men are mad jealous of their leaders for being shot. [Said by old Irish cabinet-maker after Easter Week rising. Reported in letter to Lord Haldane, see D. Sommer, *Haldane of Cloan*, Ch. 23]

25 He [Wilfred Owen] is all blood, dirt and sucked sugar stick. [*Letters on Poetry to Dorothy Wellesley*, Letter, 21 Dec. 1936]

26 People are responsible for their *opinions*, but Providence is responsible for their morals. [Quoted in Christopher Hassall, *Edward Marsh*, Ch. 6]

27 Too true, too sincere. The Muse prefers the liars, the gay and warty lads. [Of James Reeves' *The Natural Need*, quoted in Robert Graves and Alan Hodge, *The Long Weekend*]

JACK YELLEN

28 Happy Days Are Here Again. [Title of song]

YEVGENY YEVTUSHENKO

29 It's interesting to live when you are angry. [*Observer*, 'Sayings of the Week', 22 July 1962]

ANDREW YOUNG

30 For still I looked on that same star, / That fitful, fiery Lucifer, / Watching with mind as quiet as moss / Its light nailed to a burning cross. [*The Evening Star*]

31 It was the time of year / Pale lambs leap with thick leggings on / Over small hills that are not there, / That I climbed Eggardon. [*A Prehistoric Camp*]

32 Stars lay like yellow pollen / That from a flower has fallen; / And single stars I saw / Crossing themselves in awe; / Some stars in sudden fear / Fell like a falling tear. [*The Stars*]

33 The Swallows twisting here and there / Round unseen corners of the air / Upstream and down so quickly passed / I wondered that their shadows flew as fast. [*The Swallows*]

MICHAEL YOUNG

34 The Rise of the Meritocracy. [Title of book]

Z

ISRAEL ZANGWILL

1 With the audacity of true culinary genius, Jewish fried fish is always served cold. [*Children of the Ghetto*, Ch. 1, sect. iv]

2 No Jew was ever fool enough to turn Christian unless he was a clever man. [*Ib.* I. vii]

3 She was a pale, bent woman, with spectacles, who believed in the mission of Israel, and wrote domestic novels to prove that she had no sense of humour. [*Ib.* 2. i]

4 There she lies, the great Melting Pot – listen! Can't you hear the roaring and the bubbling? . . . Here shall they all unite to build the Republic of Man and the Kingdom of God. [*The Melting Pot*, Ch. 4]

5 The world bloodily minded, / The church dead or polluted, / The blind leading the blinded, / And the deaf dragging the muted. [1916]

6 Fortunately . . . religion depends as little upon theology as love upon phrenology. [*Speeches, Articles and Letters*, 'On Doctor Schaechter']

7 The law of dislike for the unlike will always prevail. And whereas the unlike is normally situated at a safe distance, the Jews bring the unlike into the heart of *every milieu*, and must there defend a frontier line as large as the world. [*Ib.* 'The Jewish Race']

LUIS DE ZULUETA

8 The Church complains of persecution when it is not allowed to persecute. [Speech in the Cortes, 1936]

INDEX

Air – *contd*
an a. that kills 100:15
room full of good a. 133:33
far away from the cold night a. 135:81
fresh a. . . . kept in its proper place 143:4
a. travel . . . as a retirement-accelerator 175:51
fancy and the empty a. 188:23
infect the a. with banal dreams 191:82
the vivid a. signed with their honour 216:24
or climb the a. 250:21
round unseen corners of the a. 251:33
Aircraft: loud fluttering a. 81:55
Airfield: the silver pall over the a. 81:56
Airships: looks down on a. 96:12
Aitches: nothing to lose but our a. 171:48
Ajar: left her all a. 196:18
Alamein: before A. we never had a victory
46:61
Alarm: when the event outran the a. 88:47
Alcohol: to deprive himself of a. 47:72
dirty sheets and stale a. 143:15
discovered that a. was a food 246:32
whether the narcotic be a. 118:54
Ale: a. money, said Burbage 27:42
he drank a pint of English a. 39:70
merrily taking twopenny a. 39:71
plucked from a can of a. 148:12
I have drunk a. 250:12
Alexander: known as A. the Great 56:15
Alfred: in the court of King A. the Great
139:87
Algebra: what is a. exactly? 12:61
Alice: but A. showed her pup 70:79
Alien: he is called an a. 162:50
Alienation: a. awaits us 128:5
Alienists: by the a. or the florists 96:23
Alike: the assumption that everyone is a.
123:88
and . . . Catholic . . . very much a. 171:43
Alive: to be a. in such weather 14:9
too many characters a. at the end. 27:45
Dickens' world . . . is a. 38:36
I know she's a. 72:10
it was better to be a. 76:25
if Roosevelt were a. 86:8
a wonder I'm still a. 86:21
still a. at twenty-two? 125:85
a. . . . for this reason I am a novelist 131:90
remind me I'm a. 150:58
never even knew that he was a. 174:38
All: a. things given full play 131:1
he was an a.-the-lights-on man 189:58
Alliance: who forced the Muse to this a. 34:20
Allies: not to hire a. 121:54
Alligator: with the naturalness of . . . the a.
161:27
Allowance: a. which the gay make 202:26
Almonds: don't eat too many a. 49:28
Alone: a. with my own convictions 80:33
I want to be a. 83:25
we are not a. 48:89
a. in railway carriages 157:45
I must enter, and leave a. 224:57
Aloofness: weary a. of Australia 130:49
Alp: an a. of unforgiveness 179:35

Alphabet: twenty-two letters of the a. 171:63
Altar: a. wine contains Glauber's salts 16:71
they stood before the a. 22:17
under the earth-line their a.s are 124:48
Altruism: a show of a. is respected 154:62
Amacher: you got to look like you're an a. 8:81
Amalgam: a toothsome a. of Americanisms
125:80
Amateur: a disease that afflicts a.s 42:36
the a. status must be maintained 88:66
its affinities are with a.s 204:69
America is the prize a. nation 244:70
Amatours: being ruined by a. 148:17
Amazons: A.s in homespuns 25:90
Ambiguity: a. that attends relationships 190:60
Ambition: my a. has been so great 100:10
names such as a. 244:86
temptations to social a. 136:18
lust and a. look ahead 136:19
Amble: do a. amiably here, O God 33:3
Ambulance: knocked down a doctor? With an
a.? 212:61
America: A's really only a kind of Russia 31:60
A. has a new delicacy 40:55
come back to A. . . . to live 114:46
the business of A. is business 52:9
whatever A. hopes to bring to pass 68:35
A. is so big 18:18
should we have lost A.? 109:28
an A. that is on the march 121:49
the discovery of A. 191:78
the more absolute silence of A. 130:69
in A. the successful writer 137:38
A. is a land of boys 147:79
the moral climate of A. 195:3
what makes A. what it is 218:57
to Europe she was A. 237:22
A. is the prize amateur nation 244:70
American: only clean-limbed A. boys 4:69
an A. girl who spoke scoffingly 8:70
A.s have a perfect right to exist 15:43
Contradictions of A. life 30:33
centre of A. culture 31:47
more A.s are killed in automobile accidents
31:47
a blonde nearly young A. woman 36:75
the greatest A. friend 47:74
if an A. told you 54:55
why shouldn't the A. people take half? 73:22
I don't see much future for the A.s 99:72
wrong with the A. public 120:35
a new generation of A.s 121:41
speaking with a slight A. accent 90:9
because A.s won't listen to sense 122:78
tain't A. or scientific 126:89
our A. professors 137:40
dozens of A.s do time 138:56
an A. motorist in England 140:8
in an A. ship 141:34
A. life in large cities 144:19
the A. character 144:20
best represented the modern A. woman 144:21
the A.s, who are the most efficient people
15:16
A. women know far more 154:60

American – *contd*
the most popular A. entertainments 155:85
A. crowd-mindedness 162:51
an A. is either a Jew or an anti-Semite 204:85
in the best A. clinics 206:19
terrible, newly imported A. doctrine 213:40
that strange blend . . . the A. abroad 217:45
let's talk sense to the A. people 219:80
A.s have a kind of resistance 228:57
A. girls do have regrets 232:7
A.s have dissipated their radical energy 239:55
the dream of the A. male 239:61
goodwill towards us, the A. people 243:52
the A. captain of industry 246:51
innocent-tasting A. drinks 246:53
Americanisms: amalgam of A. and epigrams
125:80
Amethyst: and weigh it against a. 28:78
Amiabilities: the three hundred pleasing a.
151:85
Amoebae: all the a. getting married 143:6
Amputate: thank God they had to a. 205:13
Amusement: tolerable, were it not for its a.s
137:31
this kind of a. is considered . . . decent 155:85
Anaemia: a sort of emotional a. 181:2
Anaemic: telling her he was not a. 59:21
Analogies: the finer a. of light and shade 28:75
Analyse: can a. his delusion 22:38
Analyst: a colour a. 64:60
Anarchists: a. who love God 37:10
Anarchy: the a. in your own heart 47:12
when we apply it, you call it a. 40:1
a well-bred sort of emotional a. 131:74
you do not even get a. 43:70
Ancestors: a. . . . at the Battle of Hastings
134:47
vices of his a. 72:6
Ancestry: a delusion about its a: 908:13
Ancient: the He-A. 210:50
Angel: Protestant a.s 17:14
the Recording A. . . . think of shorthand
19:58
a.s. can fly 42:60
this was the A. of history 85:88
an a. whose muscles . . . 91:8
a mixture of fools and a.s 96:14
the A. of the offshore wind 123:21
collect his royalties as Recording A. 147:78
my caramelly a. girl 149:36
song of the a.s sung by earth spirits 155:77
it may have been pleasing to the a. 202:30
Anger: the a. of men who have no opinions
42:39
Anglo-Catholic: becoming an A. 220:17
Anglo-Irishman: A. . . . what's that? 16:58
Anglo-Saxon: A. to his finger-tips 61:73
Angry: interesting to live when you are a.
251:29
Anguish: only the cry of a. 35:48
Animal: the green blood of the silent a.s 42:45
a decent attitude towards a.s 97:14
the a. always resuming its rights 105:32
you never see a.s going through 104:20
man is an amphibious a. 108:17

Animal – *contd*
a dozen of what appear to be a.s 188:31
this is the a. that does not exist 193:31
such unpleasant a.s 130:64
being told there's no such a. 132:11
tells oneself that the a. likes it 202:39
that sub-order of the a. kingdom 214:60
Animality: finds its own a. objectionable 137:29
Anna Livia: I want to hear all about A. 118:35
Anne: Good Queen A. 32:80
Annihilation: happy exposure to perfect a. 83:28
the a. of a people 85:71
no a. without representation 227:23
Annoyance: and the Library expressed its a.
181:87
Answer: not a wise question for me to a. 67:7
the a. 'Yes, but' 133:44
the a. is in the plural 142:61
what is the A.? 218:61
Antagonism: to replace national a. 237:19
Antagonists: piano a. liked to gloat 98:52
Anthem: the Uruguay national 1:8
Anthology: the A. of Later Works 106:59
an a. is like all the plums 187:8
Anti-American: every a. riot 121:51
Anti-Christ: the a. of Communism 31:46
Anti-clerical: makes me understand a. things
17:10
Anti-climax: everything afterwards savours of a.
74:68
Antipathies: and God knows what a. 196:15
Anti-semitic: he held strongly developed a.
views 54:53
Anti-social: an a. and dangerous character
18:35
Anti-sound: the heavens boomed with a. 239:62
Antithesis: go on to an a. in ideas 230:1
Anxiety: when an a. meets a technique 66:3
in a. states 10:2
the persecutory a. which usually follows
189:47
Anxious: a. to do the wrong thing correctly
202:34
Anybody: something that a. can do 98:68
Anyone: and a.s else (could that be right?)
61:74
Apartment: go to his a. . . . to look at etchings
197:49
Apathetic: theirs is brutal, ours is a. 226:12
Ape: my mother was an a., he said 89:74
the establishment of the a.s 47:75
a naked a. 162:55
we've got nothing against a.s 212:14
not the a. . . . nor the tiger 223:26
the average advance beyond a. – mentality
240:72
the A.s of God 138:53
Aphrodisiac: a circumambulating a. 80:31
fame is a powerful a. 89:86
Apologize: wanted to a. for it 26:17
Apologizing: a. for his occupation 154:68
Apostles: the A. kissed everybody 2:36
the Septuagint minus the A. 232:14
Apotheosis: appendicitis and a. 110:42
Apparel: a change of dry a. 28:67

Beauty – *contd*
  b. is always the first to hear 84:58
  blonde b. does not generally last 85:65
  b. is intrinsically edifying 106:57
  left it a land of b. spots 116:85
  Euclid alone has looked on b. bare 156:8
  what is b. anyway? 178:15
  b. is a sequence of hypotheses 183:52
  a b. cold and austere 199:77
  b. is only sin deep 202:36
  b. is momentary in the mind 219:77
Beaver: and cultivate a b. 102:51
Because: b. it was there 97:47
Beckon: to the farmer's children b. 8:83
Bed: musical b.s is the faculty sport 2:25
  deliver a sermon or wet the b. 4:81
  the desert sighs in the b. 9:3
  everybody to stay in b. all day 18:24
  deep peace of the double b. 33:14
  go to b. with a sewing machine 37:17
  marriage is not all b. and breakfast 53:36
  with the b. unmade 73:34
  their safe and paper b.s 81:56
  keeping open b. 102:58
  b. . . . is the poor man's opera 106:67
  Platonic way of going to b. 104:4
  we must . . . sleep in the same b. 46:110
  the third day he rose again from the b. 117:20
  getting out of a cold b. 133:32
  I have got up and I have gone to b. 151:8
  back again into b. like a martyr 160:11
  pursuing it from b. to b. 174:29
  the hero keeps getting in b. 196:25
  there shall be corals in your b.s 224:41
  gooseberried double b. of the wood 224:44
  to share his bread-pudding b. 224:50
  early to rise and early to b. 226:6
  that either . . . would recognize a double b.
    231:12
  minds like b.s always made up 242:48
  and putting it to b. when it got there 246:48
Bedposts: on the b. overnight 196:13
Bedroom: what you do in the b. 33:13
  sneaking out of the wrong b. 56:20
  the b.s were sacrificed 81:54
  a b. and a lecture-room 103:80
  an intellectualized b. 237:12
Bedsoxia: b., with its trailing stamen 162:62
Bedspread: like a b. 247:56
Beef: boiled b. and carrots 39:50
  no good without roast b. 149:38
Beehive: the b. state 171:47
Been: everything that will be has b. 110:53
Beer: b. and wine remain 3:39
  b., b., glorious b. 4:59
  your justice would freeze b.156:21
  b. drinking doesn't do half the harm 177:11
  that bitter b. that tastes sweet 192:23
  voice like b. trickling out of a jug 245:3
Bees: forget not b. in winter 201:4
Beethoven: the immense work of B. 221:23
Beetle: all men are but as the b.s 28:83
  behind every b. 163:76
Before: not b. or after but instead 4:65
Beginnings: the god of fair b. 124:44

Begins: where you leave off and it b. 65:80
Begun: that should not have b. 101:18
Behave: we have to learn to b. 64:52
  I'd have to b. myself 92:31
Behaved: b. just as I should have expected
    238:38
  everyone b. very badly 38:39
Behaving: act means b. 19:55
  b. as their ancestors had behaved 106:63
Behaviour: the quality of moral b. 105:39
Behind: with a b. like that 29:19
Beholder: eye of the b. 177:89
Bei: the b. unsers 244:86
Being: too early for b. 94:60
  knowledge is proportional to b. 106:54
  the darkness of mere b. 118:53
Beit: where those 300 fought with B. 17:4
Belgium: to think of gallant B. 147:71
  B. put the kibosh on the Kaiser 211:79
Belief: b. without evidence 22:26
  below the level of b. 70:67
  it trades on b. 32:67
  to these from birth is b. forbidden 124:48
  b. in the occurrence of the improbable 154:66
  commit himself to any religious b. 234:29
Believe: what we b. is not necessarily true
    16:79
  who really b. in themselves 42:48
  don't seem to b. in 'em enough 54:50
  it takes application to b. anything 70:67
  you would not b. in them either 148:18
  b.!, obey!, fight! 165:24
  I can b. in them all 209:13
  can b. enough in what one feels 250:22
  do we b. in winter 196:32
Believed: two things that will be b. 222:3
Believing: emphasis on the patient's b. 91:7
Bell-rope: the b. that gathers God 55:76
Bell: b. off San Salvador 55:78
  man like a b. 29:16
Belly: through his wife's b. 2:29
  embrace me b. like a bride 9:15
  their b.s were full 29:90
  look at May's b. 230:90
Belong: we know what we b. to 54:51
  b. to it as well 240:86
Belsen: no way of responding to B. 228:47
Belt: could not see a b. 8:73
Bench: grass is growing on the Front B. 8:79
  a man who sits on b.s 188:24
  held reality down fluttering to a b. 201:7
Benevolence: b. will cure everything 129:42
Bengal: way down in old B. 102:56
Bentley: a B. instead of a garden 185:88
Bergère: b., ô Tour Eiffele 7:48
Bergwerk: der Seelen wunderliches B. 192:24
Berkeley: the faith that ye share with B. Square
    124:53
  a nightingale sang in B. Square 150:60
Berlitz: glibness of the B. school 173:36
Bernhardt: even to please Sarah B. 14:22
Bert: that he likes to be called B. 180:68
Best: do your worst and we will do our b. 44:7
  and that will be the b. 100:13
Best-seller: the world's b. 24:73

Bore: B., a person who talks 22:20
　an intolerable b. – ourselves 109:21
　the capacity of human beings to b. 153:48
　proof that God is a b. 154:68
　he b.s for England 164:1
　an old b.; even the grave yawns 227:39
　in hell you will b. them 240:84
　sent our b.s abroad 24:68
　and crushing b.s 34:26
Bored: b. by knowing 58:11
　I want to be b. to death 61:83
　as nearly b. as enthusiasm would permit 87:35
　indefinitely b. 126:14
　I still get very b. with washing 144:27
　rather b. with their parents 151:81
　when you're b. with yourself 185:87
Boredom: death from exposure to b. 3:55
　no society . . . succumbed to b. 82:5
　cultivating b. 94:61
　the b. of the six hours in the Abbey 109:35
　b. becomes a sort of natural state 153:42
　bound in the end to suffer intolerable b. 199:75
Boring: deliberate and intentional b. 17:5
　not so b. as thought 232:8
Born: b. 1820, still going strong 4:68
　b. during the late war 8:80
　one is not b. a woman 13:80
　we are all b. mad 13:90
　unless he can remember being b. 23:51
　b. with a detective novel 52:74
　to be b. into a romance 41:32
　the slogan, B. to Lose 50:14
　when I was b. I was nearly fourteen 110:68
　if I had not been b. 177:83
　b. because it was a habit 194:57
　broke the law when he was b. 209:12
　it's unwise to be b. 208:2
　thought of all this before you were b. 212:13
　it's we who are b. . . . . in constant ratios 214:51
　I, b. of flesh and ghost 223:35
Borrowed: everything they had was b. 168:48
Borrowers: but we are B. 168:51
Bös: und nicht b. zu sein 192:10
Boshaft: b. ist er nicht 68:28
Bosom: their b.s blossoming 36:72
　rest your wounded b. against a grindstone 210:42
　her b. was heaving 176:79
Boss: Satan is a hard b. 96:13
　the hand of the b.'s daughter 10:9
　got the b. down the bottom of a well 171:50
Bossing: nobody b. you about 170:39
Boston: businessmen from B. 164:7
Botanist: not the business of the b. 174:43
Botticelli: if B. were alive 231:15
Bottle: crack a b. of fish sauce 40:75
　arm yourself with a quart b. 122:67
　to fill old b.s with banknotes 122:80
　faith and hope at twelve-and-six a b. 181:12
　hitting ginger-ale b.s with small rocks 225:83
　Aunt Agatha, who eats broken b.s 244:90
Bottled: an agony until she had b. it 201:1

Bottom: knocked the b. out of Bottom's dream 40:84
　their b.s are so gay 5:5
　putting the b. in again 104:1
　in the way my spiritual b. would 161:37
Boudoir: no sentimental b. 103:80
Bough: Ulysses' b. 70:79
　the one great b. of gold 224:60
Bought: had even b. the stars 102:66
Bouillabasse: b. is only good because 63:20
Bounce: in the plural they b. 142:60
Boundaries: rectification of national b. 22:23
Bouquet: that the b. is better than the taste 180:72
Bourbon: exacerbated by gin and b. 54:56
Bourgeois: domination by the b. spirit 19:59
　b. marriage has put our country into slippers 34:42
　the exhaustion of b. social relations 38:30
　worth far less than the b. dream 148:21
　a person of b. origin 170:32
　a b. revolution is absolutely necessary 134:60
Bourgeoisie: most democratic republican b. 134:62
　the English and French b. 228:57
　the English b. have spoken of themselves 234:19
Bournemouth: B. is one 21:3
Bovril: alas, they are B. now 181:4
Bow-wow: atrocious b. public-park manner 12:63
　Daddy wouldn't buy me a b. 222:1
Bowels: how are your b. working 149:28
Bowl: roll or b. a ball 94:59
　a good game of b.s 30:31
Boy: only clean-limbed American b.s 4:69
　so that the b.s will take you out 6:38
　a b. does not put his hand into his pocket 12:54
　the b.s know best 21:83
　the proper solemnity of an old b. 42:42
　b.s who seem born old 51:80
　unrestricted b. 52:20
　mad about the b. 54:62
　being read to by a b. 69:39
　every nice young girl's b. 145:50
　America is a land of b.s 147:79
　the b. can be thrown away 176:68
　your b.s will not be sent 195:5
　for fiery b.s that star was set 219:74
　the b. I love is up in the gallery 233:12
　liked little b.s too little 234:41
　doesn't take to your b. 244:80
　he speared the b. 141:27
　a b.'s best friend 157:55
　never had a b. friend 217:46
　my rogue's gallery of repulsive small b.s 247:65
Boyish: b. like Disraeli 51:86
Braces: the colour of his b. 73:37
　waving their b. like a banner 93:53
　absconded with a pair of red b. 112:4
　I had b. on my teeth 144:28
　rots b. at the distance of a mile 163:70
Bradley: Mr B.'s inimitable riot 161:44

INDEX

Distinguished: so here it is at last, the d. thing 114:45
Distress: the cruel goddess of D. 98:56
Distressed: sacrifice that I was d. to make 93:33
Disturb: do not d. 2:21
Dithering: Mumsy was . . . d. 23:50
Diva: the d. is descending 17:81
Diversity: make the world safe for d. 121:48
Divides: nothing d. them like Picasso 158:81
Divine: D. relations officers 78:66
sacrifice the d. passion 84:54
Diving: d. deeper than anyone else 105:45
Divorce: the surface of d. 18:31
the members of the d. colony 153:40
d. is the sign of knowledge 242:49
Divorced: demand to be d. 40:79
d. couples hobnobbed with each other 54:58
Do: confronted with what men d. 7:57
what'll we d. with ourselves 75:79
I d. these things which I d. 161:27
I don't d. anything 173:10
let's d. it, let's fall in love 179:53
we did what God wanted us to d. 232:15
Doc: never play cards with any man named D. 3:38
Dock: waving good-bye to himself on the d. 150:57
Doctor: only birth or death brought a d. 12:53
when a d. does go wrong 64:46
stick out your tongue at the insurance d. 148:6
arm them against the d.s 209:19
knocked down a d.? 212:11
take off for the d. 38:35
d. what do you say? 196:33
d's . . . know men 205:1
Doctoring: literature is due to bad d. 105:34
Doctrinaires: we have to go to the d. 42:38
d. are the vultures of principle 140:22
Documents: signed d. they did not read 92:27
Dodgson: that man Charles D. 54:67
Dog: all the d.s of Europe bark 9:87
where the d.s go on with their doggy life 9:2
I wish I'd bought a d. 11:34
the woman who is really kind to d.s 15:40
hates children and d.s 73:18
stop running those d.s 94:57
love each other like d.s do 62:15
than I like d.s 216:20
he was Brown D. to himself 102:41
don't let's go to the d.s tonight 97:30
a d.'s life without a d.'s decencies 125:81
their famous ill-bred d. 135:73
Englishmen taking mad d.s for walks 157:65
a beaten d. beneath the hail 181:90
too big a d. in the garden 219:1
provide a d.'s toilet 235:44
for an old woman to outlive her d.s 242:36
your own d. doesn't take to your boy 244:80
Dogmas: they do not even know they are d. 42:40
dulls the edges of all our d. 165:16
Doing: paying attention and d. 106:56
Doll: any d. will go to his apartment 197:49
Charlotte is not such a d. 197:51

Dollar: who has a million d.s 8:78
a d. in another man's hands 96:17
the recent gyrations of the d. 122:77
life printed on d. bills 169:10
Dolly: he's had more d. 178:28
Dolphin: that d.-torn sea 254:40
Domesticated: can become d. too 89:81
Domination: the d. of the planet 109:31
Don: one's a d. 17:89
a long littleness of d.s 51:89
imperfectly recalled by a senile d. 187:2
Don Juan: if D.s only obeyed their desires 104:10
a D. without the courage 105:40
woman-worshipping D.s 131:4
Don Quixote: only . . . original creation . . . D. 152:41
Done: what have we d. to each other? 50:54
more I could have d. to prevent this 67:6
something must be d. 68:23
do what you want d. 247:70
Donkey: lions led by d.s 100:89
that I fear; it is the d. 223:26
Donor: find something that excites the d. 146:54
Donsmanship: D. he defines as 180:67
Doom: the fiat of D. 114:47
Doomed: we recognize a d. people 85:77
Doomsday: D. weapons 128:1
Door: oh for d.s to be open 9:16
a d. of good reputation 76:20
a city of d.s slamming 188:22
someone at the d. wanting you 211:85
the D. in the Wall was a real d. 238:27
Doorsteps: on my grandfather's d. 88:48
Dose: normal f. for an adult defeatist 247:57
or give it in strong d.s 149:31
Dostoyevsky: learn from D. and Chekhov 131:87
Double: a guarded kind of d.-talk 226:8
Double-bed: this d. of a world 80:35
Doubt: a recurring d. 15:46
when man begins to d. 131:2
curiosity, freckles and d. 174:25
faith without d. is nothing but death 231:1
Douche: accompaniment of a thousand d. bags 142:53
Dough: stamped from the d. of suffering 239:52
Douleurs: je reste roi de mes d. 7:52
Dover: too ludicrous to be believed in D. 90:6
Down: D., upsey! 120:23
goes d. as far as you want to go 149:46
Downs: our whale-backed D. 124:49
Downsmanship: d. he defines as the art of 180:67
Downstairs: Christopher Robin has fallen d. 163:68
Downstart: being taken by the d. 155:4
Dragon: before he killed the d. 39:70
a gaping silken d. 88:45
Dragoons: horse, foot and d. 23:52
Drainpipe: a municipal d. 140:20
Draught: what we at home call d. 84:51
Drawers: disordered backs of cupboard d. 88:51
Drawing: the d. is on the level of 23:59
Drawing-rooms: floating through my d. 67:11
Dread: the d of games 21:82
wise with d. 70:79

Egg – *contd*
continued to lay e.s 105:30
I have laid five e.s in six days 171:60
even the Tough E.s liked it 245:28
Egosim: the artist's e. is outrageous 152:27
Egotist: e., n. a person of low taste 22:25
Egregious: the high E. is fairly on 236:80
Egypt: you can't judge E. by *Aïda* 73:27
Eiffel: shepherdess, oh E. Tower 7:48
Eiger-Sinn: nichtexistent in E. 161:39
Eighteen: she was e. in the attics 102:64
Eighteenth: in the e. century 103:82
Eilende: das E. wird schon vorüber sein 193:29
Ein: nor can anyone understand E. 5:88
Einfache: zeig ihm das E. 192:22
Einig: wir sind nicht e. 191:7
Einstein: ten conversations with E. 34:39
E., the greatest Jew since Jesus 91:3
the genius of E. leads to Hiroshima 178:14
Elbow: intellectual e.-room 112:14
Elderly: distrust of the e. 8:81
e. people [do not take interest] in sport 76:35
not fit for e. people to see 210:57
Elders: a party taken over by the e. 75:84
the red-eyed e. watching 76:219
Election: no go the e.s 147:73
the loss of the e. more certain 10:13
trust in various methods of e. 175:47
Electrical: e. charge . . . exerts e. force 67:3
Electricity: current of strong, leaking e. 36:81
Element: yield their names to the e.s 222:4
always on his e. 228:44
Elephant: e.s . . . are seldom lost 2:20
gave lectures from an e. 66:88
easier to hide five e.s 138:72
he stalls above me like an e. 142:51
Elijah: plays bridge like E. 92:17
Eliot: the work of Mr E. is respected 26:15
if Mr E. had been pleased to write in 147:81
Elizabeth: Blessed St E. Bathilde 74:49
Ellis: she knew her Havelock E. 103:72
Elm: the green e. with the one great bough 224:60
Eloquence: spoke with homicidal e. 205:15
Embers: blow on a dead man's e. 88:60
Embracement: licensed now for e. 20:77
Emendation: any theory based on an e. 39:61
Emergency: one e. following another 74:55
Emigranz: Seine E. 244:87
Emil: password E. 120:18
Emma: look as if they were called E. 161:48
Emotion: the degree of my aesthetic e. 16:75
secondhand and therefore incalculable e.s 12:49
men don't register e. when we meet 97:34
what would happen without negative e. 172:77
tranquillity remembered in e. 173:11
the most voluble of the e.s 48:16
Emotional: the practical and the e. 12:62
Emperor: even e.s can't do it all 29:7
for the big stealin' dey makes you e. 169:16
the e. of ice-cream 219:72
Empire: liquidation of the British E. 44:9
run the E. without neglecting form 48:13

Empire – *contd*
looks for his glasses to find the e. 80:21
the ridiculous e.s break 81:55
a great e. will be destroyed 98:66
under the brutal e. of the masses 170:19
the British E. was mostly acquired 175:48
and acquired the e. 24:68
to build the British E. 143:35
Employed: e. on things already done 82:4
the rise in the total of those e. 174:40
Employee: e. tends to rise 177:87
e.s who have not reached 177:88
Employer: an e. I'm trying out 241:18
Empty: I am a returned e. 63:22
Emulsion: a feeling of e. 176:69
Enamoured: e. of married women 176:80
Encouragement: smiling like a dentist 147:86
End: this is not the e. of me 11:29
I stuck with them to the e. 75:81
now I move softly towards the e. 116:87
chickens or insurance, I could hold my e. up 144:29
education . . . is not an e. in itself 149:37
laid e. to e. 174:35
the e. is not yet 208:9
dangerous at both e.s 76:29
cheerful at the e. 236:84
come to a bad e., very enjoyable 224:43
it will be the e. of everything we stand for 27:39
Ending: a sorting out and a happy e. 27:39
the best . . . hoped for from the e. 212:4
Endeavour: inspires a man to high e. 154:71
Enemy: three kinds of e. face 9:7
alone among smiling e.s 25:88
sombre e. of good art 51:70
I cannot get any sense of an e. 132:10
whatever goes on two legs is an e. 171:58
designing mausoleums for his e.s 139:83
our real e.s go in sheepskin by 142:52
the resistance of its class e.s 217:40
an e. of the human race 157:42
if the e. don't get you 226:11
you cannot get a better class of e. 158:61
Energy: the only big present source of e. 58:7
Engaged: to each of whom she had become e. 208:34
if Adam and Eve had been merely e. 237:17
one of the nicest girls I was ever e. to 245:8
Engineers: the age of the e. 100:90
artists are not e. of the soul 121:47
England: the middle-class woman of E. 12:41
concerts in E. have no future 14:18
in E. politicians seem 37:29
the men that worked for E. 39:68
alas, alas for E. 39:69
E. is a curious country 45:45
even the Jews in E. 51:86
the law of E. is a very strange one 58:4
the last King of E. 68:21
the kings of E., diamonds, hearts 72:51
slow pattern of Victorian E. 75:83
E. is a living guide-book 85:80
you can tell you're not in E. 151:87
for E., home and beauty 93:46

England – *contd*
he bores for E. 164:1
E., too, was led by adventurers 98:64
and E. over 101:19
suspended in favour of E. 210:45
in what perfection E. produces them 112:16
found E. a land of beauty 116:85
E. shall bide 125:59
a winsome bit of Merrie E. 125:78
the old savage E. 130:66
E. is only a little island 140:8
who made old E.'s name 145:41
in E. it is bad manners to be clever 155:88
that E. and I first set foot on each other
155:1
a world where E. is finished and dead 156:13
the national sport of E. 227:31
E. will have her neck wrung 239:57
English: no E. name for *esprit-de-corps* 1:12
within these breakwaters E. is spoken 9:85
E. without an accent 18:28
E. novelists 19:45
the E. muse 34:25
we E. are quite honest 98:53
the E. look for the serious message 90:13
E. women do not like me 25:14
telling the E. some interesting things 33:12
the oligarchic character of the modern E.
41:34
his E. education 42:42
the E. statesman 43:64
the E. never draw a line 44:15
I am myself an E.-speaking union 47:80
civilization built up by the E. 51:90
anything but the most dignified E. 59:25
the E. and the Irish are very much alike 65:84
the E.-speaking races against the world 85:84
most E. talk 112:14
the baby doesn't understand E. 126:10
when the E. began to hate 123:90
but marks our own E. dead 123:2
in an E. ship 141:34
the E. will penetrate 143:3
nothing unites the E. like war 158:81
there's enough E. to go round 162:60
a dull man writing broken E. 166:5
E. women in general 188:35
E. genius is anti-professional 204:69
wholesome and really nice E. people 210:44
by teaching them to speak E. 211:83
the E. and French bourgeoisie 228:57
E. as she is spoke 229:80
the E. sent their bores 24:68
Englishman: escape out of an E.'s hand 12:62
born an E. and remained one for years 16:57
if an E. told you 54:55
the E. at his best 73:41
it is not that the E. can't feel 77:50
Leopold could easily pass for an E. 84:55
an E. is 90:7
the E. is naturally wasteful 151:76
every E. has to survive one insult 162:50
no E. is ever fairly beaten 210:53
you never find an E. among the underdogs
235:43

Englishmen: most E. . . . born with a detective
novel 32:74
we do not regard E. as foreigners 128:16
E. taking mad dogs for walks 157:65
Engraved: so deeply e. 232:3
Enhale: as though she would e. them 73:35
Enigma: a mystery inside an e. 44:4
Enjoy: I just e. more and more things 26:18
except how to e. it 94:73
Enjoyable: come to a bad end, very e. 224:43
Enjoyed: demoralizing when consciously e.
126:13
Enjoyment: no individual e. in nature 240:75
Enjoys: miserable fellow, he e. everything 19:51
Enlightenment: sing for his own e. 98:51
Enquiry: the finger of e. 76:19
Enslavement: madness potential e. 128:8
Enterprise: it is e. which builds 122:79
Entertain: whom it is difficult to e. 159:83
Entertained: I go to the theatre to be e. 52:5
e. within an inch of their lives 215:90
e. by some of your grosser reminiscences
248:8
Entertainment: no connection with e. 33:10
disaster or e. of some kind 191:5
Enthusiasm: mixture of e. with cowardice 51:81
as nearly bored as e. would permit 87:35
Enthusiastic: they're as e. as you are 84:63
Entry: happens to be a second e. 1:13
Envelope: life is . . . a semi-transparent e.
248:78
Environment: the . . . e.-proof bulk 218:68
Ephemeral: only the e. is of lasting value 110:63
jealousies, each of which is e. 183:38
Epic: the e. poem and . . . metaphysics 153:48
Epigram: impelled to try an e. 173:16
purrs like an e. 148:24
Ep's: E. statues are junk 5:88
Equal: everybody should have an e. chance
243:59
Equality: rabid e.-mongrels 131:4
democratic e. is the most efficacious 194:52
Equanimity: e. bordering on indifference 84:48
Equator: no more a united nation than the E.
44:1
a yard and a half round the e. 133:40
Equine: an e. attribute 19:43
Erastianism: discovered E. in the village 246:33
Erben: und werden keinen E. haben 193:35
Erde: die E. ist wie ein Kind 193:28
Erdenklichen: quer zu E. völlig gehörig 192:18
Erickin': to have any beastly E. 126:86
Ermine: white e. was meant to express 43:66
Erotic: conceals e. purposes 79:80
Error: few e.s they have ever avoided 44:13
one way to recognize e. 85:178
possibility of e. must be ruled out 119:3
e.s of those who think they are strong 21:16
Esau: E. that swapped his copyright 95:90
E.'s fables 96:27
Escape: separates e. . . . from exile 167:37
Escutcheons: the receipts for their e. 48:4
Esmé: for E. with Love and Squalor 203:51
Esprit: no English name for *e.-de-corps* 1:12
Esquire: we are all e.s now 87:40

Fatheads: one of the most pronounced f. 246:40
Father: another letter from my F. 27:50
  now I have to call him f. 49:34
  you are your f.'s f. 55:71
  a substitute for the f. 79:83
  what is the f. up to? 181:8
  to show F. bathing the twins 193:44
  the f. in the modern suburban family 199:83
  my F. can have it 224:54
Fatherhood: mirrors and f. are abominable
  24:78
Fatherlands: Europe of the f. 60:38
Fathoming: may not even be worth f. 18:33
Fatigue: f. makes women talk more 136:25
Fatuity: and plages of dear f. 191:82
Faubourg: I belong to the F. St Patrice 117:24
Fauces: feared he would misplace his f. 118:42
Fault: I have my f.s 14:6
  pointing out . . . the f.s of his mistress 183:37
  it had only one f. 226:10
Fauns: heard the f. chiding Proteus 180:82
Favour: but it's a f. like? 238:46
Fear: can she who shines so calm be f.? 23:54
  as though under constant f. 72:12
  let us never f. to negotiate 121:52
  he is F., little hunter 124:47
  I have killed f. 125:83
  f. . . . and ambition look ahead 136:19
  f.s, prejudices . . . are the peers 140:15
  f. of death and f. of life both 153:46
Feared: f. rather than loved 199:89
Feasible: only f. indoors 74:46
Feather: down f.s out of an old cushion 36:1
  struck down by death's f. 223:35
Feats: the f. of his literary memory 48:17
Features: f. hold them 168:42
  the distance . . . her f. will have travelled
  184:56
  crisping her most striking f. 2:33
February: the 23rd of F. 228:55
Fee: as though it were a doctor's f. 136:12
Feed: throw a f. into her 197:44
Feeding: f. the mouth that bites you 61:86
  spoon-f. . . . teaches us 77:55
Feel: to f. hot and think cold 36:89
  their language convey more than they f. 50:61
  art . . . f.s and presents 55:81
  he paints . . . what he f.s 178:17
Feeling: can't put them out of his f.s 37:25
  though we all disguise our f.s very well 53:37
  f. is bad form 77:50
  f.s you haven't really got 131:83
  but I had me f.s 161:52
  even to know what the f. is 250:22
  deal with simple f.s 204:86
  conventional f. patterns 131:81
Feet: the f. of the bottle-laden 31:51
  I feel sick and me f. hurt 53:41
  looking at people's f. 75:70
  Henry IV's f. and armpits 106:64
  until thy f. have trod the road 123:3
  leaves the marks of his f. 133:36
  die on your f. 108:1
  it was always under your f. 158:76
  tends . . . to make their f. ache 215:86

Fehler: wenn Frauen F. machen wollen 120:16
Felicity: f. on the far side of baldness 214:59
Fell: he f. down a great deal 225:87
Fellow: to love my f. man 40:83
Fellowship: the right hand of f. 116:90
Female: the fly-specked abdominous f. 55:87
  interviewing a faded f. 92:30
  why should human f.s become sterile 105:30
  the seldom f. in a world of males 178:31
Feminine: craving . . . for the eternal f. 12:40
  enthuses the f. mind 94:54
Feminization: the f. of the white European
  138:66
Femme: on ne naît pas f. 13:80
  la f. est faite pour l'homme 160:18
  Il faut du temps pour être f. 5:1
Fence: sat so long on the f. 140:21
  the f. is just too high 152:17
Fernsprechbeamtin: F. has . . . a vision 115:66
Ferrovialis: f. naturaliter 104:21
Ferry: a ship's party on a f. boat 75:8
  a voice that used to shake the f. boats 148:15
Fertile: in such a fix to be so f. 167:25
Fever: your sensations during f. 143:12
  of chills and f.s she died 187:11
Few: rationalism for the f. 31:50
  the f. who have grasped the history of ideas
  156:19
Fiction: my one form of continuous f. 21:13
  made palatable by the jam of f. 152:28
  casting my mind's eye over the whole of f.
  152:29
  poetry is a comforting piece of f. 154:64
  poetry is the extreme f. 219:73
Fiddle: who has been taught to play the f. 4:61
  burn while Rome f.s 51:74
  help us f. while Rome burns 179:42
Field: the f. and wood, all bone-fed loam 23:56
  ten ploughed f.s like ten full-stops 150:69
Field-Marshal: the last F. I shall promote
  99:70
Fifth: triumphant in the f. 150:74
  the Himmler of the Lower F. 187:12
Fifty: I come back every f. years 70:82
  f. It's the age when 104:14
Fifty-three: north of f. 124:40
Fight: thought it wrong to f. 17:83
  it's not what men f. for 72:14
  and he is dead who will not f. 89:87
  and are longing for a f. 91:1
  to f. against the shoddy design 177:5
  the best part of married life is the f.s 241:14
  tell me what's right and I'll f. for it 244:72
Fighting: to think they're worth f. for 54:50
  when we ain't f. . . . ack like sojers 153:32
Figleaf: modernity here wore a f. 146:58
Figtrees: f. for a long time now 192:13
Figure: f. painting, the type of all 20:62
  not even a public f. 57:29
  a mourning f. walks, and will not rest 139:79
  permitted to draw hooded f.s 249:10
Filbert: for Gilbert, the F. 244:74
Filing: watch them f. out 50:59
  fussy about f. 175:49
Fill: f. yourself right up to here 4:59

Folk: advise not wayside f. 123:3
  except incest and f. dancing 33:71
  if the enemy don't get you, your own f. may
    226:11
Follow: I must f. them 24:66
  that doesn't mean we must f. it 126:15
  tell the boys to f. 114:51
Folly: he knew human f. 9:86
  trained f. 83:38
  why do people lament their f. 100:5
  moved to f. by a noise 132:24
Food: if music be the breakfast f. of love 2:21
  the f. had . . . the merit of being tasteless
    61:84
  the f. is simple 149:32
  the f. was incredibly bad 179:49
  and the f. a tragedy 181:6
  the problem is f. 62:11
  merely to put f. out of my mind 212:5
  something the Pure F. Committee had rejected
    246:30
  discovered that alcohol was a f. 246:32
Foodstuffs: his lowness creeped out via f. 118:34
Fool: men were mostly f.s 41:28
  any f. can criticize 83:24
  a mixture of f.s and angels 96:14
  to be bigger f.s than in everyday life 110:56
  he f.s nobody as completely 122:68
  the old man who will not laugh is a f. 204:66
  making a f. of himself about her 207:47
  let him remain a f. 223:24
  a damned f. if I didn't 224:42
  only f.s and passengers drink at sea 232:16
  a f. among f.s 241:20
Fooling: thought he was only f. 56:16
Foolish: such f. things as you have tried 120:38
  average man's opinions are much less f. 200:6
Foot: f. and note disease 21:1
  the whole of creation to produce my f. 101:30
  upadiddle and old man's f. 162:62
  one f. on a bar of soap 185:90
  the way you give a hot f. 197:46
Football: a f. game with everyone offside 74:62
  the sixth day is for f. 32:62
  I see the world as a f. 135:78
  tall thin men watching a f. match 146:56
Footmarks: his f. with his destination 200:10
Footmen: to be enjoyed by f. 106:70
Footnotes: f. to Plato's philosophy 240:78
Footprints: my f. They're . . . in my socks
  149:51
Forbidden: hinting at the f. 8:83
Force: the action of blind mechanical f. 114:56
  victories of consciousness over blind f.s 229:69
  F. one day was served to him 70:74
  other nations use 'f.' 235:55
Footsteps: waiting for the familiar f. 246:49
Forebears: my f. were successful crooks 7:62
Forehead: his hair and f. 201:16
Foreign: so f. indeed that 33:11
  I do not relish f. relations 36:86
  to pronounce f. names as he chooses 46:67
  blown constantly by f. winds 153:44
  the moment he lands on f. soil 162:50
  my f. policy 165:18

Foreign – contd
  depress by the use of f. words 180:63
  he saw f. policy 140:20
  can't see that f. stories are ever news 235:50
Foreigners: sympathy for being f. 26:16
  few f. can understand 45:45
  went off to fight the f. 52:11
Foretold: all was f. me 224:59
Forget: never f. any moment 25:5
  I never f. a face 149:48
  as accurately as he f.s 166:20
  three things I always f. 221:41
Forgetting: f. each time to post it 79:82
  live by f. 30:26
Forgive: will f. a man anything 43:80
Forgiveness: after such knowledge, what f.?
  69:42
Forgotten: I had entirely f. the statement 79:79
Fork: hold on to our toasting f.s 87:32
  sure he had a f. in the other 136:16
  a knife and two f.s left at the end 191:1
  a f. in his inexperienced hand 237:7
Form: without neglecting the study of f. 48:13
  a passionate appreciation of f. 16:73
  you hew f. truly 55:89
  significant f. 16:72
  have you filled in the necessary f.s 80:24
  suffocation by f.s 36:78
  a mass of purely nonsensical f.s 81:48
  a fair amount of f.-filling 175:51
  the purest mobile f. 126:3
Forming: the time you took at f. yourself 54:48
Formula: matter – a convenient f. 199:86
Fornicate: always f. between clean sheets 80:29
Fornicated: f. and read the papers 34:34
Fornication: important matters . . . f. 152:16
  an unrivalled garment for f. 151:77
Forsyte: no F. had as yet died 82:18
Fort: some moral f. of a lifetime 24:83
Fortnight: I came for a f. 155:1
Fortune: the f. we awaited so anxiously 85:88
Forty: the age of f. 24:77
Fou: un f. qui se croyait Hugo 48:14
Foundation: let the f. be bacon and eggs 96:29
  the f.s of that which it intends to reform
    229:63
Founders: which hesitates to forget its f.
  240:77
Fountain: their f.s piped an answer 129:39
  the f. given by Baroness Burdett-Coutts 177:6
Four: f. be the things 174:25
  goes in a f.-wheeler to the theatre 31:43
Fourteen: won in f. days 91:13
  when I was born I was nearly f. 110:68
Fourth: the f. person singular 72:11
Fox: the f. came home 150:70
  crazy like a f. 176:64
  inferior forms of f. hunting 234:27
Fractions: I like . . . vulgar f. 47:70
Français: ce n'est pas f. 18:36
France: in F. there are politicians 37:29
  F. has lost the battle 83:29
  only one illusion – F. 122:73
  F. was neither led nor governed 177:84
  it's a picture about F. 196:28

Fruitful: the command, be f. and multiply 109:25

Frustration: predominant emotion a puzzled f. 25:13

the age of f. 175:49

Fry: Dear Roger F. 149:33

Frying-pan: spoilt the best f. 112:6

Fuchsia: like the split buds of a black f. 169:15

f. drenched with rain 2:19

Fucking: cold-hearted f. 131:75

Fuel: gathering f. in vacant lots 69:49

Fufluns: call the god of wine F. 103:74

Fühlt: im Weltall, wo es fühlender f. 192:22

Führer: the will of the F. 78:63

Fulfil: ought to f. sacredly their desires 132:18

Fulfilment: every f. is slavery 35:61

Full: going to find this f. of quotations 65:65

can't do it on a f. one either 190:68

Full-stops: ten ploughed fields, like ten f. 150:69

Fume: the captured f. of space 54:68

Fun: what on earth was all the f. for? 21:89

work is much more f. 54:64

nothing more f. than a man 174:26

f. to be poor 6:44

f. to be in the same decade 195:7

the f. brigade 213:37

now I must pay for my f. 123:17

Function: the principle of the Führer's f. 78:63

Funeral: if you don't go to other men's fs. 59:27

but there are f.s 61:75

chosen the day of the . . . match for the f. 102:44

f. marches round your heart 156:20

when Doctor Dougall attended a f. 213:32

one f. makes many 236:89

off to a f. supper 29:2

Funny: f. because I had said it 42:47

f. without being vulgar 84:49

a f. streak 134:49

everything is f. 195:84

just as f. as politicians 196:12

Fur: voice like hot, damp f. 121:64

Furious: f. that she had not been asked 234:39

Furniture: fill their rooms with useless f. 227:31

Furry: the fire was f. as a bear 212:21

Further: always a little f. 76:27

Fury: no f. like a non-combatant 160:15

a blind f. of creation 208:68

Future: f., n. in which our affairs prosper 22:27

concerts in England have no f. 14:18

the f. is black 10:6

the orgiastic f. 75:82

the great dead language of the f. 103:75

to predict the f. 108:6

Russia will certainly inherit the f. 131:85

passing . . . to the sphere of the f. 135:65

the f. is something which everyone reaches 136:21

revealed to me the structure of the f. 223:21

has drowned the f. and the past 224:56

the f. is the most expensive luxury 241:9

from the infinite f. 104:1

G

Gabriel: check with G. himself 220:9

Gadarene: ready for the G. gallop 83:28

Gai: toujours g., toujours g. 148:4

Gaiety: the only concession to g. 225:69

Gains: no g. without pains 219:80

Gal: I'm the laziest g. in town 179:52

Gallery: the boy I love is up in the g. 233:12

Galloping: g. . . . in search of an idea 248:80

Gallows: the miniature g. of her ears 102:46

Gambling: the g. known as business 22:39

a g. streak 134:49

Game: there is no returning g. 13:83

the Socratic manner is not a g. 15:49

the dread of g.s 21:82

may be a damned amusing g. 74:65

this – skin g. 83:22

the g. is ended 101:18

and think they know the g. 145:41

that aesthetic g. of the eye 178:15

twenty-five years playing team g.s 219:89

Gamekeeper: open his g's letters first 228:43

Gangster: have always acted the g. 127:20

Gaol: woman's place is in the g. 27:55

Gap: the g. between Dorothy and Chopin 2:15

Garbo: one sees in G. sober 230:4

Garden: sorry you should see the g. now 65:67

the g. of Art

weed the g., wind the clock 76:24

everything in the g.'s lovely 93:45

only going into their own back g. 141:44

don't go into Mr McGregor's g. 179:57

the g. boy is leading the cranes home 233:4

the g.s of the west 15:27

Gare: you can't say, au-dessus de sa g. 187:13

Gargoyle: a g. . . . for a Methodist chapel 15:52

Garlic: edged off with a whisper of g. 96:20

passed on . . . of an overdose of g. 203:53

Garter: g., n. an elastic band 22:8

Gas: the g. was on in the Institute 20:78

it is certainly not a ball of flaming g. 132:6

we built our g. chambers to accommodate 99:83

trying on g. masks here 38:45

Gate: our g.s to the glorious 77:39

in the park. The g. was open 117:16

Gaullist: I myself have become a G. 83:30

Gawd: even bein' G. ain't a bed of roses 50:56

Gay: their bottoms are so g. 5:5

Gazette: the Rabbit Fanciers' G. 103:68

Gebärde: binden dich an Bild und G. 193:34

Gebild: schlägt sich erdachtes G. 192:18

Gee-whiz: makes a reader say G. 145:39

Geheimnis: drängst dein reines G. 192:13

Genealogy: g., n., an account 22:29

General: a g. and a bit of shooting 16:65

they're all of him, the G. 52:15

where one can intimidate g.s 77:49

the weakness of strong g.s 84:60

in a civil war, a g. must know 189:42

g.s also are proletarian 200:9

the French g.s looked much brainier 205:16

Itinerary: to trace out the imaginary i. 25:7
Ivory: for peacocks, apes and i. 124:34

J

Jab: to j. the life out of the Germans 205:15
Jacob: Jem is joky for J. 118:33
Jahweh: J. . . . spends . . . part of his time 153:49
Jail: do you know you can go to j.? 121:62
Jam: one look at the rush-hour j. 47:83
  j.s meticulously jarred 76:26
  j. tomorrow and one often sees 215:85
Jamais: j. trist, Archy, j. triste 148:34
Jane: I'd call 'em all J. 237:2
Japan: means the defeat of J. 195:9
  regard J. as barbarous 169:14
Japanese: seek the society of J. generals 41:31
  that the J. would, in quite a friendly way 188:20
Jaw: she moved her lower j. monotonously 8:80
  blood, swift despatching j.s 217:30
Jawbacious: high old j. argument 236:87
Jazz, music means j. 19:55
  though the j. age continued 75:84
Jealous: I should never dream of being j. 112:6
Jealousy: 'tis all j. to the bride 12:66
  j. is . . . feeling alone 25:88
  beware of j. 28:70
  an infinity . . . of different j.s 183:38
Jehovah: a J. complex 94:63
  J. of the Thunders 123:14
Jellyfish: with as little uproar as a j. 246:42
Jem: as J. is joky for Jacob 118:33
Jest: aye, even j. in Zion 125:66
Jesuit: in camphor . . . with the J. Fathers 105:33
Jesus: stand around like J. in Gethsemane 29:6
  the greatest Jew since J. 91:3
  as good as Renan's Life of J. 133:25
  the thing J. really would have liked 203:49
  whether you think J. was God or not 209:32
  J. of Matthew 209:29
Jew: never call a J. a J. 3:48
  half of Christendom worships a J. 4:78
  even the J.s in England 51:86
  the greatest J. since Jesus 91:3
  good or bad, like J.s 110:74
  what one J. copies 142:58
  I decide who is a J. 142:59
  must be a J. . . . such a Scotch name 168:45
  J.s and Protestants who adore the world 204:80
  either a J. or an anti-Semite 204:85
  no J. was ever fool enough 252:2
  the J.s bring the unlike 252:7
Jewish: total solution of the J. question 86:90
  their dark, compact, J. lives 102:54
  best that is in the J. blood 130:53
  just J., not the whole hog 157:44

Jewish – *contd*
  and he is slightly J. 197:52
  J. fried fish is always served cold 252:1
  a J. financier 191:78
Jewry: an instrument of J. 227:20
Jewellery: don't ever wear artistic j. 49:27
  I always recognize the j. 85:69
Jezebel: you should hear him throw down J. 59:34
Jigging: always j. a jog 118:41
Jim: I've had my eye on J. 135:79
Jingo: against the j.s at its close 45:34
  acclaim your glorious name – by j. 56:2
Joans: hunting with the polly j. 118:39
Job: taken the trouble to learn his j. 19:45
  we have finished the j. 91:2
  I got my j. by hollering 95:87
  the only j. left 95:5
  undertook to do a j. 115:75
  hypocrisy . . . is a whole-time j. 152:27
  when your neighbour loses his j. 229:74
John-Sebastian: a little more J.-like 104:22
John Thomas: J. marrying Lady Jane 131:76
Joined: what God hath j. together 210:65
Joke: it's our only j. 16:65
  to forget a poor j. 25:12
  they look for the j. 90:13
  the coarse j. proclaims 137:29
  I don't make j.s 195:74
  no more j.s in music-halls 205:10
  it's the funniest j. in the world 208:3
  go on finding the same j. funny 239:52
Jonah: belly J. hunting 118:39
Jones: never knew Lord J. was alive 40:88
  our Mr J. 75:76
Jordan: do not take a bath in J., Gordan 212:23
Journalism: but why j.? 11:22
  j. largely consists in 40:88
  j. . . . will be grasped at once 50:64
  j. gains as much as literature loses 109:24
Journalist: bribe . . . the British j. 247:67
Journey: dead, but cannot make the j. 129:36
  whenever I prepare for a j. 147:90
  lots I could tell you of this j. 206:27
Joy: bursting out of his collar with j. 37:15
  and rent spontaneous j. 250:8
  each for the j. of working 125:61
Joyce: the words Mr J. uses 211:68
Joyed: I j. in the passing day 60:44
Joyicity: hoppy on akkant of his j. 118:41
Judaized: American society half J. 99:72
Judas: J. is the last god 130:68
Judge: Christ says J. not 109:38
  a j. is not supposed to know 173:1
  more difficult to j. oneself 201:11
Judgement: don't wait for the Last J. 34:43
  when the Day of J. comes 80:24
  commit oneself to any critical j. 133:41
  their personal j. of hardly any account 137:47
Juice: full of j. *de spree* 125:77
Julia: a speech from J. Sees Her 73:30
July: J. 1917 was the month 228:59
Jumble: J. Jim, who shall remain nameless 135:77
Jumbo: J. asleep 212:22

Literature – *contd*
  the distinction between l. and journalism 109:24
  like their l. clear and cold 137:40
  assigned him a place in our l. 160:22
  l. and butterflies are the two sweetest 166:8
  English l.'s performing flea 169:9
  great l. is simply language 180:73
  l. . . . attempts to illuminate 220:16
  sit on the edge of the chair of l. 225:84
  our . . . ideology has produced a large l. 228:49
  'why, it's l.!' 236:78
Little: people resent . . . having too l. 50:40
  this l. once, O Lord 73:21
  how shall we turn to l. things 44:46
  l. minds are interested in 101:27
Littleness: spoiled by the l. 29:7
Litero-criminal: l. New York circles 138:56
Live: London is a splendid place to l. in 11:24
  the aim is to l. lucidly 35:57
  you don't actually l. longer 78:71
  I'll l. too, if it kills me 80:30
  if I had to l. in conditions like that 83:34
  finding something to l. for 92:20
  l. forever or die in the attempt 94:65
  despise sex and l. for it 131:73
  a woman who l.s for others 136:23
  to l. is not like walking through a field 175:54
  we l., forever taking leave 192:20
  a firm believer in l. and let l. 212:9
  that he wants to l. humbly 218:64
  interesting to l. when you are angry 251:29
  what does a man l. by 30:26
  never to l. 114:46
  so l. that you wouldn't 195:87
  to oppose is to l. 119:1
Lives: a splendid moment in our small l. 44:12
  entertained within an inch of their l. 215:90
Liveth: their name l. for ever 205:12
Living: l. in the past . . . is cheaper 5:8
  l. is no more than a trick 7:52
  and partly l. 69:53
  the absent l. 16:69
  l. half in a cemetery 30:29
  does not owe us a l. 67:15
  if l. isn't a seeking for the grail 74:65
  the worst of l. 101:25
  a l. corpse if there ever was one 110:44
  the l. are getting rarer 111:78
  evolution is far more important than l. 118:56
  tired of l., and scared of dying 121:58
  the possibilities of fine l. 133:45
  gets his l. by such depressing devices 153:42
  different l. is not l. in different places 216:22
  that the l. do not talk at all 229:82
  a l. is made 241:6
Lloyd George: L. spoke for 117 minutes 19:49
Loaf: half a l. is better 43:65
  buy a l. of bread with one 43:76
Loafer: for the sportsman and the l. 155:76
Loafing: looked on cricket as organized l. 223:25

Lob: generally figure as nothing but a l. 198:71
Locally: history than they can consume l. 202:23
Locomotion: for purposes of human l. 63:16
Locomotives: say it with l. 138:61
Locust: the years that the l. hath eaten 109:40
Logs: manifested itself only by dead l. 165:27
Logic: the l. of our times 59:32
  upon the l. rather than upon the crime 63:31
  when l. and science were the fashion 103:2
Loincloth: wearing l.s and aprons 89:76
  l., loosely slung over the right shoulder 189:40
Loins: gird your blue-veined l. 2:31
Loisirs: la guerre . . . avec . . . ses longs l. 6:45
Lollocks: these dusty-featured l. 88:51
London: L. is a splendid place 11:24
  to speak against L. 77:43
  L. doesn't love the latent 112:9
  there would be in L. . . . more of that kind 113:19
  and I'm learning 'ere in L. 124:30
  L. spread out in the sun 129:24
  L. is chaos incorporated 155:84
  around the world, or the West End of L. 185:86
  the lamps of L. uphold the dark 248:85
Loneliness: pray that your l. may spur you 92:20
  burning in your l. 156:16
  l. can be conquered 226:15
Lonely: for fear I may be l. 116:83
  write to Miss L.-hearts 239:49
Long: in the l. run we are all dead 48:12
  failure . . . to be l. for this world 113:21
  the L. Man of Wilmington 124:52
Longer: it just seems l. 78:71
Looey: the period of L. Cans 96:7
Look: l. at yourself with one eye 110:66
  a strange but burly l. 135:71
  some men never l. at you 174:23
  everyone bore a hopeful l. 191:5
Looked: I stopped, I l., and I listened 193:43
Looking: not at that moment l. round 196:27
  although she was l. all the time 224:46
  women have served . . . as l.-glasses 248:90
Loon: crazy as a l. 35:69
Looney-bin: a sort of janitor to the l. 245:20
Lord: our L.'s sex life 90:3
  the L. survives the rainbow of his will 142:50
  those who did not excessively fear the L. 158:80
Lords: taken his seat in the L. 15:37
  every man has a House of L. in his head 140:15
Lord's: the risk of anyone being lynched at L. 244:81
Lose: the slogan, born to l. 90:14
  we don't want to l. you 197:38
  nothing you can l. by dying 204:79
Losing: l. or regaining faith 74:58
  I'm terrified to l. it 92:28
Lost: elephants are seldom l. 2:20
  l. everything except his reason 42:50
  almost certainly have been l. without him 100:6

313

S

Saturday – *contd*
  the youngest being christened S. 140:4
  it is S. before you realize it's Thursday
  178:19
  on S. I'm willing 244:76
Sauce: crack a bottle of fish s. 40:75
  art is not a special s. 136:4
Saucy: you buy s. savings stamps 120:24
Sauntering: you can go s. along 33:12
Saurian: the eyes of some old s. in decay
  179:43
Sausinges: where's the s.? 158:70
Savage: when Britain had a s. culture 11:26
  if an uneducated s. can do that 52:12
  the young man who has not wept is a s.
  204:66
  the conversion of a s. to Christianity 209:30
Save: he need not exist in order to s. us 61:66
  whenever you s. five shillings 122:75
  rushed through life trying to s. 194:68
Saviour: I imitate the S. 102:51
Saw: as I never s. myself 182:17
Saxons: The S. have stolen my balls 16:63
Saxophone: learnt the s. to amuse 30:39
  sweet, sweet and piercing, the s. 102:55
Say: till I see what I s. 5:86
  s. what you have to s. in twenty minutes
  25:10
  do not know what they are going to s. 43:82
  hardly anybody has got anything to s. 58:1
  I mean every word you s. 95:80
  that is, never s. anything 133:41
  more to s. when I am dead 193:48
  that what people s. of us in true 214:49
Saying: do not know what they are s. 43:82
  s. the same things over and over 65:81
  seldom interested in what he is s. 70:68
  the S.s Attributive of H. C. Earwicker
  117:26
  what is it s. to us 236:83
Scaffold: never on the s. 43:83
Scaly: about as s. as I had expected 245:26
Scandal: only silence or s. 153:33
  s. is merely the compassionate allowance
  202:26
Scandalous: never been openly s. 171:56
Scarecrows: to measure the s. 163:74
Scarlatti: S. condensed so much music 31:57
Scavengers: the red-eyed s. are creeping 69:37
Scenery: too much s. 96:28
  she was all for s. 113:19
Schedule: mechanically kept to his s. 215:74
Scheherezade: S. is the classic example 249:13
Scheming: the s. look of an ex-cathedral 74:47
Schizophrenia: s. cannot be understood 128:3
Schlief: sah ich, dass ich s. 128:3
Schnee: kann den Alten in den S. pissen 139:76
Schnorrer: did anyone say *s.*? 149:42
Scholar: the last humiliation of an aged s.
  49:29
  better s. than Wordsworth 101:21
  as you're not a s. 110:59
Scholarship: slender indications of s. 44:20
School: the s. went up last 16:70
  love and the Board s. 15:50

School – *contd*
  they take me to see girls' s.s 25:4
  went to s. without any boots 31:54
  such a thing as a state s. 41:11
  has all the faults of a public s. 51:79
  all s.s are hell 52:20
  some of us have to go to summer s. 62:89
  I think I'll not send him to s. 64:54
  tried to make our s. days happy 32:70
  and a hundred s.s of thought centred 148:3
  she would set fire to the s. 206:32
  worse than being taught in a church s. 209:27
  she has been late for s. 224:45
  provided jails called s.s 231:11
  leading s., first-rate s., good s., and s.
  234:16
  the ready-made blackcoat s. of costume
  238:28
Schoolboy: the method that of a s. 23:59
  an elderly s. 42:42
  a s. is a novelist 51:81
Schoolgirl: a s. answered the question 2:20
  like a shocked s. 84:61
  raw and astringent as a s. 96:26
Schoolmaster: the s. of ever afterwards 76:13
  the moment the s.'s back is turned 209:27
  I expect you'll be becoming a s., sir 233:15
Schoosz: denn S. ist alles 192:19
Schreibe: ich s. für Heute 235:62
Sciatica: soft as Eve and sharp as s. 224:50
Science: the jilted bachelor of s. 34:20
  spoilt for all purposes of s. 41:26
  s. in the modern world has many uses 41:29
  the s. of the spirit 55:82
  s. . . . is really anti-intellectual 154:58
  s. should leave off making pronouncements
  115:88
  for the destruction of Nordic s. 227:20
  a s. which hesitates to forget 240:77
  s. is what one Jew copies from another 142:58
Scientific: t'ain't American or s. 126:89
Scientist: the s. who yields anything 153:45
  just an old mad s. at bottom 176:65
  in the company of s.s. 9:20
  every genuine s. must be a metaphysician
  210:47
  when s.s are faced with culture 215:86
Scold: Sergeant, I am wishful to s. you 12:58
Scorn: s. of irregular perquisites 234:19
Scortacolour: Matisse, odalisque in s. 37:12
Scotch: working on a bottle of S. 18:30
  certainly Irish, or S.? 91:10
  you've got such a S. name 168:45
Scots: you S. are such a mixture 12:62
  Keir Hardie taught them to speak S. 211:83
Scotsman: a S. with a grievance 245:14
Scotsmen: an island governed by S. 90:7
Scott: said Liddell to S. 93:37
Scoundrel: a thorough, convinced s. 207:48
Scourger: the s. almighty 117:20
Scout: interest in the S. movement 184:14
Scowl: a six-and-a-half-foot s. 221:26
Scrap: nosing for s.s in the galley 124:33
  never seen one decent bar s. 237:1
Scrapes: what s. you do get us into 214:76

MORE ABOUT PENGUINS

Penguinews, which appears every month, contains details of all the new books issued by Penguins as they are published. From time to time it is supplemented by *Penguins in Print*, which is a complete list of all available books published by Penguins. (There are well over three thousand of these.)

A specimen copy of *Penguinews* will be sent to you free on request, and you can become a subscriber for the price of the postage. For a year's issues (including the complete lists) please send 30p if you live in the United Kingdom, or 60p if you live elsewhere. Just write to Dept EP, Penguin Books Ltd, Harmondsworth, Middlesex, enclosing a cheque or postal order, and your name will be added to the mailing list.

Some other books published by Penguins are described on the following pages.

Note : *Penguinews* and *Penguins in Print* are not
available in the U.S.A. or Canada

Penguin Reference Books

THE PENGUIN DICTIONARY
OF QUOTATIONS
J. M. and M. J. Cohen

The reader, the writer, the after-dinner speaker, the crossword-puzzle solver and the browser will find what they want among the 12,000 or so quotations, which include the most celebrated lines from Shakespeare, the Bible or *Paradise Lost* side by side with remarks and stray lines by almost unknown writers.

THE PENGUIN ENGLISH DICTIONARY
G. N. Garmonsway

Specially commissioned for Penguins, this dictionary is unrivalled as a catalogue of English words as they are now used in print and speech.

'This is, above all else, a *modern* dictionary... The editors have performed an immensely difficult task with tact and skill' – Eric Partridge in the *Guardian*

ROGET'S THESAURUS
Robert A. Dutch

'This must surely be the most indispensable publication ever compiled. In its revised form it is even more invaluable' – *John O'Londons*

This revised edition includes thousands of new entries, increased cross-references and an entirely new index. (*Not for sale in the U.S.A. or Canada.*)

USAGE AND ABUSAGE
Eric Partridge

Language is everybody's business and enters into almost every part of human life. Yet it is all too often misused: directness and clarity disappear in a whirl of clichés, euphemisms, and woolliness of expression. This book wittily attacks linguistic abuse of all kinds, and at the same time offers constructive advice on the proper use of English.